21世纪英语专业系列教材

新编英国文学选读

SELECTED READINGS OF ENGLISH LITERATURE

（第5版）

(The 5th Edition)

主编 胡亚敏 李公昭

编者（按姓氏音序排序）

陈礼珍 谷 伟 胡亚敏 黄 川 李梦雨

陆志阳 石平萍 夏 辉 张运恺

西安交通大学出版社
XI'AN JIAOTONG UNIVERSITY PRESS

国家一级出版社
全国百佳图书出版单位

图书在版编目（CIP）数据

新编英国文学选读 / 胡亚敏，李公昭主编. —5版. —西安：西安交通大学出版社，2022.8
ISBN 978-7-5693-2620-8

Ⅰ.①新… Ⅱ.①胡…②李… Ⅲ.①英语—阅读教学—高等学校—教材②英国文学—文学欣赏 Ⅳ.①H319.37

中国版本图书馆CIP数据核字（2022）第091165号

书　　名　新编英国文学选读（第5版）
　　　　　XINBIAN YINGGUO WENXUE XUANDU
主　　编　胡亚敏　李公昭
责任编辑　庞钧颖　蔡乐芊
责任校对　李　蕊

出版发行　西安交通大学出版社
　　　　　（西安市兴庆南路1号　邮政编码710048）
网　　址　http://www.xjtupress.com
电　　话　（029）82668357　82667874（市场营销中心）
　　　　　（029）82668315（总编办）
传　　真　（029）82668280
印　　刷　西安五星印刷有限公司

开　　本　787mm × 1092mm　1/16　印张　25.25　字数　575千字
版次印次　2022年8月第5版　2022年8月第1次印刷
书　　号　ISBN 978-7-5693-2620-8
定　　价　59.80元

如发现印装质量问题，请与本社市场营销中心联系调换。
订购热线：（029）82665248　（029）82667874
投稿热线：（029）82665371

第 5 版前言

Preface to the 5th Edition

《新编英国文学选读》（第 4 版）出版至今已有五年，到了该对教材进行修订的时候。根据我国高等教育的改革需求、教材的使用情况及教师和学生们提出的意见与建议，我们在《新编英国文学选读》（第 5 版）中进行了如下修订。

第一，新版教材中新增了 V. S. 奈保尔、朱利安·巴恩斯、伊恩·麦克尤恩和石黑一雄这四位当代作家的介绍及代表作。同时，由于教材篇幅的限制，不得不忍痛删除了亚历山大·蒲伯、威廉·麦克皮斯·萨克雷、E. M. 福斯特、D. H. 劳伦斯的相关内容，并根据教材使用的实际情况，对部分选文和内容进行了不同程度的调整和更新。

第二，我们补充和更新了部分选文后的思考题，旨在启发学生洞察文学作品蕴含的思想价值和精神内涵，体会人类共同情感和全人类共同价值，引导学生在评析英国文学作品、开展跨文化比较和研究时，能够坚持马克思主义世界观和方法论，既坚持文化自信，也展现国际视野，提升思辨能力。

第三，我们对之前教材出现的错误也进行了更正。

另外，需要说明的是，《新编英国文学选读》（第 5 版）保留了先前各版的主要特色，在作品后提供“简评”或“解读举例”，以拓展学生的思路和视野。

参加此次修订工作的有战略支援部队信息工程大学洛阳校区（原解放军外国语学院）的（按姓氏音序）谷伟、胡亚敏、黄川、李梦雨、陆志阳、石平萍、夏辉、张运恺和杭州师范大学外国语学院的陈礼珍。胡亚敏和李公昭负责审定全书，并统稿润色。需要指出的是，本书是在先前四个版本的基础上完成的，没有之前各版作者的辛勤努力，是不可能有《新编英国文学选读》（第 5 版）的，在此再向他们表示感谢。另外，研究生刘可心参与了新版教材的校对工作，在此一并表示感谢。

最后要感谢西安交通大学出版社和出版社负责《新编英国文学选读》（第5版）的编辑为本教材付出的辛勤努力。

编　者

2022年8月

第 1 版前言

Preface to the 1st Edition

《新编英国文学选读》是适合大学英语本科高年级英国文学课需要的，编排方法更为新颖、合理、实用的英国文学选读本。我们在研究、参考了国内外现有的同类型教材的基础上，针对我国本科英语专业英国文学课教学的实际情况，精选了英国文学重要时期的代表作家与作品，反映了英国文学的大致轮廓。除了借鉴其他教材特色外（如重要时代、作家、作品附简介，作品附注释和思考题等），《新编英国文学选读》还有如下三个特色。

首先，重要作品后附解读举例，提出两三种可能的解读方法供学生参考，以拓展学生的思路。对不适合进行多种解读的作品则提供简评，以起抛砖引玉之作用。

其次，每位作家及其作品后附推荐书目，以供对该作家或作品感兴趣的学生进一步研究使用。

最后，在全书末尾附欧洲与英国历史、文学的大事记年表，将英国文学置于欧洲文化的大背景下，勾勒出英国历史、文学的发展线索，以方便读者。《新编》除原著与问题外，其余均用中文编写，以扩大读者面。

《新编英国文学选读》对《新编英国文学教程》进行了较大的修订，主要方面有：①删减了部分内容，以压缩篇幅；②订正了原书中的错误；③修改了部分思考题，使之更具操作性；④改写了部分“简评”或“解读举例”；⑤充实了部分推荐书目。

参加编写工作的同志有（按姓氏音序）陈国华、陈榕、高继海、何荣东、李公昭、王岚、许德金、朱荣杰、周汶。另外，高芳编写了哈代部分，陈荣东、梁小波编写了附录的一部分，李公昭对全书进行了修订。由于多人执笔，风格难以统一，各种错误也在所难免，恳请广大读者批评指出。

编　者

2009 年 8 月

目　录

Contents

English Romanticism

1789–1832

English Literature of the Victorian Age

1832–1901

English Literature in the Twentieth Century

1900–1945

Comtemporary English Literature

1945–

Middle English Literature

449–1485

英国中世纪文学史大致可分为盎格鲁 – 撒克逊 (The Anglo-Saxon Period, 449—1066) 和中古英语 (The Middle English Period, 1066—1485) 两个时期。

公元前凯尔特人迁入不列颠岛，成为英国最早的居民。公元一世纪至 410 年，英伦三岛为罗马人统治。449 年开始，随着西罗马帝国的衰落，罗马人逐渐撤出了英伦三岛，北欧日耳曼部族的朱特人 (Jutes)、盎格鲁人 (Angles) 和撒克逊人 (Saxons) 开始陆续入侵不列颠。他们的语言——盎格鲁 – 撒克逊语 (Anglo-Saxon) 或古英语 (Old English)——也开始广为传播。597 年，圣奥古斯丁 (St. Augustine, ?—605) 率 40 余名修士来到英格兰传教，基督教开始在不列颠岛盛行。

盎格鲁 – 撒克逊时代最重要的文学作品是长达三千多行的头韵史诗《贝奥武甫》(*Beowulf*, 700—750)，讲述了一个斯堪的纳维亚的民间传说。古英语散文的杰出代表是比德 (the Venerable Bede, 673/674—735) 的《英吉利人民宗教史》(*The Ecclesiastical History of the English People*, 731—732)，描写了英国第一位宗教诗人开德蒙 (Caedmon, 657—680) 充满神奇色彩的生平事迹。该作品用拉丁文写成，后译成英文，是了解早期英国历史的珍贵史料。891 年，韦塞克斯 (Wessex) 国王艾尔弗雷德大帝 (Alfred the Great, 849—899) 开始组织修士汇编《盎格鲁 – 撒克逊编年史》(*The Anglo-Saxon Chronicle*)，后人一直续编至 1154 年。这是第一部用英语写成的散文巨著，文风简约、质朴，对英国散文的发展产生了深远的影响。

1066 年，诺曼底公爵威廉 (William, Duke of Normandy, 1028—1087) 打败英军，夺得王位，成为英王威廉一世 (William I)，史称“诺曼征服”(the Norman Conquest)。此后近 300 年的时间里，法语一直是英国统治阶层的语言，教会学者则用拉丁文写作，英语只在普通民众中使用，以至于在 12 世纪之前几乎没有用英文写成的文学作品。

然而诺曼征服之后，英国的封建制度得到完善，新的社会等级产生。处于统治阶级最高层的是国王，国王以下为贵族、骑士、大主教、主教和封臣。处于社会底层的则是农民。骑士是社会的中心人物，据传他们英勇善战又风流倜傥。他们所体现的骑士风度 (chivalry) 成为当时最主要的文学形式——浪漫传奇 (romance)——的基本主题。浪漫传奇既有诗的形式，也有散文的形式，其中最著名的要数讲述亚瑟王及其圆桌骑士 (King Arthur and His Knights of the Round Table) 冒险经历的故事。在这些故事中最为生动精彩的则数《高文爵士和绿衣骑士》(*Sir Gawain and the Green Knight*)。1485 年托马斯 · 马洛礼 (Thomas Malory, c.1415—1471) 于 1469 至 1470 年间完成的散文传奇《亚瑟王之死》(*Le Morte d'Arthur*) 由威廉 · 卡克斯顿 (William Caxton, 1422—1491) 在英国建立的首家印刷所 (1476 年建立) 印刷出版。该作品文字简朴、节奏优美，不失为这一题材的集大成作品和中世纪最后一部伟大的散文作品。

威廉·兰格伦 (William Langland, c.1332—c.1400) 聚集对下层人民生活的描写，他的《农夫皮尔斯之梦》(*The Vision of Piers Plowman*) 是最伟大的英语诗篇之一，流传下来的三个版本分别于 1363 年、1371 年和 1395 年写成。在这首长达七千多行的头韵长诗中，作者通过一系列的梦境，对 14 世纪英国的社会状况进行了生动形象的描述，既表达了对统治阶层的尖锐讽刺，也抒发了对穷苦人民悲惨生活的同情。这首诗对 1381 年约翰·鲍尔 (John Ball, 1338—1381) 和瓦特·泰勒 (Wat Tyler, c.1341—1381) 领导的农民起义起到了推波助澜的作用。

对 1381 年起义产生更大影响的是约翰·威克里夫 (John Wycliffe, c.1330—1384) 和他的罗拉德派 (Lollards)。他们反对寺院占有土地，驳斥教会的古老教义，为传布新的教义和维护普通百姓的利益而四处奔波。威克里夫对文学的贡献在于他首次组织将《圣经》从拉丁文翻译成英文，并为后人留下了两卷庄重古雅的布道词。

在整个中世纪文学中，成就最大的首推杰弗里·乔叟 (Geoffrey Chaucer, c.1343—1400)。他经历丰富，与社会各阶层都有广泛的接触，这为他提供了旁人难以获得的创作素材。他一生勤奋好学，精通法文、拉丁文和意大利文，并虚心学习同时代文学大师们的创作方法和思想主题，尤其注意汲取意大利人文主义者的先进思想。乔叟的艺术成就，首先在于他以现实主义的笔触逼真、全面地描绘了当时英国社会的全貌，开创了英国现实主义文学的传统。其次，他的作品，尤其是《坎特伯雷故事集》(*The Canterbury Tales*, c.1387—1400) 表达了自己的人文主义思想，淋漓尽致地揭露了宗教的腐败、贵族的奢靡生活及当时社会的其他丑陋现象，同时歌颂了人的智慧、对生活的热爱和对幸福的追求。他是英国人文主义的先驱，是中世纪和英国文艺复兴之间承上启下的人物。再者，他的《坎特伯雷故事集》构思巧妙，叙事方式多样，对 18 世纪后的英国小说产生了不可估量的作用。最后，乔叟首次把“英雄双韵体”(heroic couplet) 从法语诗作引入英诗，以取代古英语的头韵诗。此外他还是第一位用中古英语写作的伟大诗人，为近代英国文学语言奠定了基础。他被卡克斯顿誉为英国的“诗歌之父”。

在乔叟的耀眼光芒之后，15 世纪的英国文坛显得黯然失色，值得一提的名家只有马洛礼一人。但在这个通俗文学盛行的时期涌现出了许多优美动人的抒情诗 (Lyrics)、民间故事 (Folk Tales) 和民谣 (Ballads)。它们长期以来在民间由吟游诗人口头传唱，12 世纪后开始被记录下来，并于 15 世纪达到极盛。其中最著名的民间故事有《猫头鹰和夜莺》(*The Owl and the Nightingale*)。民谣则以歌颂绿林好汉罗宾汉的《罗宾汉的事迹》(*The Gest of Robyn Hode*) 流传最广。此外以宗教内容为题材的神秘剧 (Mystery Play) 和道德剧 (Morality Play) 也是中世纪的主要文学形式。

作者简介

Geoffrey Chaucer
c.1343—1400

杰弗里·乔叟出身于伦敦一个殷实的酒商家庭，早年接受高于一般平民阶层的教育，兼之家庭与宫廷素有往来，14岁时给国王爱德华三世之子莱昂纳尔 (Lionel) 当差。16岁时乔叟参加英王远征军赴法作战被俘，后被赎回。1366年，乔叟与菲丽帕 (Philippa) 结婚。菲丽帕是王后的侍女，王子龚特 (Gaunt) 第三个妻子的姐姐。1367年乔叟成为爱德华三世的贴身仆从。1372年，他被派往意大利热那亚安排通商事宜。1374年，龚特成为他的庇护人。随后，乔叟担任了一系列官职：伦敦海关羊毛税收官、肯特郡治安官及该郡爵士、国王的工程官和索默塞特郡某地的林务次官等。其间他还多次被派往法国和意大利执行公务。1400年10月25日，乔叟逝世，葬于西敏寺，从此西敏寺一角 (Poets' Corner, Westminster Abbey) 成为文学大师的长眠之所。

从如此粗略的生平轮廓中，我们仍可看出乔叟一生丰富的经历，他与社会各阶层都有广泛的接触：他来自平民阶层，又长期在宫廷贵族中间周旋；他在英国国内担任过多种官职，又多次被派往欧洲大陆执行公务。这为他提供了旁人很难获得的创作素材。他一生勤奋好学，拥有60多册藏书（当时已属不易），精通法文、拉丁文和意大利文。他刻苦钻研古罗马哲学家波伊提乌 (Boethius, c.470/475—524) 的《哲学的慰藉》(*The Consolation of Philosophy*)，从中汲取深邃的哲学思想。他与当时英国的高尔 (John Gower, 1330—1408)、法国的傅华萨 (Jean Froissart, 1337—1405)、意大利的薄伽丘 (Giovanni Boccaccio, 1313—1375) 和弗兰齐斯科·彼特拉克 (Francesco Petrarch, 1304—1374) 等文坛巨匠都有或多或少的联系，向他们学习如何挖掘主题和熟练的创作手法，他尤其汲取了意大利人文主义者的先进思想。就生活阅历、知识面、想象力和文学创造力而言，与乔叟同时代的英国人难以望其项背。

与他的生活经历相对应，乔叟的文学创作活动可以分为三个阶段。在第一阶段 (1372年之前)，他主要翻译了一首13世纪的法国诗歌《玫瑰传奇》(*Romaunt of the Rose*)，另写有《公爵夫人之书》(*The Book of the Duchesse*)，这是1369年乔叟奉龚特之命为其死去的第一任夫人所写的挽歌。该作品无论内容还是形式均深受法国诗人的影响。第二阶段 (1372—1385) 的作品具有明显的意大利文学的痕迹，如《声誉之堂》(*The House of Fame*, 1370) 可以看作是对但丁 (Dante Alighieri, 1265—1321)《神曲》(*The Divine Comedy*, 1307—1321) 的模仿，而薄伽丘的影子在乔叟的主要作品中更是随处可见，比如《禽鸟议会》(*The Parlement of Foules*, 1380) 和《特罗勒与克丽西德》(*Troylus and Cryseyde*,1385)。后者是乔叟最长的完整诗篇，长达八千多行，是借用薄伽丘一首诗的主题改写而成。在第三阶段 (1386—1400)，乔叟除了在 1386 年完成了《好女人的故事》(*The Legend of Good Women*) 外，主要把精力放在《坎特伯雷故事集》的创作上。尽管故事集最终未能如愿完成，但仍不失为英国文学史上的一座丰碑。

乔叟的艺术成就，首先在于他以现实主义的笔触逼真、全面地描绘了当时英国社会的全貌，开创了英国现实主义文学的传统。其次，他在作品中，尤其在《坎特伯雷故事集》中表达了自己的人文主义思想，淋漓尽致地揭露了宗教的腐败、贵族的奢靡及当时社会的其他丑陋现象，同时歌颂了人类的智慧、对生活的热爱和对幸福的追求。他是英国人文主义的先驱，是中世纪和英国文艺复兴之间承上启下的人物。再次，他的故事集构思巧妙，叙述方式多样。有的故事在叙述过程中会被旁人打断，甚至引起争论；有些故事的观点针锋相对，像磨坊主与地方官、行乞修道士与法庭差役各自讲的故事。另外，有些故事从不同角度对同一主题进行阐述，像巴斯夫人、牛津学者和地主都在各自的故事中融入了他们对婚姻的看法。这样，故事之间有了一种内在的联系，避免了以往故事集的零碎拼凑感。最后，在语言上，乔叟引入了法语诗作中的英雄双韵体，用以取代古英语的头韵诗。同时，他是第一位用中古英语进行文学创作的伟大诗人。正是乔叟使伦敦方言成为现代标准英语，奠定了近代英国文学语言的基础。

The Canterbury Tales

【题解】

《坎特伯雷故事集》是乔叟在生命最后十年倾尽心血构筑的一座文学丰碑。故事集的总引交代了讲故事的缘由：诗人和其他 29 名朝觐者一起由伦敦出发，前去约 60 公里以外的坎特伯雷朝圣，在旅店老板的提议下，他们决定每人在来回旅途中各讲两个故事，之后由老板评判，讲得最好的人回到旅店后大家合请他吃饭。这个庞大的计划本应包括 120 个故事，但乔叟最后只完成了总引和 22 个故事，另有两个未完成的故事。即便如此，该书汇集了中古文学的各种主要体裁，如宫廷传奇、寓言、游历和冒险故事、圣徒传、劝善书等。乔叟以其细腻幽默的笔调真实、生动地描写了代表当时社会各个阶层的众朝觐者的性格、职业和爱好，并记录了他们所讲述的符合各自身份的故事。其中武士讲的骑士故事、女修道士讲的圣母传奇传说、侍从讲的浪漫传奇故事、赦罪僧讲的说教示例故事、巴斯夫人讲的示例童话故事等最为有名。以下所选诗节为《坎特伯雷故事集》总引开场白的原文，及其现代英语译文，可对照阅读。

From The Canterbury Tales

The General Prologue

(excerpt)

When that Aprill with his shoures sote
The droghte of Marche hath perced to the rote,
And bathed every veyne in swich licour
Of which vertu engendred is the flour;
Whan Zephirus eek with his swete breeth
Inspired hath in every holt and heath
The tendre croppes, and the yonge sonne
Hath in the Ram his halfe cours y-ronne,
And smale foules maken melodye,
That slepen al the night with open ye
(So priketh hem Nature in hir corages):
Than longen folk to goon on pilgrimages
And palmers for to seken straunge strondes,
To ferne halwes, couthe in sondry londes;
And specially, from every shires ende
Of Engelond, to Caunterbury they wende,
The holy blisful martir[1] for to seke
That hem hath holpen, whan that they were seke.
Bifel that in that seson on a day,
In Southwerk at the Tabard as I lay,
Redy to wenden on my pilgrimage
To Caunterbury with ful devout corage,
At night was come into that hostelrye

Wel nyne and twenty in a companye
Of sondry folk, by aventure y-falle
In felawshipe, and pilgrims were they alle,
That toward Caunterbury wolden ryde.
The chambres and the stables weren wyde,
And wel we weren esed atte beste.
And shortly, whan the sonne was to reste,
So hadde I spoken with hem everichon,
That I was of hir felawshipe anon,
And made forward erly for to ryse,
To take our wey, ther as I yow devyse.
But natheles, why I have tyme and space,
Er that I ferther in this tale pace,
Me thinketh it acordaunt to resoun,
To telle yow al the condicioun
Of ech of hem, so as it semed me,
And whiche they weren, and of what degree,
And eek in what array that they were inne:
And at a knight than wol I first biginne.

The Modern English translation of the above lines:

The General Prologue

When April with his sweet showers has
Has pierced the drought of March to the root,
And bathed every vein in such moisture
As has power to bring forth the flower;
When, also, Zephyrus with his sweet breath
Has breathed spirit into the tender new shoots
In every wood and meadow, and the young sun
Has run half his course in the sign of the Ram,
And small birds sing melodies and

Sleep with their eyes open all the night
(so Nature pricks them in their hearts):
Then people long to go on pilgrimages,
And palmers long to seek strange shores
And far-off shrines known in various lands,
And, especially, from the ends of every shire
In England they come to Canterbury,
To seek the holy, blissful martir[1]
Who helped them when they were sick.
It befell that one day in that season,
As I was in Southwark at the Tabard Inn,
Ready to go on my pilgrimage
To Canterbury with a most devout heart,
At night there came into that hostelry
A company of nine-and-twenty people—
All sorts of people, who had met by chance;
And all of them were pilgrims
Who were riding toward Canterbury.
The chambers and the stables were spacious,
And we were made most comfortable.
And shortly, when the sun had gone down,
I had spoken with every one of them
So that I had soon become one of their group,
And made an arrangement to rise early
To be on our way, as I shall tell you.
But none the less, while I have time and space,
Before I pass on further in this tale,
It seems to me in order
To tell you all about
Each of them, as they seemed to me—
And who they were, and of what rank in life,
And also what they wore—
And with a knight, then, I will begin.

【注释】

1. martir: martyr, 指 St.Thomas Becket, 因与英王亨利二世 (Henry Ⅱ, 1133—1189) 发生争执，于 1170 年在坎特伯雷大教堂被谋杀。

【思考题】

1. How does Chaucer paint the setting of his story in the first forty-two lines of the Prologue?
2. What is Chaucer's view of the Canterbury pilgrimage?
3. In the opening lines, what might be the significance of transition from descriptions of nature to divinity?

English Renaissance

1485–1603

文艺复兴是欧洲从中世纪向近代过渡期间发生的一场意义深刻、影响深远的思想文化运动，始于14世纪意大利的佛罗伦萨，后迅速席卷德国、法国、西班牙、英国等国，并于16世纪达到高潮。

这一时期的欧洲社会经历了深刻的变化。工商业的发展、王权的巩固、海外的扩张与殖民，地理与科学的新发现，社会生活的世俗化，德、英、法等国先后进行的宗教改革等极大开阔了人们的眼界，促进了资本主义经济的发展，鼓励人们进一步探索人存在的价值和现实生活的意义。1453年东罗马帝国灭亡，大批学者携带古希腊、古罗马作品的手抄本和文物逃往西欧，同时在罗马城废墟中又发掘出许多古罗马雕像，给人们展示了一个与中古世纪截然不同的古代文化，掀起了一股研究古典学术和追求新知识的热潮，也极大地推动了人文主义运动的开展。因此总的来说，文艺复兴具有三个主要特征：第一，古希腊、古罗马文化的复兴；第二，知识的复兴；第三，人文主义运动的发展。

人文主义思想 (Humanism) 的核心就是强调以人为本，宣传个性解放、现世幸福，积极推进学术交流，传播科学知识和国家统一等新思想，对封建制度、宗教禁欲主义和上层僧侣的腐败虚伪进行无情的嘲讽与抨击。文艺复兴时期的文学正是以人文主义思想为主要内容的。意大利诗人但丁、彼特拉克，小说家薄伽丘等人是意大利和欧洲早期人文主义文学的杰出代表， 他们在文学领域取得的重大成就为近代欧洲文学的发展开辟了道路。法国文艺复兴运动中涌现出来的弗朗索瓦·拉伯雷 (François Rabelais, 1494—1553) 的小说，七星诗社 (La Pléiade)① 和米歇尔·德·蒙田 (Michel de Montaigne, 1533—1592) 的散文等极大丰富了法国乃至欧洲的人文主义文学。

16世纪后，西班牙、英国的资本主义得到迅速发展，产生了洛佩·德·维迦卡尔皮奥 (Lope de Vega Carpio, 1562—1635)、米格尔·德·塞万提斯 (Miguel de Cervantes, 1547—1616)、埃德蒙·斯宾塞 (Edmund Spenser, 1552/1553—1599)、克里斯托弗·马洛 (Christopher Marlowe, 1564—1593)、威廉·莎士比亚 (William Shakespeare, 1564—1616) 等一批杰出的人文主义作家。在西班牙和英国，诗歌、小说、戏剧和散文创作全面繁荣，欧洲文艺复兴文学达到了高峰。

英国人文主义文学是欧洲人文主义文学的顶峰，可上溯到英国的“诗歌之父”乔叟。他创作的富有浪漫色彩的《坎特伯雷故事集》，通过对教会、僧侣的腐败虚伪的批判和对现实美好生活的肯定与追求为英国后来的文艺复兴运动定下了基调。1485年都铎王朝 (The Tudor Dynasty, 1485—1603) 的建立结束了英国连年的内战，统一了王权，重振了英国的政治与经济，恢复了其在欧洲的地位，加强了英国与欧

① 16世纪中期法国的一个文学团体，由七位人文主义诗人组成。

洲各国的联系。从英王亨利七世 (Henry Ⅶ, 1457—1509) 开始，英国文艺复兴运动得到了迅猛的发展。托马斯·莫尔爵士 (Sir Thomas More, 1478—1535) 是这一时期重要的人文主义作家。他创作的《乌托邦》(*Utopia*, 1516) 借一位回到英国的水手之口描绘了一个理想的社会，开启近代欧洲描述空想社会理想著作的先河。这一时期的英国新诗也开始崭露头角。英国最早的新诗作者托马斯·怀亚特 (Sir Thomas Wyatt, 1503—1542) 和萨里伯爵亨利·霍华德 (Henry Howard, Earl of Surrey, 1517—1547) 将彼特拉克的诗歌形式引入英国，并用这一形式创作了许多爱情十四行诗，为当时的英国诗坛带来了一股新鲜的空气。到了伊丽莎白时代，随着英国国家的日益强盛，英国的文艺复兴运动达到了高潮。斯宾塞的《仙后》(*The Faerie Queene*, 1590) 运用非凡的想象创造出一个瑰丽多姿的世界，也为英国诗歌创造出一种独特的诗节，即有名的斯宾塞诗节 (Spenserian Stanza)，他的诗歌成就代表着文艺复兴时期英国非戏剧文学的高峰。

除了抒情诗外，英国文艺复兴文学的另一重要形式是戏剧。伊丽莎白时代的英国戏剧是英国文艺复兴时期所有文学形式中最辉煌的一种，代表了英国乃至整个欧洲文艺复兴时期文学创作的最高成就。伊丽莎白中期的英国戏剧代表人物有以约翰·黎里 (John Lyly, 1554?—1606)、马洛、托马斯·基德 (Thomas Kyd, 1558—1594)、罗伯特·格林 (Robert Greene, 1558—1592) 等“大学才子”(University Wits)，他们是英国文艺复兴戏剧的先驱，其作品表明英国文艺复兴时期的戏剧已趋向成熟，而莎士比亚的戏剧则将英国文艺复兴戏剧推向高峰。莎士比亚之后的剧作家主要有托马斯·米德顿 (Thomas Middleton, 1580—1627)、约翰·韦伯斯特 (John Webster, 1580—1632) 等人。他们的戏剧作品，如《白魔》(*The White Devil*) 和《玛菲公爵夫人》(*The Duchess of Malfi*) 等由于过多加入流血与恐怖的场面而大大削弱了剧本所要表现的道德力量，因此被称为“流血悲剧”(Bloody Tragedy)。此外许多迂腐和低级的闹剧式喜剧也纷纷登场。这些都表明，在莎士比亚以后，英国的文艺复兴运动已开始走向衰败。

1642 年英国内战爆发，同年 9 月，英国议会两院发布命令，封闭全国的剧院。至此，轰轰烈烈的英国文艺复兴运动落下了帷幕。

作者简介

William Shakespeare

1564—1616

威廉·莎士比亚出生于英国中部沃尔威克郡埃文河畔斯特拉特福镇 (Stratford-upon-Avon) 一个中层阶级家庭。父亲约翰·莎士比亚曾做过羊毛生意，后当过镇民政官、镇长。莎士比亚是家里的长子，少年时期就读于当地的文法学校，学过古典文学、修辞学、拉丁语和法语等课程。18 岁那年莎士比亚娶年长自己 8 岁的安妮·海瑟威 (Anne Hathaway) 为妻，生有一男二女。三年后莎士比亚只身离开家乡来到伦敦，先在剧院门口给人看管马匹，后被剧院看中演了几个小角色。当时莎士比亚的戏剧才华很快就显露出来。1592 年，当时已名噪一时的剧作家罗伯特·格林在临终前给朋友的信中警告马洛等“大学才子”，要提防一只“新近用我们的羽毛装扮起来的乌鸦，因为在他戏子的外表下包藏着虎狼之心……他自以为是国内独一无二的‘擅场’(Shake-scene) 能手。”其实这时莎士比亚的戏剧生涯才刚刚开始，只写了《亨利六世》(*Henry VI, Part I/Part II/Part III*)。

1592 至 1593 年间，伦敦由于流行鼠疫，关闭了所有的剧院。此间，莎士比亚写了两首长诗：《维纳斯和阿童尼》(*Venus and Adonis*, 1593) 和《鲁克丽丝受辱记》(*The Rape of Lucrece*, 1594)。鼠疫过后，当剧院重新开张时，莎士比亚已成为他所在剧团的大股东。

在莎士比亚的戏剧创作生涯中，他和形形色色的人打过交道，其中既有花一便士到公共剧院站着看戏的平民百姓，又有花大钱到私人剧院看戏的王公贵族。剧团还频频出入宫廷为英女王伊丽莎白一世 (Elizabeth Ⅰ, 1533—1603) 和后来的詹姆士一世 (James Ⅰ, 1566—1625) 进行演出。莎士比亚与下层人民的交往极大丰富了他的语言，使之充满机智、幽默、诙谐，而他与王公贵族的交往也使他得以深入了解宫廷生活。在二十多年的创作生涯中，莎士比亚笔耕不辍，共创作了 38 个剧本，2 部长诗，154 首十四行诗和几首杂诗。1613 年他离开伦敦回乡定居，1616 年 4 月 23 日与世长辞，享年 52 岁。

莎士比亚的创作生涯经常被不同的评论家分为不同的阶段，较为普遍的是分为三个阶段，即以历史剧和喜剧创作为主的第一阶段 (1590—1600)；以悲剧创作为主的第二阶段 (1601—1608) 和以传奇剧（又称悲喜剧）创作为主的第三阶段 (1609—1613)。莎士比亚的历史剧围绕英国百年战争、玫瑰战争等史实表现英国 15 世纪以来一百多年的战乱史，反映了他拥护王权、反对内乱的政治主张和历史观点。莎士比亚的喜剧大多发生在南欧，表现的却是一个“快乐的英国”，其基本主题是爱情和友谊。多数喜剧充满欢乐与阳光，反映了人文主义者对新生活的渴望和打破宗教禁欲的封建道德观的要求。莎士比亚的悲剧则表现了人文主义理想与英国现实矛盾的冲突，以及理想在冲突中的幻灭等主题，其笔触之严峻、思想之深刻、语言之精湛是莎士比亚前期作品无法比拟的。莎士比亚的传奇剧往往在开头时矛盾重重、危机四伏，但最终却为爱情、友谊、宽容所调和，以大团圆结局告终，表现了莎士比亚后期创作淡泊、宽容、宁静的一面。

莎士比亚戏剧是文艺复兴的高峰。他的作品早已跨越时空界限，成为全人类巨大的精神财富。“他不属于一个时代，而属于所有世纪。”

Hamlet

【题解】

《哈姆雷特》(全名为 *Hamlet, Prince of Denmark*) 是莎士比亚四大悲剧中的第一部，也是他的代表作。丹麦王子哈姆雷特的故事最早见于12世纪丹麦历史学家萨克索·格拉玛提库斯 (Saxo Grammaticus, 1150—1220) 写的《丹麦史》(*The History of the Danes*)，后法、英两国剧作家将其改编成剧本。一般认为莎士比亚的《哈姆雷特》系根据同时代作家基德一部现已失传的《厄哈姆雷特》(*Ur-Hamlet*) 改编而来。改编后的剧本保留了原剧本的主要框架，但却被赋予了原剧本所没有的思想深度与艺术魅力。丹麦王子哈姆雷特在德国威登堡上大学期间突闻父亲死讯，回国奔丧后又经历了叔叔称王和母亲改嫁。哈姆雷特开始怀疑叔叔克劳迪斯弑君篡位，不久他便从先王的鬼魂和戏中戏里得到证实。为了复仇，哈姆雷特开始装疯卖傻，就是为了不引起国王的怀疑，但国王还是从哈姆雷特的种种疯话中觉察到后者居心叵测，于是派出大臣、哈姆雷特的恋人及儿时好友等前来试探，并在哈姆雷特误杀大臣波洛涅斯后派其出使英国，欲借英王之手置哈姆雷特于死地。哈姆雷特识破国王阴谋，安全返回丹麦。国王又令波洛涅斯之子雷欧提斯与之比剑，并事先在剑上涂上毒药。为确保阴谋得逞，国王又设下毒酒。然而雷欧提斯与哈姆雷特双双中毒剑，毒酒又被王后喝下。在临终之际，雷欧提斯指证国王为罪魁祸首。哈姆雷特一剑刺去，终于以沉重的代价报了杀父之仇，自己也倒地死去。下文选自《哈姆雷特》第三幕第一场。

From Hamlet

Act 3 Scene 1

Enter King, Queen, Polonius, Ophelia, Rosencranz, Guildenstern, and Lords.

King. And can you by no drift of circumstance[1]
Get from him why he puts on this confusion:
Grating so harshly all his days of quiet
With turbulent and dangerous lunacy?

Ros. He does confess he feels himself distracted,
But from what cause he will by no means speak.

Guild. Nor do we find him forward to be sounded[2],
But with a crafty madness keeps aloof
When we would bring him on to some confession
Of his true state.

Queen. Did he receive you well?

Ros. Most like a gentleman.

Guild. But with much forcing of his disposition[3].

Ros. Niggard of question[4], but of our demands
Most free in his reply.

Queen. Did you assay him to any pastime[5]?

Ros. Madam, it so fell out, that certain players
We o'er-raught[6] on the way: of these we told him,
And there did seem in him a kind of joy
To hear of it: They are about the court,
And (as I think) they have already order
This night to play before him.

Pol. 'Tis most true:
And he beseech'd me to entreat your majesties
To hear and see the matter.

King. With all my heart, and it doth much content me
To hear him so inclined. Good Gentlemen,
Give him a further edge[7], and drive his purpose on
To these delights.

Ros. We shall, my Lord

［*Exeunt Rosencranz and Guildenstern.*］

King. Sweet Gertrude, leave us too,
For we have closely sent for Hamlet hither,
That he, as'twere by accident, may there
Affront Ophelia. Her father and myself (lawful espials)
Will so bestow ourselves that, seeing unseen,
We may of their encounter frankly judge,
And gather by him, as he is behaved[8],
If't be th' affliction of his love or no
That thus he suffers for[9].

Queen. I shall obey you,
And for your part［,］Ophelia, I do wish
That your good beauties be the happy[10] cause
Of Hamlet's wildness: so shall I hope your virtues
Will bring him to his wonted way[11] again,
To both your honours.

Oph. Madam, I wish it may.

［*Exit Queen with Lords.*］

Pol. Ophelia, walk you here. Gracious［,］so please ye[12],
We will bestow ourselves.［*To Ophelia*］Read on this book[13],
That show of such an exercise[14] may colour
Your loneliness[15]. We are oft to blame in this,
'Tis too much proved, that with devotion's visage[16],
And pious action, we do sugar o'er
The devil himself.

King.［*Aside*］O, 'tis too true!
How smart a lash that speech doth give my conscience!
The harlot's cheek beautied with plast'ring art[17]
Is not more ugly to the thing that helps it[18],
Than is my deed to my most painted word.
Oh heavy burthen!

Pol. I hear him coming, let's withdraw, my Lord.

[*Exeunt Claudius and Polonius.*]

Enter Hamlet.

Ham. To be, or not to be, that is the question:
Whether'tis nobler in the mind to suffer[19]
The slings and arrows of outrageous fortune,
Or to take arms against a sea of troubles,
And by opposing end them[20]: to die, to sleep—
No more[21]; and by a sleep, to say we end
The heart-ache, and the thousand natural shocks
That flesh is heir to[22]; 'Tis a consummation[23]
Devoutly to be wish'd. To die to sleep,
To sleep, perchance to dream; I[24], there's the rub[25],
For in that sleep of death, what dreams may come,
When we have shuffled off this mortal coil[26],
Must give us pause. There's the respect[27]
That makes calamity of so long life:
For who would bear the whips and scorns of time[28],
The oppressor's wrong, the proud man's contumely[29],
The pangs of dispriz'd[30] love, the law's delay,
The insolence of office[31], and the spurns[32]
That patient merit of the unworthy takes[33],
When he himself might his quietus make
With a bare bodkin[34]? Who would fardels bear
To grunt and sweat under a weary life,
But that the dread of something after death
The undiscovered country, from whose bourn[35]
No traveler returns, puzzles the will,
And makes us rather bear those ills we have,
Than fly to others that we know not of?
Thus conscience[36] does make cowards of us all,
And thus the native hue of resolution
Is sicklied o'er, with the pale cast of thought[37],

And enterprises of great pith and moment[38]
With this regard[39] their currents turn awry
And lose the name of action. Soft you[40] now,
The faire Ophelia? Nymph, in thy orisons
Be all my sins remembered.

Oph. Good my lord[41],
How does your honor for this many a day?

Ham. I humbly thank you: well, well, well.

Oph. My lord, I have remembrances of yours,
That I have longed long to re-deliver.
I pray you now, receive them.

Ham. No, no, I never gave you aught.

Oph. My honor'd Lord, you know right well you did,
And with them words of so sweet breath compos'd,
As made the things more rich. Their perfume lost:
Take these again, for to the noble mind
Rich gifts wax[42] poor, when givers prove unkind.
There my lord.

Ham. Ha, ha: Are you honest[43]?

Oph. My Lord?

Ham. Are you fair?

Oph. What means your lordship?

Ham. That if you be honest and faire, your honesty should admit[44] no discourse to your beauty.

Oph. Could beauty [,] my lord, have better commerce[45] than with[46] honesty?

Ham. Ay truly: for the power of beauty, will sooner transform honesty from what it is to a bawd[47], than the force of honesty can translate beauty into his likeness. This was sometime a paradox[48], but now the time gives it proof. I did love you once.

Oph. Indeed my lord, you made me believe so.

Ham. You should not have believed me. For virtue

cannot so inoculate our old stock, but we shall relish of it[49]. I loved you not.

Oph. I was the more deceived.

Ham. Get thee to a nunnery. Why would'st thou be a breeder of sinners? I am myself indifferent[50] honest, but yet I could accuse me of such things, that it were better my mother had not borne me. I am very proud, revengeful, ambitious, with more offences at my beck, than I have thoughts to put them in, imagination to give them shape, or time to act them in. What should such fellows as I do, crawling between earth and heaven? We are arrant knaves all, believe none of us. Go thy ways to a nunnery. Where's your father?

Oph. At home, my lord.

Ham. Let the doors be shut upon him, that he may play the fool nowhere, but in's own house. Farewell.

Oph. O help him, you sweet heavens.

Ham. If thou dost marry, I'll give thee this plague for thy dowry. Be thou[51] as chaste as ice, as pure as snow, thou shalt not escape calumny[52]. Get thee to a nunnery. Go, farewell. Or if thou wilt needs marry, marry a fool: for wise men know well enough what monsters[53] you make of them. To a nunnery go, and quickly too. Farewell.

Oph. O heavenly powers, restore him.

Ham. I have heard of your paintings too well enough.God has given you one face, and you make your self another: you jig[54], you amble, and you lisp[55], and nickname Gods creatures, and make your wantonness your ignorance[56]. Go to[57], I'll[58] no more on't[59], it hath made me mad. I say, we will have no more marriages. Those that are married already, all but one shall live, the rest shall keep as they are. To a nunnery, go.

[*Exit Hamlet.*]

Oph. O what a noble mind is here o'er-thrown!
The courtier's, soldier's, scholar's: eye, tongue, sword,
Th' expectancy and rose of the faire state[60],
The glass of fashion[61], and the mould of form[62],
Th' observ'd of all observers[63], quite, quite down.
And I of ladies most deject[64] and wretched,
That suck'd the honey of his music vows:
Now see that noble, and most sovereign reason,
Like sweet bells jangled out of tune, and harsh,
That unmatch'd form and feature of blown youth[65],
Blasted with ecstasy[66]. Oh woe is me,
T' have seen what I have seen: see what I see.

[*Enter King and Polonius.*]

King. Love? His affections[67] do not that way tend,
Nor what he spoke, though it lack'd form[68] a little,
Was not like madness[69]. There's something in his soul
O'er which his melancholy sits on brood[70],
And I do doubt[71] the hatch, and the disclose[72]
Will be some danger, which for to prevent
I have in quick determination
Thus set it down. He shall with speed to England[73]
For the demand of our neglected tribute:
Haply[74] the seas and countries different
With variable objects[75], shall expel
This something settled matter in his heart:
Whereon his brain ['s] still beating[76], puts him thus
From fashion of himself[77]. What think you on't?
Pol. It shall do well. But yet do I believe
The origin and commencement of his grief
Sprung from neglected love. How now Ophelia?
You need not tell us what Lord Hamlet said,

We heard it all. My lord, do as you please,
But if you hold it fit after the play,
Let his queen mother all alone entreat him
To show his grieves[78]: let her be round[79] with him,
And I'll be plac'd (so please you) in the ear
Of all their conference[80]. If she find him not[81],
To England send him: Or confine him where
Your wisdom best shall think.
King. It shall be so:
Madness in great ones must not unwatch'd go.
Exeunt.

【注解】

1. drift of circumstance: 迂回曲折，拐弯抹角。
2. forward to be sounded: 愿意被人试探底细。
3. with much forcing of his disposition: 相当不自然。
4. Niggard of question: 不愿主动说话。
5. assay him to any pastime: 引他找一找乐子。
6. o'er-raught: 相当于 overtook 赶上并超过。
7. Give him a further edge: 再给他加点油。
8. gather by him, as he is behaved: 根据他的言谈举止判断。
9. suffers for: 相当于 suffers from。
10. happy: 幸运。
11. wonted way: 常态。
12. so please ye: 相当于 if you please，一种敬语。
13. book:《圣经》或祈祷书。
14. show of such an exercise: 摆出这副念经的样子。
15. colour your loneliness: 解释你为何独自在此。
16. devotion's visage: 虔诚的表情。
17. plast'ring art: 美容术，化妆术。
18. to the thing that helps it: 与美容之物相比。
19. suffer: 忍受。
20. by opposing end them: 相当于 end them by opposing them。
21. No more: 此处可以有两种解释：①对 to die, to sleep 的补充说明，即 to die is no more than to sleep; ②对 end them 的补充说明，即 no more trouble。
22. thousand natural shocks that flesh is heir to: 肉体承受的千百种病恙。

23. consummation: 归宿。
24. I: 相当于 Ay，感叹词。
25. rub: 难点，麻烦，原指草地滚球中使球偏离目标的障碍物或地面凹凸之处。
26. shuffled off this mortal coil: 摆脱人世的纷扰。
27. respect: 考虑。
28. time: 尘世；时世。
29. contumely: 鄙视，白眼。
30. dispriz'd: 不被珍视的。
31. office: 官吏。
32. spurns: 侮辱。
33. That patient merit of the unworthy takes: "patient merit" 指宽忍的君子，"the unworthy" 指缺德的小人。
34. . . . his quietus make with a bare bodkin: 仅用一把匕首就能了结他的生死簿上的账。
35. bourn: 疆域。
36. conscience: 内心的盘算。
37. Is sicklied o'er . . . of thought: 蒙上了一层瞻前顾后的苍白病容。
38. pith and moment: 实质和重要性。
39. With this regard: 由于这个原因。
40. Soft you: 停住，别说了。
41. Good my Lord: 相当于 My good Lord。
42. wax: 变得。
43. honest: 贞洁；诚实。
44. admit: 允许。
45. commerce: 交易；交往。
46. with: 也作 your。
47. bawd: 娼妓。
48. paradox: 谬论。
49. . . . virtue cannot so inoculate our old stock, but we shall relish of it: 美德无论怎样嫁接到我们原有的砧木上，我们也尝得出砧木的味道。but 相当于 without。
50. indifferent: 有些。
51. Be thou: 相当于 Even if thou be。
52. calumny: 诽谤。
53. monsters: 根据英国民间说法，妻子如果不忠，丈夫头上就会长出两只角。这里的 monsters 指这种头上长角的怪物。
54. jig: 哼小调或随小调扭动起舞。
55. lisp: 装腔作势。
56. make your wantonness your ignorance: 把你们的肆无忌惮说成是天真无知。
57. Go to: 相当于 Go away。
58. I'll: 相当于 I want。

59. on't: 相当于 of it。
60. expectancy and rose of the faire state: 我们美丽国家的期待和玫瑰。“期待”指人们对王子最终要继承王位的期待；“玫瑰”常被视为花中之王，象征青春年华。
61. The glass of fashion: 时尚的楷模。
62. the mould of form: 仪表的典范。
63. Th' observ'd of all observers: 所有仰慕者敬仰的对象。
64. deject: 相当于 dejected。
65. blown youth: 风华正茂的青年。
66. Blasted with ecstasy: 被癔症摧残。
67. affections: 心思。
68. lack'd form: 语无伦次。
69. Nor . . . not . . . : 这里的双重否定并不表示肯定，只起强调作用。
70. sits on brood: 谋划。这里借用母鸡孵蛋来比喻慢慢谋划。
71. doubt: 担心。
72. disclose: 成熟后的想法。
73. He shall with speed to England: 我要立即派他去英国。shall 表达说话人的意愿。早期现代英语中，shall、will、must 等情态动词后面常直接跟 to，表示去某一地方。
74. Haply: 或许，但愿。
75. variable objects: 各种景色。
76. Whereon his brain's still beating: 这样一来他脑子里不停地想着事情。“still”意为不停、不断。
77. puts him thus from fashion of himself: 使他改变自己近来的举止。
78. show his grieves: 倾诉他的苦水。
79. round: 直截了当。
80. And I'll be plac'd . . . conference: 我将藏在能听到他们所有谈话的地方。
81. find him not: 探不出个究竟。

【思考题】

1. In the beginning lines of Scene 1, the king uses phrases like “puts on this confusion”, “dangerous lunacy”, etc. What can you infer from the king's idea of Hamlet's madness?
2. When Polonius says “ . . . with devotion's visage,/ And pious action, we do sugar o'er/ The devil himself”, the king responds by an aside, saying, “O'tis true: . . . /Oh heavy burthen!” Do you think the king feels guilty of his crime?
3. The famous soliloquy beginning with “To be, or not to be” is Hamlet's meditation on the issues of life and death. Discuss Hamlet's (or Shakespeare's) notion of earthly life in view of the intellectual background of Renaissance.

【简评】

《哈姆雷特》是莎士比亚的戏剧艺术达到巅峰时期他创作的代表作，是莎士比亚作品中最成熟、最深刻的一部。通过复仇剧的形式，《哈姆雷特》表达了莎士比亚对国家、王权、统一、理想、人生、死亡等重大问题的思考。第三幕是全剧的高潮。在此场中不仅有哈姆雷特最为著名的独白，还有戏中戏、国王祈祷、哈姆雷特误杀波洛涅斯等关键情节，在结构上起到了一个承上启下的作用。在本场给观众印象最深的还是哈姆雷特上场时念的那段著名独白。它深刻地表现了哈姆雷特在父亲突然死去、母亲改嫁、叔父继位等一系列变故后产生的复杂思想、矛盾心理与内心冲突。如果说奥菲利娅在痛苦之余对哈姆雷特发出的评价 (The courtier's, soldier's, scholar's eye . . .) 反映了哈姆雷特人文主义的一面，那么哈姆雷特自己的这段独白则表现了这位“忧郁王子”对人文主义思想怀疑与动摇的一面。哈姆雷特是一个具有丰满的人物，在英国甚至世界文学中也是最具争议的人物形象之一。有一百个读者，就可能有一百个哈姆雷特，而各个时代又可能有各个时代的哈姆雷特。《哈姆雷特》思想上的深刻性、情节上的生动性、人物上的复杂性、语言上的丰富性——所有这些使得该剧成为世界文学史上一颗璀璨夺目的明星。

Sonnets

【题解】

十四行诗起源于 13 世纪的意大利，16 世纪上半叶由英国诗人萨里伯爵霍华德和怀亚特引入英国，风靡一时。莎士比亚的十四行诗早在 1609 年发表前就以手抄本的形式在民间流传，其主题思想以歌颂爱情与友谊为主。但这种爱情、友谊又完全不同于与莎士比亚同时代大多数人的爱情、友谊观，总是伴随着一种感官上的激情，与同时代人约翰·多恩 (John Donne, 1572—1631) 的爱情诗十分接近。这些诗共 154 首，分为三组。第一组 (第 1 至 126 首) 是诗人写给一位青年男子的，告诫他要早些结婚，生儿育女；第二组 (第 127 至 152 首) 描写了一位姿色不佳的黑肤女郎 (dark lady)，诗人表达了对她毫不掩饰的情欲；第三组 (第 153 至 154 首) 与前两组毫无关系，好像是同一首诗写了两遍。在韵脚上，莎士比亚创作了自己的诗韵，即有名的莎士比亚十四行诗韵：abab, cdcd, efef, gg。以下两首为莎士比亚十四行诗第 18 首、第 29 首。

18

Shall I compare thee to a summer's day?[1]
Thou art more lovely and more temperate.
Rough winds do shake the darling buds of May,[2]
And summer's lease[3] hath all too short a date[4];
Sometime[5] too hot the eye of heaven[6] shines,
And often is his gold complexion dimm'd,[7]
And every fair from fair sometime declines,[8]
By chance or nature's changing course[9] untrimm'd[10]:
But thy eternal summer shall not fade
Nor lose possession of that fair thou ow'st,[11]
Nor shall Death brag thou wander'st in his shade,[12]
When in eternal lines[13] to time thou grow'st.[14]
So long as men can breathe or eyes can see,
So long lives this[15], and this gives life[16] to thee.

【注解】

1. Shall I compare thee to a summer's day?: 这是一个 rhetorical question。A summer's day 相当于 summer，用 summer's day 是为了和第三行的 May 押韵。英国的夏季除 7 月下旬的十几天外，气候一般舒适宜人，和中国北方地区的晚春比较接近，会让人产生愉快、美好的联想。莎剧《仲夏夜之梦》(*A Midsummer Night's Dream*, 1595/1596) 就是一个例子。
2. May: 英国人一般把 5 月中旬到 8 月中旬这段时间看作夏天。
3. lease: 租约。任何季节都像人类从大自然那里租来的一件东西，有时间限制，时间一到就被收回。
4. date: 时间，期限。
5. Sometime: 相当于 Sometimes。
6. the eye of heaven: 天的眼睛，此处喻指太阳。
7. his gold complexion dimm'd: 他金光闪闪的面庞被（乌云）遮蔽。
8. every fair from fair sometime declines: 相当于 every fair sometime declines from fair。第一个 fair 指美好的事物，如美人、美丽的面孔等；第二个 fair 和下面第十行的 fair 指美本身。sometime 在这里的意思是到一定时候。
9. nature's changing course: 大自然的演变进程。
10. untrimm'd: 卸去美的装束。
11. ow'st: 拥有。
12. shade: shadow。
13. eternal lines: 不朽的诗句。

14. to time thou grow'st: 你长到时间身上。
15. this: 这首诗。
16. life: 永生。

【思考题】

1. What is the theme of the poem?
2. Why is the speaker's loved one more lovely than a summer's day? What qualities of a summer's day does he compare his loved one to?
3. There is obviously a shift of tone and subject matter in line 9. Describe such a shift.
4. What rhetorical devices are used in this sonnet?
5. Love is a recurring theme in world literature and is presented in many ways by writers of different time periods and from various parts of the world. Can you cite any love poems in Chinese literature that have the same charm as this Sonnet of Shakespeare?

29

When in disgrace with fortune and men's eyes[1],
I all alone beweep[2] my outcast state[3],
And trouble deaf heaven with my bootless[4] cries,
And look upon myself and curse my fate,
Wishing me like to[5] one more rich in hope[6],
Featur'd[7] like him, like him with friends posses'd[8],
Desiring this man's art[9], and that man's scope[10],
With what I most enjoy contented least[11],
Yet in these thoughts[12] myself almost despising[13],
Haply I think on thee, and then my state,
(Like to the lark at break of day arising)
From sullen earth, sings hymns at heaven's gate.
For thy sweet love remembered such wealth brings[14]
That then I scorn to change my state with kings.[15]

【注解】

1. in disgrace with fortune and men's eyes: 穷困潦倒，世人鄙夷。"in disgrace" 意为失去……的宠爱。

2. beweep: 哭泣。
3. outcast state: 孤苦伶仃的处境。这里的 state 与第 14 行里的 state 意思相同。
4. bootless: 徒劳的。
5. like to: 像……一样，意同第 11 行的 like to。
6. one more rich in hope: 一个更有前程的人。
7. Featur'd: 有好容貌。
8. with friends posses'd: 有亲朋好友。
9. art: 才艺。
10. scope: 渊博。
11. With what I most enjoy contented least: 我对自己最喜欢的事最不满足。
12. in these thoughts: 想到这里。
13. myself almost despising: 几乎鄙视自己。
14. thy sweet love . . . wealth brings: 一想起你甜蜜的爱，我就有了无尽的财富。
15. change my state with kings: 相当于 exchange my state for that of kings。

【思考题】

1. In the first two thirds of the sonnet, the speaker is complaining about the misfortunes in his life. What suddenly lifts him out of his bad mood?
2. Explain and comment on these two lines: "Like to the lark at break of day arising/From sullen earth, sings hymns at heaven's gate."
3. In the last line, the speaker scorns to change his state with kings. What does the word "state" mean?

English Literature of the Early/ Mid Seventeenth Century

1603–1660

在英国历史上，17 世纪前六十年，是一个动荡不安、风云际会的时代，其间爆发了震惊世界的英国清教徒革命，史称英国内战。事实上，早在 16 世纪末伊丽莎白女王统治晚期，英国社会已危机四伏。1588 年，英国海军击败了西班牙无敌舰队，英国取得海上霸主的地位。外患既去，内忧渐起，一致对外时被搁置一旁的种种矛盾逐渐暴露了出来，并迅速激化：以宗教改革为目的的清教势力日益壮大，矛头直指黑暗腐败的国教；议会和王室间摩擦频繁，新兴资产阶级羽翼渐丰，不甘屈居于王权之下；兼之两任斯图亚特王 (Stuart Kings) 詹姆士一世 (James I，1566—1625)，以及查理一世 (Charles I，1600—1649) 缺乏政治才能，政府腐化，人民的不满情绪高涨，1642 年英国内战终于爆发。1649 年，保皇党大败，查理一世被议会激进派送上断头台。然而，随后成立的共和政府实际上处在奥利弗·克伦威尔 (Oliver Cromwell, 1599—1658) 的军事独裁之下。人们对严酷的清教统治渐感失望。1660 年，英王查理二世 (Charles II，1630—1685) 回国，斯图亚特王权复辟。虽然从表面上看，复辟后的国家结构与内战之前并无二致，但这一历史性的大变革却对英国社会生活的各个方面产生了强烈的冲击。在不足百年的时间里，英国从一个君权至上、等级森严的社会变成了一个充满活力、多种势力并存的新型社会。

17 世纪上半叶，影响英国的不仅是清教徒革命，一场思想革命也在悄然展开。现代天文学家尼古拉·哥白尼 (Nicolaus Copernicus，1473—1543) 大胆提出了日心说，推翻了地球是宇宙中心的观念。英国在 17 世纪 60 年代初成立了科学团体“皇家学会”(The Royal Society)，当时人们热衷于进行天文、医学、物理、化学等方面的研究和实验。如果说大革命有形地摧毁了王权统治，那么这些早期的科学探索则在无形间从思想上摇撼了君权神授的世界观。在这两股势力的合力下，英国社会向多元化发展。

社会的动荡，思想的革新，对这一时期的文学作品产生了深远的影响。伊丽莎白时代华丽铺排的文风不见了，自信乐观的口吻消失了，对“乌托邦”式的理想世界的浪漫向往被人所淡忘。17 世纪的作家们身处在一个多种价值观念激烈交锋的时代，他们赋予这个时代的文学全新的内涵。

首先，玄学派 (Metaphysical School) 诗歌异军突起。这派诗人虽然继承了伊丽莎白时代诗歌复杂精妙的语言特色，却尽弃那一时代甜腻空泛、故作优雅的文风。他们的诗歌较口语化，韵脚复杂、不规则、思辨性强、涵盖面广，主题包括天文、地理、哲学、物理等各方面，充满了奇思妙想 (conceit)，将各种看似毫不相干的意象冶于一炉。塞缪尔·约翰逊博士 (Dr. Samuel Johnson，1709—1784) 批评这派诗人全凭蛮力将杂七杂八的思想拉到一处。虽然玄学派诗人的确有卖弄学问之嫌，喜欢语出惊人，但是，约翰逊博士所认为的“蛮力”(violence) 恰恰揭示出这类诗作里隐藏着的裹挟一切的巨大能量。那些看似庞杂无章的意象恰恰是这个动荡混乱的时代的一种反映。玄学派诗人正是通过复杂的哲学思辨试图对复杂的现实社会加以再现。他们的作品也影响了20世纪初同样身处动荡时代的现代派诗人，使他们从中找到了共鸣。玄学派诗人中的佼佼者是约翰·多恩，他因创作《歌与短歌》(*Songs and Sonnets*, 1633) 和《圣十四行诗》(*Holy Sonnets*, 1633) 闻名于世。乔治·赫伯特 (George Herbert, 1593—1633) 被誉为"玄学派诗圣"，他的诗歌带有强烈的宗教色彩，代表作是《圣殿》(*The Temple*, 1633)。安德鲁·马维尔 (Andrew Marvell, 1621—1678) 的《花园》("The Garden", 1681) 和《致他羞怯的女友》("To His Coy Mistress", 1681) 都是英国诗歌不可多得的精品。虽然马维尔的想象没有多恩那么瑰丽突兀，但他的诗风平静清新，有一种庄严典雅之美。

这一时期另一个主要诗歌流派的人物以本·琼生 (Ben Jonson, 1572—1637) 为代表，人们称他们为"The Tribe of Ben"。因为这派诗人 (Sons of Ben) 多是乡绅出身，有保皇倾向，因此又称为"骑士派诗人" (the Cavalier Poets)。他们的诗歌遵循古典主义原则，推崇理性、和谐与规律，讲究古典精炼的形式和严格的韵脚，对其后兴起的新古典主义 (Neo-Classicism) 诗歌，尤其是约翰·德莱顿 (John Dryden, 1631—1700) 和亚历山大·蒲伯 (Alexander Pope, 1688—1744) 的作品，产生了重大影响。其代表人物本·琼生的诗歌简洁明快，表达干净洗练，说理确切有力。他的继承者罗伯特·赫里克 (Robert Herrick, 1591—1674)，约翰·萨克林 (John Suckling, 1609—1642) 和理查德·勒夫莱斯 (Richard Lovelace, 1618—1657) 则文风优雅，措辞精妙。他们的作品流露出一种贵族式的淡然，缺少了琼生的严肃，却完整保留了琼生讲究琢磨、推崇精细的特色。

进入17世纪，伊丽莎白时代最为盛行的文学形式——戏剧，受到了清心寡欲的清教徒和道德家的强烈抨击，戏剧家们不得不依附于宫廷权贵，寻求他们的庇护。这一时期的戏剧创作以复仇剧和闹剧式的喜剧为主，充满了暴力、血腥、疯狂、腐败和恣肆的激情，其中最成功的作品要数本·琼生的喜剧。琼生的喜剧专门讽刺社会，抨击时代，剧中人物多受某种情绪 (humours) 或情欲的支配，无法自控。他的喜剧既有高雅的古典主义成分，又有低俗、滑稽荒诞的玩笑，充溢了活力，开创了英国喜剧的传统。他的代表作有《狐狸》(*Volpone*, 1606)、《炼金士》(*The Alchemist*, 1610) 等。1642年，英国内战爆发，剧院被迫关闭，直到1660年王权复辟后才重新开放，戏剧这一伟大的艺术形式走下了文艺复兴时代的巅峰。

17世纪上半叶是英国散文发展的重要阶段。在这个多种思想激烈冲突的时代，散文以它灵活的形式、宽广的适应范围，为人们提供了阐发各自观点的快捷方式。这一时期的宗教纷争造就了一批伟大的布道者。兰斯洛特·安德鲁斯 (Lancelot

Andrews, 1555—1626) 和约翰 · 多恩的布道文在英国散文中独具一格。这个时代还诞生了出色的散文家弗兰西斯 · 培根 (Francis Bacon，1561—1626)。他选用短小精悍的随笔 (essay) 形式，分析处世之道，探讨人生哲理。他的散文笔锋犀利，文字简练质朴、风格庄重，比喻虽不多，但形象生动。尽管培根的散文重说理，重简洁，但是 17 世纪上半叶的散文仍以华美的巴洛克 (Baroque) 风格为主。医生出身的托马斯 · 布朗爵士 (Sir Thomas Browne，1605—1682) 的《医生哲学》(*Religio Medici*, 1643)、《瓮葬》(*Urn-Burial*, 1658) 等作品虽然缺乏培根式的缜密逻辑思维，但文字郁茂，行文细腻，是诗意的散文。罗伯特 · 伯顿 (Robert Burton，1577—1640) 的《忧郁的解剖》(*The Anatomy of Melancholy*，1621) 辞藻华丽，想象怪诞，或幽默或夸张或愤懑，情感多变。这个时代还诞生了传记散文家以萨克 · 沃尔顿 (Izaak Walton，1593—1683)，日记作家塞缪尔·皮普斯 (Samuel Pepys, 1633—1703) 和撰写《天路历程》(*The Pilgrim's Progress*, 1678) 的清教徒作家约翰 · 班扬 (John Bunyan, 1628—1688)。

17 世纪英国文坛最伟大的作家非约翰 · 弥尔顿 (John Milton, 1608—1674) 莫属。他的作品包括英国文学中最精美的十四行诗、最优秀的田园挽诗《黎西达斯》(*Lycidas*, 1637) 和最伟大的史诗《失乐园》(*Paradise Lost*, 1667)。他的散文具有雄辩色彩，气势磅礴，堪称英国散文经典之作。他是这个时代在文学方面的集大成者。

17 世纪中前期的英国文学依稀带有文艺复兴时代的痕迹，但它孕育着变革，孕育着一个崭新的文学时代。虽然这一时期的历史跨度不到六十年，却为英国文学史这幅长卷增添了它独特的色彩和印记。

John Donne
1572—1631

约翰·多恩出生在一个笃信天主教的富有商人家庭。他 4 岁丧父，母亲半年后再婚。多恩早年在家接受正统的天主教教育，1583 年进入牛津大学学习，后转入剑桥大学，前后读书六年，但由于他是天主教徒，未能获得学位。多恩 19 岁到伦敦林肯法律协会 (Lincoln's Inn of Court) 学习法律，却又因为他的信仰，无法执业做律师。1593 年，多恩的弟弟因藏匿天主教徒入狱而死，此后不久，多恩放弃了天主教信仰。多恩曾在 16 世纪 90 年代中期去欧洲大陆旅游，游历过意大利和西班牙。1596 年，他自愿追随埃塞克斯伯爵二世罗伯特·德弗罗 (Robert Devereux Essex, Earl of Essex Ⅱ, 1567—1601) 远征加的斯港 (Cadiz)；1597 年，又随沃尔特·雷利爵士 (Sir Walter Raleigh, 1554—1618) 在亚速尔群岛 (the Azores) 与西班牙人作战。在此期间，他结识了当时的掌玺大臣托马斯·埃格顿 (Thomas Egerton, 1540—1617) 的儿子。1598 年，在他的推荐下，多恩成为埃格顿的私人秘书。1601 年，多恩和埃格顿的内侄女，年仅 17 岁的安·摩尔 (Ann More) 秘密完婚。虽然他们婚后感情甚笃，但这段婚姻却断送了多恩的前程。他不仅丢了差事，还一度锒铛入狱。其后十四年，多恩不得不为养家糊口费尽心思。在 16 世纪 90 年代，多恩还是个意气风发的风流才子，生活浪荡；步入中年后，却被疾病贫穷所困，失意潦倒。在这一时期，多恩公开改信国教，参加了反对天主教的笔战。1607 年，多恩得到在国教供职的机会，但拒绝就任。1612 年，他被引荐给国王詹姆士一世。詹姆士国王很欣赏多恩的才华，认为他能成为一名伟大的教士，便下令不允许多恩以其他形式为朝廷效命，逼他出任教职。几经犹豫，1615 年，多恩终于做了国教牧师，在林肯法律协会宣讲宗教。多恩的听众中有不少是受过高等教育的人，这要求他不仅需要有对宗教的热忱，更需要有智慧、知识和技巧。多恩的才华终于得到施展，事实证明他是一位出色的演说家。1617 年，多恩的妻子去世，此后他更加全身心地投入宗教事业。1621 年，他被任命为圣保罗大教堂的教长 (Dean of St. Paul's)。1631 年，多恩去世。

约翰·多恩为后世留下了 160 篇布道文。他的布道文有炽热的情感、生动的形象，结构合理，文辞雄辩，其中不少是英国散文不可多得的名篇。尤其是《紧急时刻祈祷文》(*Devotions upon Emergent Occasions*, 1640, 1649, 1661; 分三集出版) 中的第 17

篇“Meditation 17”，直到20世纪还广为传颂。海明威的名著《丧钟为谁而鸣》(*For Whom the Bell Tolls*, 1940)的书名就出自这篇文章。

当然，多恩最大的成就还是他的诗歌创作。在他生前，他写的诗仅在私下流传，这是因为他早期诗作常涉及爱情主题，与他虔诚持重的教长身份不符，所以不宜公开。直到1633年，多恩的《诗歌》(*Poems*)才得以付梓出版。伊丽莎白时代晚期，诗歌大都文字华丽，意象陈腐空洞，节奏甜腻而缺乏生气。多恩的诗作尽扫前人的浮靡之气。他的作品语藏机锋(wit)，富于奇思妙想，擅长将各种看似风马牛不相及的意象交织在一处，制造一种新颖的和谐。比如，他在《别离辞：哭泣》(“A Valediction: Of Weeping”)中曾将情人分别时的泪滴分别比作印有爱人肖像的钱币、绘有大千世界的地球仪、被月球引力引来的大海的狂波，使人不由自主地为他奇妙的想象力拍案叫绝。多恩诗歌的另一特点是哲学性、逻辑性强，明明是在抒发感情，却又糅合着敏捷活泼的思维活动。读多恩的诗，如同参加一项智力游戏，唯有开动脑筋，方能追赶上诗人飞驰的想象，品味出他精妙的思辨。多恩的诗歌格律复杂，经常打破常规限制，令他的同辈人大为震惊。这些自成一格的诗歌因多恩的生花妙笔常常流动着一种特别的音韵美。

多恩的诗歌毁誉参半。17世纪的桂冠诗人约翰·德莱顿认为多恩虽聪明机智，但算不上一个好诗人。18世纪的约翰逊博士更是对多恩这一派文学诗人不屑一顾，认为他们“全凭蛮力将杂七杂八的思想拉到一处”。20世纪现代派代表艾略特(T. S. Eliot，1888—1965)却对多恩赞美有加。他指出唯有真正的天才才能写出如此精妙的诗作，并认为多恩远胜于那些感情与思想相脱节(dissociation of sensibility)的诗人，如弥尔顿。他能用感情捕捉思想，将思想化为感情，使感情与思想水乳交融(unified sensibility)。无论毁之誉之，约翰·多恩的诗歌凭借它独特的魅力，成为英国文学中一道永恒的风景。

A Valediction: Forbidding Mourning

【题解】

根据以萨克·沃尔顿(Izaak Walton, 1953—1683)所作的多恩传记(*Bibliography of Donne*)，这首多恩送给妻子的赠别诗写于1611年。当时多恩正准备随罗伯特·特鲁里爵士(Sir Robert Drury, 1575—1615)出使欧洲大陆。他的妻子在他出国期间产下一死胎。据传记作家推测，多恩动身之前即有不祥预感，所以这首诗语气严肃，感情深沉，一改多恩平日艳情诗的浪荡口吻。

A Valediction: Forbidding Mourning

As virtuous men pass mildly away,
And whisper to their souls to go,
Whilst some of their sad friends do say
The breath goes now, and some say, No;

So let us melt, and make no noise,
No tear-floods, nor sigh-tempests move,
'Twere profanation of our joys
To tell the laity our love[1].

Moving of th' earth[2] brings harms and fears,
Men reckon what it did and meant;
But trepidation of the spheres,
Though greater far, is innocent[3].

Dull sublunary[4] lovers' love
(Whose soul[5] is sense)cannot admit
Absence, because it doth remove
Those things which elemented[6] it.

But we, by a love so much refined
That our selves know not what it is,
Inter-assured[7] of the mind,
Care less[8], eyes, lips, and hands to miss.

Our two souls therefore, which are one,
Though I must go, endure not yet
A breach, but an expansion,
Like gold to airy thinness beat[9].

If they be two, they are two so,

As stiff twin compasses are two[10];
Thy soul, the fixed foot, makes no show
To move, but doth, if th' other do.

And though it in the center sit,
Yet when the other far doth roam,
It leans and hearkens after it,
And grows erect, as that comes home.

Such wilt thou be to me, who must
Like th' other foot, obliquely[11] run;
Thy firmness makes my circle just,
And makes me end where I begun.

【注解】

1. 'Twere profanation of our joys / To tell the laity our love: 'Twere: 相当于 it were。"profanation" 意为亵渎、不敬。"laity" 指俗人(有别于教士和僧侣)。这两句旨在表明他们的爱神圣而高尚。
2. Moving of th' earth: 地震。
3. . . . trepidation of the spheres . . . is innocent: "trepidation of the spheres" 指天体震动。文艺复兴时代的人相信托勒密的天文学理论，他们认为地球是宇宙的中心，周围运行的轨道有九层，构成九重天。其中最外面的一层是水晶天，它的运动变化会影响内部几重天。这句的意思是，尽管天体震颤比地震更猛烈，但它不会对人类产生太大影响，所以是无害的 ("innocent")。
4. sublunary: 相当于 below the moon，指月亮之下的，地球的，世俗多变的。根据文艺复兴时代的天文观，月亮之下的地区，包括地球在内，处在动荡变化和衰败之中，与永恒不变的星际形成对比。
5. soul: essence，本质。
6. elemented: composed，构成。
7. Inter-assured: 用来修饰 "we"，指我们心心相印。
8. care less: 相当于 careless。这句话正常语序应是 Careless to miss eyes, lips, and hands。
9. Like gold to airy thinness beat: 这句话的正常结构是 Like gold beat to airy thinness，意思是别离是爱的延展，如同黄金能打成薄薄的金页。诗人将他们的爱比作黄金，它的 "airy thinness" 与凡俗的 (sublunary)、必须依靠感官的厚重、浑浊的爱成鲜明对比。
10. As a stiff twin compasses are two: 多恩将相恋的人比作圆规的两只脚，这是玄学派最著名的奇思妙想之一。圆规象征坚贞，画出的圆象征完美和圆满。
11. obliquely: 倾斜。圆规的圆周脚画圆时总有所倾斜。

【思考题】

1. Why does Donne's "Valediction" (a poem of farewell) forbid mourning?
2. The poem is organized around a contrast of two kinds of lovers: the "laity", and as their implied opposite, the "priesthood". Are these terms literary or metaphysical? What is the essential difference between these two kinds of love? How, according to the speaker, does their behaviour differ when they must separate from each other?
3. If the poem ended with line 24, what would it mean? How would it differ from the complete version?
4. Comment on the relation of the various images to each other. Is there a development of some kind?

John Milton
1608—1674

约翰·弥尔顿是英国文学史上当之无愧的巨匠。他出生于伦敦的一个殷实家庭，12 岁师从博学多才的学者托马斯·扬 (Thomas Young, 1587—1655)，15 岁进入圣保罗学校 (St. Paul's School)，1629 年获剑桥大学基督学院 (Christ's College, Cambridge) 学士学位，1632 年获该学院硕士学位。毕业后，由于不满当时教会贪污腐化的黑暗现实，弥尔顿放弃了到教会任职的机会。他先搬到伦敦东郊的哈默史密斯，继而又隐居于温莎附近的霍顿乡间别墅，潜心研究学问达六年之久，遍览英文、拉丁文、希腊文、意大利文、希伯来文等书写的重要典籍。1638 年，为了增广见闻，他踏上了去欧洲大陆的旅程，参观了巴黎、佛罗伦萨、罗马等文化名城，结识了不少知名学者，其中包括伟大的天文学家伽利略，后因英国国内政治风云剧变，于 1639 年返回英国，随即投身于反王权、反教会的斗争之中。1642 年，他与年仅 16 岁的玛丽·鲍威尔 (Mary Powell) 结婚，但婚姻并不美满，新娘婚后一个月即返回娘家居住，直到 1645 年才回到他身旁，并于 1652 年早逝。1649 年，英王查理一世被送上断头台，弥尔顿欣然领命，在克伦威尔政府中担任国务会议拉丁文秘书一职，用笔为武器，坚决捍卫英国人民斗争得来的民主和自由。由于终日埋头工作，过于疲劳，弥尔顿于 1651 年双目几近失明。1656 年，他再次结婚，娶凯瑟琳·伍德科克 (Catherine Woodcock) 为妻，但她在 1658 年死于难产。1660年，斯图亚特王朝复辟，弥尔顿一度身陷囹圄，有生命之忧，多亏朋友相助，才幸免于难。1663年，他第三次结婚，妻子是伊丽莎白·明斯豪 (Elizabeth Minshull)。弥尔顿晚年双目失明，疾病缠身，生活拮据，但就是在这种恶劣的环境下，仍将一腔心血投注于创作。1674年，这位文学巨匠溘然辞世。

弥尔顿生活的时代，轰轰烈烈的文艺复兴已近尾声，启蒙运动尚在襁褓之中。弥尔顿就是这两股洪流交汇处的过渡人物。因此，从他的作品中既能看到强烈的人文主义色彩和雄奇瑰丽的气势，又能看到清教徒式的严峻内敛的倾向。弥尔顿的创作大致可分为三个时期。1628至1639年间是求学时期，作品以抒情诗为主，代表作有写于21岁生日的《圣诞清晨歌》("On the Morning of Christ's Nativity")，1631年左右创作的姊妹诗《快乐的人》("L'Allegro") 和《忧思的人》("Il Penseroso")，以及为纪念溺水而死的好友爱德华·金 (Edward King) 而作的《黎西达斯》。这一时期的作品风格明净，多如出水芙蓉般清新自然，虽然尚缺乏后期史诗那种雷霆万钧的气势，但作者卓然不群的诗才已得到充分的展示。1640至1660年是弥尔顿的创作中期，除了十四行诗外，他几乎放弃了写诗，将主要精力投注于撰写富有宣传鼓动性的论辩文和政治小册子。主要作品有1644年为争取出版自由高声疾呼的《论出版自由》(*Areopagitica*)，1651年为驳斥欧洲大陆保皇学者克劳狄乌斯·萨尔马修斯 (Clandius Salmasius, 1588—1653) 而作的《为英国人民声辩》(*Defence of the English People*) 和1653年的《再为英国人民声辩》(*Second Defence of the English People*)。弥尔顿的论辩文，说理清晰，雄辩有力。1660至1674年是弥尔顿的创作晚期。出版于1667年的《失乐园》取材《圣经·旧约·创世记》，描述了人类始祖受撒旦诱惑，违背上帝意志偷食禁果而被逐出乐园，它是英国文学最伟大的作品之一。1671年出版的《复乐园》(*Paradise Regained*) 取材于《圣约·新约·马太福音》，记述了耶稣基督在撒旦的百般诱惑面前毫不动摇，坚持信仰，战胜考验，从而恢复了乐园。诗人坦言《复乐园》是他偏爱的作品，因为耶稣基督的形象远比《失乐园》中的亚当坚定。但是，《复乐园》的文学价值却远逊于《失乐园》，行文有凝滞呆板之嫌，缺乏激情与壮阔。同年出版的《力士参孙》(*Samson Agonistes*) 典出《圣经·旧约·士师记》，是一部继承古希腊悲剧传统的诗剧。参孙是犹太大力士，与非利士人屡战屡胜，但受妻子大利拉 (Delilah) 的哄骗，被俘为囚，双目被刺瞎。他斗争到底，与非利士人同归于尽。事实上，弥尔顿正是以参孙自喻，尽管双目失明，但革命斗志不减。他虽然在没有光的世界里度过后半生，却为后人创作出了辉映百代的不朽诗篇。

Paradise Lost

【题解】

《失乐园》这部气势恢宏的史诗是英国文学的骄傲。全书共分 12 部。第一至四部叙述了撒旦叛军大败，堕入地狱，建万魔宫，撒旦为了复仇潜回地球。第五至八部用倒叙手法介绍了撒旦叛军与上帝之间的天界大战，以及上帝造人的过程。第九部是全书高潮，亚当与夏娃在撒旦的诱惑下偷食禁果。第 10 至第 12 部讲述亚当与夏娃被逐出乐园，居于尘世，人类历史由此展开。

弥尔顿写《失乐园》的时候，轰轰烈烈的英国大革命已告失败，与失去乐园中的亚当、夏娃一样，英国人民也生活在痛苦之中。弥尔顿创作这部史诗，就是为了“向世人昭示天理的公道”(justify the ways of God to men)，借古喻今，告诉英国人民要学会坚持和忍耐，等待被赎救的那天到来。史诗中，人类始祖亚当与夏娃的形象高大秀美。虽然他们因为自身的弱点而失去乐园，但他们默默承受苦难时所表现出的勇气和坚韧，充分展示了人性的力量，更让人看到恢复乐园的曙光。

《失乐园》采用无韵体 (the blank verse)，诗行通常是五步抑扬格。句子结构错杂繁复，短语层层叠加，从句互相嵌套，往往十几行、甚至几十行才组成一个完整的句子，是典型的“弥尔顿式的语言”(the Miltonic language)。全诗节奏紧凑，语言瑰丽，气势雄浑。

以下选自《失乐园》第一部的第 1 至第 124 行。这些诗行具有明显的史诗特征。第 1 至第 26 行中，作者向神乞求赐予他灵感 (invocation)，这是荷马的《奥德赛》(*The Odyssey*)、维吉尔的《埃涅阿斯纪》(*The Aeneid*) 等史诗惯用的开篇形式。第 27 至第 44 行是史诗式设问 (the epic question)，诗人探问人类失去乐园的原因，引入了撒旦的形象。第 44 至第 75 行描绘了撒旦叛军大败，堕入火湖饱受煎熬的场面。第 76 至第 124 行是撒旦反抗上帝“暴政”的“豪言壮语”。

From Paradise Lost

Book 1

(excerpt)

Of man's first disobedience, and the fruit[1]
Of that forbidden tree whose mortal[2] taste
Brought death into the world, and all our woe,

With loss of Eden, till one greater Man[3]
Restore us, and regain the blissful seat,
Sing, Heavenly Muse, that on the secret top
Of Oreb, or of Sinai, didst inspire
That shepherd who first taught the chosen seed[4]
In the beginning how the heavens and earth
Rose out of Chaos: or, if Sion hill
Delight thee more, and Siloa's brook that flowed
Fast by the oracle of God[5], I thence
Invoke thy aid to my adventurous song,
That with no middle flight intends to soar
Above th'Aonian mount, while it pursues
Things unattempted yet in prose or rhyme[6].
And chiefly thou, O Spirit[7], that dost prefer
Before all temples th'upright heart and pure,
Instruct me, for thou know'st; thou from the first
Wast present, and, with mighty wings outspread,
Dovelike sat'st brooding on the vast abyss[8],
And mad'st[9] it pregnant: what in me is dark
Illumine; what is low, raise and support;
That to the height of this great argument[10]
I may assert Eternal Providence,
And justify the ways of God to men.
　Say first (for Heaven hides nothing from thy view,
Nor the deep tract of Hell), say first what cause
Moved our grand parents[11], in that happy state,
Favored of Heaven so highly, to fall off
From their Creator, and transgress his will
For[12] one restraint, lords of the world besides[13]?
Who first seduced them to that foul revolt?
　Th'infernal serpent; he it was, whose guile,
Stirred up with envy and revenge, deceived
The mother of mankind, what time[14] his pride

Had cast him out from Heaven, with all his host
Of rebel angels, by whose aid aspiring
To set himself in glory above his peers[15],
He trusted to have equaled the Most High,
If he opposed; and with ambitious aim
Against the throne and monarchy of God
Raised impious war in Heaven and battle proud,
With vain attempt[16]. Him the Almighty Power
Hurled headlong flaming from th' ethereal sky
With hideous ruin and combustion down
To bottomless perdition, there to dwell
In adamantine chains and penal fire,
Who durst defy th' Omnipotent to arms[17].
 Nine times the space that measures day and night
To mortal men, he with his horrid crew
Lay vanquished, rolling in the fiery gulf
Confounded though immortal. But his doom
Reserved him to more wrath; for now the thought
Both of lost happiness and lasting pain
Torments him; round he throws his baleful[18] eyes,
That witnessed huge affliction and dismay,
Mixed with obdurate pride and steadfast hate.
At once, as far as angels ken[19], he views
The dismal situation waste and wild:
A dungeon horrible, on all sides round
As one great furnace flamed; yet from those flames
No light[20], but rather darkness visible
Served only to discover sights of woe,
Regions of sorrow, doleful shades, where peace
And rest can never dwell, hope never comes
That comes to all[21], but torture without end
Still urges[22], and a fiery deluge[23], fed
With ever-burning sulphur unconsumed:

Such place Eternal Justice had prepared
For those rebellious; here their prison ordained
In utter darkness[24] and their portion set
As far removed from God and light of Heaven
As from the center[25] thrice to th'utmost pole.
O how unlike the place from whence they fell!
There the companions of his fall, o'erwhelmed
With floods and whirlwinds of tempestuous fire,
He soon discerns; and, weltering by his side,
One next himself in power, and next in crime,
Long after known in Palestine, and named
Beelzebub[26]. To whom th' Arch-Enemy,
And thence in Heaven called Satan[27], with bold words
Breaking the horrid silence, thus began:—
'If thou beest he—but O how fallen[28]! how changed
From him who, in the happy realms of light
Clothed with transcendent brightness, didst outshine
Myriads[29], though bright!—if he whom mutual league,
United thoughts and counsels, equal hope
And hazard in the glorious enterprise
Joined with me once, now misery hath joined
In equal ruin; into what pit thou seest
From what height fallen: so much the stronger proved
He with his thunder[30]; and till then who knew
The force of those dire arms[31]? Yet not for those,
Nor what the potent Victor in his rage
Can else inflict, do I repent, or change,
Though changed in outward lustre, that fixed mind,
And high disdain from sense of injured merit,
That with the Mightiest raised me to contend,
And to the fierce contentions brought along
Innumerable force of Spirits armed,
That durst dislike his reign, and, me preferring,

His utmost power with adverse power opposed
In dubious[32] battle on the plains of Heaven,
And shook his throne. What though the field be lost?
All is not lost—the unconquerable will,
And study[33] of revenge, immortal hate,
And courage never to submit or yield:
And what is else not to be overcome[34]?
That glory never shall his wrath or might
Extort from me. To bow and sue for grace
With suppliant knee, and deify his power
Who, from the terror of this arm, so late
Doubted[35] his empire—that were low indeed;
That were an ignominy and shame beneath
This downfall; since, by fate, the strength of gods[36],
And this empyreal substance, cannot fail[37];
Since, through experience of this great event,
In arms not worse, in foresight much advanced,
We may with more successful hope resolve
To wage by force or guile eternal war,
Irreconcilable to our grand Foe,
Who now triumphs, and in th' excess of joy
Sole reigning holds the tyranny of Heaven.'

【注解】

1. fruit: 双关语，既指禁果，又指偷食禁果后被逐出乐园的结果。
2. mortal: 相当于deadly，双关语，指逐出乐园后，人类的生命有限，终有一死，也指凡间的、人类的(to mortals)，指人类因尝禁果被贬至尘世。
3. one greater Man: 指耶稣基督。
4. Sing . . . the chosen seed: "Heavenly Muse" 指天庭诗神缪斯。"Oreb" 即 Horeb，何烈山，又称Sinai，西奈山，在埃及和迦南之间。"That shepherd" 指犹太宗教领袖摩西 (Moses)，他曾经在西奈山旁的米甸荒原牧羊。"the chosen seed" 指上帝的选民犹太人。弥尔顿按照传统史诗体例，向神乞求赐予灵感。但是，有别于荷马、维吉尔，他祈求的诗神不是古希腊神话中的神，而是上帝。根据《圣经 · 旧约 · 出埃及记》(*Exodus*) 第 19 章记载，上帝在西奈山顶激励摩西写下十诫，将法律传给犹太人。传说中，摩西也是包括《创世记》在内的《摩西五经》的作者。

5. if Sion hill . . . the oracle of God: "Sion Hill" 即 Zion, 锡安山。"Siloa's Brook" 指西罗亚溪。"Fast" 即 close，近旁。"the oracle of God" 指上帝的圣殿，上帝通过预言家向世人昭示他的意旨。位于耶路撒冷 (Jerusalem) 的圣殿就坐落在锡安山上，西罗亚溪从旁边流过。古希腊神话中艺术之神缪斯常出没于山林泉水之间，弥尔顿祈求的神灵也住在高山上、流水旁。

6. That with no middle flight . . . rhyme: "middle flight" 指中天。古人将地球分为三层。第一层是地面，第二层到达山顶，称为中天。"th' Aonian Mount" 即赫利孔山 (Helicon)，希腊神话中缪斯诸神的居住地，属于中天。"Things unattempted yet in prose or rhyme" 一句译自文艺复兴时期意大利诗人卢多维科 · 阿里奥斯托 (Ludovico Ariosto, 1474—1533) 的传奇诗《疯狂的罗兰》(*Orlando Furioso*)。这一段话表明弥尔顿欲与荷马等著名诗人一争高下，飞跃中天，到达真正的天界，写出前人未敢涉足的题目，超越前人。

7. Spirit: 相当于 Holy Spirit, or Heavenly Muse。

8. Dove-like sat'st brooding on the vast abyss: 这一句是《钦定本圣经》(King James Version Bible) 中几段语录的糅合。

9. mad'st: 相当于 made。

10. argument: 相当于 theme，意为主题。

11. grand parents: "grand" 有多个含义。首先含人类始祖之意 (first in time)；又指上帝初创之时，亚当夏娃形象高大美丽 (splendid in appearance or style)；兼指最重要的祖先，没有他们就没有人类繁衍于世 (first in importance)。

12. for: 相当于 except for。

13. besides: 相当于 in every other respect。

14. what time: 相当于 at the time when。

15. his peers: 相当于 his equals，即与他地位相同的人，指其他的天使。天界大战前，撒旦曾担任天使长，是天使中的一员。

16. With vain attempt: 从第 34 行开始到第 44 行 "With vain attempt" 止，是一个整句。这句话较复杂，短语叠短语，从句套从句，直至 "With vain attempt " 全句戛然而止。句子结构象征撒旦的苦心经营终于一瞬间化为泡影。

17. Him the Almighty Power . . . arms: 这个句子的结构深受拉丁文法影响。弥尔顿大胆地将动词 "hurled" 的宾语 "him" 提前，将句子倒装，形象刻画了撒旦一个倒栽葱满身火焰堕入地狱的场景。同时, "Him""Hurled""headlong""hideous" 组成压头韵。"th' ethereal sky" 指天庭; "perdition" 指地狱; "adamantine chains" 指牢固的锁链。"durst" 即 dared。

18. baleful: 双关语, 既含有邪恶 (malignant) 之意, 与 Satan 的恶魔身份相符; 又含有痛苦 (suffering) 之意，因为 Satan 正身处地狱，身心俱受煎熬。

19. as far as angels ken: 相当于 as far as angels can see，天使目力所及之处。

20. from those flames/No light: 这个句子没有动词，突出强调了地狱里有火无光 (fire without light)。

21. hope never comes / That comes to all: 这句话与但丁的诗句 "All hopes abandon, ye who enter here" 相似。这种说法逻辑上有矛盾 —— 既然是 "All", 指全部，就该包括那些身处地狱的人 (Hell-dwellers)。弥尔顿借这种逻辑悖论表明他们甚至不属于 "All"。

22. urges: 相当于 afflicts。

23. a fiery deluge: 铺天盖地的火焰像洪水一样。"deluge" 指洪水。

24. utter darkness: “utter” 既表示全部 (complete)，又因谐音，含 outer 之意。这里特指远离天国的黑暗地狱。
25. the center: 指地球。弥尔顿在《失乐园》中引用了两种宇宙观。一种是托勒密的宇宙观，即在整个创造出来的宇宙中，地球是中心，周围分成九重，各有轴心。另一种宇宙观认为地球及整个创造出来的宇宙不过是个附属物，置身于一个更大的混沌宇宙之中，由一条金链 (golden chain) 与天国 (Heaven) 相连。文中撒旦穿过混沌宇宙自天堂堕入地狱的距离，相当于托勒密宇宙观中从地球到最外层轴心距离的三倍。
26. Beelzebub: 别卜西 (腓尼基人的神)，也称 Baal (巴尔)，意为蝇王 (Lord of Flies)，《圣经·新约·马太福音》12.24 中的邪恶王子。与其他堕落天使一样，别卜西被剥夺了其原有的天使姓名，因此只能以“邪神”称之。
27. Satan: 在希伯来语中，Satan (撒旦) 的意思是敌人。
28. . . . how fallen!: 此处援引《圣经·旧约·以赛亚书》(Isaiah 14.12)：“How are thou fallen from heaven, O Lucifer, Son of the morning”。
29. Myriads: 众生。
30. thunder: 相当于 thunderbolt，霹雳。
31. . . . and till then . . . dire arms: 这里的意思是，在我们反抗堕落前，谁知道上帝竟有那么威力巨大的武器。
32. dubious: 胜败难料。
33. study: 强烈的愿望。
34. what is else not to be overcome? : 相当于 what else does it mean not to be overcome? 还有什么比这些更难战胜?
35. doubted: 相当于 feared for。
36. gods: 诸神，诗歌中常用来形容天使。但此处撒旦暗示自己也是神。
37. cannot fail: 相当于 cease to exist，不能灭亡。

【简评】

在《失乐园》的开头，弥尔顿开宗明义，表明自己创作这部作品的目的是要“justify ways of God to men” (I, 26)，即上帝如此惩罚人类 (使人失去乐园) 的正当性。紧接着诗人把矛头直指那被打入地狱中的蛇 (Th’ infernal Serpent)，正是那该死的蛇“设下奸计 / 欺骗了人类之母” (I, 35—36)，也正是如此，上帝将它和它的叛军同伙打入地狱，遭受地狱烈火的烤炙。然而从第 84 行撒旦开口说话起，其魔鬼的形象突然发生了巨大变化，似乎已经不再是那条令人厌恶的蛇，而成为一个虽遭迫害，却不甘堕落、不屈不挠、不惜牺牲、挑战权威和上帝在“天界暴政”的英雄。

……战败又有何妨，
并非失去了一切，不挠的意志、
复仇的誓言、不灭的仇恨，

以及永不屈服、永不退让的勇气，
还有什么比这些更难战胜？(105—109)

在描写撒旦"豪言壮语"这些诗行中，弥尔顿似乎呈现了一个悖论，挑战了读者的阅读期待，造成了理解混乱，引发了各种迥异的解读，其中最著名的莫过于英国浪漫主义诗人布莱克的看法，他认为弥尔顿在描写天使和上帝时缩手缩脚，但在写到恶魔和地狱时却发挥得淋漓尽致，这是因为弥尔顿是一个真正的诗人，自己站在恶魔一边却不自知。年轻一代的英国浪漫主义诗人拜伦、雪莱等更是对魔鬼撒旦所体现的英雄气概和崇高美推崇备至，认为在《失乐园》中撒旦才是真正的英雄，甚至对自己被说成是"撒旦派"诗派 ("Satanic" school) 而深感认同。然而随着读者阅读的不断深入，撒旦在《失乐园》中的形象日渐渺小，最终还原了其蛇的猥琐形象，呼应了诗人在作品开头表明的主旨。尽管如此，对于撒旦的不同解读还是极大地扩展与丰富了《失乐园》的思想性。

【思考题】

1. Milton believed himself to be a divinely inspired writer. Can you find any clues in this excerpt? What are they?
2. *Paradise Lost*, ranked with Homer's *Odyssey* and Virgil's *The Aeneid*, is considered to be one of the greatest epics of the world. Comment on the conventions of classical epic used in this extract.
3. Who is the looming figure in this excerpt? Do you think his image attractive or not? Why?
4. Joseph Addison (1672–1719) once argues that Milton "has carried our language to a greater height than any of the English poets have ever done before or after him, and made the sublimity of his style equal to that of his sentiments." But Dr. Johnson (1709–1784), who disliked Milton, complains that Milton "has founded his style by a perverse and pedantic principle. He was desirous to use English words with foreign idiom . . . of him, at last, may be said what Jonson says of Spenser, that he wrote no language." Which side would you stand by? Can you illustrate the features of the "Miltonic style" with examples from the excerpt?
5. As we can see from this poem, Satan serves as the dual image of a destroyer who brings the downfall of man and a rebel against authority that is akin to a hero in some people's minds. What is your comment on the duality in people's personality?

The Restoration and Eighteenth Century English Literature

1660–1789

背景介绍

1640年，英国资产阶级革命开始，其后的二十年里，英国政局动荡，战火连绵不断。以克伦威尔为代表的资产阶级极权统治未能平息统治阶层内部及统治阶级与劳动人民之间的矛盾。克伦威尔死后，斯图亚特王朝卷土重来，查理二世于1660年登上王位， 这就是王政复辟时期 (The Restoration, 1667—1685)。这个时期天灾人祸接踵而来：大批共和派人士被屠杀，1665年暴发瘟疫，1666年的大火使伦敦变成一片废墟。1688年英国爆发了光荣革命 (The Glorious Revolution)，目的是阻止国王实行君主专制统治。斯图亚特王朝被推翻，资产阶级和贵族互相妥协，建立了君主立宪制。18世纪的英国政局相对稳定，资本主义经济得以持续发展，国力强盛，英国政府不断发动对外战争，在世界各地建立了许多殖民地和半殖民地。工业革命方兴未艾，圈地运动仍在继续。资产阶级与劳动人民的矛盾日益突出，各地爆发了无数次起义。爱尔兰人民也掀起了民族解放运动。

这一时期的英国文学大致可分为三个阶段：第一阶段从1660年到1700年约翰·德莱顿逝世，新古典主义 (Neo-classical) 文学及其批评原则形成；第二阶段为新古典主义文学的鼎盛时期，从1700年到1745年乔纳森·斯威夫特 (Jonathan Swift, 1667—1745) 逝世；第三阶段从1745年到1784年约翰逊博士逝世。在这一时期，新古典主义受到浪漫主义新思想的挑战。1798年威廉·华兹华斯 (William Wordsworth, 1770—1850) 和塞缪尔·泰勒·柯勒律治 (Samuel Taylor Coleridge, 1772—1834) 共同出版《抒情歌谣集》(*Lyrical Ballads*)，正式宣告浪漫主义时期的到来。

德莱顿是第一阶段最重要的人物，是王政复辟时期的桂冠诗人，著有长诗《押沙龙和阿奇托菲尔》(*Absalom and Achitophel*, 1681) 和其他一些时事主题的诗作。其戏剧代表作、无韵体悲剧《一切为了爱情》(*All for Love*, 1677)，根据新古典主义的创作原则重新演绎莎士比亚的《安东尼与克莉奥佩特拉》(*Antony and Cleopatra,* 1606/1607) 的故事。德莱顿也是一位重要的批评家，其散文名作《论戏剧诗》(*An Essay of Dramatic Poesy*, 1668) 既把英国文学批评推向新的高度，其本身又是一种清新、简朴和自然的散文风格的典范。

王政复辟时期的戏剧中最具有代表性的是风俗喜剧 (Comedy of Manners)。其中最著名的有乔治·埃思里奇爵士 (Sir George Etherege, c.1635—1691) 的《时髦男子》(*The Man of Mode*, 1676)，威廉·威彻利 (William Wycherley, 1640—1716) 的《乡村妇女》(*The Country Wife*, 1675) 和《坦率的人》(*The Plain Dealer*, 1676)，以及威廉·肯格里夫 (William Congreve, 1670—1729) 的《为爱而爱》(*Love for Love*, 1695) 和《世道》(*The Way of the World*, 1700) 等。

这一时期的散文有了新的开端。散文作者一反此前多恩的布道词、弥尔顿的政治小册子和托马斯·布朗爵士的作品里所运用的华丽辞藻和宏伟沉郁的文风，开始朝着平实、亲切和实用的方向发展。在哲学和科学领域，有托马斯·霍布斯 (Thomas Hobbes, 1588—1679) 的《利维坦》(*Leviathan*, 1651) 和约翰·洛克 (John Locke, 1632—1704) 的《论人类的理解》(*An Essay Concerning Human Understanding*, 1689)。新散文还体现在塞缪尔·佩皮斯 (Samuel Pepys, 1633—1703) 的日记中，他生动描述了私人生活的详情细节，令人耳目一新。杰里米·科利尔 (Jeremy Collier, 1650—1726) 在《略论英国戏剧的不道德与不圣洁》(*A Short View of the Immorality and Profaneness of the English Stage*, 1698) 中，以一种严密的学者文风，对复辟时期喜剧的猥琐进行了抨击。

这一时期最著名的诗作是约翰·弥尔顿的《失乐园》《复乐园》和悲剧《力士参孙》。弥尔顿主要活跃在资产阶级革命时期，写了大量支持革命、极具战斗性的小册子，正是这些诗作使他成为英国文学史上最伟大的史诗作者。约翰·班扬是 17 世纪最伟大的小说作家。他的《天路历程》以梦境寓意的方式描写了当时英国的现实生活。同时，弥尔顿和班扬在各自的作品中表达了在当时已颇具影响力的清教思想。

第二阶段的代表人物是蒲伯和斯威夫特。蒲伯是古典主义诗歌最重要的代表人物，他自如地运用英雄双韵体并将其发挥到极致。他也是一位讽刺大师，其讽刺诗《夺发记》(*The Rape of the Lock*, 1712—1714) 通过"夺发"这件琐事，用极为夸张的语言讽刺了上流社会的无聊和可笑。斯威夫特更是一个毫不妥协的讽刺作家。他的系列讽刺作品——《书籍之战》(*The Battle of Books*, 1704)、《一只桶的故事》(*A Tale of a Tub*, 1704) 及《格利佛游记》(*Gulliver's Travels*, 1726) 等对当时社会的各个领域、阶层，乃至人类本身的丑陋进行了无情和辛辣的讽刺。

随着政治生活的活跃和城市人口的增加，伦敦各种报刊激增，散文创作空前活跃，为现实主义小说的发展奠定了基础。丹尼尔·笛福 (Daniel Defoe, 1660—1731) 因创办《评论》(*The Review*, 1704—1713) 杂志而成为英国报刊业的奠基人。当然，笛福之所以扬名后世，更是因为他取得的以《鲁滨孙漂流记》(*Robinson Crusoe*, 1719) 为代表的小说创作成就。约瑟夫·爱迪森 (Joseph Addison, 1672—1719) 和理查德·史蒂尔 (Sir Richard Steele, 1672—1729) 共同创办的《闲话报》(*The Tatler*, 1709—1711) 和《旁观者》(*The Spectator*, 1711—1712) 面向中产阶级读者，起到了传播文化和道德说教的作用。

第三阶段可以被称为散文时代 (The Age of Prose)。各个领域的散文巨著竞相面世：文学评论以约翰逊博士编辑的《莎士比亚戏剧集序言》(*Preface*, 1765) 和《诗人传》(*The Lives of the Poets*, 1779—1781) 为代表；最著名的传记当推詹姆斯·鲍斯威尔 (James Boswell, 1740—1795) 的《塞缪尔·约翰逊传》(*Life of Johnson*, 1791)。

埃德蒙·伯克 (Edmund Burke, 1729—1797) 的一系列政论小册子用精辟的语言表述了自己的政见。爱德华·吉本 (Edward Gibbon, 1737—1794) 的历史巨著《罗马帝国衰亡史》(*The Decline and Fall of the Roman Empire*, 1776—1788) 和亚当·斯密 (Adam Smith, 1723—1790) 的《国富论》(*An Enquiry into the Nature and Causes of the Wealth of Nations*, 1776) 等亦在史学界和经济学领域引起了轰动。

这一阶段英国小说取得了新的发展。小说家们更注重描写中下层人民的形象，小说题材更贴近现实生活，结构更加完整，语言更加通俗易懂。塞缪尔·理查逊 (Samuel Richardson, 1689—1761) 的书信体小说《帕美拉，或德行有报》(*Pamela; or, Virtue Rewarded,* 1740) 首次以处于社会底层的女佣为主人公，注重以情动人，为小说发展开辟了新天地。亨利·菲尔丁 (Henry Fielding, 1707—1754) 则代表了 18 世纪英国小说的最高成就，其代表作《弃儿汤姆·琼斯》(*The History of Tom Jones, a Foundling*, 1749) 标志着英国小说已臻成熟。托比·斯摩莱特 (Tobia Smollett, 1721—1771) 的《兰登传》(*Roderick Random*, 1748) 和《亨弗雷·克林克》(*Humphrey Clinker*, 1771) 也是这一时期的名作。怪才劳伦斯·斯特恩 (Laurence Sterne, 1713—1768) 创作的奇书《项迪传》(*Life and Opinions of Tristram Shandy*, 1759—1767) 打破常规叙事模式，穿插无休止的离题话、不完整的句子、空白页、古怪的句法结构、幽默的奇思和伤感情调等，成为 20 世纪后现代主义小说的开山鼻祖。小说发展的另一个特点是恐怖小说或哥特式小说 (Gothic Novel) 的盛行：霍勒斯·沃尔波尔 (Horace Walpole, 1717—1797) 的《奥特兰托堡》(*The Castle of Otranto*, 1765)、威廉·贝克福德 (William Beckford, 1759—1844) 的《瓦塞克》(*Vathek*, 1786)、安·拉德克利佛夫人 (Mrs Ann Radcliff, 1764—1823) 的《尤多福的奥秘》(*The Mysteries of Udolpho*, 1794) 等，展示了一个个稀奇古怪、神秘莫测的幻想世界，表达了对当时社会重商主义的不满。

与小说相比，18 世纪后半叶的戏剧则相形见绌。理查德·布林斯雷·谢立丹 (Richard Brinsley Sheridan, 1751—1816) 是这一时期最重要的喜剧作家，其《造谣学校》(*The School for Scandal*, 1777) 以精巧的语言和生动的场面尖锐讽刺了上流社会的虚伪和荒淫。奥利弗·哥尔德斯密斯 (Oliver Goldsmith, 1728—1774) 的《屈身求爱》(*She Stoops to Conquer*, 1773) 也不失为一部出色的喜剧，在揭露社会现实的同时，表达了一种田园牧歌般的幻想。这种幻想也充溢于他的小说《威克菲牧师传》(*The Vicar of Wakefield*, 1766) 和诗歌《荒村》("The Deserted Village", 1770) 中。

这一阶段的诗歌可以说是一大突破，因为它预示着浪漫主义的到来。年轻一代诗人打破蒲伯极力推崇的诗歌标准和创作方法，强调灵感和独创的重要性。托马斯·格雷 (Thomas Gray, 1716—1771) 的《墓地挽歌》("Elegy Written in a Country Churchyard", 1750) 和《诗人》("The Bard", 1757)，威廉·柯林斯 (William Collins,

1721—1759) 的《咏黄昏》("Ode to Evening", 1747) 和《咏苏格兰山地流行的迷信》("Ode on the Popular Superstitions of the Highlands", 1749)，威廉 · 考珀 (William Cowper, 1731—1800) 的《约翰 · 吉尔平》(*John Gilpin*, 1785) 等都是不可多得的佳作。威廉 · 布莱克 (William Blake, 1757—1827) 和苏格兰民族诗人罗伯特 · 彭斯 (Robert Burns, 1759—1796) 则为浪漫主义的到来吹响了前奏。

作者简介

Daniel Defoe

1660—1731

丹尼尔·笛福出身于伦敦一个信奉长老会的中产阶级家庭。青年笛福并未如其父所愿成为长老会牧师，而是投身商海，却经营不当，负债累累，甚至破产入狱。1683 年笛福发表了第一本政治小册子。1685 年他参加蒙毛斯公爵 (The Duke of Monmouth) 反詹姆士二世的叛乱。1688 年他发表文章支持革命，随后长期为威廉三世效劳，并发表了一系列效忠于威廉王的政治小册子，如《真正的英国人》(*The Trueborn Englishman*, 1701) 等。为讽刺英国国教对其他教派的迫害，他写了《消灭不同教派的捷径》(*The Shortest Way with the Dissenters*, 1702)，并因此被捕入狱，判处枷刑示众三次，但他旋即回敬了《立枷颂》(*Hymn to the Pillory*, 1703)。伦敦市民视其为英雄，在他受刑期间向他献花、欢呼，以示支持。1704 年至 1713 年，笛福创办并编辑《评论》杂志，写了许多政治、经济和宗教方面的文章，针砭时弊，宣扬新兴资产阶级的思想。在文学上笛福可谓大器晚成，59 岁发表第一部小说《鲁滨孙漂流记》，随后多部小说相继问世，包括《辛格尔顿船长》(*Captain Singleton*, 1720)、《摩尔·弗兰德斯》(*Moll Flanders*, 1722)、《杰克上校》(*Colonel Jacque*, 1722) 和《罗克查娜》(*Roxana*, 1724) 等。这些小说大多以第一人称叙述主人公离奇曲折的生活遭遇，描绘出一幅幅 17 世纪末至 18 世纪初英国中下层人民贫困、艰难的生活状况。与他所创造的许多人物相似，笛福一生经济窘迫，债务缠身，最后为躲债而客死他乡。

笛福一生著述颇丰，共达 250 部之多，给后人留下了丰厚的文学遗产。尽管他并未受过高等教育，却通晓七国语言，在作品中表现出了惊人的学识。尽管他的作品没有蒲伯的古典风范，也没有斯威夫特的辛辣讽刺，却能自成一家，于平直晓畅、细枝末节中见真实，使读者不知不觉中产生一种认同感。笛福是一位具有独创精神的天才，是英国报刊业的奠基人和重要的现实主义小说家。

Robinson Crusoe

【题解】

《鲁滨孙漂流记》取材于苏格兰水手亚历山大·赛尔柯克 (Alexander Selkirk) 独自在荒岛生活五年的真实经历。鲁滨孙从小志向远大，一心想干出一番轰轰烈烈的大事来。19 岁时，他不顾家人反对，出海当了水手，有过不少冒险。他曾被强盗掳去，沦为奴隶，后获救到了巴西。在一次去非洲的航行中船遇风暴触礁，大家弃船逃亡，只有鲁滨孙一人幸免于难，登上一个无人居住的荒岛，开始了长达 28 年 2 个月零 19 天的荒岛生活。他自制木排，将船上尚未沉没、并能分解搬运的食物、火药、工具、帆布、木块等悉数运到岛上。他搭建篷屋，开荒种粮，制磨磨粉，烧制陶罐，凿挖独木舟(却又无力让它下水)，猎取野兽，腌制咸肉，缝制皮衣，驯养山羊等，这一切都是他依靠自己的勤奋和智慧，根据所积累的生活常识，在极其艰苦的条件下独立完成的。他详细记录岛上所发生的每一件事，并描述他发现沙滩上有一个脚印时产生的警觉和震惊。后来，他目睹了一些野人来岛上庆祝胜利并烤食俘虏。他设法救出了一个俘虏，并给他取名“星期五”(Friday)。后来“星期五”成了他忠实的仆人和同伴。最后，一艘英国船停泊在某岛附近，鲁滨孙协助船长平息船员的哗变，终于随船返回英国。后来他返回该岛视察岛上情况，而“星期五”在一次印第安人的袭击中不幸身亡。

所选部分为鲁滨孙在沙滩上发现人的脚印后的震惊，以及所采取的应急措施。

From Robinson Crusoe

A Footprint (excerpt)

From Chapter 11

. . . It happen'd[1] one Day about Noon going towards my Boat, I was exceedingly surpriz'd with the Print of a Man's naked Foot on the Shore, which was very plain to be seen in the Sand: I stood like one Thunder-struck, or as if I had seen an Apparition; I listen'd, I look'd round me, I could hear nothing, nor see any Thing, I went up to a rising Ground[2] to look farther, I went up the Shore and down the Shore, but it was all one, I could see no other Impression but that one, I went to it again to see if there were any more, and to observe if it might not be my Fancy; but there was no Room for that, for there was exactly the very Print of a Foot, Toes, Heel, and every Part of a Foot; how it came thither, I knew not, nor could in the least imagine. But after innumerable fluttering Thoughts, like a Man perfectly confus'd and out of my self, I came Home to my Fortification[3], not feeling, as we say, the Ground I went on, but terrify'd to the last Degree, looking behind me at every two or three Steps, mistaking every Bush and Tree, and fancying every Stump at a Distance to be a Man; nor is it possible to describe how many various Shapes affrighted Imagination represented Things to me in, how many wild Ideas were found every Moment in my Fancy, and what strange unaccountable Whimsies came into my Thoughts by the Way.

When I came to my Castle, for so I think I call'd it ever after this, I fled into it like one pursued; whether I went over by the Ladder as first contriv'd, or went in at the Hole in the Rock, which I call'd a Door, I cannot remember; no, nor could I remember the next Morning, for never frighted Hare fled to Cover, or Fox to Earth, with more Terror of Mind than I to this Retreat.

I slept none that Night; the farther I was from the Occasion of my Fright, the greater my Apprehensions were, which is something contrary to the Nature of such Things, and especially to the usual Practice of all Creatures in Fear: But I was so embarrass'd with my own frightful Ideas of the Thing, that I form'd nothing but dismal Imaginations to my self, even tho'[4] I was now a great way off of it. Sometimes I fancy'd it must be the Devil; and Reason joyn'd in with me upon this Supposition: For how should any other Thing in human Shape come into the Place? Where was the Vessel that brought them? What Marks was there of any other Footsteps? And how was it possible a Man should come there? But then to think that Satan should take human Shape upon him in such a Place where there could be no manner of Occasion for it, but to leave the Print of his Foot behind him, and that even for no Purpose too, for he could not be sure I should see it; this was an Amusement[5] the other Way; I consider'd that the Devil might have found out abundance of other Ways to have terrify'd me than this of the single Print of a Foot. That as I liv'd quite on the other Side of the Island, he would never have been so simple to leave a Mark in a Place where 'twas Ten Thousand to one whether I should ever see it or not, and in the Sand too which the first Surge of the Sea upon a high Wind would have defac'd entirely: All this seem'd inconsistent with the Thing it self, and with all the Notions we usually entertain of the Subtilty of the Devil[6].

Abundance of such Things as these assisted to argue me out of all Apprehensions of its being the Devil: And I presently concluded then, that it must be some more dangerous

Creature, (viz.)That it must be some of the Savages of the main Land over against me, who had wander'd out to Sea in their Canoes; and either driven by the Currents, or by contrary Winds had made[7] the Island; and had been on Shore, but were gone away again to Sea, being as loth[8] perhaps, to have stay'd in this desolate Island, as I would have been to have had them.

While these Reflections were rowling upon my Mind, I was very thankful in my Thoughts, that I was so happy as not to be thereabouts at that time, or that they did not see my Boat, by which they would have concluded that some Inhabitants had been in the Place, and perhaps have search'd farther for me: Then terrible Thoughts rack'd my Imagination about their having found my Boat, and that there were People here; and that if so, I should certainly have them come again in greater Numbers, and devour me; that if it should happen so that they should not find me, yet they would find my Enclosure[9], destroy all my Corn, carry away all my Flock of tame Goats, and I should perish at last for meer[10] Want.

Thus my Fear banish'd all my religious Hope; all that former Confidence in God which was founded upon such wonderful Experience as I had had of his Goodness, now vanished, as if he that had fed me by Miracle hitherto, could not preserve by his Power the Provision which he had made for me by his Goodness: I reproach'd my self with my Easiness, that would not sow any more Corn one Year than would just serve me till the next Season, as if no Accident could intervene to prevent my enjoying the Crop that was upon the Ground; and this I thought so just a Reproof, that I resolv'd for the future to have two or three Years Corn beforehand, so that whatever might come, I might not perish for want of Bread.

How strange a Chequer Work of Providence is the Life of Man[11]! and by what secret differing Springs are the Affections hurry'd about as differing Circumstance[12] present! To Day we love what to Morrow[13] we hate; to Day we seek what to Morrow we shun; to Day we desire what to Morrow we fear; nay even tremble at the Apprehensions of; this was exemplify'd in me at this Time in the most lively Manner imaginable; for I whose only Affliction was, that I seem'd banished from human Society, that I was alone, circumscrib'd by the boundless Ocean, cut off from Mankind, and condemn'd to what I call'd silent Life; that I was as one who Heaven thought not worthy to be number'd among the Living, or to appear among the rest of his Creatures; that to have seen one of my own Species, would have seem'd to me a Raising me from Death to Life, and the greatest Blessing that Heaven it self, next to the supreme Blessing of Salvation, could bestow; I say, that I should now tremble at the very Apprehensions of seeing a Man, and was ready to sink into the Ground at but the Shadow or silent Appearance of a Man's having set his Foot in the Island.

Such is the uneven State of human Life: and it afforded me a great many curious Speculations afterwards, when I had a little recover'd my first Surprize; I consider'd that this was the Station of Life the infinitely wise and good Providence of God had determin'd for me, that as I could not foresee what the Ends of Divine Wisdom might be in all this, so I was not to dispute his Sovereignty, who, as I was his Creature, had an undoubted Right by Creation to govern and dispose of me absolutely as he thought fit; and who, as I was a Creature who had offended him, had likewise a judicial right to condemn me to what Punishment he thought fit; and that it was my Part to submit to bear his Indignation, because I had sinn'd against him.

I then reflected that God, who was not only Righteous but Omnipotent, as he had thought fit thus to punish and afflict me, so he was able to deliver me; that if he did not think fit to do it, 't was my unquestion'd Duty to resign my self absolutely and entirely to his Will; and on the other Hand, it was my Duty also to hope in him, pray to him, and quietly to attend the Dictates and Directions of his daily Providence.

These Thoughts took me up many Hours, Days; nay, I may say, Weeks and Months; and one particular Effect of my Cogitations on this Occasion, I cannot omit, viz. One Morning early, lying in my Bed, and fill'd with Thought about my Danger from the Appearance of Savages, I found it discompos'd me very much, upon which those Words of the Scripture came into my Thoughts, Call upon me in the Day of Trouble, and I will deliver, and thou shalt glorify me[14].

Upon this, rising chearfully out of my Bed, my Heart was not only comforted, but I was guided and encourag'd to pray earnestly to God for Deliverance: When I had done praying, I took up my Bible, and opening it to read, the first Words that presented to me, were, Wait on the Lord, and be of good Cheer, and he shall strengthen thy Heart; wait, I say, on the Lord[15]. It is impossible to express the Comfort this gave me. In Answer, I thankfully laid down the Book, and was no more sad, at least, not on that Occasion.

In the middle of these Cogitations, Apprehensions and Reflections, it came into my Thought one Day, that all this might be a meer Chimera of my own; and that this Foot might be the Print of my own Foot, when I came on Shore from my Boat: This chear'd me up a little too, and I began to perswade[16] my self it was all a Delusion; that it was nothing else but my own Foot, and why might not I come that way from the Boat, as well as I was going that way to the Boat; again, I consider'd also that I could by no Means tell for certain where I had trod, and where I had not; and that if at last this was only the Print of my own Foot, I had play'd the Part of those Fools, who strive to make stories of Spectres, and Apparitions; and then are frighted at them more than any body.

Now I began to take Courage, and to peep abroad again; for I had not stirr'd out of my Castle for three Days and Nights; so that I began to starve for Provision; for I had little or nothing within Doors, but some Barley Cakes and Water. Then I knew that my Goats wanted to be milk'd too, which usually was my Evening Diversion; and the poor Creatures were in great Pain and Inconvenience for want of it; and indeed, it almost spoil'd some of them, and almost dry'd up their Milk.

Heartning my self therefore with the Belief that this was nothing but the Print of one of my own Feet, and so I might be truly said to start at my own Shadow, I began to go abroad again, and went to my Country House, to milk my Flock; but to see with what Fear I went forward, how often I look'd behind me, how I was ready every now and then to lay down my Basket, and run for my Life, it would have made any one have thought I was haunted with an evil Conscience, or that I had been lately most terribly frighted, and so indeed I had.

However, as I went down thus two or three Days, and having seen nothing, I began to be a little bolder; and to think there was really nothing in it, but my own Imagination: But I cou'd not perswade my self fully of this, till I should go down to the Shore again, and see this Print of a Foot, and measure it by my own, and see if there was any Similitude or Fitness, that I might be assur'd it was my own Foot: But when I came to the Place, First, It appear'd evidently to me, that when I laid up my Boat, I could not possibly be on Shore any where there about. Secondly, When I came to measure the Mark with my own Foot, I found my Foot not so large by a great deal; both these Things fill'd my Head with new Imaginations, and gave me the Vapours again, to the highest Degree; so that I shook with cold, like one in an Ague: And I went Home again, fill'd with the Belief that some Man or Men had been on Shore there; or in short, that the Island was inhabited, and I might be surpriz'd before I was aware; and what course to take for my Security I knew not.

O what ridiculous Resolution Men take, when possess'd with Fear! It deprives them of the Use of those Means which Reason offers for their Relief. The first Thing I propos'd to my self, was, to throw down my Enclosures, and turn all my tame Cattle wild into the

Woods, that the Enemy might not find them; and then frequent the Island in Prospect of the same, or the like Booty: Then to the simple[17] Thing of Digging up my two Corn Fields, that they might not find such a Grain there, and still be prompted to frequent the Island; then to demolish my Bower, and Tent, that they might not see any Vestiges of Habitation, and be prompted to look farther, in order to find out the Persons inhabiting.

These were the Subject of the first Night's Cogitation, after I was come Home again, while the Apprehensions which had so over'run my Mind were fresh upon me, and my Head was full of Vapours, as above: Thus Fear of Danger is ten thousand Times more terrifying than Danger it self, when apparent to the Eyes; and we find the Burthen of Anxiety greater by much, than the Evil which we are anxious about; and which was worse than all this, I had not that Relief in this Trouble from the Resignation I used to practise, that I hop'd to have. I look'd, I thought, like Saul[18], who complain'd not only that the Philistines were upon him; but that God had forsaken him; for I did not now take due Ways to compose my Mind, by crying to God in my Distress, and resting upon his Providence, as I had done before, for my Defence and Deliverance; which if I had done, I had, at least, been more cheerfully supported under this new Surprise, and perhaps carry'd through it with more Resolution.

This Confusion of my Thoughts kept me waking all Night; but in the Morning I fell asleep, and having by the Amusement of my Mind, been, as it were, tyr'd, and my Spirits exhausted; I slept very soundly, and wak'd much better compos'd than I had ever been before; and now I began to think sedately; and upon the utmost Debate with my self, I concluded, that this Island, which was so exceeding pleasant, fruitful, and no farther from the main Land than as I had seen, was not so entirely abandon'd as I might imagine: That altho' there were no stated Inhabitants who liv'd on the Spot; yet that there might sometimes come Boats off from the Shore, who either with Design, or perhaps never, but when they were driven by cross Winds, might come to this Place.

That I had liv'd here fifteen Years now, and had not met with the least Shadow or Figure of any People yet; and that if at any Time they should be driven here, it was probable they went away again as soon as ever they could, seeing they had never thought fit to fix there upon any Occasion, to this Time.

That the most I cou'd suggest any Danger from, was, from any such casual accidental Landing of straggling People from the Main, who, as it was likely if they were driven hither, were here against their Wills; so they made no stay here, but went off again with all possible Speed, seldom staying one Night on Shore, lest they should not have the Help of the Tides, and Day'light back again; and that therefore I had nothing to do but to consider of some safe Retreat, in Case I should see any Savages land upon the Spot.

Now I began sorely to repent, that I had dug my Cave so large, as to bring a Door through again, which Door, as I said, came out beyond where my Fortification joyn'd to the Rock; upon maturely considering this therefore, I resolv'd to draw me a second Fortification, in the same Manner of a Semicircle, at a Distance from my Wall, just where I had planted a double row of Trees, about twelve Years before, of which I made mention: These Trees having been planted so thick before, they wanted but a few Piles to be driven between them, that they should be thicker, and stronger, and my Wall would be soon finish'd.

So that I had now a double Wall, and my outer Wall was thickned with Pieces of Timber, old Cables, and every Thing I could think of, to make it strong; having in it seven little Holes, about as big as I might put my Arm out at: In the In'side of this, I thickned my Wall to above ten Foot thick, with continual bringing Earth out of my Cave, and laying it at the Foot of the Wall, and walking upon it; and through the seven Holes, I contriv'd to plant the Musquets, of which I took Notice, that I got seven on Shore out of the Ship; these, I say, I planted like my Cannon, and fitted them into Frames that held them like a Carriage, that so I could fire all the seven Guns in two Minutes Time: This Wall I was many a weary Month a finishing, and yet never thought my self safe till it was done.

When this was done, I stuck all the Ground without my Wall, for a great way every way[19], as full with Stakes or Sticks of the Osier like Wood, which I found so apt to grow, as they could well stand; insomuch, that I believe I might set in near twenty thousand of them, leaving a pretty large Space between them and my Wall, that I might have room to see an Enemy, and they might have no shelter from the young Trees, if they attempted to approach my outer Wall.

Thus in two Years Time I had a thick Grove and in five or six Years Time I had a Wood before my Dwelling, growing so monstrous thick and strong, that it was indeed perfectly impassable; and no Men of what kind soever, would ever imagine that there was any Thing beyond it, much less a Habitation: As for the Way which I propos'd to my self to go in and out, for I left no Avenue; it was by setting two Ladders, one to a Part of the Rock which was low, and then broke in, and left room to place another Ladder upon that; so when the two Ladders were taken down, no Man living could come down to me without mischieving himself; and if they had come down, they were still on the Out'side of my outer Wall.

Thus I took all the Measures humane Prudence could suggest for my own Preservation; and it will be seen at length, that they were not altogether without just Reason; though I foresaw nothing at that time, more than my meer Fear suggested to me.

While this was doing, I was not altogether Careless of my other Affairs; for I had a great Concern upon me, for my little Herd of Goats; they were not only a present Supply to me upon every Occasion, and began to be sufficient to me, without the Expence of Powder and Shot; but also without the Fatigue of Hunting after the wild Ones, and I was loth to lose the Advantage of them, and to have them all to nurse up over again.To this Purpose, after long Consideration, I could think of but two Ways to preserve them; one was to find another convenient Place to dig a Cave Under'ground, and to drive them into it every Night; and the other was to enclose two or three little Bits of Land, remote from one another and as much conceal'd as I could, where I might keep about half a Dozen young Goats in each Place: So that if any Disaster happen'd to the Flock in general, I might be able to raise them again with little Trouble and Time: And this, tho' it would require a great deal of Time and Labour, I thought was the most rational Design.

Accordingly I spent some Time to find out the most retir'd Parts of the Island; and I pitch'd upon one which was as private indeed as my Heart could wish for; it was a little damp Piece of Ground in the Middle of the hollow and thick Woods, where, as is observ'd, I almost lost my self once before, endeavouring to come back that Way from the Eastern Part of the Island: Here I found a clear Piece of Land near three Acres, so surrounded with Woods, that it was almost an Enclosure by Nature, at least it did not want near so much Labour to make it so, as the other Pieces of Ground I had work'd so hard at.

I immediately went to Work with this Piece of Ground, and in less than a Month's Time, I had so fenc'd it round, that my Flock or Herd, call it which you please, who were not so wild now as at first they might be supposed to be, were well enough secur'd in it. So, without any farther Delay, I removed ten young She-Goats and two He-Goats to this Piece; and when they were there, I continued to perfect the Fence till I had made it as secure as the other, which, however, I did at more Leisure, and it took me up more Time by a great deal.

All this Labour I was at the Expence of, purely from my Apprehensions on the Account of the Print of a Man's Foot which I had seen; for as yet I never saw any human creature come near the Island, and I had now liv'd two Years under these Uneasinesses, which indeed made my Life much less comfortable than it was before; as may well be imagin'd by any who know what it is to live in the constant Snare of the Fear of Man; and this I must observe with Grief too, that the discomposure of my Mind had too great Impressions also upon the religious Part of my Thoughts, for the Dread and Terror of falling into the hands of Savages and Cannibals, lay so upon my spirits, that I seldom found my self in a due Temper for Application to my Maker, at least not with the sedate Calmness and Resignation of Soul which I was wont to do; I rather pray'd to God as under great Affliction and Pressure of Mind, surrounded with Danger, and in Expectation every Night of being murther'd[20] and devour'd before Morning; and I must testify from my Experience, that a Temper of Peace, Thankfulness, Love and Affection, is much more the proper Frame for Prayer than that of Terror and Discomposure; and that under the Dread of Mischief impending, a Man is no more fit for a comforting Performance of the Duty of praying to God, than he is for Repentance on a sick Bed: For these Discomposures affect the Mind as the others do the Body; and the Discomposure of the Mind must necessarily be as great a Disability as that of the Body, and much greater, Praying to God being properly an Act of the Mind, not of the Body.

【注解】

1. happen'd: 相当于 happened。下文中的 surpriz'd、listen'd、look'd 等也是同样的道理。
2. a rising Ground: 高处。
3. Fortification: 指在此之前鲁滨孙为防野兽侵袭修筑的堡垒。
4. tho': 相当于 though。
5. Amusement: 困惑的原因。
6. the Subtilty of the Devil: "Subtilty"即 subtlety，指恶魔的诡秘。
7. made: 抵达。
8. loth: 相当于 loathsome，不愿意的。
9. Enclosure: 围垦种粮的地方。
10. meer: 相当于 mere。
11. a Chequer Work of Providence is the Life of Man: 人生变幻无常。
12. Circumstance: 相当于 Circumstances。
13. To Day, to Morrow: 相当于 today, tomorrow。
14. Call upon me . . . glorify me: 引自《圣经·诗篇》第 50 章第 15 节。
15. Wait on the Lord, . . . on the Lord: 引自《圣经·诗篇》第 27 章第 14 节。
16. perswade: 相当于 persuade。

17. simple: 愚蠢的。
18. Saul: 该典故出自《旧约·撒母耳记》第28章第15节："撒母耳对扫罗说：'你为什么搅扰我，招我上来呢？'扫罗回答说：'我甚窘急，因为非利士人攻击我，上帝也离开我。'撒母耳说：'耶和华已经离开你，且与你为敌，你何必问我呢？'"
19. without my Wall, for a great way every way: 在我的围墙外的空地四周，直到很远的地方都……
20. murther'd: 相当于murdered。

【思考题】

1. How does Robinson Crusoe persuade himself that the footprint has not been left by the Devil?
2. What foolish things does Robinson Crusoe propose to himself when he is possessed with fear?
3. In *Robinson Crusoe*, there are many epigrammatic sentences that tell universal truths, such as "To Day we love what to Morrow we hate" and "Fear of danger is ten thousand Times more terrifying than Danger it self." Can you find more examples in the selection?
4. James Joyce once notes that Defoe's figure Robinson Crusoe is a true symbol of the rising British middle-class colonists during that time: "He is the true prototype of the British Colonist. The whole Anglo-saxon spirit is in Crusoe: the manly independence, the unconscious cruelty, the persistence, the slow yet efficient intelligence, the sexual apathy, the caculating taciturnity." How do you understand Joyce's words?

【简评】

《鲁滨孙漂流记》是英国文学史上第一部伟大的小说。笛福从新兴资产阶级和殖民主义的立场出发，歌颂了在鲁滨孙身上所体现出来的百折不挠、冒险进取的精神。这在当时是进步的，较之那些不思进取、不事劳作的封建贵族阶层，资产阶级是推动社会进步的一支重要力量。同时，我们也应该清醒地认识到鲁滨孙作为资产阶级和殖民主义一员的局限性：他参与黑奴贸易，自封总督，对小岛实行的是典型的殖民统治，即使对与他朝夕相处、相依为命的"星期五"，他也难以摆脱主人的姿态，平等待人。在创作方法上，笛福用第一人称的叙述方式，以朴实无华的语言，通过大量的细节描写，营造出一种真实感，逼真再现了鲁滨孙在三十年当中所遇、所见、所思、所感和所为的一切。诗人柯勒律治曾评价说，鲁滨孙是"一个普遍的代表人物，每位读者都可以取而代之。"由此可见鲁滨孙这一人物的真实性和典型性。几百年来，该小说已被陆续译成多种语言，在世界广为流传。

Jonathan Swift
1667—1745

乔纳森·斯威夫特出生于都柏林，父母都是英国人。他早年的生活和教育由伯父葛德汶 (Godwin) 负担。14 岁时，斯威夫特进入都柏林三一学院，1686 年获学士学位，接着攻读硕士，但由于 1688 年爱尔兰政局动荡，只好弃学从政，回英格兰给辉格党政客威廉·坦布尔爵士 (Sir William Temple) 当秘书，虽结识了大批学者和达官显要，却始终未能获得理想的职位。在此期间，斯威夫特阅读了大量的书籍，先后于 1691 年和 1701 年获得硕士和博士学位。同时他尝试诗歌创作，但佳作不多。

他的才华首先展现在讽刺作品的创作中。1696 至 1697 年间，斯威夫特创作了《一只桶的故事》和《书籍之战》，并于 1704 年同时出版。这两部作品分别对宗教的腐朽和学术界的偏颇进行了讽刺和抨击。1710 年，由于对辉格党的宗教政策不满，斯威夫特转而支持托利党，为其编辑党报并撰写大量政论文章和小册子，深受赏识。同年他开始给恋人艾瑟·约翰逊 (Esther Johnson) 去信，后人将他四年的书信汇集成《致斯黛拉的信》(*Journal to Stella*, 1766) 出版，从中可窥知斯威夫特当时的生活与情感。他与另一女子海斯特·梵奴迈 (Hester Vanhomrigh) 的微妙关系则记述于诗作《凯德尼斯与梵奈莎》(*Cadenus and Vanessa*, 1713) 之中。1713 年，斯威夫特由于得不到渴盼已久的主教职位，迫不得已回到爱尔兰充任都柏林圣帕特里克大教堂教长。不久，斯威夫特摆脱个人得失，开始更多地关注爱尔兰人民的利益，成为反抗英国政治压迫和经济剥削、争取民族自由的领头人，被爱尔兰人民尊奉为民族英雄、自由卫士。他撰写的有关爱尔兰问题的小册子极大地唤醒和鼓舞了爱尔兰人民的斗志。1724 年，他发表了《布商来信》(*Drapier's Letters*)，揭露了英国政府在爱尔兰铸造成色分量均不足的铜币以牟取暴利、摧垮爱尔兰经济的企图。为此英国政府悬赏 300 镑捉拿作者，但爱尔兰无一人出卖他。1726 年，斯威夫特发表了《格列佛游记》(*Gulliver's Travels*)，引起巨大轰动。1729 年，他又深感爱尔兰人民的疾苦，奋笔疾书，写出了讽刺文《一个温和的建议》("A Modest Proposal")，用“爱尔兰穷人唯一的出路便是将自己的婴孩卖给英国富人供他们食用”这一“温和”建议，讽刺了英国政府对爱尔兰的压迫。该文振聋发聩，其讽刺之辛辣令人叹为观止。1739 年，斯威夫特发表了《斯威夫特博士死亡之诗》(*Verses on the Death of Dr. Swift*)，对自己的一生做了客观的评价，并驳斥了社会上对他的种种非难。1745年，斯威夫特离世，遗嘱中他把所有财产都捐献给慈善机构。

斯威夫特的一生尽管仕途不顺，却并不像他的政敌所说的那样因此而耿耿于怀，仇恨整个人类。他那犀利无比的笔锋如长剑一般，毫不留情地刺向社会的陈规陋习、宗教的虚伪腐败、贵族社会的荒淫无耻、政治的阴险毒辣和学术界的孤陋偏执，又以满腔热忱为穷苦人民和受压迫民族的利益摇旗呐喊。他的作品立场鲜明，针对性强，具有强烈的时代感，这也得益于其作品所具有的独特文体。斯威夫特认为"用得恰到好处的词即是最好的文体"(Proper words in proper places make the best style.)。他用词简单、具体、清晰，句法毫不繁复，语言简洁明了。他的文体摒弃一切虚饰和怪异，不失为优雅的上乘之作。

Gulliver's Travels

【题解】

斯威夫特与蒲伯、爱迪森、史蒂尔和肯格里夫等同时代的文学巨匠关系密切，他们成立了一个俱乐部，定期聚会，分工命题，针砭时事。《格列佛游记》正是这样的命题之作，而斯威夫特却把它写成了一部世界名著。自1726年10月它的第一部分面世以来，小说深受全世界各类读者的喜爱，这可能是斯威夫特始料未及的。

小说描写外科医生(后成为船长)格列佛(Gulliver)自述的四次航行。第一次航行由于航船失事，他流落到小人国(Lilliput)。尽管小人国国民只有6英寸(约0.15米)高，为普通人的十二分之一，却自高自大，野心勃勃，钩心斗角，阴险毒辣。小人国的两大政党以穿高跟鞋和低跟鞋来区分，宗教派别的争论焦点是打鸡蛋应该从大头还是从小头。这些描述其实是对英国政党和宗教的讽刺。

在第二部中，格列佛被放逐到了巨人国(Brobdingnag)，那里的人身高60英尺(约18.29米)，却并不凶残，相反，他们心地善良，富有同情心，不知政治和火药为何物。当格列佛向巨人国国王介绍英国的风土人情和政治制度，并以此为荣时，巨人国国王却视英国乃至欧洲为蚁丘，认为人类不过是大自然容许爬行于地表的最有害的小野兽而已。

在第三部中，格列佛到了飞岛(Laputa)之上，发现那里的贤人一离开自己圈定的领域便一无所知，还发现科学家们试图从黄瓜中分离出阳光。与古代伟人们的交谈使他意识到后人所写的历史断章取义，以讹传讹，歪曲了先哲们的思想。这是批判当时的科学家、哲学家、历史学家及经济学家等身上表现出来的丑陋一面。

在最后一部中，格列佛来到慧骃国(Houyhnhnms)。慧骃是一种有理智的马，心灵高贵，举止得体，而人形动物 (Yahoo) 却残暴、猥琐，令人恶心。作者运用这种反差无情地揭露了人类的丑陋，这也是许多评论家们责难斯威夫特仇恨人类的主要原因。而实际上，斯威夫特想要强调的正是人类理智的重要性，一旦丧失理智，人类将与其他动物无异。所选章节为全书第一部第一章，其中格列佛介绍了自己的家庭和航行的动机，以及航船沉没后他游到小人国成为阶下囚的经过。

From Gulliver's Travels

A Voyage to Lilliput

Chapter 1

The author gives some account of himself and family—his first inducements to travel—He is shipwrecked and swims for his life—Gets safe on shore in the country of Lilliput, is made a prisoner, and carried up the country.

My father had a small estate in Nottinghamshire; I was the third of five sons. He sent me to Emanuel college in Cambridge at fourteen years old, where I resided three years, and applied myself close to my studies: but the charge of maintaining me (although I had a very scanty allowance) being too great for a narrow fortune, I was bound apprentice to Mr. James Bates, an eminent surgeon in London, with whom I continued four years, and my father now and then sending me small sums of money, I laid them out in learning navigation and other parts of the mathematics useful to those who intend to travel, as I always believed it would be some time or other my fortune to do; When I left Mr. Bates, I went down to my father; where, by the assistance of him and my uncle John and some other relations I got forty pounds, and a promise of thirty pounds a year to maintain me at Leyden[1]; there I studied physics[2] two years and seven months, knowing it would be useful in long voyages.

Soon after my return from Leyden, I was recommended, by my good master Mr. Bates, to be surgeon to the *Swallow*, Captain Abraham Pannell commander, with whom I continued three years and a half, making a voyage or two into the Levant[3], and some other parts. When I came back, I resolved to settle in London, to which Mr.Bates, my master, encouraged me; and by him I was recommended to several patients. I took part of a small house in the Old Jury[4], and being advised to alter my condition, I married Mrs.[5] Mary Burton, second daughter to Mr. Edmond Burton, hosier, in Newgate Street, with whom I received four hundred pounds for a portion[6].

But, my good master Bates dying in two years after, and I having few friends, my business began to fail; for my conscience would not suffer me to imitate the bad practice of too many among my brethren[7]. Having, therefore, consulted with my wife and some of my acquaintance, I determined to go again to sea. I was surgeon successively in two ships, and made several voyages for six years to the East and West Indies, by which I got some addition to my fortune. My hours of leisure I spent in reading the best authors, ancient and modern, being always provided with a good number of books, and when I was ashore in observing the manners and dispositions of the people, as well as learning their language, wherein I had a great facility by the strength of my memory.

The last of these voyages not proving very fortunate, I grew weary of the sea, and intended to stay at home with my wife and family. I removed from the Old Jury to Fetter Lane, and from thence to Wapping[8], hoping to get business among the sailors, but it would not turn to account. After three years' expectation that things would mend, I accepted an advantageous offer from Captain William Prichard, master of the Antelope, who was making a voyage to the South Sea. We set sail from Bristol, May 4th, 1699, and our voyage at first was very prosperous.

It would not be proper, for some reasons, to trouble the reader with the particulars of our adventures in those seas; let it suffice to inform him that in our passage from thence to the East Indies we were driven by a violent storm to the north-west of Van Diemen's Land[9]. By an observation, we found ourselves in the latitude of 30 degrees 2 minutes south. Twelve of our crew were dead by immoderate labour, and ill food; the rest were in a very weak condition. On the fifth of November, which was the beginning of summer in those parts, the weather being very hazy, the seamen spied a rock, within half a cable's length[10] of the ship, but the wind was so strong, that we were driven directly upon it, and immediately split. Six of the crew, of whom I was one, having let down the boat into the sea, made a shift to get clear of the ship and the rock. We rowed by my computation about three leagues, till we were able to work no longer, being already spent with labour while we were in the ship. We therefore trusted ourselves to the mercy of the waves, and in about half an hour the boat was overset by a sudden flurry from the north. What became of my companions in the boat, as well as of those who escaped on the rock or were left in the vessel, I cannot tell, but conclude they were all lost. For my own part I swam as fortune directed me, and was pushed forward by wind and tide. I often left my legs drop, and could feel no bottom; but when I was almost gone and able to struggle no longer, I found myself within my depth; and by this time the storm was much abated. The declivity was so small that I walked near a mile before I got to the shore, which I conjectured was about eight o'clock in the evening. I then advanced forward near half a mile, but could not discover any sign of houses or inhabitants—at least, I was in so weak a condition that I did not observe them. I was extremely tired, and with that, and the heat of the weather, and about half a pint of brandy that I drank as I left the ship, I found myself much inclined to sleep. I lay down on the grass, which was very short and soft, where I slept sounder than ever I remember to have done in my life, and, as I reckoned, above nine hours; for when I awaked, it was just daylight. I attempted to rise, but was not able to stir, for as I happen'd to lie on my back, I found my arms and legs were strongly fastened on each side to the ground, and my hair, which was long and thick, tied down in the same manner. I likewise felt several slender ligatures across my body from my armpits to my thighs. I could only look upwards; the sun began to grow hot and the light offended my eyes. I heard a confused noise about me, but, in the posture I lay, could see nothing except the sky. In a little time I felt something alive moving on my left leg, which, advancing gently forward over my breast, came almost up to my chin, when, bending my eyes downwards as much as I could, I perceived it to be a human creature not six inches high, with a bow and arrow in his hands, and a quiver at his back. In the mean time, I felt at least forty more of the same kind (as I conjectured) following the first. I was in the utmost astonishment, and roared so loud that they all ran back in a fright; and some of them, as I was afterwards told, were hurt with the falls they got by leaping from my sides upon the ground. However, they soon returned, and one of them, who ventured so far as to get a full sight of my face, lifting up his hands and eyes by way of admiration, cried out in a shrill, but distinct voice, 'Hekinah degul[11]!' The others repeated the same words several times, but I then knew not what they meant . . . . I lay all this while, as the reader may believe, in great uneasiness; at length, struggling to get loose, I had the fortune to break the strings and wrench out the pegs that fastened my left arm to the ground; for, by lifting it up to my face, I discovered the methods they had taken to bind me, and at the same time, with a violent pull, which gave me excessive pain, I a little loosened the strings that tied down my hair on the left side, so that I was just able to turn my head about two inches. But the creatures ran off a second time, before I could seize them; whereupon there was a great shout in a very shrill accent, and after it ceased, I heard one of them cry aloud, Tolgo phonac; when in an instant I felt above an hundred arrows discharged on my left hand, which pricked me like so many needles, and besides they shot another flight into the air, as we do bombs in Europe, whereof many, I suppose, fell on my body (though I felt them not) and some on my face, which I immediately covered with my left hand. When this shower of arrows was over, I fell a groaning with grief and pain; and then striving again to get loose, they discharged another volley larger than the first, and some of them attempted with spears to stick me in the sides; but, by good luck, I had on me a buff jerkin which they could not pierce. I thought it the most prudent method to lie still, and my design was to continue so till night, when, my left hand being already loose, I could easily free myself; and as for the inhabitants, I had reason to believe I might be a match for the greatest armies they could bring against me, if they were all of the same size with him that I saw. But fortune disposed otherwise of me. When the people observed I was quiet they discharged no more arrows; but by the noise I heard, I knew their numbers increased and about four yards from me, over against my right ear, I heard a knocking for above an hour, like people at work; when, turning my head that way, as well as the pegs and strings would permit me, I saw a stage erected about a foot and a half from the ground, capable of holding four of the inhabitants, with two or three ladders to mount it: from whence one of them, who seemed to be a person of quality, made me a long speech, whereof I understood not one syllable. But I should have mentioned, that before the principal person began his oration, he cried out three times, 'Langro dehul san!' (these words and the former were afterwards repeated and explained to me). Whereupon immediately about fifty of the inhabitants came and cut the strings that fastened the left side of my head, which gave me the liberty of turning it to the right, and of observing the person and gesture of him who was to speak. He appeared to be of a middle age, and taller than any of the other three who attended him, whereof one was a page who held up his train, and seemed to be somewhat longer than my middle finger; the other two stood one on each side to support him. He acted every part of an orator, and I could observe many periods[12] of threatenings, and others of promises, pity and kindness. I answered in a few words, but in the most submissive manner, lifting up my left hand and both eyes to the sun, as calling him for a witness; and being almost famished with hunger, having not eaten a morsel for some hours before I left the ship, I found the demands of nature so strong upon me, that I could not forbear showing my impatience (perhaps against the strict rules of decency) by putting my finger frequently on my mouth to signify that I wanted food. The Hurgo (for so they call a great lord, as I afterwards learnt) understood me very well. He descended from the stage, and commanded that several ladders should be applied to my sides, on which above an hundred of the inhabitants mounted and walked towards my mouth, laden with baskets full of meat, which had been provided and sent thither by the King's orders upon the first intelligence he received of me. I observed there was the flesh of several animals, but could not distinguish them by the taste. There were shoulders, legs and loins shaped like those of mutton, and very well dressed, but smaller than the wings of a lark. I ate them by two or three at a mouthful, and took three loaves at a time, about the bigness of musket bullets. They supplied me as fast as they could, showing a thousand marks of wonder and astonishment at my bulk and appetite. I then made another sign that I wanted drink. They found by my eating that a small quantity would not suffice me; and being a most ingenious people, they slung up with great dexterity one of their largest hogsheads, then rolled it towards my hand, and beat out the top; I drank it off at a draught, which I might well do, for it hardly held half a pint, and tasted like a small wine of Burgundy, but much more delicious. They brought me a second hogshead, which I drank in the same manner, and made signs for more, but they had none to give me. When I had performed these wonders, they shouted for joy, and danced upon my breast, repeating several times as they did at first, 'Hekinah degul.' They made me a sign that I should throw down the two hogsheads, but first warning the people below to stand out of the way, crying aloud, 'Borach mivola!' and when they saw the vessels in the air, there was an universal shout of 'Hekinah degul!' I confess I was often tempted, while they were passing backwards and forwards on my body, to seize forty or fifty of the first that came in my reach, and dash them against the ground. But the remembrance of what I had felt, which probably might not be the worst they could do, and the promise of honour I made them, for so I interpreted my submissive behaviour, soon drove out those imaginations. Besides, I now considered my self as bound by the laws of hospitality to a people who had treated me with so much expense and magnificence. However, in my thoughts I could not sufficiently wonder at the intrepidity of these diminutive mortals, who durst[13] venture to mount and walk on my body, while one of my hands was at liberty, without trembling at the very sight of so prodigious a creature as I must appear to them. After some time, when they observed that I made no more demands for meat, there appeared before me a person of high rank from his Imperial Majesty. His Excellency, having mounted on the small of my right leg, advanced forwards up to my face, with about a dozen of his retinue. And producing his credentials under the Signet Royal, which he applied close[14] to my eyes, spoke about ten minutes, without any signs of anger, but with a kind of determinate resolution; often pointing forwards, which, as I afterwards found, was towards the capital city, about half a mile distant, whither it was agreed by his Majesty in council that I must be conveyed. I answered in a few words, but to no purpose, and made a sign with my hand that was loose, putting it to the other (but over his Excellency's head, for fear of hurting him or his train) and then to my own head and body, to signify that I desired my liberty. It appeared that he understood me well enough, for he shook his head by way of disapprobation, and held his hand in a posture to show that I must be carried as a prisoner. However, he made other signs to let me understand that I should have meat and drink enough, and very good treatment. Whereupon I once more thought of attempting to break my bonds; but again, when I felt the smart of their arrows upon my face and hands, which were all in blisters, and many of the darts still sticking in them, and observing likewise that the number of my enemies increased, I gave tokens to let them know that they might do with me what they pleased. Upon this the Hurgo and his train withdrew, with much civility and cheerful countenances. Soon after I heard a general shout, with frequent repetitions of the words, 'Peplom selan', and I felt great numbers of the people on my left side relaxing the cords to such a degree, that I was able to turn upon my right, and to ease myself with making water, which I very plentifully did, to the great astonishment of the people, who conjecturing by my motions what I was going to do, immediately opened to the right and left on that side to avoid the torrent which fell with such noise and violence from me. But before this, they had daubed my face and both my hands with a sort of ointment very pleasant to the smell, which in a few minutes removed all the smart of their arrows. These circumstances, added to the refreshment I had received by their victuals and drink, which were very nourishing, disposed me to sleep. I slept about eight hours, as I was afterwards assured; and it was no wonder, for the physicians, by the Emperor's order, had mingled a sleeping potion in the hogsheads of wine.

It seems that upon the first moment I was discovered sleeping on the ground after my landing, the Emperor had early notice of it by an express, and determined in council that I should be tied in the manner I have related (which was done in the night while I slept), that plenty of meat and drink should be sent me, and a machine prepared to carry me to the capital city.

This resolution perhaps, may appear very bold and dangerous, and I am confident would not be imitated by any prince in Europe on the like occasion; however, in my opinion, it was extremely prudent as well as generous. For supposing these people had endeavoured to kill me with their spears and arrows while I was asleep, I should certainly have awaked with the first sense of smart, which might so far have roused my rage and strength, as to enable me to break the strings wherewith I was tied; after which, as they were not able to make resistance, so they could expect no mercy:

These people are most excellent mathematicians, and arrived to a great perfection in mechanics by the countenance and encouragement of the Emperor, who is a renowned patron of learning. This prince hath several machines fixed on wheels, for the carriage of trees and other great weights. He often builds his largest men of war, whereof some are nine foot long, in the woods where the timber grows, and has them carried on these engines[15] three or four hundred yards to the sea. Five hundred carpenters and engineers were immediately set at work to prepare the greatest engine they had. It was a frame of wood raised three inches from the ground, about seven foot long and four wide, moving upon twenty—two wheels. The shout I heard was upon the arrival of this engine, which, it seems, set out in four hours after my landing. It was brought parallel to me as I lay. But the principal difficulty was to raise and place me in this vehicle. Eighty poles, each of one foot high, were erected for this purpose, and very strong cords of the bigness of packthread were fastened by hooks to many bandages, which the workmen had girt round my neck, my hands, my body, and my legs. Nine hundred of the strongest men were employed to draw up these cords by many pulleys fastened on the poles, and thus, in less than three hours, I was raised and slung into the engine, and there tied fast. All this I was told, for while the whole operation was performing, I lay in a profound sleep, by the force of that soporiferous medicine infused into my liquor. Fifteen hundred of the Emperor's largest horses, each about four inches and a half high, were employed to draw me towards the metropolis, which, as I said, was half a mile distant.

About four hours after we began our journey, I awaked by a very ridiculous accident; for, the carriage being stopped a while to adjust something that was out of order, two or three of the young natives had the curiosity to see how I looked when I was asleep; they climbed up into the engine, and advancing very softly to my face, one of them, an officer in the guards, put the sharp end of his half-pike a good way up into my left nostril, which tickled my nose like a straw, and made me sneeze violently, whereupon they stole off unperceived, and it was three weeks before I knew the cause of my awaking so suddenly. We made a long march the remaining part of the day, and rested at night with five hundred guards on each side of me, half with torches, and half with bows and arrows, ready to shoot me if I should offer to stir. The next morning at sunrise we continued our march, and arrived within two hundred yards of the city gates about noon. The Emperor and all his court came out to meet us, but his great officers would by no means suffer his Majesty to endanger his person by mounting on my body.

At the place where the carriage stopped, there stood an ancient temple, esteemed to be the largest in the whole kingdom, which, having been polluted some years before by an unnatural murder, was, according to the zeal of those people, looked on as profane, and therefore had been applied to common use, and all the ornaments and furniture carried away. In this edifice it was determined I should lodge. The great gate fronting to the north was about four foot high, and almost two foot wide, through which I could easily creep. On each side of the gate was a small window not above six inches from the ground: into that on the left side, the King's smiths conveyed fourscore and eleven chains, like those that hang to a lady's watch in Europe, and almost as large, which were locked to my left leg with six and thirty padlocks. Over against this temple, on the other side of the great highway, at twenty foot distance, there was a turret at least five foot high. Here the Emperor ascended with many principal lords of his court, to have an opportunity of viewing me, as I was told, for I could not see them. It was reckoned that above an hundred thousand inhabitants came out of the town upon the same errand; and in spite of my guards, I believe there could not be fewer than ten thousand, at several times, who mounted upon my body by the help of ladders. But a proclamation was soon issued to forbid it upon pain of death. When the workmen found it was impossible for me to break loose, they cut all the strings that bound me; whereupon I rose up with as melancholy a disposition as ever I had in my life. but the noise and astonishment of the people at seeing me rise and walk are not to be expressed. The chains that held my left leg were about two yards long, and gave me not only the liberty of walking backwards and forwards in a semicircle, but, being fixed within four inches of the gate, allowed me to creep in, and lie at my full length in the temple.

【注解】

1. Leyden: 荷兰一所著名的医科大学。
2. physics: 相当于 medicine。
3. Levant: 东地中海地区。
4. the Old Jury: the old Jewry，中世纪伦敦的犹太区。

5. Mrs.: Mistress 的缩写，当时适用于已婚和未婚女子。
6. portion: 嫁妆。
7. brethren: 古英语，相当 brothers。
8. Fetter Lane . . . Wapping: “Fetter Lane”和“Wapping”都是当时伦敦中下层人民的聚居地。
9. Van Diemen’s Land: 指塔斯马尼亚 (Tasmania)，当时被认为是澳大利亚本土的一部分。
10. a cable’s length: 相当于 185.3 米。
11. Hekinah degul: 作者虚构的小人国语言，相当于英语 what in the devil。下文中类似语言确切意义不详。
12. periods: 整句。
13. durst: 古英语，dare 的过去式。
14. applied close: 凑近，移近。
15. engines: 机械装置。

【思考题】

1. Gulliver is said to be Mr. British Middle Class (a representative of the middle class) of his time. Find as many proofs as possible in this chapter to support this statement.
2. What is the advantage of making Lilliputians so tiny?
3. Can you sense the irony in Gulliver’s gradual realization that he becomes the prisoner of men only six inches tall? Are you aware of the fact that the name Gulliver implies that he is “gullible”, a man who believes what he is told?
4. Like many narratives about voyages to nonexistent lands, Jonathan Swift in *Gulliver’s Travels* explores the utopian elements. But his description of the imaginary community is quite different from that of Tao Yuanming’s (陶渊明) “The Peach Blossom Spring” (《桃花源记》). How do you evaluate Swift’s attitudes towards the idea of utopia?

【简评】

斯威夫特的政敌曾诬蔑他是个病态的厌世者，认为他在《格列佛游记》尤其是第四部中对一种人形动物 Yahoo 的描述是出于对整个人类的仇恨。其实在这里斯威夫特要强调的正是人类理智的重要性，一旦丧失理智，人类将与其他动物无异。他希望人类把理性和仁爱当作一种生活正道，安排好自身的生活，抵制纷争，制止腐败，然后从事一项雄心勃勃的事业。正是他那尖锐无比的讽刺背后朴实而又美好的思想，使他的小说历经几个世纪仍为全世界广大读者所喜爱。

作者简介

Samuel Richardson
1689—1761

塞缪尔·理查逊出身于英国德比郡一个细木工家庭，家境贫困，只受过相当有限的教育。17岁时，理查逊在伦敦一家出版公司当学徒。他虚心好学，进步很快，深得老板赏识，后来娶老板之女为妻。到30岁时，理查逊已拥有自己的出版公司，事业蒸蒸日上，成为托利党机关报、下院期刊、法律报告和多家报纸的指定出版商，并于1754年成为出版行业协会会长。理查逊涉足小说创作纯属偶然。1739年，已知天命的理查逊应朋友之邀编撰一本书信写作手册，面向不会写信的乡村青年男女。在编写过程中，他突发奇想，开始写一本书信体小说 (the epistolary novel)，这就是《帕美拉，或德行有报》。该书前两卷于1740年出版，后两卷于次年面世，立即成为英伦三岛乃至整个欧洲的畅销书，并被译成法语、德语等七种语言，人们争相购阅，成为茶馆里、饭桌上的谈论焦点。

1747年，理查逊的第二部小说《克莱丽莎·哈洛》(*Clarissa Harlowe*) 的前两卷出版，次年又出版了后五卷，获得了甚于《帕美拉，或德行有报》的成功。在这部堪称英语小说长度之最的小说里，理查逊讲述了一个催人泪下的故事：年轻美貌的克莱丽莎·哈洛不屈从父母包办的婚姻，却误入浪荡子拉佛累斯 (Lovelace) 的圈套，虽百般抵抗仍不幸失身，最后羞愧而死。此书是为了警示“在婚姻问题上父母和子女双方的不良行为可能带来不幸”。1754年，理查逊的又一作品《查尔斯·格兰迪森爵士的历史》(*The History of Sir Charles Grandison*) 出版。查尔斯·格兰迪森爵士是一个近乎完美的男子：出身高贵、家境殷实、品格高尚、相貌英俊。一个偶然的机会他搭救了被劫持的哈里艾特·拜伦 (Harriet Byron)，两人一见钟情。但由于与另一女子订婚在先，为信守誓言，查尔斯只好忍痛割爱。经过一番周折，女方解除婚约，查尔斯与哈里艾特终成眷属。就艺术成就而言，该小说不及前两部，但在当时仍大受读者青睐，简·奥斯汀 (Jane Austen, 1775—1827) 也对它推崇备至。

现代读者对理查逊失去兴趣甚至淡忘他，主要是由于他的作品篇幅过长，以及读者价值观的改变。帕美拉是真有美德还是只是处心积虑地诱惑B先生，这在当时便有人提出疑问，而现代读者对此的疑惑可能更为强烈。但无论如何，理查逊在英国文学史上占有一席之地毋庸置疑。首先，理查逊是他那个时代人民生活的忠实记录者。他的作品揭示了像帕美拉这样的女孩的无助境况、普通人生活的艰辛和穷人与富人之间的隔阂与对立。其次，理查逊独创性地大量运用书信体的方式，不仅展示了人物的言行举止，还细腻地描述了人物的内心世界，剖析他们的动机，表现他们的情感。这为英国文学乃至整个欧洲文学开辟了一个新天地，甚至对卢梭、歌德和普希金都有极大影响。理查逊的作品在叙述技巧上也颇具特色，作者自始至终保持沉默，不作任何评论，为人物提供了一个个充分表露自己的舞台。

Pamela; or, Virtre Rewarded

【题解】

《帕美拉，或德行有报》整部小说由帕美拉·安德鲁斯 (Pamela Andrews) 与父母之间的书信和帕美拉的日记组成。在第一部分里，15 岁的美丽少女帕美拉是个女仆，故事开始时，她的女主人去世，少爷 B 先生伺机骚扰，想方设法占有她。帕美拉竭尽全力保住自己的贞洁。后来 B 先生把她带到偏僻的庄园，眼看就要阴谋得逞，但帕美拉的晕厥阻止了他。最后，B 先生被她的美德打动，决定娶她为妻。帕美拉的美德得到了回报。小说第二部描述了帕美拉的婚姻生活。她不亢不卑地忍受夫家亲戚对出身低贱的她冷淡甚至鄙视的态度，以自己的美德征服了他们，最后为他们所接受。她举止得体地面对丈夫的私生子，阻止丈夫做出更多的荒唐事。最后，她成了一个人人敬重的女主人。

下文为帕美拉写的日记“星期二晚上”，日记描述 B 先生在女管家的协助下，假冒女佣闯入帕美拉寝室，最后因为晕厥保住了自己的贞洁。这次经历竟激发了 B 先生的怜爱之心，并最终向帕美拉正式求婚。

From Pamela; or, Virtue Rewarded

Tuesday Night

For the future, I will always mistrust most, when appearances look fairest. O your poor daughter! what has she not suffered since Sunday night!—My worst trial, and fearfullest danger! O how I shudder to write you an account of this wicked interval of time! For, my dear parents, will you not be too much frightened and affected with my distress, when I tell you, that his journey to Stamford was all abominable pretence? For he came home privately, and had well'nigh effected all his vile purposes[1] in the ruin of your poor daughter! And that by such a plot as I was not in the least apprehensive of: and you'll hear what a vile unwomanly part that wicked wretch, Mrs. Jewkes[2], acted in it!

I left off with letting you know how much I was pleased that I had one night's reprieve added to my honesty. But I had less occasion to rejoice than ever, as you will judge by what I have said already. Takes then, the greadful story, as well as I can relate it.

The maid Nan is a little apt to drink if she can get at it; and Mrs. Jewkes happened, or designed, as is too probable, to leave a bottle of cherry-brandy in her way, and the wench drank more of it than she should; and when she came to lay the cloth, Mrs. Jewkes perceived it, and rated at[3] her most sadly. The wretch has too many faults of her own, to suffer any of the like sort in any body else, if she can help it; and she bade her get out of her sight, when we had supped, and go to bed, to sleep off her liquor, before we came to bed. And so the poor maid went muttering upstairs.

About two hours after, which was near eleven o'clock, Mrs. Jewkes and I went up to go to bed; I pleasing myself with what a charming night I should have. We locked both doors, and saw poor Nan, as I thought, sitting fast asleep, in an elbow-chair, in a dark corner of the room, with her apron thrown over her head and neck. But oh! it was my abominable master, as you shall hear by and by. And Mrs. Jewkes said, 'There is that beast of a wench fast asleep! I knew she had taken a fine dose.''I will wake her,' said I. No, don's, said she; 'Let her sleep on,' answered she, 'we shall lie better without her.' 'So we shall,' said I; 'but won't she get cold?'

'I hope,' said the vile woman, 'you have no writing to-night.' 'No,' replied I, 'I will go to bed when you go, Mrs. Jewkes.''That's right,' answered she, 'indeed I wonder what you can find to write about so continually. I am sure you have better conveniences of that kind, and more paper, than I am aware of. Indeed I had intended to rummage you, if my master had not come down; for I spied a broken tea-cup with ink, which gave me a suspicion: but as he is come, let him look after you, if he will. If you deceive him, it will be his own fault.'

All this time we were undressing ourselves; and I fetching a deep sight, 'What do you sigh for?' said she. 'I am thinking, Mrs. Jewkes,' answered I, 'what a sad life I live, and how hard is my lot. I am sure the thief that has robbed is much better off than I, bating[4] the guilt; and I should, I think, take it for a mercy to be hanged out of the way, rather than live in these cruel apprehensions.' So, being not sleepy, and in a prattling vein[5], I began to give a little history of myself, in this manner.

'My poor honest parents,' said I, 'in the first place, took care to instil good principles into my mind, till I was almost twelve years of age; and taught me to prefer goodness and poverty, if they could not be separated, to the highest condition of life; and they confirmed their lessons by their own practice; for they were of late years remarkably poor, and always as remarkably honest, even to a proverb; for, As honest as goodman ANDREWS, was a bye-word.

Well, then comes my late dear good lady, and takes a fancy to me, and said she would be the making of me, if I was a good girl; and she put me to sing, to dance, to play on the harpsichord, in order to divert her melancholy hours; and also taught me all manner of fine needle-works; but still this was her lesson, 'My good Pamela, be virtuous, and keep the man at a distance.' Well, so I did; and yet, though I say it, they all respected me; and would do any thing for me, as if I were a gentlewoman.

But then, what comes next? Why, it pleased God to take my good lady; and then comes my master; and what says he? Why, in effect, it is 'Be not virtuous, Pamela.'

So here have I lived above sixteen years in virtue and reputation; and, all at once, when I come to know what is good, and what is evil, I must renounce all the good, all the whole sixteen years' innocence, which, next to God's grace, I owed chiefly to my parents and to my lady's good lessons and examples, and chuse[6] the evil; and so, in a moment's time, become the vilest of creatures! And all this, for what, I pray? Why, truly, for a pair of diamond earrings, a solitaire, a necklace, and a diamond ring for my finger; which would not become me; for a few paltry fine clothes; which, when I wore them, would make but my former poverty more ridiculous to every body that saw me; especially when they knew the base terms I wore them upon. But, indeed, I was to have a great parcel of guineas beside; I forget how many; for had there been ten times more, they would not have been so much to me, as the honest six guineas you tricked me out of, Mrs. Jewkes.

Well, but then I was to have I know not how many pounds a year for my life; and my poor father (fine encouragement indeed!) was to be the manager for the abandoned prostitute, his daughter; and then, (there was the jest of it!) my kind, forgiving, virtuous master would pardon me all my misdeeds!

And what, pray, are all these violent misdeeds? Why, they are, for daring to adhere to the good lessons that were taught me; for not being contented, when I was run away with, in order to be ruined; but contriving, if my poor wits had been able, to get out of danger, and preserve myself honest.

Then was he once jealous of poor John[7], though he knew John was his own creature, and helped to deceive me.

Then was he outrageous against poor Mr. Williams[8]! and him has this good, merciful master thrown into gaol! and for what? Why, truly, for that being a divine, and a good man, he was willing to forego all his expectations of interest, and assist a poor creature, whom he believed innocent!

But, to be sure, I must be forward, bold, saucy, and what not! to dare to attempt an escape from certain ruin, and an unjust confinement. Poor Mr. Williams! how was he drawn in to make marriage proposals to me! O Mrs. Jewkes! what a trick was that! The honest gentleman would have had but a poor catch of me, had I consented to be his wife; but he, and you too, know I did not want to marry any body. I only wanted to go to my poor parents, and not to be laid under an unlawful restraint, and which would not have been attempted, but only that I am a poor destitute young creature, and have no friend that is able to right me.

'So here, Mrs. Jewkes,' said I, 'have I given my history in brief. I am very unhappy; and whence my unhappiness? Why, because my master sees something in my person that takes his present fancy; and because I would not be ruined; why, therefore, to choose, I must, and I shall be ruined! And this is all the reason that can be given!'

She heard me run on all this time, while I was undressing, without any interruption; and I said, 'Well, I must go to the two closets, ever since an affair of the closet at the other house, though he is so far off. And I have a good mind to wake this poor maid.' 'No, don't,' said she, 'I charge you. I am very angry with her, and she'll get no harm there; and if she wakes, she will find her way to bed well enough, as there is a candle in the chimney.'

So I looked into the closets, and kneeled down in my own, as I used to do, to say my prayers, and this with my underclothes in my hand[9]; and passed by the supposed sleeping wench, in my return. But little did I think, it was my wicked, wicked master in a gown and petticoat of hers, and her apron over his face and shoulders. To what meannesses will not Lucifer make his votaries stoop, to gain their abominable ends!

Mrs. Jewkes by this time was got to bed, on the further side, as she used to do; and I lay close to her, to make room for the maid, when she should awake. 'Where are the keys?' said I, 'and yet I am not so much afraid to-night.' 'Here,' said the wicked woman, 'put your arm under mine, and you shall find them about my wrist, as they used to be.' I did so, and the abominable designer held my hand with her right hand, as my right arm was under her left.

In less than a quarter of an hour, hearing the supposed maid in motion, 'Poor Nan is awake,' said I; 'I hear her stir.''Let us go to sleep,' replied she, 'and not mind her: she'll come to bed, when she's quite awake.' 'Poor soul!' said I, 'I'll warrant she will have the headache finely to-morrow for this.''Be silent,' answered she, 'and go to sleep; you keep me awake. I never found you in so talkative a humour in my life.' 'Don't chide me,' said I; 'I will say but one thing more: do you think Nan could hear me talk of my master's offers?' 'No, no,' replied she, 'she was dead asleep.''I am glad of that,' said I, 'because I would not expose my master to his common servants, and I knew you were no stranger to his fine articles.''I think they were fine articles,' replied she, 'and you were bewitched you did not close with them: but let us go to sleep.'

So I was silent, and the pretended Nan (O wicked, base, villainous designer! what a plot, what an unexpected plot was this!) seemed to be awaking; and Mrs Jewkes, abhorred creature! said, 'Come, Nan! What, are you awake at last? Pr'ythee come to-bed, for Mrs. Pamela is in a talking fit, and won't go to sleep one while.

At that, the pretended she came to the bed-side; and sitting down in a chair concealed by the curtain, began to undress. 'Poor Mrs Ann,' said I, 'I warrant your headaches most sadly! How do you do?' No answer was returned. 'You know I have ordered her not to answer you,' said the abominably wicked woman. This plot, to be sure, was laid when she gave her these orders the night before.

The pretended Nan (how shocking to relate!) then came into bed, trembling like an aspen-leaf; and I (poor fool that I was!) pitied her much. But well might the barbarous deceiver tremble at his vile dissimulation, and base designs.

What words shall I find, my dear mother (for my father should not see this shocking part), to describe the rest, and my confusion, when the guilty wretch took my left arm, and laid it under his neck as the vile procuress held my right; and then he clasped me round the waist!

'Is the wench mad?' said I. 'Why, how now, confidence?' thinking still it had been Nan. But he kissed me with frightful vehemence; and then his voice broke upon me like a clap of thunder, 'Now, Pamela,' said he, 'is the time of reckoning come, that I have threatened!' I screamed out for help; but there was nobody to help me: and both my hands were secured, as I said. Sure never poor soul was in such agonies as I. 'Wicked man!' said I; 'wicked, abominable woman! Good Heaven, this one time! this one time, good Heaven, deliver me, or strike me dead this moment!' And then I screamed again and again.

'One word with you, Pamela!' said he. 'Hear me but one word! Hitherto you find I offer nothing to you.' 'Is this nothing,' said I, 'to be in bed here? To hold my hands between you?'

'Hear me, Pamela.' 'I will hear, if you will this moment leave the bed, and take this vile woman from me!'

Said she, (O disgrace of womankind!) 'Don't stand dilly-dallying, sir. She cannot exclaim worse than she has done; and will be quieter when she knows the worst.'

'Silence!' said he to her. 'I must say one word to you, Pamela: it is this; you now see, that you are in my power! You cannot get from me, nor help yourself: yet have I not offered any thing amiss to you. But if you resolve not to comply with my proposals, I will not lose this opportunity. If you do, I will yet leave you. I abhor violence[10]. Your compliance, my dear girl, shall intitle you to all I offered you in my proposals.'

'O sir,' exclaimed I, 'leave me, do but leave me, and I will do anything I ought to do.' 'Swear then to me,' said he, 'that you will accept my proposals!' And then (for this was all detestable grimace[11]) he put his hand in my bosom.

With struggling, fright, terror, I quite fainted away, and did not come to myself soon; so that they both, from the cold sweats I was in, thought me dying. And I remember no more, than that, when, with great difficulty, they brought me to myself, she was sitting on one side of the bed, with her clothes on; and he on the other with his, and in his gown and slippers.

When I saw them there, I sat up in my bed, nothing about my neck, without any regard to what appearance I must make, and he soothing me with an aspect of pity and concern, I put my hand to his mouth, and said, 'O tell me, yet tell me not, what I have suffered in this distress!' And I talked quite wild, and knew not what: for I was on the point of distraction.

He most solemnly, and with a bitter imprecation, vowed, that he had not offered the least indecency; that he was frightened at the terrible manner I was taken with the fit: that he would desist from his attempt; and begged but to see me easy and quite, and he would leave me directly, and go to his own bed. 'O then,' said I, 'take with you this most wicked woman, this vile Mrs Jewkes, as an earnest that I may believe you!'

'And will you, sir,' said the wicked wretch, 'for a fit or two, give up such an opportunity as this? I thought you had known the sex better. She is now, you see, quite well again!'

This I heard; more she might say; but I fainted away once more, at these words, and at his clasping his arms about me again. And when I came a little to myself, I saw him sit there, and the maid Nan, holding a smelling-bottle to my nose, and no Mrs Jewkes.

He said, taking my hand, 'Now will I vow to you, my dear Pamela, that I will leave you the moment I see you better, and pacified. Here's Nan knows, and will tell you, my concern for you. I vow to Heaven, that I have not offered any indecency to you. And since I found Mrs Jewkes so offensive to you, I have sent her to the maid's bed. The maid only shall stay with you to-night; and but promise me, that you will compose yourself, and I will leave you.' 'But,' said I, 'will not Nan also hold my hand? And will not she let you come in again?' He swore that he would not return that night. 'Nan,' said he, 'do you go to-bed to the dear creature, and say all you can to comfort her; and now, Pamela, give me but your hand, and say you forgive me, and I will leave you to your repose.'

I held out my trembling hand, which he vouchsafed to kiss; and again demanding my forgiveness, 'God forgive you, sir,' said I, 'as you will be just to what you promise!' And he withdrew, with a countenance of remorse, as I hoped; and Nan shut the doors, and, at my request, brought the keys to bed.

【注解】

1. . . . had well-nigh effected all his vile purposes: 几乎让他的卑鄙目的得逞。
2. Mrs Jewkes: B先生的女管家，种种阴谋的帮凶。
3. rated at: 责骂。
4. bating: 除……之外。
5. in a prattling vein: 谈兴正浓。
6. chuse: 相当于 choose。
7. John: B先生收买的信使，帕美拉的信送递其父母前必先交B先生过目。
8. Mr. Williams: B先生的牧师。B先生曾假装要把帕美拉许配给他。
9. with my underclothes in my hand: 在以前的版本里作者特意强调帕美拉当时一丝不挂。
10. I abhor violence: 这句话是作者于1801年修订时加进去的，为了使B先生的转变不显得太唐突。
11. grimace: 哄骗。

【思考题】

1. Do you think Mr. B's change from a base wretch to a considerate lover convincing?
2. What social reality has been revealed in Pamela's helpless situation?
3. What techniques does the author use to appeal to the sympathy of the readers for Pamela?

解读举例

1. 帕美拉工于心计，一心想往上爬，成为贵夫人。她一再拒绝B先生的纠缠，并非真有美德，而是为了增加自己的筹码，诱使B先生娶自己。她写给父母的信也是装腔作势，煽情十足。

2. 帕美拉是当时受压迫人民呼天不应、欲哭无泪的无助状况的真实写照。她为生活所迫去当女佣，不光在经济上受尽剥削，还失去了人身自由，连自己的贞操都难以保全。这是对资本主义制度的控诉。而最后帕美拉满足于成为贵夫人的现实，也表现了作者的阶级局限性。

3. 帕美拉是一个反叛者的形象。女佣因为主人的胁迫而失身，这在当时司空见惯，甚至合情合理。但帕美拉以弱小之躯抵抗B先生编织的淫毒之网，并对B先生所拥有的这种为世人默许的权利提出挑战：我怎么就成了他的财产？他有什么权利这样做？这与窃贼占有他的赃物又有何异？

Henry Fielding
1707—1754

作者简介

亨利·菲尔丁出生于萨默塞特郡，祖上为伯爵，其父曾当过将军。他由家教启蒙，后进入伊顿公学接受中等教育，又于1728年春入莱顿大学专攻法律，因家境穷困于次年秋辍学。上大学之前，菲尔丁已开始其文学生涯：1728年初，他的第一部剧作《几场假面舞会中的爱》(*Love in Several Masques*)公演并出版。在随后的9年时间里，他先后推出25部剧作，大多指点江山、评点时事，其讽刺之尖锐大胆尤以最后两部《帕斯昆》(*Pasquin*, 1736)和《1736年历史纪事》(*The Historical Register for the Year 1736*, 1737)为甚。为此他激怒了当时的首相罗伯特·沃尔蒲尔(Robert Walpole, 1676—1745)，在后者的直接干预下，议会于1737年6月通过《戏剧审查法》(the Theatrical Licensing Act)，限制剧院数量，并禁止上演影射国王和政府官员的剧目。菲尔丁被迫结束戏剧创作，重新开始学习法律，并于1740年取得律师资格。他是一位出色的法律工作者，1748年被任命为伦敦地方治安法官，并于 1751 年组建了伦敦第一支现代警察队伍。同时，他又是一位成功的期刊主编，在 1739 至 1748 年间先后主编过 4 种期刊。1734 年菲尔丁与夏洛特·克莱多克 (Charlotte Cradock) 结婚。她是菲尔丁心目中的理想女性，之后他的小说中多位女主人公的形象都以她为原型。1744 年夏洛特去世，三年后，他不顾政敌的取笑，娶前妻侍女玛丽·丹尼尔 (Mary Daniel) 为妻。1753 年，菲尔丁积劳成疾，于次年 6 月前往葡萄牙里斯本，希望在温和的气候下康复，但于同年 10 月 8 日与世长辞，年仅 47 岁。

1740 年，理查逊的小说《帕美拉，或德行有报》出版并引起轰动，而菲尔丁却质疑帕美拉的所谓美德及其作者的道德观，于是便有了他的第一部小说《约瑟夫·安德鲁斯》(*Joseph Andrews*, 1742)。小说前十章的情节安排与《帕美拉》反其道而行之：帕美拉之弟约瑟夫在波比先生 (Mr Booby，即 Mr. B) 的姑妈波比夫人家当佣工，经常受到女主人及其侍女的性骚扰，他严正拒绝，女主人恼羞成怒，将其赶出家门。其后的章节里，菲尔丁的主要兴趣已不再是戏仿《帕美拉，或德行有报》，而是着重描写约瑟夫与亚当斯牧师 (Parson Adams) 在流浪途中所遭遇的光怪陆离的事情和形形色色的人物。这种流浪汉小说 (Picaresque Novel) 全面反映时代生活和社会现实，是英国小说创作的又一发展。

翌年，菲尔丁出版第二部小说《大伟人乔纳森·瓦尔德传》(*The Life of Jonathan Wild the Great*, 1743)。小说取材于真人真事：强盗头子瓦尔德于 1725 年被处以绞刑。菲尔丁极富想象力地叙述了罪犯从出生、洗礼到成为不可一世的匪首及最后被捕处死的“伟大”一生，意在影射那些成功的政客与瓦尔德无异，为达目的而不择手段，毫无德行可言。

1749 年菲尔丁的代表作《弃儿汤姆·琼斯》出版，大获成功。1751 年菲尔丁的最后一部小说《阿美莉亚》(*Amelia*) 问世。通过主人公阿美莉亚及其丈夫的艰辛生活和悲惨遭遇，作者抨击了英国的债务法和监狱的黑暗。

菲尔丁是 18 世纪英国最伟大的小说家。他曾把自己作品的体裁归纳为“散文滑稽史诗”(the comic epic in prose)。他参照古希腊史诗作家荷马的创作实践，借鉴哲学家亚里士多德的理论，采用西班牙作家塞万提斯《堂·吉诃德》所用的流浪汉小说形式，写出了《约瑟夫·安德鲁斯》和《汤姆·琼斯》这两部不朽之作。尤其是后者，无论就内容抑或形式而言，都是 18 世纪英国现实主义小说成就的巅峰。《阿美莉亚》则为 19 世纪英国批判现实主义小说开辟了道路。

菲尔丁的小说与同时代其他小说不同的是，它们不是书信体或主人公自述形式，而是直接由作者叙述，并适当加以解释，使得叙述更加直截了当，更加自由、清晰和完整，有助于形象、生动、全面地刻画人物。菲尔丁的文体多样，因人因事而异，有时近乎漫谈，有时粗俗滑稽，有时高贵典雅。他的小说情节生动曲折，布局巧妙奇特，人物有血有肉、栩栩如生，为读者展现了18世纪中叶英国社会的全景图。诗人乔治·戈登·拜伦 (George Gordon Byron, 1788—1824) 曾称菲尔丁为“展示人性的散文荷马”(the prose Homer of Human Nature)，实在恰如其分。

Tom Jones

【题解】

汤姆·琼斯是个弃儿，被富有的乡绅奥尔沃西收养。奥氏另外收养了其妹之子布利非尔，并将其作为自己的合法继承人。两个孩子一起长大，显示出截然不同的性格和人品。两人又都追求乡绅韦斯顿之女索菲娅。阴险狡诈的布利非尔极力排挤善良诚实的汤姆，多次向奥氏告密中伤汤姆。兼之年轻的汤姆生活上有不检点之处，曾与猎场看守人之女有染，又因为不愿讨好谄媚而引起家庭教师的敌意，汤姆最终被逐出家门。他四处流浪，想去伦敦参军。此时，索菲娅因不满父亲逼她嫁给布利非尔而离家投奔伦敦的亲戚。两人在路上及伦敦历尽艰险。其间汤姆受伯莱斯顿夫人 (Lady Bellaston) 的诱惑与其纠缠不清，后又为布利非尔暗算而被捕。索菲娅也落入伯莱斯顿夫人的圈套而险遭侮辱。后来，布利非尔的阴谋败露，汤姆的身世终于大白于天下。原来，他是奥氏妹妹的亲生儿子，奥氏的亲外甥。最后，奥氏取消了布利非尔的继承人资格，改立汤姆为合法继承人。索菲娅原谅了汤姆的不忠行为，有情人终成眷属。

《汤姆·琼斯》共18部，每部的引子中包括菲尔丁优美的散文。下文节选自小说第三部第二、四两章。作者通过一些小事呈现了汤姆和布利非尔各自的态度，从中可看出两人性格和人品的差异。

From Tom Jones

Book 3

Chapter 2

The Heroe of this great History appears with very bad Omens. A little Tale of so Low a Kind, that some may think it not worth their Notice. A Word or two concerning a Squire, and more relating to a Gamekeeper, and a Schoolmaster.

As we determined, when we first sat down to write this history, to flatter no man, but to guide our pen throughout by the directions of truth, we are obliged to bring our heroe on the stage in a much more disadvantageous manner than we could wish; and to declare honestly, even at his first appearance, that it was the universal opinion of all Mr. Allworthy's family that he was certainly born to be hanged.

Indeed, I am sorry to say, there was too much reason for this conjecture; The lad having, from his earliest years, discovered a propensity to many vices, and especially to one which hath as direct a tendency as any other to that fate which we have just now observed to have been prophetically denounced against him; he had been already convicted of three robberies, viz, of robbing an orchard, of stealing a duck out of a farmer's yard, and of picking Master Blifil's pocket of a ball.

The vices of this young man were, moreover, heightened, by the disadvantageous light in which they appeared when opposed to the virtues of Master Blifil, his companion: a youth of so different a cast from little Jones, that not only the family, but all the neighbourhood, resounded his praises. He was, indeed, a lad of a remarkable disposition; sober, discreet, and pious, beyond his age; qualities which gained him the love of everyone who knew him, whilst Tom Jones was universally disliked; and many expressed their wonder, that Mr Allworthy would suffer such a lad to be educated with his nephew, lest the morals of the latter should be corrupted by his example.

An incident which happened about this time will set the characters of these two lads more fairly before the discerning reader than is the power of the longest dissertation.

Tom Jones, who, bad as he is, must serve for the heroe of this history, had only one friend among all the servants of the family; for as to Mrs Wilkins[1], she had long since given him up, and was perfectly reconciled to her mistress. This friend was the gamekeeper, a fellow of a loose kind of disposition, and who was thought not to entertain much stricter notions concerning the difference of meum and tuum[2], than the young gentleman himself. And hence this friendship gave occasion to many sarcastical remarks among the domestics, most of which were either proverbs before, or, at least, are become so now; and, indeed, the wit of them all may be comprised in that short Latin proverb, "Noscitur a socio," which, I think, is thus expressed in English, "You may know him by the company he keeps."

To say the truth, some of that atrocious wickedness in Jones, of which we have just mentioned three examples, might perhaps, be derived from the encouragement he had received from this fellow, who, in two or three instances, had been what the law calls an accessary after the fact[3]: you the whole duck, and great part of the apples, were converted to the use of the gamekeeper, and his family; Tho', as Jones alone was discovered, the poor lad bore not only the whole smart, but the whole blame; both which fell again to his lot on the following occasion.

Contiguous to Mr Allworthy's estate was the manor of one of those gentlemen who are called preservers of the game. This species of men, from the great severity with which they revenge the death of a hare or a partridge, might be thought to cultivate the same superstition with the Bannians[4] in India; many of whom, we are told, dedicate their whole lives to the preservation and protection of certain animals; was it not that our English Bannians, while they preserve them from other enemies, will most unmercifully slaughter whole horse-loads themselves; so that they stand clearly acquitted of any such heathenish superstition.

I have, indeed, a much better opinion of this kind of men than is entertained by some, as I take them to answer the order of Nature, and the good purposes for which they were ordained, in a more ample manner than many others. Now, as Horace tells us, that there are a set of human beings,

Fruges consumere nati.

"Born to consume the fruits of the earth;" So, I make no manner of doubt but that there are others,

Feras consumere nati.

"Born to consume the beasts of the field;" or, as it is commonly called, the game; and none, I believe, will deny, but that those squires fulfil this end of their creation.

Little Jones went one day a shooting with the gamekeeper; when, happening to spring a covey of partridges, near the border of that manor over which Fortune, to fulfil the wise purposes of Nature, had planted one of the game consumers, the birds flew into it, and were marked (as it is called) by the two sportsmen, in some furze bushes, about two or three hundred paces beyond Mr. Allworthy's dominions.

Mr. Allworthy had given the fellow strict orders, on pain of forfeiting his place, never to trespass on any of his neighbours; no more on those who were less rigid in this matter than on the lord of this manor. With regard to others, indeed, these orders had not been always very scrupulously kept; but as the disposition of the gentleman with whom the partridges had taken sanctuary was well known, the gamekeeper had never yet attempted to invade his territories. Nor had he done it now, had not the younger sportsman, who was excessively eager to pursue the flying game, over-persuaded him; but Jones being very importunate, the other, who was himself keen enough after the sport, yielded to his persuasions, entered the manor, and shot one of the partridges.

The gentleman himself was at that time on horse-back, at a little distance from them; and hearing the gun go off, he immediately made towards the place, and discovered poor Tom; for the gamekeeper had leapt into the thickest part of the furze-brake, where he had happily concealed himself.

The gentleman having searched the lad, and found the partridge upon him, denounced great vengeance, swearing he would acquaint Mr. Allworthy. He was as good as his word: for he rode immediately to his house, and complained of the trespass on his manor in as high terms and as bitter language as if his house had been broken open, and the most valuable furniture stole out of it. He added, that some other person was in his company, tho' he could not discover him; for that two guns had been discharged almost in the same instant. And, says he, "We have found only this partridge, but the Lord knows what mischief they have done."

At his return home, Tom was presently convened before Mr Allworthy. He owned the fact, and alleged no other excuse but what was really true, viz, that the covey was originally sprung in Mr. Allworthy's own manor.

Tom was then interrogated who was with him, which Mr. Allworthy declared he was resolved to know, acquainting the culprit with the circumstance of the two guns, which had been deposed by the squire and both his servants; but Tom stoutly persisted in asserting that he was alone; yet, to say the truth, he hesitated a little at first, which would have confirmed Mr. Allworthy's belief, had what the squire and his servants said, wanted any further confirmation.

The gamekeeper, being a suspected person, was now sent for, and the question put to him; but he, relying on the promise which Tom had made him, to take all upon himself, very resolutely denied being in company with the young gentleman, or indeed having seen him the whole afternoon.

Mr. Allworthy then turned towards Tom, with more than usual anger in his countenance, and advised him to confess who was with him; repeating, that he was resolved to know. The lad, however, still maintained his resolution, and was dismissed with much wrath by Mr. Allworthy, who told him he should have to the next morning to consider of it, when he should be questioned by another person, and in another manner.

Poor Jones spent a very melancholy night, and the more so, as he was without his usual companion: for Master Blifil was gone abroad on a visit with his mother. Fear of the punishment he was to suffer was on this occasion his least evil; his chief anxiety being, lest his constancy should fail him, and he should be brought to betray the gamekeeper, whose ruin he knew must now be the consequence.

Nor did the gamekeeper pass his time much better. He had the same apprehensions with the youth; for whose honour he had likewise a much tenderer regard than for his skin.

In the morning, when Tom attended the reverend Mr. Thwackum[5], the person to whom Mr. Allworthy had committed the instruction of the two boys, he had the same questions put to him by that gentleman, which he had been asked the evening before, to which he returned the same answers. The consequence of this was, so severe a whipping, that it possibly fell little short of the torture with which confessions are in some countries extorted from criminals.

Tom bore his punishment with great resolution; and tho' his master asked him, between every stroke, whether he would not confess, he was contented to be flead rather than betray his friend, or break the promise he had made.

The gamekeeper was now relieved from his anxiety, and Mr. Allworthy himself began to be concerned at Tom's sufferings: for, besides that Mr. Thwackum, being highly enraged that he was not able to make the boy say what he himself pleased, had carried his severity much beyond the good man's intention, this latter began now to suspect that the squire had been mistaken; which his extreme eagerness and anger seemed to make probable; and as for what the servants had said in confirmation of their master's account, he laid no great stress upon that. Now, as cruelty and injustice were two ideas of which Mr. Allworthy could by no means support the consciousness a single moment, he sent for Tom, and after many kind and friendly exhortations, said, "I am convinced, my dear child, that my suspicions have wronged you; I am sorry that you have been so severely punished on this account." And at last gave him a little horse to make him amends; again repeating his sorrow for what had past.

Tom's guilt now flew in his face more than any severity could make it. He could more easily bear the lashes of Thwackum, than the generosity of Allworthy. The tears burst from his eyes, and he fell upon his knees, crying, "Oh! sir, you are too good to me. Indeed you are. Indeed, I don't deserve it." And at that very instant, from the fullness of his heart, had almost betrayed the secret; but the good genius of[6] the gamekeeper suggested to him what might be the consequence to the poor fellow, and this consideration sealed his lips.

Thwackum did all he could to dissuade Allworthy from shewing any compassion or kindness to the boy, saying, "He had persisted in an untruth;" and gave some hints that a second whipping might probably bring the matter to light.

But Mr. Allworthy absolutely refused to consent to the experiment. He said, the boy had suffered enough already, for concealing the truth, even if he was guilty, seeing that he could have no motive but a mistaken point of honour for so doing.

"Honour!" cryed Thwackum, with some warmth, "mere stubbornness and obstinacy! Can honour teach anyone to tell a lie, or can any honour exist independent of religion?"

This discourse happened at table when dinner was just ended; and there were present Mr. Allworthy, Mr. Thwackum, and a third gentleman who now entered into the debate, and whom, before we proceed any farther, we shall briefly introduce to our reader's acquaintance.

Chapter 4

Containing a necessary Apology for the Author; and a childish Incident, which perhaps requires an Apology likewise.

Before I proceed farther, I shall beg leave to obviate some misconstructions into which the zeal of some few readers may lead them; for I would not willingly give offence to any, especially to men who are warm in the cause of virtue or religion.

I hope, therefore, no man will, by the grossest misunderstanding, or perversion, of my meaning, misrepresent me, as endeavouring to cast any ridicule on the greatest perfections of human nature; and which do, indeed, alone purify and ennoble the heart of man, and raise him above the brute creation. This, reader, I will venture to say (and by how much the better man you are yourself, by so much the more will you be inclined to believe me), that I would rather have buried the sentiments of these two persons in eternal oblivion, than have done any injury to either of these glorious causes.

On the contrary, it is with a view to their service that I have taken upon me to record the lives and actions of two of their false and pretended champions. A treacherous friend is the most dangerous enemy; and I will say boldly, that both religion and virtue have received more real discredit from hypocrites, than the wittiest profligates or infidels could ever cast upon them: nay, farther, as these two, in their purity, are rightly called the bands of civil society, and are indeed the greatest of blessings; so when poisoned and corrupted with fraud, pretence, and affectation, they have become the worst of civil curses, and have enabled men to perpetrate the most cruel mischiefs to their own species.

Indeed, I doubt not but this ridicule will in general be allowed: my chief apprehension is, as many true and just sentiments often came from the mouths of these persons, lest the whole should be taken together, and I should be conceived to ridicule all alike. Now the reader will be pleased to consider, that, as neither of these men were fools, they could not be supposed to have holden none but wrong principles, and to have uttered nothing but absurdities; what injustice, therefore, must I have done to their characters, had I selected only what was bad! and how horribly wretched and maimed must their arguments have appeared!

Upon the whole, it is not religion or virtue, but the want of them which is here exposed. Had not Thwackum too much neglected virtue, and Square[7], religion, in the composition of their several systems, and had not both utterly discarded all natural goodness of heart, they had never been represented as the objects of derision in this history, in which we will now proceed.

This matter, then, which put an end to the debate mentioned in the last chapter, was no other than a quarrel between Master Blifil and Tom Jones, the consequence of which had been a bloody nose to the former; for though Master Blifil, notwithstanding he was the younger, was in size above the other's match, yet Tom was much his superior at the noble art of boxing.

Tom, however, cautiously avoided all engagements with that youth: for besides that Tommy Jones was an inoffensive lad amidst all his roguery, and really loved Blifil; Mr Thwackum being always the second of the latter[8], would have been sufficient to deter him.

But well says a certain author, no man is wise at all hours; it is therefore no wonder that a boy is not so. A difference arising at play between the two lads, Master Blifil called Tom a beggarly bastard. Upon which the latter, who was somewhat passionate in his disposition, immediately caused that phenomenon in the face of the former, which we have above remembered.

Master Blifil now, with his blood running from his nose, and the tears galloping after from his eyes, appeared before his uncle and the tremendous Thwackum. In which court an indictment of assault, battery, and wounding, was instantly preferred against Tom, who in his excuse only pleaded the provocation, which was indeed all the matter that Master Blifil had omitted.

It is indeed possible, that this circumstance might have escaped his memory; for, in his reply, he positively insisted, that he had made use of no such appellation; adding, "Heaven forbid such naughty words should ever come out of his mouth!"

Tom, though against all form of law, rejoined in affirmance of the words. Upon which Master Blifil said, "It is no wonder. Those who will tell one fib, will hardly stick at another. If I had told my master such a wicked fib as you have done, I should be ashamed to shew my face."

"What fib, child?" cries Thwackum pretty eagerly.

"Why, he told you that nobody was with him a shooting when he killed the partridge; but he knows (here he burst into a flood of tears), yes, he knows, for he confessed it to me, that Black George the gamekeeper was there. Nay, he said, —yes you did, —deny it if you can, that you would not have confest the truth, though master had cut you to pieces."

At this the fire flashed from Thwackum's eyes, and he cried out in triumph: "Oh! ho! This is your mistaken notion of honour! This is the boy who was not to be whipped again!" But Mr. Allworthy, with a more gentle aspect, turned towards the lad, and said, "Is this true, child? How came you to persist so obstinately in a falshood?"

Tom said, "He scorned a lie as much as anyone; but he thought his honour engaged him to act as he did; for he had promised the poor fellow to conceal him; which," he said, "he thought himself farther obliged to, as the gamekeeper had begged him not to go into the gentleman's manor, and had at last gone himself in compliance with his persuasions." He said, "this was the whole truth of the matter, and he would take his oath of it;" and concluded with very passionately begging Mr. Allworthy, "to have compassion on the poor fellow's family, especially as he himself had been only guilty[9], and the other had been very difficultly prevailed on to do what he did. Indeed, sir," said he, "it could hardly be called a lie that I told; for the poor fellow was entirely innocent of the whole matter. I should have gone alone after the birds; nay, I did go at first, and he only followed me to prevent more mischief. Do, pray sir, let me be punished, take my little horse away again; but pray sir, forgive poor George."

Mr. Alloworthy hesitated a few moments, and then dismissed the boys, advising them to live more friendly and peaceably together.

【注解】

1. Mrs Wilkins: 奥尔沃西家一女佣，曾同情汤姆。
2. meum and tuum: 拉丁文，我的和你的(就财产所有权而言)。此处比喻他常把别人的东西据为己有。
3. an accessary after the fact: [法] 事后从犯。
4. Bannians: 指印度社会中严格信奉印度教的商人，他们不捕食任何动物。
5. Mr Thwackum: 汤姆和布利非尔的家庭教师之一，英国国教牧师，一个见风使舵、阿谀奉承的小人。
6. the good genius of . . . : 某人的守护神。
7. Square: 汤姆和比利非尔的另一家庭教师，哲学家，崇尚美德自然神论者，实际却是个伪君子，与看林人之女私通。
8. Mr Thwackum being always the second of the latter: Mr Thwackum 是布利非尔的支持者，会偏袒布利非尔。
9. he himself had been only guilty: 只有我自己（指汤姆）是有罪的。

【思考题】

1. Irony is a figure of speech in which one says the opposite of what he means. Fielding makes an effective use of irony in the selected chapters. Point out the ironies used in these two chapters and tell in what way they effectively reveal the different characters of Tom Jones and Master Blifil.
2. What kind of person is Mr. Allworthy? And Mr. Thwackum?
3. In paragraph one, just before he introduces Tom Jones to the reader, the narrator says that "we are obliged to bring our Heroe on the Stage in a much more disadvantageous Manner that we could wish; and to declare . . . that it was the universal Opinion of all Mr. Allworthy's Family that he was certainly born to be hanged." From these words, can you tell what Fielding will depict his hero Tom Jones?

【简评】

《汤姆·琼斯》之所以能取得如此巨大的成就，是因为小说的情节安排和人物刻画比较成功。更为重要的是，它以史诗般的规模和气势，描绘了 18 世纪中叶英国社会生活的全景：从乡村到都市，从下层社会到上流社会，各个阶层、各色人等无不涉及。这部小说达到了作者想使之成为“那个时代的一面镜子”(a mirror of its age) 和“描写人性的本来面目”(describe human nature as it is) 的目的。

English Romanticism

1789–1832

背景介绍

“浪漫主义”(romanticism)一词源于中世纪欧洲的“浪漫传奇”(romance)，讲述的常常是英雄救美之类的故事。欧洲文学上的浪漫主义时期是指18世纪末19世纪初在整个欧洲盛行的反对理性、推崇想象的文学运动。

英国的浪漫主义文学时期通常从1798年华兹华斯和柯勒律治合著的《抒情歌谣集》(*Lyrical Ballads*)发表算起，到1832年沃尔特·司各特爵士(Sir Walter Scott, 1771—1832)去世为止。这段时期的文学创作显示出了与18世纪前期(Age of Swift)、中期(Age of Pope)及中后期(Age of Johnson)古典主义文学创作的巨大差异：18世纪的作家强调理性与判断，而浪漫主义作家则重视想象和情感；18世纪作家强调经验的普遍性和一般性，而浪漫主义作家则重视个人的主观感受和经验的特殊性；18世纪作家强调社会的总体价值，而浪漫主义作家则重视个人价值的挖掘和实现；18世纪作家主要从古典文学特别是希腊文学中寻求模仿的对象和灵感，而浪漫主义作家则从中世纪的民间故事中寻求灵感和创作的源泉。这些都构成了英国浪漫主义时期文学创作的独特风格。

更具体地说，英国的浪漫主义文学除了具有各国浪漫主义文学所共有的以自我为中心来歌颂自我、抒发自我情感的特征以外，还有自身独有的特色。该特色可从被称为英国浪漫主义宣言书的《抒情歌谣集》的序言中略见一斑。在序言里，诗人华兹华斯满怀豪情地宣称，“一切好的诗歌都是强烈情感的自然流露”，“在所有这些诗歌里，我自己给自己制定的主要目标是要从普通人的生活中选取事件和情景，并尽可能地使用普通人的语言去讲述或描述它们。”华兹华斯不但从理论上告别了18世纪诗坛的陈词滥调，而且还与密友柯勒律治一起在《抒情歌谣集》里成功地实践了他崭新的创作观。

英国乃至世界的浪漫主义运动发生在18世纪与19世纪之交并非偶然。它与当时世界性的革命运动思潮息息相关。美洲的民族独立解放运动、法国大革命及欧洲各国，特别是英国的工业革命都对浪漫主义运动的兴起产生了巨大的推动力。法国大革命是浪漫主义运动首先发生在欧洲的主要原因，对英国浪漫主义运动的蓬勃开展更是产生了重大影响。追根溯源，浪漫主义作家在思想上深受德国唯心主义古典哲学的影响，开始重视人的自由、自在和自为性，并开始重新认识自我，审视自我，从而进一步追求自我价值的实现。正是由于对自我内心情感的抒发和追求，英国的浪漫主义作家与欧洲各国的先驱们一起开始以作品为宣泄口，追求强烈情感的自然流露，张扬个性解放，以锐不可当之势冲垮了理性统治长达一百多年的文学大堤。

就英国文学而言，1798年《抒情歌谣集》的发表标志着英国文学进入新纪元：文学作品的创作从此摆脱了理性的束缚，由传统的描摹自然、重视理性转向了描摹自我的内心世界、重视自我情感的抒发，以自我为中心来建构浪漫世界是英国乃至世界浪漫主义文学所共有的本质特征。此外，重视想象、崇拜自然、强调个性也是英国浪漫主义文学的三大特征。在具体的创作实践中，英国的浪漫主义作家从民间文学创作中大量汲取营养，摆脱了古典主义的种种束缚，发挥自由的想象，表达强烈的情感，并从内容、语言、形式等诸多方面进行了新的改革尝试。这一切都构成了英国浪漫主义文学独特的艺术风格，在当时吸引了众多读者。

英国浪漫主义常常分为三个时期：第一个时期为前浪漫主义时期，代表作家有布莱克、彭斯；第二个时期为早期浪漫主义时期，主要作家有华兹华斯、柯勒律治等人；第三个时期为后期浪漫主义时期，代表作家为雪莱 (Percy Bysshe Shelley, 1792—1822)、拜伦和济慈 (John Keats, 1795—1821)。

值得注意的是，以上提到的英国浪漫主义作家都是诗人，这主要是因为在浪漫主义文学运动中，浪漫主义诗歌无论是在理论上还是实践上都影响巨大，是同期的散文和小说所无法比拟的。当然，诗歌上的成就并不能掩盖浪漫主义时期新型散文和小说的贡献，它们都是英国浪漫主义文学运动不可分割的组成部分。就散文而言，这一时期的突出成就是“亲切文体”(familiar style) 散文随笔的出现。当时的散文大家有三位：查尔斯·兰姆 (Charles Lamb, 1775—1834)、威廉·哈兹利特 (William Hazlitt, 1778—1830) 与托马斯·德·昆西 (Thomas De Quincey, 1785—1859)。他们对英国散文随笔的发展作出了突出贡献。有趣的是，尽管作为同时代人的兰姆与哈兹利特都才情恣肆，但由于个性、经历的不同，他们的散文随笔却显示出不同的风格：兰姆的随笔注重细节，精于思考，善于用典，往往从生活琐事或日常的知识性题材谈起，或风雅幽默、情趣盎然，或缠绵悱恻、哀婉动人，极富生活气息和人情味，主要作品集有《伊利亚随笔集》(*Essays of Elia*, 1823)；哈兹利特则不同，他的散文谈古论今，气势雄伟，汪洋恣肆，“渊深如海”(史蒂文生语)，突出特点是更为奔放开朗、波澜曲折，主要散文集有《家常话》(*Table Talk*, 1821)、《素描与随笔》(*Sketches and Essays*, 1829) 等。

浪漫主义时期小说上的成就则主要体现在内容和题材的创新上。当时主要的小说类型有两种：哥特小说 (Gothic novel) 和历史小说 (historical novel)。哥特小说的名称源于中世纪的哥特传奇故事 (Gothic romance)。它在中世纪背景的映衬之下 (通常是经常闹鬼或阴森森的城堡里)，通过讲述一段离奇而又惊心动魄的经历来刺激读者，读起来令人毛骨悚然。这种小说曾在 19 世纪的上半期流行一时，是现代恐怖和神秘小说的鼻祖。历史小说的出现主要归功于司各特，正是他的努力才使历史题材进入了小说领域。在司各特的笔下，重大的历史事件和人物配上合适的历史场景又栩栩如生地展现在人们的面前。历史小说当时曾十分流行。简·奥斯汀是这一时期优秀的女小说家。她的小说以描写日常生活中的小事见长。情节简单、文体平易、观察敏锐、分析透彻是其主要特点。正是由于她对人们日常生活交往的细致观察和深刻描绘，后人把她的小说称为“风俗小说”(novel of manners)。奥斯汀的代表作品《傲慢与偏见》(*Pride and Prejudice*, 1813)、《理智与情感》(*Sense and Sensibility*, 1811)等都是英国文学的经典之作。

William Blake
1757—1827

威廉·布莱克生于伦敦，父亲是服饰用品店老板。他一生所受的正规教育只限于艺术领域。他 10 岁时进入一所画校学习，后来又在皇家艺术学院进修过一段时间。14 岁时，布莱克开始给当时伦敦一位著名的雕刻匠当学徒，一干就是 7 年。在这段时间内，他利用闲暇大量阅读各种文学作品，并开始尝试作诗。24 岁时，布莱克与一位蔬菜农场主的女儿结婚。当时，这位名叫凯瑟琳的女子一字不识，而布莱克则教会了她读书识字，以帮助他进行雕版和印刷。二人终生相依为命，没有孩子。

布莱克是英国文学史上最为多才多艺、也最注重精神生活的艺术家。说他多才多艺是因为他集刻字、雕版、绘画、作诗于一身，他的雕版绘画才能与作为手工匠人困苦的生活经历对他以后的诗歌创作产生了深远的影响。说他最重视精神生活是因为他对宗教的虔诚和对《圣经》的崇拜已达到近乎疯狂的地步。他认为艺术离不开上帝和《圣经》。

布莱克浓厚的宗教意识、艺术家的天分和丰富的人生阅历为他的诗歌提供了取之不尽的创作源泉，使他的诗歌具有明显的宗教性、预言性、哲理性和艺术性等特点。布莱克对英国诗歌，特别是浪漫主义诗歌的贡献主要表现在以下方面：首先，在语言上，布莱克的诗通俗易懂、简单明了；其次，在形式上，布莱克的诗大多采用歌谣体，读起来朗朗上口，音节也铿锵有力，特别是前期诗集，如《天真之歌》(*Songs of Innocence*, 1789)、《经验之歌》(*Songs of Experience*, 1794)；最后，在内容上，诗人一反 18 世纪新古典主义提倡的理性为上、对称为美、追求共性而贬抑个性的文风，没有去盲目崇古，而是基于个人的亲身经历和所见所闻对当时扭曲的社会现实进行了辛辣的讽刺和无情的抨击。无论从哪一方面来讲，布莱克都可称得上是英国浪漫主义诗歌的先驱。难怪华兹华斯这样评价布莱克："在此人的疯狂之中有某种东西比拜伦或沃尔特·司各特的正常更让我感兴趣。"

尽管布莱克的一生都是在困苦中度过的，诗人出色的绘画和诗歌才能在当时并没有引起读者和批评家的注意，他赖以生存的主要职业是雕版刻印工作，但他出色的诗才和求知欲却使他能够自学成才，并成为一代名家。就诗人的诗歌创作而言，前期和后期有着明显的差别。前期主要包括《诗歌素描》(*Poetical Sketches*, 1783)、《天真之歌》及《经验之歌》等。这一时期较后期而言语言上明显简单易懂，诗歌以短诗为主，音节也能短则短，题材内容主要是生活中的所见所闻。后期的诗作篇幅则明显增长，有时长达数百行乃至上千行，内容也明显地晦涩起来，以神秘、宗教及象征为主要特征。

《天真之歌》和《经验之歌》是布莱克流传最广的两个诗集，表现了人生两个不同的阶段和两次不同的经历，用布莱克自己的话来说，是“人类心灵深处的两种相反的状况”。许多诗歌往往同时出现在两个诗集中，表达的主题思想却截然不同。总体而言，《天真之歌》的讲述者多是天真的孩子或慈爱的成人，其主题是他们对现实的观感。对他们而言，现实世界是美好的，是仁慈、怜悯、和平和友爱的代名词，即使在艰难困苦的境况中也对未来充满希望。《经验之歌》的讲述者则完全不同，他们从现实世界中获得经验，清醒地认识到现实的残酷和丑恶，从而发出愤怒的呼喊。这种呼喊实际上代表了诗人布莱克自己的心声。

The Chimney Sweeper (1, 2)

【题解】

18世纪末期，英国无序的工业化进程导致“扫烟囱的孩子”的出现。当时，童工盛行，穷人家的孩子往往在四五岁就被卖去扫烟囱，清除狭窄通道里的煤灰。对幼小的孩子来说，长期从事这种工作往往导致发育畸形，罹患肺病。诗人以此为题，从不同角度对这一主题进行了阐述。《天真之歌》中的孩子尽管被父亲卖去扫烟囱，过着苦难的生活，却充满着希望与欢乐；而《经验之歌》中的孩子则不同，他对自己的不幸表示了强烈不满，并向自己笃信宗教的父母发出了愤怒的呼喊。

The Chimney Sweeper

(1)

(*From* Songs of Innocence)

When my mother died I was very young,
And my father sold me while yet my tongue
Could scarcely cry weep! weep! weep! weep![1]
So your chimneys I sweep & in soot I sleep.

There's little Tom Dacre, who cried when his head
That curl'd like a lamb's back, was shav'd, so I said,
"Hush, Tom! never mind it, for when your head's bare,
You know that the soot cannot spoil your white hair."

And so he was quiet, & that very night,
As Tom was a-sleeping, he had such a sight!
That thousands of sweepers, Dick, Joe, Ned, & Jack,
Were all of them lock'd up in coffins of black.

And by came an Angel who had a bright key,
And he open'd the coffins & set them all free;
Then down a green plain, leaping, laughing they run,
And wash in a river and shine in the Sun.

Then naked & white, all their bags left behind,
They rise upon clouds, and sport in the wind;
And the Angel told Tom, if he'd be a good boy,
He'd have God for his father & never want joy.

And so Tom awoke; and we rose in the dark
And got with our bags & our brushes to work.
Tho' the morning was cold, Tom was happy & warm;
So if all do their duty, they need not fear harm.

The Chimney Sweeper

(2)

(*From* Songs of Experience)

A little black thing among the snow
Crying "'weep,' weep," in notes of woe!
"Where are thy father & mother? say?"

"They are both gone up to the church to pray.

"Because I was happy upon the heath,
And smil'd among the winter's snow;
They clothed me in the clothes of death,
And taught me to sing the notes of woe.

"And because I am happy, & dance & sing,
They think they have done me no injury,
And are gone to praise God & his Priest & King,
Who make up a heaven of our misery."

【注解】

1. weep: 由于孩子年龄小，所以在发"sweep"一词时就吞掉了"s"音。这里的"weep"也有双关之意，可理解为孩子的哭泣。尤其是在第二首诗中，这层意思十分明显。

【思考题】

1. The boy has undergone a spiritual change from the first poem to the second one. Can you elaborate on this change? What is your comment on such a change? Is it a growth? Why or why not?
2. How do his and the poet's attitudes toward his lot in life differ in the first poem? How about the second chimney poem?
3. How do the meanings of the poet and the speaker differ in lines 3, 7–8, and 24 of the first poem?
4. Point out the significance of the sweepers' being "lock'd up in coffins of black" and the Angel's releasing them with a bright key.
5. In the first poem, the poet uses the dramatic irony in which the discrepancy is not between what the speaker says and what he means but between what the speaker says and what the author means. Read the poem thoroughly to see how dramatic irony works effectively in it. (cf. Questions 2–3.)
6. Compare the above two chimney poems and explain why the first is included in *Songs of Innocence*, while the other, in *Songs of Experience*.

Robert Burns

1759—1796

罗伯特·彭斯是苏格兰历史上迄今为止最伟大的农民诗人。尽管他英年早逝，实际创作的时间从第一本诗集出版(1786 年) 算起也不过短短的十年，但他的名声却远扬四海，在苏格兰更是家喻户晓。当时有人曾这样宣称："五湖四海的乡村到处都在吟诵他的诗……无论老的还是少的，严肃的还是活泼的，有文化的还是无文化的，都一样欣喜若狂。"

彭斯 1759 年 1 月出生于苏格兰西南部艾尔郡 (Ayrshire) 一个名叫阿罗卫 (Alloway) 的地方。他的父亲威廉·彭斯 (William Burnes) 是个贫苦的花匠和佃农。尽管家庭的贫穷使他无法供养幼年的诗人接受正规的学校教育，但他勤学善思，尊重知识，这对幼小的彭斯产生了重大的影响。彭斯在极为贫困的境遇中大量涉猎文学作品：荷马、莎士比亚、弥尔顿、蒲伯、爱迪森和史蒂尔的作品都在他的兴趣范围内。其母有一副好嗓子，从小就教儿子吟唱苏格兰民歌、民谣，鼓励彭斯学习、收集、吟唱苏格兰优秀的民歌、民谣。后来这些民歌和民谣中相当一部分被诗人改编成了不朽的诗作，如脍炙人口的《友谊天长地久》("Auld Lang Syne"，1796)。生活的艰辛与贫困并没有影响彭斯对农民生活的热爱和对美好生活的向往。彭斯 15 岁时即在劳动中对一名爱歌唱的农家少女产生了感情，并由此激发了创作的灵感，一发而不可收。1786 年，彭斯在克尔马诺克城 (Kilmarnock) 出版了首卷诗集，使他一举成名，并在苏格兰首府爱丁堡受到当地文学界的热烈欢迎和崇拜，在随后的几年中该作曾一版再版，彭斯也因此赢得了"苏格兰诗人" (Caledonia's Bard) 的声誉。但由于诗人出身贫贱，加上高傲的自尊、过分的敏感、放荡不羁的生活、桀骜不驯的性格，以及反传统、反长老会的斗争精神，他受到了爱丁堡知识分子及上层社会的排挤。1787 年春，彭斯从爱丁堡回到了故乡艾尔郡，并与长期相恋的爱人正式结婚，重新开始过普普通通的农民生活。

尽管彭斯的一生都是在艰难困苦中度过的，但生活的艰辛并没有阻碍他的创作热情。除了最著名的几首长诗外，彭斯在他第一本诗集出版时已创作了现存的几乎所有的短诗。彭斯的诗歌十分苏格兰化。就语言而论，诗人最优秀的诗篇都是以苏格兰农民的方言写成的。而他用标准英语创作的作品，除个别诗篇，如《亚顿河水》("Afton Water", 1791)，多数都不成功。事实上，诗人的第一本诗集——克尔马诺克诗集的书名就标明了该本诗集的语言特色：《诗集：主要使用苏格兰方言》(*Poems: Chiefly in Scottish Dialect*, 1786)。从内容上来看，彭斯的诗歌涉及普通苏格兰人民生活的方方面面：有世俗方面的，也有宗教方面的，有颂扬纯朴率直的，也有鞭挞贪婪丑恶的，有写人的，也有咏物的。根据诗歌内容，彭斯的作品大致可分三类：第一类为讽刺诗，如《威利长老的祷词》("Holy Willie's Prayer", 1789)、《致小老鼠》("To a Mouse", 1785)、《致虱子》("To a Louse", 1786) 等；第二类为抒情诗，包括歌颂爱情、友谊、民主及爱国主义等诗篇，如《一朵红红的玫瑰》("A Red, Red Rose", 1794)、《友谊天长地久》《不管那一套》("For a' That and a' That", 1794) 及弘扬爱国主义的诗篇《苏格兰人》("Scots Wha Hae", 1793) 等；第三类为长篇叙事诗，如《汤姆·奥尚特》(*Tam o'Shanter*, 1791) 等。

值得一提的是彭斯对苏格兰民歌谣整理、传播和发展所作出的突出贡献。诗人将毕生精力投入苏格兰民间歌谣的收集、整理和创作上，一生编写的歌谣有360多篇，其中有一百来篇传诵至今。个别歌谣，如《友谊天长地久》，已成为世界人民喜爱的佳作。正是由于诗人对苏格兰民族文化所作的特殊贡献，苏格兰人民至今没有忘记他。现在，每年数以千计的彭斯联谊会在苏格兰各地以各种形式召开，纪念这位伟大的诗人，倾诉人们对他的思念。

A Red, Red Rose

【题解】

这是一首赞美爱人的小诗。诗人采用了民谣体 (ballad metre)，每小节四行，其中奇数行为抑扬格四音步 (iambic tetrameter)，偶数行为抑扬格三音步 (iambic trimeter)。押韵格式为abab。尽管从诗境上看，这首诗并不出众，但民谣体的灵活运用却给该诗增添了活力，使其既能吟诵，又可歌唱。

A Red, Red Rose

O My Luve's like a red, red rose,
That's newly sprung in June;
O My Luve's like the melodie
That's sweetly played in tune.

As fair art thou, my bonnie lass,
So deep in luve am I;
And I will luve thee still, my dear,
Till a'[1] the seas gang[2] dry.

Till a' the seas gang dry, my dear,
And the rocks melt wi' the sun;
O I will love thee still, my dear,
While the sands o' life shall run.

And fare thee weel[3], my only luve,
And fare thee weel awhile!
And I will come again, my luve,
Tho'[4] it were ten thousand mile.

【注解】

1. a': 相当于 all。
2. gang: 相当于 go。
3. fare thee weel: 相当于 fare thee well，别了，再见。
4. Tho': 相当于 Though。

【思考题】

1. Some critics claim that in many aspects, this poem seems conventional. Do you agree? Why or why not? Does this poem remind you of any Chinese ancient poems? If yes, make a comparison between them.
2. An outstanding feature of this poem is the skillful use of many figures of speech. Draw on specific lines to explain the effect of these figures.
3. This poem reads more like a song. How do you think the poet achieves this songlike quality?
4. This short poem is actually composed of a series of overstatements. What is the function of them? Give examples to illustrate your point.

【简评】

《一朵红红的玫瑰》是彭斯在古老的苏格兰民谣的基础上加工创作的一首脍炙人口的爱情诗。诗歌以其清新质朴的语言、生动鲜明的意象、强烈真挚的情感、忠贞不渝的爱情流传甚广，经久不衰，颂声载道。诗歌一开头就用了两个人们喜闻乐见的意象，把心上人比喻为“六月里刚刚绽放的红红的玫瑰”和“旋律优美、悦耳动听的乐曲”，描写了心上人的美丽。“红红的玫瑰”，意象直观生动，象征着爱情、美丽、青春、生机和活力，描写了心上人朝气蓬勃、赏心悦目的形象。“优美的旋律”的比喻别出心裁，既可指心上人动听的声音，也可指她柔情似水、善解人意的性格。两个比喻由外到内，由远及近，由静态到动态，赞颂了心上人的外在美和内在美，形体美、心灵美和人格美。接着，诗人在下面两节中表达了对心上人深沉、真挚、忠贞不渝的爱情。纵使海枯石烂，地老天荒，宇宙毁灭，只要他一息尚存，他对心上人的爱情将坚贞不渝，超越时空，亘古不变。这不由让读者想起中国汉乐府民歌《上邪》中描写的那坚如磐石的爱情，“山无棱，江水为竭，冬雷震震，夏雨雪，天地合，乃敢与君绝！”最后一节再次强调二人之间深沉、真挚的爱情。纵使相隔万水千山，诗人一定会跋山涉水，排除万难，来到心上人的身边，与她团聚。诗歌语言朴实，意象鲜明，富有乐感，朗朗上口，情感炽热，感人肺腑，打动了千千万万恋人的心，成为人们耳熟能详、传唱不衰的经典。

Auld Lang Syne

【题解】

《友谊天长地久》是彭斯所编创的苏格兰歌谣中传唱最广的一首，可以说它不仅是苏格兰民歌，也是全世界最为著名的民歌之一。该诗描绘了老朋友在即将离别时，依依不舍、共同举杯怀念往昔好时光的情景。深切动人的歌词配上悠扬婉转的曲调，把老朋友之间的依依惜别之情表现得淋漓尽致。

Auld Lang Syne

Should auld acquaintance be forgot,
and never brought to mind?
Should auld acquaintance be forgot,

and auld lang syne[1]?
Chorus

For auld Lang syne, my jo,
for auld lang syne,
We'll tak[2] a cup o' kindness yet,
for auld lang syne.

And surely ye'll be your pint-stoup[3]!
and surely I'll be mine!
And we'll tak's cup o'kindness yet,
for auld lang syne.
Chorus

We twa hae run about the braes[4],
And pu'd the gowans[5] fine,
But we've wandered mony a weary foot,
sin' auld lang syne.
Chorus

We twa hae paidl'd in the burn[6],
from morning sun till dine[7];
But seas between us braid[8] hae roared,
sin' auld lang syne.
Chorus

And there's a hand, my trusty fiere[9]!
and gie's a hand o' thine!
And we'll tak' a right gude-willie waught[10],
for auld lang syne.
Chorus

【注解】

1. auld lang syne: 相当于 long ago，意为从前，往昔。
2. tak: 相当于 take。
3. be your pint-stowp: 付你自己那一杯的账。
4. braes: 相当于 slopes。
5. gowans: 相当于 daisies。
6. burn: 相当于 stream。
7. dine: 相当于 dinner。
8. braid: 相当于 broad。
9. fiere: 相当于 friend。
10. a right gude-willie waught: 极大的、急切的一口。

【思考题】

1. What is the dominant emotion of this poem? Love, sorrow, joy, patriotism or what?
2. Practice reading this song aloud to bring out the rhythmic quality. If possible, learn to sing this song in class.
3. Decide who is singing in the poem—Burns in his own person or an imaginary person?

【简评】

《友谊天长地久》(又名《往昔时光》)发表于1796年，是一首怀旧诗，后被人谱曲。诗歌抒发了诗人对往日时光的回忆，对真挚友谊的怀念，和对老朋友重逢的期待。诗歌的标题"友谊天长地久"在只有四行的合唱中重复三次，每节诗后合唱又重复一遍，"友谊万岁，友谊万岁！举杯痛饮，同声歌颂，友谊地久天长。"这突出了诗歌对美好真挚、天长地久的友谊的歌颂。诗歌一开始就抒发了对往日时光的追忆和对纯真友情的珍视和铭记："怎能忘记旧日朋友，心中能不怀想？旧日朋友岂能相忘，友谊地久天长？"读起来令人心潮澎湃，感慨万千。接着诗歌在第三节和第四节回忆老朋友们童年时代共同度过的美好时光，以及分别后随着年龄的增长饱尝人生艰辛、疲惫不堪的感受，但诗人并没有停留在悲观消沉和伤感中，而是在第二节、第五节、第六节把重点放在描写老朋友们久别重逢、举杯畅饮的欢乐景象上。劳燕分飞、远隔重洋、人世沧桑都无法改变老朋友之间的深情厚谊。这份友情弥足珍贵，对友谊的回忆能给人带来莫大的心灵安慰和精神享受。

这首诗本来就很有名，谱曲后更受人喜爱，尤其是1940年电影《魂断蓝桥》(*Waterloo Bridge*)把这首歌作为主题曲后，这首语言优美、旋律悠扬、动人心弦的歌谣更是家喻户晓，风靡全球。歌曲里饱含着对美好时光的回忆，以及对未来美好生活的祝福。

William Wordsworth
1770—1850

威廉·华兹华斯是19世纪初英国伟大的浪漫主义诗人，对英国乃至世界浪漫主义运动都有着很大的影响。在很小的时候，华兹华斯就喜欢独自在田间散步，欣赏大自然的美景，思考自然与人生。对于童年的这段生活经历，他到中年时仍然能够平静地回忆起来，并把它写成英国诗歌史上不朽的诗篇——《序曲》(*The Prelude*, 1850)。13岁时，华兹华斯父母相继离世，但他还是克服困难，于1787年进入剑桥大学学习。正是这段大学时光培养了华兹华斯的兴趣和爱好，也影响了他早期的思想，他强烈向往法国大革命，希望法国能通过革命建立起崭新、平等、合理、友爱的社会秩序。为此，诗人从剑桥大学毕业后还特意重返法国。然而，这时英法开战。由于经济原因，华兹华斯1791年被迫回国。法国大革命后期的恐怖行为使华兹华斯的革命理想幻灭，并一度陷入绝望。从此，诗人开始遁迹山水，过起崇拜自然的半隐士生活。1795年，华兹华斯幸运地得到了一笔来自朋友兼崇拜者的遗产，这使得他能够专心致志地进行诗歌创作。于是，华兹华斯与妹妹一起搬到了位于英格兰西北部湖区德塞郡的一个小村庄居住下来，并在那儿经介绍认识了柯勒律治，从此开始了英国文学史上最为重要、也收获最丰的一段友谊，后人把他与柯勒律治等诗人一起并称为“湖畔诗人”。他们于1798年合作发表了著名的浪漫主义诗集《抒情歌谣集》(*Lyrical Ballads*)，其中的序言(后来曾经多次修改和补充)，特别是1802年版的序言被公认为划时代的浪漫主义宣言书。

尽管1802年版的序言不过万余字，但它的意义却不可以用字数来衡量。在此序言中，诗人一反18世纪诗歌创作的原则和方法，以一种崭新的理论和实践向世人展示了浪漫主义诗歌的创作理念。理论上，诗人主张诗歌的内容应该以普通的乡村生活为主，应当歌颂自然和平凡的美好，这就摈弃了新古典主义时期诗歌创作以上层生活为核心、为上层社会服务的思想。诗人还主张诗歌的语言应当采用中下阶层普通劳动人民的语言，以符合乡村与老百姓生活。只有使用平常、生动而又真实的语言才能更好地表达诗歌的内容。诗人使用平凡语言的主张是对18世纪新古典主义诗歌创作的反叛，从根本上改变了18世纪使用专门的“诗歌辞藻”(poetic diction)及陈词滥调的创作方法，使原本仅有少数上层人才能欣赏的诗歌变成了普通人都能理解的朴素话语。

诗人认为一切好的诗歌都是“强烈情感的自然流露”，是“一切知识的开始和终结，同人心一样不朽”，由此把诗歌提高到至高无上的位置。诗人也因此成为人性最坚强的捍卫者、支持者和维护者，他所到之处都播下了人的情谊和友爱。

诗人的伟大之处并不仅仅在于他的诗歌理论，更为难能可贵的是他把伟大的理论成功地付诸实践，《抒情歌谣集》就是明证。总之，华兹华斯的诗歌内容新颖，感情真挚，意境高远，语言朴素。他的许多诗作都已成为英国诗歌中不可多得的佳作。由于诗人在诗歌创作方面的杰出成就，他于1843年被授予英国“桂冠诗人”的称号。今天，随着生态环境的恶化和生态危机的加深，华兹华斯的诗歌受到生态批评家前所未有的重视，在今天的社会仍焕发出勃勃生机。他也被称为英国浪漫主义时期伟大的生态诗人。

My Heart Leaps up

【题解】

这首仅有九行的抒情小诗写于1802年，表达了诗人对自然与美的追求和向往。一年后华兹华斯创作发表了被爱默生称为19世纪诗歌里程碑的《永生颂》(“Ode: Intimations of Immortality from Recollections of Early Childhood”, 1807)。本诗是对《永生颂》最好的注释。事实上，华兹华斯本人也把本诗的最后三行用作《永生颂》的题词。

My Heart Leaps up

My heart leaps up when I behold
　A rainbow[1] in the sky:
So was it when my life began;
　So is it now I am a man;
So be it when I shall grow old,
　Or let me die!
The Child is father of the Man[2];
And I could wish my days to be
Bound each to each by natural piety.[3]

【注解】

1. rainbow: 彩虹被认为是美丽与诚实的象征。
2. The Child is father of the Man: 在《复乐园》中，弥尔顿曾表达过相似的观点：The childhood shews the man/As morning shews the day.
3. natural piety: 此处指对自然的崇拜和虔诚，与《圣经》中的宗教与虔诚相对。

【思考题】

1. In this poem, as in “Tintern Abbey”, Wordsworth thinks of life as existing in three phases. What are they?
2. Does the poet’s response to the rainbow have anything to do with the three phases? If yes, how? If not, why not?
3. Read this poem carefully and tell the significance of the shift in lines 3–5.
4. What is the meaning of “And I could wish my days to be” as opposed to “And I am sure my days will be”?
5. Line 7 is paradoxical. In what sense is a child the “father” of the man he eventually becomes?

【简评】

《我心雀跃》是诗人 32 岁时创作的作品。短诗以彩虹为意象，表达了诗人毕生对自然的虔诚与信念。第 1 至 6 行叙述作者从儿童到成年的不同时期中看到彩虹时的激动心情；第 3 至 5 行连续以“So was it” “So is it” “So be it”的重复语法来强调这种情感；第 6 行更以短促的四音节句子，表达希望这种情感能长存到老的愿望，以及若未能如愿则宁愿赴死的情感转折及迫切心情；第 7 行“The Child is father of the Man”是本诗诗眼，由于其似非而是的性质历来有不同的解释。一种最基本的解释是成人在成长过程中受到现实、尘世的压制和污染而变得世故、圆滑，不再纯真。孩童未受文明“污染”的纯真心灵更接近自然的原生态，因此反而能够启迪成人如何感应自然、回归自然。从这个意义上说，孩童是成人的父亲。这行诗给我们的另一个启示是，由于孩童更接近自然，因此也更富有想象力、敢于想象，而自由想象也是浪漫主义诗人的不懈追求和他们诗歌的最大特征。最后两行表明，诗人不敢肯定未来是否能保有纯净天真的心（即今后看到彩虹时是否照样会“心跳”），故只能以虔诚的祈愿作结。

I Wandered Lonely as a Cloud

【题解】

《我似一朵孤独的流云》写于1804年，记述的是诗人在大自然中的感悟。在该诗的最后一节，诗人描绘了他1802年版的"序言"中所宣称的那种"平静中的回忆"。据诗人的妹妹多萝西·华兹华斯在1802年4月5日的记述，诗人两年前也有过此种感悟。

I Wandered Lonely as a Cloud

I wandered lonely as a cloud
That floats on high o'er vales and hills,
When all at once I saw a crowd,
A host, of golden daffodils;
Beside the lake, beneath the trees,
Fluttering and dancing in the breeze.

Continuous as the stars that shine
And twinkle on the milky way,
They stretched in never-ending line
Along the margin of a bay:
Ten thousand saw I at a glance,
Tossing their heads in sprightly dance.

The waves beside them danced; but they
Out-did the sparkling waves in glee:
A poet could not but be gay,
In such a jocund company:
I gazed—and gazed—but little thought
What wealth the show to me had brought:

For oft, when on my couch I lie

In vacant or in pensive mood,
They flash upon that inward eye
Which is the bliss of solitude;
And then my heart with pleasure fills,
And dances with the daffodils.

【思考题】

1. In "I Wandered Lonely as a Cloud," how does Wordsworth achieve the seemingly effortless effect of implying the unity of his consciousness with nature? Does this technique appear in any other Wordsworth lyrics?
2. Imagery is important in understanding the theme of this poem. Analyze the images in this poem to see how they are used effectively to reveal the theme of the poem.
3. What are the three "dances" of the daffodils mentioned in the poem?
4. Explain the implications of "that inward eye/Which is the bliss of solitude."
5. Read the poem aloud and try to grasp the emotional state the poet was in while writing this poem.
6. How would you think about the relationship between nature and human being, as is revealed in the poem?

解读举例

1. 《我似一朵孤独的流云》是诗人回忆的一次简单经历：面对大自然的美景而欣喜万分。这次简单的经历是通过语言和音节的完美结合，以及少量暗喻表现出来的。

2. 《我似一朵孤独的流云》尽管看起来简单，但实际包含了一种情感上的对立。这种对立主要通过以多姿多彩、生机勃勃的水仙花为代表的自然，和简单、乏味的人类之间的强烈对比得以实现。不过在诗的结尾，这种对立与冲突得到了和解。

3. 《我似一朵孤独的流云》和华兹华斯的其他自然诗一起，可作为当代生态批评的范本。这些诗作歌颂了大自然的美好、宁静与和谐，认为大自然具有抚慰人的精神、净化人的灵魂、治疗人的心灵创伤的作用，表达了人应该回归自然，与大自然和谐相处的观点。在今天生态危机的语境中，华兹华斯被称为英国浪漫主义时期伟大的生态诗人。

Samuel Taylor Coleridge
1772—1834

作者简介

塞缪尔·泰勒·柯勒律治出生于英格兰德文郡的一个乡村牧师之家，是14个孩子中最小的一个。10岁时，因父亲去世而被送到伦敦上学。这段早期的学习经历对诗人一生的影响很大。他在学堂埋头读书，既学习希腊、罗马文学，也学习哲学。对这段日子，诗人曾在他的《午夜霜寒》("Frost at Midnight", 1798)一诗中有精彩的描述："因为我是在／大城市里长大的，关在幽暗的学堂回廊里／没看到什么可爱的东西，除了天空和星星"。虽然诗人如此描述他成长时期的学习生涯，实际上他前期的努力得到了应有的回报，到他19岁进入剑桥大学学习古典文学时(1791)，他已经是一名博学多才的学者了。然而诗人此时厌倦了大学生活，于1793年偷偷离开剑桥大学去参军，后因不能忍受军队的煎熬，在哥哥们的帮助下重新回到剑桥大学继续学习。1794年，诗人又离开了剑桥大学，并于同年夏天结识了罗伯特·骚塞(Robert Southey, 1774—1843)。于是两个激进的年轻人雄心勃勃地计划去美国建立"乌托邦"式的大同社会，后以失败告终。

1795年，柯勒律治结识了华兹华斯，二人结下深厚友情，合作就此展开。1798年，两位诗人合作发表了《抒情歌谣集》，其前言被公认为浪漫主义诗歌的宣言书，而柯勒律治的《老水手谣》("The Rime of the Ancient Mariner")就是该诗集的开篇之作。在此之前，他的另两篇杰作《忽必烈汗》("Kubla Khan; or a Vision in a Dream")和《克丽斯特贝尔》("Christabel")就已公开发表。1798年冬，柯勒律治与华兹华斯兄妹一起去了德国。在哥廷根大学，他对康德哲学产生了浓厚的兴趣，开始钻研康德和其他德国哲学家的作品。他本人也因此成为把德国先进的哲学思想介绍到英国国内的重要学者之一。1800年，他随同华兹华斯兄妹迁居英国西部的湖区。他们在湖边饮酒作诗，探讨理论，后被人称为"湖畔诗人"。1810年柯勒律治与华兹华斯因见解不同，发生争执，并因此断绝交往。然而与华兹华斯交往与合作的十五年是柯勒律治一生最为辉煌多产的时期。从1808年起，柯勒律治开始了他的演讲生涯。由于他出色的口才、幽默的谈吐，诗人很快就成为英国浪漫主义时期最优秀的演讲家。他发表的有关莎士比亚及其他一些优秀的作家的演讲现已成为文学批评的经典之作。

诗人的晚年为风湿及其他多种疾病困扰，不得不服用鸦片来镇痛，并因此上瘾。

柯勒律治是英国文学史上最多才多艺的作家之一，他既是浪漫主义诗歌的先驱，同时也是伟大的文学批评家、理论家。在诗歌创作、文学批评与文艺理论方面都有建树，有些作品和理论至今还对英国文学的发展产生着深远的影响。就诗歌而言，尽管创作的数量并不多，却不乏佳作。最为人熟知的是《老水手谣》《忽必烈汗》《午夜霜寒》《沮丧颂》(“Dejection: An Ode”, 1802)《克丽斯特贝尔》等。作为一名文学批评家和理论家，柯勒律治著述颇丰，他从 1808 年开始在伦敦发表的有关莎士比亚及其他作家的系列讲座已成为英国文学批评的经典，而他于 1817 年完成并发表的《文学传记》(*Biographia Literaria*) 更是集诗人一生批评理论之大成。其中包括当时有关浪漫主义文学创作的一些主要观点和论点，以及对前期合作伙伴华兹华斯于 1798 年版《抒情歌谣集》序言中所提出的浪漫主义诗歌理想创作方法的追踪探讨。诗人认为《文学传记》是对他毕生“文学生涯和文学观点”的总结。

就艺术成就而言，柯勒律治诗歌的创造性尤为突出。他与华兹华斯一起，打破了新古典主义时期诗歌因循守旧、强调模仿、注重理性而压抑情感的清规戒律，开创了歌颂自然、弘扬自我、注重情感、语言明快晓畅的新一代诗风。诗人脍炙人口的杰作都具有奇伟瑰丽的想象、恢宏壮观的场面，以及神秘莫测的气氛。这些都形成了柯勒律治独特的浪漫主义诗风，也是对他创作理论最好的补充。

The Rime of the Ancient Mariner

【题解】

《老水手谣》(又译：《古舟子咏》)是《抒情歌谣集》1798 年版的开篇。诗中的故事系根据诗人的朋友约翰·克鲁伊尚克的一个梦改编而成，讲述的是罪与罚的因果报应：一个老水手射杀了一只信天翁，受到了热爱此鸟的南极精灵的报复，同船的水手先后死去，老水手则幸免于难，因为“死亡”与“死中生”两个精灵打赌，以“死中生”赌赢告终。但是，老水手生不如死：在茫茫大海中他每天都必须面对船上的尸体那一双双怨恨的眼睛，内心受到极大的折磨。然而他的人性并未泯灭，痛苦之余祝福另一小生物水蛇之后得以生还。返回故乡后，他必须向人倾诉自己的痛苦经历才能继续生活下去。

今天，《老水手谣》日益受到生态批评者的青睐。英国著名的生态文学研究者乔纳森·贝特评价道，《老水手谣》里咏叹的不是命运悲剧，而是自然伦理或大地伦理的悲剧，批判的是人类的骄傲、狂妄和毫无“物道”的残暴。杀死无辜的鸟儿，标志着人类与其生存环境里的其他生命彻底决裂，从此成了生物界中的局外人，成了被大地母亲所抛弃的孤儿，就像那个整夜徘徊在黑暗森林里的老水手。生态文学研究者N. 罗伯茨和特里·吉福德认为，《老水手谣》是英语文学中“最伟大的生态寓言”。就创作风格而言，本诗摒弃了传统的诗歌形式，采用了歌谣体，语言简单朴素，同时注重人物的情感表达，是诗人浪漫主义诗歌创造理念的具象化表达。

下文节选自《老水手谣》的第一部分。

From The Rime of the Ancient Mariner

Part 1

It is an ancient Mariner,
And he stoppeth one of three.
—"By thy long gray beard and glittering eye,
Now wherefore stopp'st thou me?

The Bridegroom's doors are opened wide,
And I am next of kin;
The guests are met, the feast is set:
May'st hear the merry din."

He holds him with his skinny hand;
"There was a ship," quoth he.
"Hold off! unhand me, gray-beard loon!"
Eftsoons[1] his hand dropped he.

He holds him with his glittering eye—
The Wedding-guest stood still,
And listens like a three years' child;
The Mariner hath his will[2].

The Wedding-guest sat on a stone:
He cannot choose but hear;
And thus spake on that ancient man,
The bright-eyed Mariner.

"The ship was cheered, the harbour cleared,
Merrily did we drop
Below the kirk[3], below the hill,
Below the lighthouse top.

The Sun came up upon the left,
Out of the sea came he!
And he shone bright, and on the right
Went down into the sea.

Higher and higher every day,
Till over the mast at noon[4] —"
The Wedding-Guest here beat his breast,
For he heard the loud bassoon.

The bride hath paced into the hall,
Red as a rose is she;
Nodding their heads before her goes
The merry minstrelsy.

The Wedding-Guest he beat his breast,
Yet he cannot choose but hear;
And thus spake on that ancient man,
The bright-eyed Mariner.

"And now the STORM-BLAST came, and he
Was tyrannous and strong;
He struck with his o'ertaking wings,
And chased us south along.

With sloping masts and dipping prow,
As who pursued with yell and blow
Still treads the shadow of his foe,

And forward bends his head,
The ship drove fast, loud roared the blast,
And southward aye we fled.

And now there came both mist and snow,
And it grew wondrous cold:
And ice, mast-high, came floating by,
As green as emerald.

And through the drifts the snowy clifts
Did send a dismal sheen:
Nor shapes of men nor beasts we ken—
The ice was all between.

The ice was here, the ice was there,
The ice was all around:
It cracked and growled, and roared and howled,
Like noises in a swound[5]!

At length did cross an Albatross,
Thorough the fog it came;
As if it had been a Christian soul,
We hailed it in God's name.

It ate the food it ne'er had eat,
And round and round it flew.
The ice did split with a thunder-fit;
The helmsman steered us through!

And a good south wind sprung up behind;
The Albatross did follow,
And every day, for food or play,
Came to the mariner's hollo!

In mist or cloud, on mast or shroud[6],
It perched for vespers nine;
Whiles all the night, through fog-smoke white,
Glimmered the white Moon-shine."

"God save thee, ancient Mariner!
From the fiends, that plague thee thus!—
Why look'st thou so?"—With my crossbow
I shot the ALBATROSS.

【注解】

1. Eftsoons: 相当于 immediately，立即，马上。
2. The Mariner hath his will: 老水手通过催眠术控制了婚礼上客人的意志。
3. kirk: 相当于 church，教堂。
4. Till over the mast at noon: 本行言外之意为船已行驶到了赤道 (the "Line")。
5. swound: 相当于 swoon，狂喜。
6. shroud: 桅杆上的绳子。

【思考题】

1. The accounts of the Wedding Guest's reactions in Parts I and Ⅶ serve as a frame for the Mariner's tale by giving it a beginning and an end. To what extent does the presence of the Wedding Guest influence your own reactions to the poem?
2. Select words and phrases unusual in their descriptive power and in their appeal to sight, sound, and touch. Notice the simple words in this ballad. Why are so many words of only one or two syllables used?
3. Coleridge is famous for what he calls "willing suspension of disbelief." What does "willing suspension of disbelief" mean in the context of the poem?

Kubla Khan; or, a Vision in a Dream

【题解】

《忽必烈汗》历来被奉为浪漫主义诗歌中具有丰富想象力的代表作。据诗人自述，该诗写于 1797 和 1798 年间，应另一位浪漫主义诗人拜伦的要求于 1816 年发表。

为了说明该诗的创作过程，诗人特地为该诗写了长达500多字的序言，序言中说明：诗人为了镇痛，服了两粒含有鸦片的药丸，昏昏入睡，在梦境之中创作了此诗；入睡前，诗人正在看《布切斯历程记》(*Purchas's Pilgrimage*, 1625) 一书中有关忽必烈汗在元大都下令建造"仙那都"的章节；诗人在梦醒之后记下梦中所见所思的过程中，因受到打搅而没能如愿全部写下梦中所见。为此，诗人自己特地为该诗加了一个副标题："或，梦中之境，一个片段"。

对序言中诗人的种种宣称，批评家们历来莫衷一是。有些批评家提出问题：该诗是写于1797年，还是稍晚一些？它是否是作者在梦中或鸦片造成的幻境中创作出来的？它到底是完整的，还是仅为一个片段？对该诗的不同解读决定了对这些问题的回答。

Kubla Khan; or, a Vision in a Dream

In Xanadu did Kubla Khan[1]
A stately pleasure-dome decree:
Where Alph[2], the sacred river, ran
Through caverns measureless to man
Down to a sunless sea.
So twice five miles of fertile ground
With walls and towers were girdled round:
And here were gardens bright with sinuous rills,
Where blossomed many an incense-bearing tree;
And there were forests ancient as the hills,
Enfolding sunny spots of greenery.

But oh! that deep romantic chasm which slanted
Down the green hill athwart a cedarn cover[3]!
A savage place! as holy and enchanted
As e'er beneath a waning moon was haunted
By woman wailing for her demon-lover!
And from this chasm, with ceaseless turmoil seething,
As if this earth in fast thick pants were breathing,
A mighty fountain momently was forced:

Amid whose swift half-intermitted burst
Huge fragments vaulted like rebounding hail,
Or chaffy grain beneath the thresher's flail;
And' mid these dancing rocks at once and ever
It flung up momently the sacred river.
Five miles meandering with a mazy motion
Through wood and dale the sacred river ran,
Then reached the caverns measureless to man,
And sank in tumult to a lifeless ocean;
And 'mid this tumult Kubla heard from far
Ancestral voices prophesying war!
The shadow of the dome of pleasure
Floated midway on the waves;
Where was heard the mingled measure
From the fountain and the caves.
It was a miracle of rare device,
A sunny pleasure-dome with caves of ice!

A damsel with a dulcimer[4]
In a vision once I saw:
It was an Abyssinian maid,
And on her dulcimer she played,
Singing of Mount Abora[5].
Could I revive within me
Her symphony and song,
To such a deep delight 'twould win me,
That with music loud and long,
I would build that dome in air,
That sunny dome! those caves of ice!
And all who heard should see them there,
And all should cry, Beware! Beware!
His flashing eyes, his floating hair!
Weave a circle round him thrice[6],

And close your eyes with holy dread,
For he on honey-dew hath fed,
And drunk the milk of Paradise.

【注解】

1. Kubla Khan: 元世祖忽必烈于13世纪后期创建元朝，建都上都，史称开平府，在今内蒙古自治区内。
2. Alph: 该名字源于古希腊一条名为 Alpheus 的河。在古希腊神话中，Alpheus 是追求山林仙女 Arethusa 的河神，后月神 Artemis 将 Arethusa 化为泉水，助她逃脱，他也就化为河水与泉水汇合。
3. athwart a cedarn cover: 穿过雪松厚厚的一层覆盖物。
4. dulcimer: 扬琴。在本行中意为"甜蜜的歌儿"。
5. Mount Abora: 可能指现今埃塞俄比亚的一座山脉。据传，山上也有一座类似忽必烈的游乐宫的宫殿。参见弥尔顿的《失乐园》第四部第 280 至 282 行。
6. weave a circle . . . thrice：本行说的是一种神奇的仪式，它能使受到启发的诗人不被打搅。

【思考题】

1. What is the relation of the world inside the dome to the world outside it?
2. Discuss the unity of the poem, paying special attention to the strands of imagery which connect its two parts.
3. Some critics argue that this poem, instead of being a fragment, is rather complete in itself. Do you agree? Why or why not?

解读举例

1.《忽必烈汗》是一首抒情诗的片段，充满了浪漫主义情调和令人难忘的美景。之所以说它是片段，主要是因为该诗是由不连贯的、色彩斑斓的意象和没有具体所指的意义构成。第二、三小节之间的梦中幻境也不连贯，甚至结尾也采用了不确定的和加强感情色彩的重叠手法。该诗每一部分中使用的头韵和尾韵也赋予该诗鲜明的音乐节奏。

2.《忽必烈汗》表现了一个戏剧性的冲突，其结构完整统一。在前两节中，诗人首先将地面上自然和人工的美景与地底下超自然的神秘联系起来，流经它们的"圣河"则是联结这两股力量的纽带。地面上"仙那都"的美丽景色与地下洞穴的冰冷黑暗象征着生命与死亡这两种原始力量的冲突。在第三节中，诗人通过某种宗教的召唤解决了这种冲突。

George Gordon Byron
1788—1824

乔治·戈登·拜伦出生于伦敦一个贵族家庭，三岁丧父，十岁承袭叔祖父的贵族头衔。他先后就学于哈罗私立贵族学校 (Harrow School) 和剑桥三一学院 (Trinity College)。读书期间，他发表了第一部诗集《懒散的时刻》(*Hours of Idleness*, 1807)，表达了他对社会和现实的不满，也初次展示了他的诗歌天赋，但却受到当时著名刊物《爱丁堡评论》的猛烈攻击，被斥为“死水一潭”(so much stagnant water)。两年后，作为回击，拜伦写下了第一首重要诗作《英国诗人和苏格兰评论家》(*English Bards and Scotch Reviewers*, 1809)，以 18 世纪英国诗人蒲伯的偶句体形式讽刺和抨击了英国当时几乎所有重要的浪漫主义诗人，如骚塞、华兹华斯、柯勒律治等人。1809 年，拜伦进入上院，随后踏上了为期两年的旅欧路程，游历了葡萄牙、西班牙、马耳他、阿尔巴尼亚、希腊等地，为后来的诗歌创作积累了大量素材。游历期间，拜伦创作了《恰尔德·哈罗德游记》(*Childe Harold's Pilgrimage*，1812) 第一、二章和著名抒情诗《雅典的少女》(“Maid of Athens”)，发表后引起巨大轰动，用拜伦自己的话说就是“一觉醒来成为名人”(awoke one morning and found myself famous)。

1811 年和 1813 年，拜伦在上院发表演说，以热烈的情感为诺丁汉的纺织工人辩护，谴责政府处死这些因失业而走投无路、破坏机器的工人。1813 年，拜伦以中东和远东地区的神话故事为题材创作发表了一系列叙事诗，如《阿比道斯的新娘》(“The Bride of Abydos”)、《海盗》(“The Corsair”)、《异教徒》(“The Giaour”)等，翌年又写了《异教徒》的续篇《拉拉》(“Lara”)。这些叙事诗中的男主角几乎都是所谓拜伦式英雄 (Byronic hero)。1815 年，拜伦创作了《希伯来歌曲》(*Hebrew Melodies*)，其中包括一些十分著名的爱情诗，如《她在美中漫步》(“She Walks in Beauty”) 等。

1816 年 4 月 25 日，拜伦因离婚遭到社会攻击，愤而离开英国，永不再回。在瑞士，他遇到雪莱，与之结下深厚友谊，并创作了诗剧《曼弗雷德》(*Manfred*, 1817) 前两幕和《恰尔德·哈罗德游记》第三章。同年 8 月离开瑞士到意大利定居，翌年完成《曼弗雷德》第三幕和《恰尔德·哈罗德游记》第四章和最后一章，并开始代表作《唐璜》(*Don Juan*, 1818—1823) 的创作。1819 至 1823 年间，拜伦先后迁居威尼斯、拉文纳、比萨等地。除了继续《唐璜》第三、四章的创作外，这一期间拜伦还写了一系列书斋悲剧 (Closet Tragedies)，其中最著名的为取材于圣经故事的神秘剧《该隐》(*Cain*, 1821)。1822 年，“桂冠诗人”骚塞发表长诗《审判的幻景》(*A Vision of Judgement*, 1821)，在前言部分攻击拜伦为“撒旦派”诗歌领袖。翌年，拜伦发表了同名讽刺长诗予以回敬。

在诗歌创作的同时，拜伦积极参加意大利烧炭党人的爱国斗争。1823 年他前往希腊参加当地人民反抗土耳其统治的斗争，并倾其所有，组建了一个“拜伦旅”(Byron Brigade)，极大地激励了希腊人民争取独立解放的信心。1824 年 4 月，拜伦病死营地，希腊人民为他举国致哀并将他奉为民族英雄。

作为一个浪漫主义诗人，拜伦在现代的影响日趋衰落，在当时却风靡欧美，被视作那个时代最伟大的英国诗人。德国的贝多芬、歌德，法国的司汤达、丹纳，俄国的普希金，美国的麦尔维尔等都是他的崇拜者。英裔日籍作家小泉八云 (Lafcadio Hearn, 1850—1904) 对其进行了解释：首先，他的长诗描写了西欧各国的风土人情，而当时旅行费用高昂，一般人不可能到过这么多国家，因此拜伦对异国风情的描写自然会引起读者的兴趣，而同样的作品晚五十年发表就不会产生如此的轰动；其次拜伦的长诗创造了一种新的充满反叛精神的人物形象，即所谓拜伦式英雄。在拜伦以前的英国文学史上，这种崇尚自由、反抗压迫、傲睨万物般的人物形象只有弥尔顿《失乐园》中的撒旦可与之相比，在后人创作的许多著名作品中则有《呼啸山庄》(*Wuthering Heights*, 1847) 中的希斯克利夫，《白鲸》中的埃哈伯、《叶甫盖尼·奥涅金》中的奥涅金等。不仅如此，“拜伦式英雄”还对 19 世纪和后来尼采的“超人”(Superman) 哲学也产生了重大影响。

She Walks in Beauty

【题解】

本诗为拜伦早期的抒情诗，发表在 1815 年出版的《希伯来歌曲》中。1814 年 6 月 11 日，拜伦参加了一次舞会。舞会上他首次遇到威尔莫特夫人 (Mrs. Robert John Wilmot)。当时她身着缀有金属亮片的黑色丧服，看上去哀伤又动人。拜伦为她的美所倾倒，回去后一夜之间便创作了这首典型的“骑士传统”(Cavalier tradition) 短诗。

She Walks in Beauty

1

She walks in beauty, like the night
Of cloudless climes[1] and starry skies;
And all that's best of dark and bright
Meet in her aspect and her eyes:
Thus mellowed to that tender light
Which heaven to gaudy day denies.

2

One shade the more, one ray the less,
Had half impaired[2] the nameless grace
Which waves in every raven tress,
Or softly lightens o'er her face;
Where thoughts serenely sweet express
How pure, how dear their dwelling place.

3

And on that cheek, and o'er that brow,
So soft, so calm, yet eloquent[3],
The smiles that win[4], the tints that glow,
But[5] tell of days in goodness spent,
A mind at peace with all below[6],
A heart whose love is innocent!

【注解】

1. climes: 即 climate，多用于诗歌。
2. Had half impaired: 早期现代英语中的虚拟语气，即 would have half impaired。
3. eloquent: 此处作“生动有力地表露内心情感”解。
4. win: 相当于 attractive。
5. But: 相当于 Only。
6. all below: 世间万物。

【思考题】

1. How does the speaker move from "like the night" (1) to "a mind" (17) and "a heart" (18)?

2. Why should he want to describe a woman in these terms?
3. What effect does this description have on our idea of her?
4. The lady being praised is compared to the night. What particular aspects of the night are singled out in the comparison? Why does the speaker use the word "gaudy" to describe day?
5. What is the significance of the word "wave"?

The Isles of Greece

【题解】

本诗选自拜伦代表作《唐璜》第三诗章。《唐璜》是一部未完成的长篇叙事讽刺诗，全诗有16个诗章，外加17个诗章残篇，是拜伦最长的作品，也是英国文学史上最长的诗作之一。唐璜为意大利中古罗曼文学中的传奇人物。通过这位古代传奇人物在欧洲各国的冒险经历，拜伦展示了18世纪末到19世纪初欧洲的社会现实，并对当时的社会风尚、道德伦理、政治体制和社会名流等进行了深刻辛辣的讽刺。全诗以连载的形式发表，社会各界引起了强烈反响，纷纷谴责唐璜的不道德行为。然而拜伦却坚持认为《唐璜》讽刺了当代社会的种种弊端，包括欺骗、虚伪、压迫、贪婪等，因此是所有诗歌中最道德的。他曾这样告诉布莱辛顿夫人："在我身上有两种品质是始终如一的，那就是对自由的强烈热爱和对伪善的强烈憎恨。"

"The Isles of Greece"为六行诗体，四音步，抑扬格。韵式为ababcc。在诗中，拜伦借用古希腊的灿烂文明和古希腊人民反抗外来侵略的英勇史实来激励当代希腊人民反抗土耳其统治的决心。

The Isles of Greece

1

The Isles of Greece! the isles of Greece
Where burning Sappho[1] loved and sung[2],
Where grew the arts of war and peace,
Where Delos[3] rose, and Phoebus[4] sprung!
Eternal summer gilds them yet,
But all, except their sun, is set.

2

The Scian and the Teian muse[5],
The hero's harp, the lover's lute[6],
Have found the fame your shores refuse:
Their place of birth alone is mute
To sounds which echo further west
Than your sires' "Islands of the Blest[7]."

3

The mountains look on Marathon[8]—
And Marathon looks on the sea;
And musing there an hour alone,
I dream'd that Greece might still be free;
For standing on the Persians' grave,
I could not deem myself a slave.

4

A king sate[9] on the rocky brow
Which looks o'er sea-born Salamis[10];
And ships, by thousands, lay below,
And men in nations[11];—all were his!
He counted them at break of day—
And when the sun set, where were they?

5

And where are they? And where art thou,
My country? On thy voiceless shore
The heroic lay is tuneless now—
The heroic bosom beats no more!
And must thy lyre, so long divine,
Degenerate into hands like mine?

6

'Tis something in the dearth of fame[12],
Though link'd among a fetter'd race[13],
To feel at least a patriot's shame,
Even as I sing, suffuse my face;

For what is left the poet here?
For Greeks a blush—for Greece a tear.

7

Must we but weep o'er days more blest?
Must we but blush?—Our fathers bled.
Earth! render back from out thy breast
A remnant of our Spartan[14] dead!
Of the three hundred grant but three,
To make a new Thermopylae[15]!

8

What, silent still? and silent all?
Ah! no;—the voices of the dead
Sound like a distant torrent's fall,
And answer, "Let one living head[16],
But one, arise,—we come, we come!"
'Tis but the living who are dumb.

9

In vain—in vain: strike other chords;
Fill high[17] the cup with Samian[18] wine!
Leave battles to the Turkish hordes,
And shed the blood of Scio's vine!
Hark! rising to the ignoble call[19]—
How answers each bold Bacchanal[20]!

10

You have the Pyrrhic[21] dance as yet;
Where is the Pyrrhic phalanx gone?
Of two such lessons, why forget
The nobler and the manlier one[22]?
You have the letters Cadmus[23] gave—
Think ye he meant them for a slave?

11

Fill high the bowl with Samian wine!
We will not think of themes like these!

It made Anacreon's song divine:
He served—but served Polycrates[24]—
A tyrant; but our masters then
Were still, at least, our countrymen.

12

The tyrant of the Chersonese[25],
Was freedom's best and bravest friend;
That tyrant was Miltiades[26]!
O that the present hour would lend
Another despot of the kind!
Such chains as his were sure to bind[27].

13

Fill high the bowl with Samian wine!
On Suli's rock, and Parga's shore[28],
Exists the remnant of a line[29]
Such as the Doric[30] mothers bore;
And there, perhaps, some seed is sown,
The Heracleidan blood might own[31].

14

Trust not for freedom to the Franks[32]—
They have a king who buys and sells:
In native swords and native ranks[33]
The only hope of courage dwells
But Turish force and Latin fraud
Would break your shield, however broad.

15

Fill high the bowl with Samian wine!
Our virgins dance beneath the shade—
I see their glorious black eyes shine;
But gazing on each glowing maid,
My own the burning tear-drop laves,
To think such breasts must suckle slaves.

16

Place me on Sunium's[34] marbled steep,
Where nothing, save the waves and I[35],
May here our mutual murmurs sweep;
There, swan-like[36], let me sing and die:
A land of slaves shall ne'er be mine—
Dash down yon cup of Samian wine[37]!

【注解】

1. burning Sappho: 充满激情的萨福。萨福（约公元前610年—约公元前510年），希腊岛的女诗人，以写爱情抒情诗著称。
2. sung: sang 的古语形式。
3. Delos: 爱琴海上的一座岛，为希腊神话中太阳、诗歌、音乐守护神阿波罗的出生地。
4. Phoebus: 太阳神阿波罗。
5. The Scian and Teian muse: "Scian""Teian" 分别为 Scio 和 Teos 的形容词。Scio 为古希腊的一座岛，据说是古希腊诗人荷马的诞生地。Teos 为希腊古城，是古希腊著名抒情诗人阿那克里翁 (Anacreon) 的诞生地。小写 "muse" 意思是诗才（区别于专指文艺女神的 "Muse"），此处指荷马和阿那克里翁。
6. The hero's harp, the lover's lute: 分别喻指古希腊诗人荷马和阿那克里翁的诗才。
7. Islands of the Blest: 古希腊神话中有福分的人死后居住的福地，荷马称其位于西方大洋中。
8. Marathon: 马拉松，希腊平原。公元前490年，入侵希腊的波斯军队在此全军覆没。
9. A king sate: "king" 指波斯国王薛西斯一世 (Xerxes Ⅰ，约公元前519年—公元前465年)，率大军入侵希腊，惨败而归，晚年在宫中遇刺身亡。"sate" 为 sat 的古语形式。
10. sea-born Salamis: 浮在海面上的萨拉米。萨拉米为爱琴海中的一座岛，公元前480年，希腊军队以多胜少，用380余艘战船全歼了拥有2000多艘战船的波斯船队。"born"，古语，相当于 bear 的过去分词 borne。
11. men in nations: 来自各国的士兵，即从不同国家征集来的波斯军队。
12. in the dearth of fame: 在这丧失了尊严的时代，相当于 in this ignoble age。
13. a fettered race: 一个备受奴役的民族。
14. Spartan: 斯巴达人，古希腊的一个民族，以勇武、刚强、善战著称。
15. Thermopylae: 希腊一道险关。公元前480年，300多名斯巴达战士在这里与一个军团的波斯侵略者浴血奋战，最后全部壮烈牺牲。
16. Let one living head: 只要有一个活着的人领个头。"head" 此处作动词 "领导" 解。
17. Fill high: 相当于 Fill full。
18. Samian: Samos 的形容词，Samos 为爱琴海上的一座岛，该岛出产的酒颇负盛名。
19. the ignoble call: 呼唤人们饮酒作乐。
20. Bacchanal: 酒神巴克斯 (Bacchus) 的信徒，此处指寻欢作乐，不思国耻之徒。

21. Pyrrhic: Pyrrhus的形容词。Pyrrhus为古希腊伊庇鲁斯王国(Epirus，公元前318年—公元前272年)的国王，以英勇善战著称。后面的“Pyrrhic dance”（战舞）和“Pyrrhic phalanx”（方阵）据说均为伊庇鲁斯国王所创。
22. The nobler and the manlier one: 更崇高和更英勇的舞蹈，即“Pyrrhic dance”。
23. Cadmus: 卡德摩斯，希腊神话中的腓尼基王子，杀巨龙，埋其齿，创建古希腊城邦国家Thebes，从腓尼基（今叙利亚和黎巴嫩一带）引入由16个字母组成的字母体系。
24. Polycrates: 萨摩斯岛的独裁者，崇尚文艺，对诗人阿那克里翁恩宠有加。
25. Chersonese: 半岛名。
26. Miltiades: 米太亚德（约公元前554年—约公元前489年），雅典名将、政治家，Chersonese半岛的独裁者，在马拉松战役中率希腊军队打败波斯入侵者。
27. bind: 此处为双关语，既表示束缚，又表示团结众人，但以后一层意思为主。
28. Suli’s rock, and Parga’shore: Suli，阿尔巴尼亚一山区，那里的人民骁勇善战，最早起来反抗土耳其人的侵略。Parga，爱奥尼海 (Ionian Sea) 中一座港口城市，19世纪初为英国统治 (1814—1815)，后被拱手让给土耳其人。当地人民宁愿迁居他乡也不愿受土耳其人的奴役。
29. the remnant of a line: 一个民族的后裔，即上面提到的Suli和Parga地区的人民。
30. Doric mothers: “Doric”为Doris的形容词。Doris是古希腊中部地名，Dorians为古希腊一个主要民族，斯巴达人即其中一支。
31. Heracleidan blood might own: “Heracleidan”为希腊神话中大力神Heracles的形容词，传说斯巴达人为其后裔。这里的意思是Suli、Parga两地人民的身上流动着大力神Heracles的血液，堪称他的子孙。
32. the Franks: 泛指西欧人。1815年普鲁士、奥地利、俄国等一些西欧国家结成所谓的神圣同盟(Holy Alliance)，希腊独立战争爆发后即派兵前往镇压。
33. the native ranks: 本国军队，ranks的复数形式指军队。
34. Sunium’s: 雅典一海角，建有古庙。
35. save the waves and I: 语法上句末的“I”应为me，此处用使用“I”为的是与本节第四行末尾的“die”押韵。
36. There, swan-like: 传说天鹅临死前会唱哀歌。
37. A land of slaves . . . cup of Samian wine: 最后两行表达了诗人为希腊解放而奋斗到底的决心。

【思考题】

1. In this poem, Byron contrasts the glorious past of Greece with her submissive and slavery status at present. Do you think the contrasts are effective? How?
2. In stanzas 11 and 12, Byron pays a tribute to the ancient tyrants of Greece, and wishes that the Greek people could be bound by “another despot of the kind.” Does Byron really think the Greek people need a tyrant? If not, what in fact is he trying to say?
3. Four times in this poem does the poet ask people to “fill high the bowl with Samian wine” rather than urging them to rise and fight. But obviously he is being ironical.

Discuss Byron's use of irony in these places.

4. Comment on the last two lines of this poem. What emotion is aroused by such an ending? How?

【简评】

拜伦在创作此诗时，希腊人民正忍受着土耳其侵略者的奴役。诗人怀着满腔的愤怒与激情挥笔写下了这首著名诗篇，以唤起希腊人民反抗侵略的革命斗志。全诗共16个诗节，可分为三层意思。在前四个诗节中，诗人大量列举了古希腊灿烂文明成果与反抗侵略的英勇史实来说明希腊荣耀的过去。在后四个诗节中，诗人回到现在，给我们描述了一个遭受侵略却懦弱无能的希腊，与过去的辉煌形成强烈的反差。在之后的八个诗节中，每两个诗节构成一组，每组均以重复"Fill high the cup with Samian wine!"开始，一反一正，动之以情，晓之以理，其中不乏惊人之语，希望以此唤醒希腊人民奋起反抗。全诗在一种"不自由，毋宁死"的英勇气概中结束。

"The Isles of Greece"一诗情理交融，慷慨激昂，读罢给人一种酣畅淋漓、气势蓬勃的感觉。拜伦在诗中运用了大量的修辞手法，如用典、排比、对偶、反衬，大量使用感叹句与修辞疑问句，他还把历史与现实、永恒与短暂、光荣与屈辱等放在一起进行对比，造成巨大反差，以唤醒人民起来抗争。在音韵节奏上，诗人多用单音节词，造成一种短促有力的效果，其韵脚也多为强健有力的阳韵(masculine rime)，在个别地方，诗人打破全诗抑扬格的韵律，采用扬抑格来突出想要强调的意思，如最后一节中的第一、三、六行，使全诗的气氛达到了高潮。

Percy Bysshe Shelley
1792—1822

作者简介

珀西·比希·雪莱出生于英国南部萨塞克斯(Sussex)的一个贵族家庭，先后就学于伊顿公学和牛津大学。早在伊顿上学期间，雪莱就因饱受高年级大孩子的欺负，认识到学校和社会恃强凌弱的本质，这也决定了他一生反抗压迫、与专制斗争的命运。进入大学后，雪莱广泛阅读了卢梭、潘恩(Thomas Paine, 1737—1809)、葛德汶(William Godwin, 1756—1836)等人的著作，深受他们民主思想的影响，与好友T. J. 霍格(T. J. Hogg)共同撰写了一份反宗教的小册子《无神论之必要》(*The Necessity of Atheism*, 1810)，从经验的角度证明上帝是不存在的，并因此被开除。1813 年，雪莱发表了他的第一部重要诗作《麦布女王》(*Queen Mab*, 1813)，大胆地喊出了“没有上帝”的强音。翌年 7 月，雪莱基于没有爱情的婚姻是不道德的婚姻这一立场，抛弃了已怀孕的前妻哈里艾特 (Harriet), 与葛德汶之女玛丽私奔法国，致使哈里艾特在两年后投湖自尽。雪莱的行为极大震动了当时的英国社会，受到各方的强烈谴责，包括与雪莱同样激进的葛德汶。

成为社会公敌的雪莱已无法重返英国，于 1818 年与玛丽移居意大利。1818 年至 1819 年，雪莱与玛丽所生的孩子相继夭折，在承受巨大的精神创伤和心理压力的同时，雪莱反而焕发出极大的创作热情，在这两年和随后的几年中发表了一系列重要作品，如宣扬怀念济慈的悼亡诗《阿道尼斯》(“Adonais”, 1821)、伦理悲剧《沉西》(*Cenci*, 1819)、预言性诗剧《解放的普罗米修斯》(*Prometheus Unbound*, 1820)、诗歌理论《诗辩》(“A Defence of Poetry”, 1821) 和许多著名抒情诗，如《西风颂》(“Ode to the West Wind”, 1819)、《致云雀》(“To a Skylark”, 1820) 等。与此同时，雪莱还创作了一系列充满革命精神的散文和诗歌，如以自由、革命、改革等为内容的政论文《改革的哲学观》(“A Philosophical View of Reform”, 1820)，号召英国人民拿起武器反抗压迫的战斗诗《致英国人民的歌》(“A Song: ‘Men of England’”, 1819) 和以彼得卢屠杀 (Peterloo Massacre) 为背景，抗议专制暴政的《1819 年的英国》(“England in 1819”, 1819) 等。1822 年，受希腊人民反抗土耳其统治的独立解放运动的鼓舞，雪莱创作发表了他最后一部完整的诗剧《希腊》(*Hellas*, 1822)。同年 7 月 8 日，雪莱和朋友乘坐以拜伦代表作命名的“唐璜”号游艇去意大利西部港口城市里窝那 (Livorno) 看望拜伦和李・亨特 (Leigh Hunt, 1784—1859)，返回途中遭遇风浪，翻船身亡。噩耗传来，拜伦悲痛万分。在给出版商穆雷的信中，他猛烈地谴责了社会对雪莱的不公：“你们对雪莱的看法真是大错特错，他是我所认识的人里最优秀、最无私的一个，是绝无仅有的。任何人，只要跟他一比，就都成了一头野兽。”

雪莱一生勤奋好学，他的许多论述文旁征博引、气势宏大，不仅反映出他对西方宗教、哲学、历史、文学等方面的深入理解，还显示出他在科学方面的知识积累。他是一个柏拉图主义者，也是一位伟大的理想主义者，他的一生似乎都在为实践自己所信奉的各种理念顽强奋斗。恩格斯称他为“天才的预言者”。在诗歌创作方面，雪莱也取得了巨大成就。他的诗节奏明快，音调和谐，形象优美，激情澎湃，乐观向上，成为英国诗歌中不可多得的珍品。他本人也被公认为英国最伟大的抒情诗人之一。华兹华斯曾明确指出“雪莱是我们当中最优秀的艺术家，我指的是在艺术风格方面。”

Ode to the West Wind

【题解】

《西风颂》是雪莱1819年秋在意大利佛罗伦萨所作。一日雪莱在附近的树林散步，突然狂风大作，电闪雷鸣，秋雨滂沱，诗人不禁诗兴大发而作此诗。

“风”(wind)一词在希伯来语、拉丁语、希腊语及其他许多语言中与呼吸、灵魂、精灵、灵感等属同义词，因此雪莱诗中的西风是一个精灵，是一个“秋之生命的呼吸”，一到秋天便摧毁天地海洋间一切腐朽的事物，为新春孕育出新的生命。在诗的末尾，雪莱吟出了他的千古绝唱：“如果冬天来临，春天还会远吗？”

在形式上，《西风颂》是十四行诗与意大利三行诗节相融合的结果。如同十四行诗，《西风颂》每一诗节均为十四行，最后两行为偶句诗，但前十二行诗的韵式为意大利三行诗的aba bcb cdc ded，最后两行为ee。这种前后相互衔接的韵式传神地模仿了西风飞旋、席卷一切的气势。《西风颂》运用比喻、象征的手法，将写景与抒情、内心情感与外部气势融为一体，给读者以丰富的想象，是雪莱抒情诗中写得最成功的一首。

Ode to the West Wind

1

O wild West Wind, thou breath of Autumn's being,
Thou, from whose unseen presence the leaves dead
Are driven, like ghosts from an enchanter fleeing,

Yellow, and black, and pale, and hectic[1] red,
Pestilence-stricken multitudes: O thou,
Who chariotest[2] to their dark wintry bed

The winged seeds, where they lie cold and low,
Each like a corpse within its grave, until
Thine azure sister of the Spring[3] shall blow

Her clarion[4] o'er the dreaming earth, and fill

(Driving sweet buds like flocks to feed in air)
With living hues and odors plain and hill:

Wild Spirit[5], which art moving everywhere;
Destroyer and Preserver; hear, O hear!

2

Thou on whose stream, 'mid the steep sky's commotion,
Loose clouds like Earth's decaying leaves are shed,
Shook from the tangled boughs of Heaven and Ocean[6],

Angels[7] of rain and lightning: there are spread
On the blue surface of thine aery surge,
Like the bright hair uplifted from the head

Of some fierce Maenad[8], even from the dim verge
Of the horizon to the zenith's height,
The locks of the approaching storm[9]. Thou Dirge

Of the dying year, to which this closing night
Will be the dome of a vast sepulchre,
Vaulted with all thy congregated might

Of vapours[10], from whose solid atmosphere
Black rain, and fire, and hail will burst: O hear!

3

Thou who didst waken from his summer dreams
The blue Mediterranean, where he lay,
Lulled by the coil[11] of his crystalline streams,

Beside a pumice isle in Baiae's bay[12],
And saw in sleep old palaces and towers
Quivering within the wave's intenser day[13],

All overgrown with azure moss and flowers
So sweet, the sense faints picturing them! Thou
For whose path the Atlantic's level powers[14]

Cleave themselves into chasms, while far below
The sea-blooms and the oozy woods which wear
The sapless foliage of the ocean, know

Thy voice, and suddenly grow grey with fear,
And tremble and despoil themselves[15]: O hear!

4

If I were a dead leaf thou mightest bear;
If I were a swift cloud to fly with thee;
A wave to pant beneath thy power, and share

The impulse of thy strength, only less free
Than thou, O Uncontrollable! If even
I were as in my boyhood, and could be

The comrade of thy wanderings over Heaven,
As then, when to outstrip thy skyey speed[16]
Scarce seemed a vision[17]; I would ne'er have striven

As thus with thee in prayer in my sore need.
Oh, lift me as a wave, a leaf, a cloud!
I fall upon the thorns of life! I bleed!

A heavy weight of hours has chained and bowed
One too like thee: tameless, and swift, and proud.

5

Make me thy lyre[18], even as the forest is:
What if my leaves are falling like its own!
The tumult of thy mighty harmonies

Will take from both a deep, autumnal tone,
Sweet though in sadness. Be thou, Spirit fierce,
My spirit! Be thou me, impetuous one!

Drive my dead thoughts over the universe
Like withered leaves to quicken a new birth!
And, by the incantation of this verse,

Scatter, as from an unextinguished hearth
Ashes and sparks, my words among mankind!
Be through my lips to unawakened Earth

The trumpet of a prophecy[19]! O Wind,
If Winter comes, can Spring be far behind?

【注解】

1. hectic: 指肺结核患者面部呈现的颜色。
2. chariotest: 驾车飞驰。在雪莱诗中，“chariot”（四轮马车）象征着一股势不可挡的力量。
3. azure sister of the Spring: 西风有两种，一是秋天的西风，即诗中说的“Destroyer and Preserver”；二是春天刮起的西风，即“azure sister of the Spring”，也有人解释为南风。
4. clarion: 清脆的号角声。
5. Wild Spirit: 西风。
6. Shook from . . . Ocean: shook 为 shake 过去分词 shaken 的古语形式。“tangled boughs of Heaven and Ocean”指高空中纠缠在一起的云，如同盘根交错的树枝。
7. Angels: 此处指云和闪电的使者，即风。
8. Maenad: 美奈德，古希腊神话中酒神巴克斯的女祭司。据说酒神每年秋天死去，春天又复活。
9. The locks . . . storm: 为“there are spread”的主语。用“locks”来比 Maenad 的头发，此处喻指云层。
10. of vapors: 乌云。
11. coil: 一说是地中海的波涛拍击沙滩声；一说是地中海水流常呈现的不同颜色。
12. pumice isle . . . bay: “pumice”指火山熔岩形成的浮石；“Baiae’s bay”即巴亚湾，在意大利那不勒斯以西，是古罗马的名胜，曾建有古罗马皇帝恺撒行宫，后被撒拉逊 (Seracen) 人摧毁。
13. wave’s intenser day: 雪莱曾说，在水面倒映的作用下，各种颜色看起来“更鲜艳，也更柔和”。
14. Atlantic’s level powers: 对“level”一词有两种解释：①同等的，即与强劲猛烈的西风相匹敌，故译为“大西洋的汹涌的浪波”（查良铮译）；②平坦的，因此 level powers 指大西洋平静的洋面，只有西风刮来时才掀起汹涌的波涛。
15. despoil themselves: 枯败萎缩。据雪莱解释，海底的植物也像陆地的那样有盛有衰。

16. thy skyey speed: 在天空飞驰的速度，相当于 the speed through the skies。
17. vision: 幻影，此处指不可为之事。
18. lyre: 风弦琴，当风吹过时这种风琴会发出悦耳的音乐声。lyre 也暗指古希腊诗人品达 (Pindar, 约公元前 518 年—公元前 438 年)，据说他作的颂歌均需风琴伴奏。
19. trumpet of a prophecy: 即第 10 行中的“clarion”，“trumpet of a prophecy”也暗指《圣经·启示录》中最后一声预言的号声。

【思考题】

1. Write a summary of each of this ode's five sections.
2. What does wind signify in this ode? How is it used symbolically?
3. Determine the meter and rhyme of the first five stanzas. How do these elements contribute to the ode's movement? Is this pattern continued in the other four sections?
4. What are the three dominant images in the first three sections of the poem? How does the effect of the wind on each of these elements in nature bear out Shelley's characterization of the wind as "destroyer and preserver"?
5. The speaker's relation to the wind develops in a dramatic way during the course of the poem, particularly in sections 4 and 5. What is the speaker's attitude toward himself and his relation to the wind at the end of section 4? How does this change in section 5?
6. The autumn wind is also a frequent topic in Chinese literature. What similarities and differences of the images of the autumn wind in Shelley's "Ode to the West Wind" and those in Chinese poems?

解读举例

1. 《西风颂》是一首革命的颂歌。西风象征着革命力量，它是一个“破坏者兼保护者”，它要破坏的是英国的反动势力和腐朽的政治体制，它要保护和创造的则是一个光明的新世界。《西风颂》表达了诗人想通过西风（诗歌）将革命思想传播四方的愿望。

---

2. 《西风颂》是一首表达灵感与想象的诗。在前三节，诗人充分发挥想象，淋漓尽致地表现了西风横扫一切的气势与威力。在后两节中，诗人表达了自己化入西风，通过诗歌与想象向宇宙倾诉心声的愿望。

To a Skylark

【题解】

《致云雀》作于1820年夏。当时雪莱和妻子玛丽住在意大利靠近地中海的朋友家中。据玛丽回忆，一天傍晚他们在林中散步，突然听到夜莺发出一声声婉转的啼鸣，雪莱有感而作此诗。

《致云雀》是一首欢乐、空灵、优美的诗歌。诗人通过丰富的想象，将云雀描写成一种“无形的欢乐”(unbodied joy)、一个自由的精灵，一名大自然的歌手。在盛赞云雀美妙歌声的同时，也表达了雪莱本人对美好、欢乐、自由的渴望与追求。全诗意境深远，想象丰富，描写细腻，比喻生动，是一篇不朽的艺术珍品。

To a Skylark

Hail to thee, blithe spirit!
  Bird thou never wert[1]—
That from Heaven, or near it,
  Pourest thy full heart[2]
In profuse strains of unpremeditated art[3].

Higher still and higher
  From the earth thou springest
Like a cloud of fire;
  The blue deep thou wingest,
And singing still dost soar, and soaring ever singest.

In the golden lightning
  Of the sunken Sun—
O'er which clouds are bright'ning,
  Thou dost float and run;
Like an unbodied joy whose race is just begun.

The pale purple even

Melts around thy flight[4];
Like a star of Heaven
In the broad daylight
Thou art unseen, but yet I hear thy shrill delight,

Keen as are the arrows
Of that silver sphere[5],
Whose intense lamp narrows
In the white dawn clear[6],
Until we hardly see—we feel that it is there.

All the earth and air
With thy voice is loud,
As when Night is bare,
From one lonely cloud
The moon rains out her beams, and Heaven is overflowed.

What thou art we know not;
What is most like thee?
From rainbow clouds there flow not
Drops so bright to see,
As from thy presence showers a rain of melody[7].

Like a Poet hidden
In the light of thought,
Singing hymns unbidden,
Till the world is wrought
To sympathy with hopes and fears it heeded not[8]:

Like a highborn maiden
In a palace-tower,
Soothing her love-laden
Soul in secret hour

With music sweet as love—which overflows her bower:

Like a glow-worm golden[9]
  In a dell of dew,
Scattering unbeholden
  Its aerial hue
Among the flowers and grass, which screen it from the view:

Like a rose embowered
  In its own green leaves—
By warm winds deflowered—
  Till the scent it gives
Makes faint with too much sweet those heavy-winged thieves[10]:

Sound of vernal showers
  On the twinkling grass,
Rain-awakened flowers,
  All that ever was
Joyous, and clear and fresh, thy music doth surpass:

Teach us, Sprite or Bird,
  What sweet thoughts are thine;
I have never heard
  Praise of love or wine
That panted forth a flood of rapture so divine.

Chorus Hymeneal[11],
  Or triumphal chaunt,
Matched with thine would be all
  But an empty vaunt,
A thing wherein we feel there is some hidden want[12].

What objects are the fountains

Of thy happy strain?
What fields or waves or mountains?
What shapes of sky or plain?
What love of thine own kind? what ignorance of pain?

With thy clear keen joyance
Languor cannot be—
Shadow of annoyance
Never came near thee;
Thou lovest—but ne'er knew love's sad satiety.

Waking or asleep,
Thou of death must deem
Things more true and deep
Than we mortals dream,
Or how could thy notes flow in such a crystal streams[13]?

We look before and after,
And pine for what is not—
Our sincerest laughter
With some pain is fraught—
Our sweetest songs are those that tell of saddest thought[14].

Yet if we could scorn
Hate and pride and fear;
If we were things born
Not to shed a tear,
I know not how thy joy we ever should come near[15].

Better than all measures[16]
Of delightful sound—
Better than all treasures
That in books are found—

Thy skill to poet were, thou Scorner of the ground[17]!

Teach me half the gladness
  That thy brain must know,
Such harmonious madness[18]
  From my lips would flow,
The world should listen then—as I am listening now.

【注解】

1. Bird thou never wert: 你从不是一只（普通的）鸟。因上一行云雀被比作一个“欢乐的精灵”，故有此说。
2. Pourest thy full heart: 这里雪莱不说“Pourest thy songs of full heart”（倾泻你心灵的歌），因此更富想象。
3. unpremeditated art: 无须琢磨，发自内心的乐音。
4. The pale purple even / Melts around thy flight: 不说翱翔的鸟溶于淡紫的夜色中，而说夜色融合在鸟的翱翔中，这样更具诗意，与第一节第四行有异曲同工之妙。
5. silver sphere: 相当于 the morning star，指晨星、金星。
6. Whose intense lamp . . . dawn clear: 天色越来越亮，耀眼的晨星此刻也失去了原有的光芒。“clear”本应置于“dawn”前，此处置于行尾是为了与本节第二行的“sphere”押韵。
7. From rainbow . . . a rain of melody: 这三行诗的正常语序应是 Drops that flow from rainbow clouds are not so bright to see as the rain of melody that showers from the presence. 从彩虹的云间滴雨 / 那雨滴固然明亮 / 但怎及得由你遗下的一片音响？（查良铮译）
8. Till the world . . . it heeded not: “sympathy”即共鸣。这两行的意思是，云雀唱的歌使全世界由冷漠（“it heeded not”）到产生共鸣，有感于他所歌唱的希望与忧虑。
9. glow-worm golden: 正常语式应为 golden glow-worm，此处“golden”后置，与本节第三行的“unbeholden”押韵。
10. Makes faint . . . thieves: thieves 指本节第三行的“warm winds”，此句意思是花的芬芳竟然醉倒了前来偷香的暖风。
11. Chorus Hymeneal: 婚礼的合唱。Hymeneal 为 Hymen 的形容词，Hymen 系希腊神话中的婚礼之神。
12. hidden want: 一种看不见的缺陷。
13. Thou of death . . . crystal streams: 云雀对死亡的理解一定比我们凡夫俗子来得更为真切深刻，正因为这样，云雀才会唱出如此晶莹动听的歌。在以下两节中诗人表达了相同的意思。
14. Our sweetest songs . . . saddest thought: 最诉哀愁的歌才是最甜美的歌，这行诗表达了一种辩证的思想。
15. Yet if we could scorn . . . come near: 这节诗的意思是，如果我们失去了怨恨、骄傲、悲伤等凡人的情感，我们又怎能体会到云雀那样的欢乐。
16. measures: 曲调，常用于诗歌。

17. thou Scorner of the ground: 这里指云雀藐视凡世的诗人，又说泛指凡俗的一切。
18. harmonious madness: 和谐的狂热，即云雀唱出的热情但又和谐的歌。

【思考题】

1. The poem can be tentatively divided into three parts, each having its own emphasis. How do you divide them, and what are the respective emphases?
2. Why is it important that the bird is "unseen"? Which words in the poem suggest that the bird does not seem to be a physical being?
3. The poet compares the skylark to different things. What are they? What qualities do they have in common with the bird? Are these qualities more lovely than the bird's?
4. Line 90 says "Our sweetest songs are those that tell of saddest thought." How do you understand this line? What is the difference between the skylark's song and the song of the human poet?

John Keats
1795—1821

作者简介

约翰·济慈出生于一个贫寒的家庭，很小的时候父母便离开人世。15 岁那年济慈被监护人送去当外科医生的学徒，后到伦敦一家医院继续学习，但他不久便弃医从文。促使济慈作出这一决定的因素很多，但主要有两个原因：第一，早在恩菲尔德私立学校读书期间，济慈就因受教师查尔斯·考顿·克拉克 (Charles Cowden Clarke) 的影响，对古典文学艺术产生了浓厚的兴趣；第二，济慈在伦敦学医期间结识了评论家李·亨特，并通过亨特结识了当时英国文艺界其他一些著名人士，如散文家哈兹利特、兰姆，诗人雪莱，画家黑顿 (Benjamin Robert Haydon, 1786—1846) 等。与他们的交往自然加深了济慈对文学的兴趣。1816 年 10 月，济慈发表了著名的彼特拉克体 (Petrarchan) 十四行诗《初读查普曼译荷马史诗有感》(“On First Looking into Chapman's Homer”)，初次展示了自己的文学才华，并于翌年发表了第一本诗集《诗歌》(*Poems*, 1817)， 但没有引起评论界的注意。1818 年，济慈完成并发表了长达 4000 多行的神话诗《恩底弥翁》(*Endymion*)，遭到《黑林》(*Blackwood*)、《季度评论》(*The Quarterly Review*) 等一些保守刊物的非难，并被蔑称为“伦敦派”[①](Cockney School)。然而济慈并没有像一些人想象的那样垮了下来[②]，而是振作精神，于同年夏天开始创作以古代神话为题材的长篇史诗《赫坡里昂》(*Hyperion*)，但没有完成。这一年济慈还不顾潮湿阴冷的天气徒步游历了英国湖区、苏格兰、爱尔兰等地，并于深秋季节与 18 岁的范妮·布朗 (Fanny Brawne) 订婚。从 1818 年到 1819 年是济慈在经济、身体和情感上最艰难的一段时期，但也是他在文学创作上最辉煌的时期。在不到一年的时间里，济慈写下了一首又一首的佳作，如《圣阿格尼丝前夜》("The Eve of St. Agnes")、《无情的美女》("La Belle Dame Sans Merci")、《拉米亚》("Lamia") 和六首著名的颂歌。1819 年下半年，济慈开始重新创作《赫坡里昂》，并易名为《赫坡里昂的末日》(*The Fall of Hyperion*)。然而好景不长，1820 年 2 月，济慈开始咯血，同年秋前往意大利，翌年 2 月 23 日在罗马去世，年仅 26 岁。在著名的挽诗《阿道尼斯》中，雪莱称济慈是“最活跃、最年轻的诗人”，是“一颗露珠培养出来的鲜花”。

在文学创作手法上，济慈曾受斯宾塞、弥尔顿等人影响，但很快摆脱了这种影响，他甚至与亨特、雪莱等人也保持一定距离，以保证自己作品的独创性，而他最大的独创就是对大自然深切的感性理解。与其他浪漫主义诗人不同，济慈在诗歌创作中往往淡化自己的主观因素与个性特征。他曾说过：“诗人是世上最不具诗意的生物……诗人没有个性。”换句话说，就是诗人在创作时应忘却自己的存在，完全沉浸在对诗歌主题的感受中，接受一切神秘与不可知的事物而不刨根问底。这就是著名的“消极能力”(Negative Capability)。只有这样，诗人才能创作出真正的美。对济慈来说，美就是真，真就是美。

济慈的诗歌具有唯美主义倾向，但也并非完全无视现实，在追求美的同时，他也创作了一些具有民主思想的诗歌，如反对欧洲掠夺战争、歌颂和平的《和平十四行诗》("Sonnet on Peace", 1814)，献给波兰爱国志士的《致考苏斯科》("To Kosciusko", 1816)，以及针砭时事的长诗《伊莎贝拉：或那盆罗勒》(*Isabella, or the Pot of Basil*, 1820) 等。济慈所有的重要诗篇都表达了这样一种哲学观点，即人生充满着各种无法避免、又不可调和的矛盾，因此喜悦中有忧郁，快乐中有痛苦，极乐之时便可能是死亡之际。

从初露锋芒到登峰造极，济慈的诗歌创作生涯只有短短的八年。有评论家认为，他在 24 岁时取得的成就远远超过了乔叟、莎士比亚和弥尔顿等巨匠在同一年龄段

---

① 伦敦派：以李·亨特等人组成的、活跃在伦敦文坛的激进分子。

② 雪莱和拜伦都认为，正是洛克哈特 (John Lockhart, 1794—1854) 等人在《黑林》等杂志上对《恩底弥翁》的恶毒攻击使得济慈英年早逝。

的成就。他把自己对外部世界的感受与对美的理解完美地结合起来，对后人的诗歌创作产生了不可估量的影响。

Ode to a Nightingale

【题解】

《夜莺颂》作于1819年5月。当时济慈住在朋友查理·布朗家中。据布朗回忆，1819年春，一只夜莺在他家附近树上筑了个鸟巢。夜莺的歌声常常使济慈感到心旷神怡。一天清晨他把椅子搬到李子树下，一连坐了三四个钟头，回来时将手中几张纸片随手塞在了书本底下。布朗好奇地翻开纸片，发现原来上面是一首有感于夜莺的歌声而作的颂诗，这就是济慈最有名的颂诗之一——《夜莺颂》。

《夜莺颂》是诗人对夜莺不朽的歌声和人类短暂的生命所进行的对比与思索。在诗的开头，济慈描述了夜莺欢乐的歌声和自己如痴如醉的感受。诗人好像进入了一个幻境，欲随夜莺一同融入自然，忘却人生的烦恼。沐浴着午夜温柔的月色，聆听着夜莺美妙的歌声，沉醉于百花沁人心脾的芬芳……趁此极乐之时，毫无痛苦地告别人世，难道还有什么比这更美妙的吗？然而这时诗人从梦幻中醒来，告别夜莺，重返现实，并发出幻想毕竟不是现实的感叹。

在《夜莺颂》中，夜莺的歌声象征着不朽的艺术，而观照艺术的永恒与人生的短暂是浪漫主义诗歌中一个重要主题。雪莱的《奥西曼德斯》("Ozymandias", 1818)、《致云雀》，以及济慈的《希腊古瓮颂》("Ode on a Grecian Urn", 1819)、《忧郁颂》("Ode on Melancholy", 1819) 等诗都表达了这样的思想。

美国著名作家菲茨杰拉德 (F. Scott Fitzgerald, 1896—1940) 曾说自己每次吟诵《夜莺颂》都禁不住会热泪盈眶，无怪乎他会用《夜莺颂》中的“夜色温柔” (tender is the night) 一词来为自己的小说命名。《夜莺颂》不仅描写精致，感情强烈，在音韵上也很有特色，如第五节最后两行用了大量的“m”音，模仿了昆虫飞行时发出的嗡嗡嘤嘤的声音，成为英国诗史上的千古绝唱。

Ode to a Nightingale

1

My heart aches, and a drowsy numbness pains
  My sense, as though of hemlock[1] I had drunk,

Or emptied some dull opiate to the drains[2]
One minute past,[3] and Lethe-wards[4] had sunk:
'Tis not through envy of thy happy lot,
But being too happy in thine happiness—
That thou, light-wingèd Dryad[5] of the trees,
In some melodious plot[6]
Of beechen green, and shadows numberless,[7]
Singest of summer in full-throated ease.

2

O, for a draught of vintage! that hath been
Cool'd a long age in the deep-delved earth,
Tasting of Flora[8] and the country green,
Dance, and Provencal[9] song, and sunburnt mirth![10]
O for a beaker full of the warm South[11],
Full of the true, the blushful Hippocrene[12],
With beaded bubbles winking at the brim,
And purple-stained mouth;
That I might drink, and leave the world unseen,
And with thee fade away into the forest dim[13].

3

Fade far away, dissolve, and quite forget
What thou among the leaves hast never known,
The weariness, the fever, and the fret
Here, where men sit and hear each other groan;
Where palsy shakes a few, sad, last gray hairs,
Where youth grows pale, and spectre-thin, and dies;[14]
Where but to think is to be full of sorrow
And leaden-eyed despairs,
Where Beauty cannot keep her lustrous eyes,
Or new Love pine at them beyond tomorrow.[15]

4

Away! away! for I will fly to thee,
Not charioted by Bacchus and his pards[16],

But on the viewless wings of Poesy[17],
Though the dull brain perplexes and retards:
Already with thee! tender is the night,
And haply the Queen-Moon is on her throne,
Cluster'd around by all her starry Fays[18];
But here there is no light,
Save what from heaven is with the breezes blown
Through verdurous[19] glooms and winding mossy ways.

5

I cannot see what flowers are at my feet,
Nor what soft incense hangs upon the boughs[20],
But, in embalmed[21] darkness, guess each sweet
Wherewith the seasonable month endows
The grass, the thicket, and the fruit-tree wild;
White hawthorn, and the pastoral eglantine[22];
Fast fading violets cover'd up in leaves;
And mid-May's eldest child[23],
The coming musk-rose, full of dewy wine,
The murmurous haunt of flies on summer eves.

6

Darkling[24] I listen; and, for many a time
I have been half in love with easeful Death,
Call'd him soft names in many a mused rhyme[25],
To take into the air my quiet breath;
Now more than ever seems it rich to die,
To cease upon the midnight with no pain,
While thou art pouring forth thy soul abroad
In such an ecstasy!
Still wouldst thou sing, and I have ears in vain—
To thy high requiem become a sod[26].

7

Thou wast not born for death, immortal Bird!
No hungry generations tread thee down[27];

The voice I hear this passing night was heard
  In ancient days by emperor and clown:
Perhaps the self-same song that found a path
  Through the sad heart of Ruth[28], when, sick for home,
    She stood in tears amid the alien corn;
      The same that oft-times hath
  Charm'd magic casements[29], opening on the foam
    Of perilous seas, in faery lands forlorn.

8

Forlorn[30]! the very word is like a bell
  To toll me back from thee to my sole self!
Adieu! the fancy[31] cannot cheat so well
  As she is fam'd[32] to do, deceiving elf.
Adieu! adieu! thy plaintive anthem[33] fades
  Past the near meadows, over the still stream,
    Up the hill-side; and now'tis buried deep
      In the next valley-glades:
  Was it a vision, or a waking dream?
    Fled is that music:—Do I wake or sleep[34]?

【注解】

1. hemlock: 一种有毒的植物，服其汁可引起昏迷和死亡。据说古希腊哲学家苏格拉底即服此毒死亡。
2. to the drains: 一饮而尽，drain 单数表示一口之量，复数表示畅饮。
3. One minute past: 一分钟前。
4. Lethe-wards: 即 toward Lethe。Lethe，忘川，古希腊神话中冥界 (Hades) 的一条河流，人死后需饮此水，以忘却阳间一切事物。
5. Dryad: 希腊、罗马神话中的树神。此处指栖息于树上的夜莺。
6. melodious plot: 夜莺歌唱的地方。melodious 本不能修饰 plot，此处作转喻 (transferred epithet) 用。第三节中的 "leaden-eyed despair" 也属此类。
7. shadows numberless: "numberless" 后置，与下行的 "ease" 押韵。第二节中的 "forest dim" 同属此类。
8. Flora: 罗马神话中的花神，或指花本身。
9. Provencal: Provence 的形容词。普罗旺斯为法国东南部的一个地区，中世纪后期曾盛行吟唱和创作爱情歌曲，故有 Provencal song 一说。
10. sunburnt mirth: 这两个词形成一个搭配冲突 (collocative clash)，意思是 the mirth of the sunburnt people。诗歌中常用这样的手法以达到凝练的效果。

11. the warm South: 此处以“warm South”代表温暖的南方所产的酒，在修辞学上称换喻(metonymy)，其他例子如“The pen is mightier than swords.”，其中“pen”表示 the force of literature，“swords”表示 political force。
12. Hippocrene: 古希腊神话中赫利孔山(Mount Helicon)上文艺女神缪斯之泉。诗人饮此水可获灵感，此处喻指 a beaker of wine。
13. forest dim: 幽暗的树林。“dim”后置与上行的“unseen”押韵。
14. Where youth grows pale . . . dies: 济慈之弟汤姆因患肺病于 1818 年 12 月去世，评论家一般认为这里的“youth”实指汤姆。
15. Or new Love pine at them beyond tomorrow: 新欢难持久。因上行中已有否定词“cannot”，所以这一行中的否定词省略。“beyond tomorrow”为夸张用法。
16. Bacchus and his pards: 酒神巴库斯乘坐的车由豹拉行。
17. the viewless wings of Poesy: 诗人虽不能乘坐酒神的豹车飞行，但却可以借助想象这一无形的翅膀飞向夜莺。“Poesy”即 poetic fancy。
18. Fays: 相当于 Fairies。
19. verdurous: 郁郁葱葱的。
20. soft incense hangs upon the boughs: 此处借用“incense”（香味）来代表 fragrant flowers，以达到更生动的效果。
21. embalmed: 香气扑鼻的。
22. eglantine: 野蔷薇。
23. eldest child: 此处指 5 月中旬最早开放的花。
24. Darkling: 相当于 In the dark。
25. mused rhyme: 相当于 meditated rhyme，苦苦思索出来的诗句。
26. To thy high requiem become a sod: 虽然夜莺将不停地高唱安魂曲，但我已化作尘土，再也听不到。
27. No hungry generations tread thee down: 无论哪一代人，即使再苦再饿，也不会来捕猎你。
28. Ruth: 路德，《圣经》中的人物，其丈夫死后随婆婆迁居伯利恒，并下麦地干农活。下行中的“alien corn” (wheat) 即指此事。
29. Charm'd magic casements: 迷住了囚禁魔牢之人。“casements”是囚室的窗口，此处喻指囚禁在魔牢中的人被夜莺的歌声吸引到窗边。
30. Forlorn: 此处有双重意思，既与上行末尾的“forlorn”相同，表示遥远的过去，又表示 sorrowful 的意思。因此这里的 Forlorn 表示诗人从梦幻中惊醒，回到可悲的现实。
31. fancy: 指第 33 行所说的“viewless wings of Poesy”，也指下行中的“deceiving elf”。
32. fam'd: 相当于 reported。
33. plaintive anthem: 哀歌。因诗人已回到现实，故夜莺美妙的歌声此刻听起来也顿觉悲哀。
34. Do I wake or sleep: 当诗人张开想象的翅膀，吟诗作赋时，他很难分清自己是在作诗还是在做梦，故诗的末尾有此一问。在“Ode to Psyche”中，济慈也有此问：Surely I dreamt today, or did I see/The winged Psyche with awaken'd eyes?

【思考题】

1. What is the speaker's mental and emotional state at the opening of the poem? What emotions are aroused in him by the song of the nightingale?
2. The poet expresses a desire to escape from his world into the world of the nightingale. What is unsatisfactory about his world? In what two ways especially do his world and the world of the nightingale contrast (stanzas 3, 6, 7)?
3. Dying under the conditions described in stanza 6 is made to seem very attractive. How do the last two lines of the stanza affect this attractiveness? Why has the poet often been "half in love" with death? Why has he been only "half in love" with it?
4. In what sense (or senses) is the nightingale "immortal"? How is this immortality illustrated in stanza 7?
5. In what way is the imagination (or fancy) a "deceiving elf"? What is the difference between a "vision" and a "waking dream"? Does Keats expect the readers to answer the questions in the last two lines?
6. At the end of stanza 7, the "faery lands" are described as "forlorn." How does the word "forlorn" in line 71 bring the speaker back to reality? Are its meanings the same in stanza 8 as in stanza 7?

解读举例

1.《夜莺颂》描写了夜莺不朽与美妙的歌声。全诗笼罩在一片幽暗之中，我们可以听到夜莺的歌声却看不到夜莺的身影，这就更突出了夜莺的精神特性。尽管诗人无法化作不朽的夜莺，但他仍可以领略到外部世界的美。

2.《夜莺颂》表达了审美体验的短暂性与欺骗性。诗人对莺歌的反应是麻木 (drowsy numbness)、眩晕 (intoxication)、幻觉和对死亡的渴求。在诗的末尾，诗人指责想象 (fancy) 是一个"骗人的小精灵"(deceiving elf)，怀疑夜莺的幻觉只不过是一个"醒着的梦" (a waking dream)。

3.《夜莺颂》的主题表达了审美体验中两种相悖的因素与情感。对夜莺的歌声，诗人既感到喜悦 (ecstatic)，又感到悲哀 (plaintive)。我们看到的一方面是夜莺的不朽与欢快，另一方面则是人生的短暂与痛苦。

To Autumn

【题解】

《秋颂》作于1819年9月19日，是济慈作的最后一首颂诗，也是在很多读者看来最优秀的一首。创作此诗两天后，济慈在给朋友的信中这样说：

> 我从没像今天这样喜欢过收割后的田野——真的，比春寒料峭的绿色还要喜欢。不知怎的，收割后的田野看上去给人一种温暖的感觉——就像有些油画那样——礼拜天在外散步时，这种景象给我留下了深刻的印象，于是就作了这首诗。

在《秋颂》中，诗人以绚烂的笔调描写了秋天丰硕与收获的景色。全诗共三节，分别从景色、形态和声音三个方面着手，生动地表现了秋天的丰收美景。这是一首写景诗，读来宛如身临画境，但又是一首充满天籁的交响乐。更为重要的是，《秋颂》一诗有景有情，情景交融，在摹写大自然的同时也淋漓尽致地表达了诗人喜悦的情感。在给朋友的一封信中，济慈曾提到，诗人应具有一种“消极感受”的能力，即任凭自己沉浸在大自然的美景中，而不假思索与疑问，因为只有这样诗人才能最大限度地领略自然的美。《秋颂》一诗可被视为是对这个观点的最好注释。

To Autumn

Season of mists and mellow fruitfulness[1],
  Close bosom-friend of the maturing sun[2];
Conspiring with him how to load and bless
  With fruit the vines that round the thatch-eves run;
To bend with apples the mossed cottage-trees,
  And fill all fruit with ripeness to the core;
    To swell the gourd, and plump the hazel shells
With a sweet kernel; to set budding more,
  And still more, later flowers for the bees,
  Until they think warm days will never cease,
    For Summer has o'er-brimmed their clammy cells[3].

Who hath not seen thee[4] oft amid thy store?
Sometimes whoever seeks abroad may find
Thee sitting careless[5] on a granary floor,
Thy hair soft-lifted by the winnowing wind[6];
Or on a half-reaped furrow sound asleep,
Drows'd with the fume of poppies, while thy hook[7]
Spares[8] the next swath and all its twined flowers:
And sometimes like a gleaner thou dost keep
Steady thy laden head across a brook;
Or by a cider-press, with patient look,
Thou watchest the last oozings hours by hours.

Where are the songs of Spring? Ay, where are they?
Think not of them, thou hast thy music too—
While barred clouds[9] bloom the soft-dying day,
And touch the stubble-plains with rosy hue;
Then in a wailful choir the small gnats mourn
Among the river sallows[10], borne aloft
Or sinking as the light wind lives or dies;
And full-grown lambs loud bleat from hilly bourn[11];
Hedge-crickets sing; and now with treble soft
The red-breast whistles from a garden-croft[12];
And gathering swallows twitter in the skies.

【注解】

1. Season of mists and mellow fruitfulness: 在文学创作中，秋天往往是一个悲凉的季节，但在济慈的《秋颂》中，我们看到的却是一幅浓艳的深秋丰收图。
2. maturing sun: 使万物成熟的太阳。
3. For Summer has o'er-brimmed their clammy cells: 蜂房由于装满了蜜汁而流溢出来。这行诗中，诗人一连用了六个［m］音，给人一种天气暖洋洋和蜂蜜黏糊糊的感觉。
4. thee: 此处的 thee 和下面的 "thy" "thou" 均指秋天或秋之神，是一种拟人的手法。thee、thy、thou 分别为 you（宾格）、your 和 you（主格）的古体。这是因为《秋颂》以源于古希腊的颂体 (ode) 写成，其格调典雅，用字也自然较为古朴，这也体现在济慈或雪莱的其他颂诗中。
5. careless: 相当于 carefree，无忧无虑的。

6. winnowing wind: 簸谷的风。
7. hook: 相当于 scythe，镰刀。
8. Spares: 原意为饶恕，此处为留着未割的意思。
9. barred clouds: 一片片的晚霞。
10. river sallows: 一说指河边的柳树，“sallows” 等于 willows；又说指河边的浅滩，“sallow” 即 shallows。该诗 1820 年重印时，“sallows” 改为 shallows。
11. bourn: 一说小溪，“bourn” 等于苏格兰方言中的 burn；也有说法等于地区 (domain)。莎士比亚的《哈姆雷特》中有 “The undiscover'd country, from whose bourn/No traveller returns” 的台词。
12. garden-croft: 相当于 garden plot，园子。

【思考题】

1. What particular aspects of autumn does Keats focus on in stanza 1? And stanzas 2 and 3? How is your feeling about autumn affected by these aspects?
2. How is autumn personified in each stanza of the poem?
3. How many kinds of images do you find in the poem? Are the images carefully arranged?
4. Although the poem describes the beauty and fruitfulness of autumn, there is also an implicit comment on the transience of beauty. What do you think is Keats's attitude toward this reality?
5. The dominant images of autumn in traditional Chinese poems are different from those in Keat's "To Autumn." Please make a comment on the relationship between a nation's culture and its literary expression.

Jane Austen
1775—1817

作者简介

简·奥斯汀 1775 年 12 月 16 日出生于英格兰中南部汉普郡斯蒂文顿镇的一个牧师家庭，是家里的第七个孩子。自 1765 至 1801 年，奥斯汀的父亲乔治·奥斯汀 (George Austen) 一直担任斯蒂文顿教区的牧师，曾当过牛津大学的学监，学识渊博，家中藏书丰富。母亲卡桑德拉出身于当地显赫的贵族家庭。她的几位哥哥中，有从事圣职的，有成为银行家的，有在军队服役的。奥斯汀和姐姐接受过几年短暂的学校教育，之后主要在家里自学。姐妹俩一生关系很好。奥斯汀对读书有着浓厚的兴趣，通读莎士比亚剧作、英国历史和 18 世纪文学。理查逊、菲尔丁、蒲伯、哥尔德斯密斯、约翰逊、司各特、拜伦等作家作品都在她阅读之列。她尤其喜欢喜理查逊的作品。奥斯汀很早就开始写作。据说她的作品是在客厅里的一张小桌子上完成的，当有客人来访时，她会迅速把写作的东西藏起来。但家人对她的写作始终给予理解和支持，经常一起阅读、探讨文学作品，父兄们的指导和讨论也使她受益匪浅。书香气息浓厚的家庭环境为奥斯汀成长为小说家提供了有利条件。

1796 年，奥斯汀与爱尔兰青年汤姆 · 洛弗罗伊 (Tom Lefroy) 坠入爱河，但男方家人反对，要求洛弗罗伊迅速返回爱尔兰，二人被迫分手，从此再未相见。1800 年，奥斯汀的父亲退休，全家迁往巴斯。1802 年，将继承大笔财产的青年哈里斯 · 比格威瑟 (Harris Bigg-Wither) 向奥斯汀求婚。她起先答应了，但第二天早上又改变了主意，因为她不爱他。1805 年，父亲去世，奥斯汀和母亲、姐姐一起迁往南安普敦，1809 年又移居朝顿 (Chawton)，和哥哥爱德华一家住在一起。1816 年，奥斯汀身患重病，健康每况愈下，1817 年 5 月被送往温切斯特治疗，终因医治无效，于 7 月 18 日去世。奥斯汀终生未嫁，死后葬在温彻斯特大教堂。

简 · 奥斯汀的小说以出版年代为序，分别是《理智与情感》(*Sense and Sensibility*, 1811)、《傲慢与偏见》(*Pride and Prejudice*, 1813)、《曼斯菲尔德庄园》(*Mansfield Park*, 1814)、《爱玛》(*Emma*, 1815)、《诺桑觉寺》(*Northanger Abbey*, 1817) 和《劝导》(*Persuasion*, 1817)。奥斯汀生活时代的英国，阶级意识强烈，社会等级森严，性别歧视严重。社会反对妇女涉足公共领域，女性只能把自我命运的改善寄希望于婚姻。婚姻被视为女性寻求改变自我命运的机会。奥斯汀以现实主义手法把以理查逊的《帕美拉，或德行有报》为代表的伤感小说和风俗喜剧 (Comcdy of Manners) 结合在一起，专门描写英国乡镇中产阶层的女士和先生们的言行举止、舞会、茶会、散步和野餐等。读者在她的作品中看不到当时法国大革命动荡的局势和拿破仑战争的滚滚硝烟。因此，有评论家指责奥斯汀不关心普通民众的生活和情感，然而这主要基于她坚持的创作原则，即只写自己熟悉的领域。虽然她的小说取材范围狭小，然而却“荟萃了人情世故和世间百态”，“折射了大千世界和普遍的人类关系”。同时，其作品观察世事细致入微，人物对话生动逼真，人物形象栩栩如生，情节安排紧凑完整，反讽 (irony) 手法运用出色，这些都使奥斯汀的故事引人入胜，备受青睐。读者往往对作品人物命运产生强烈共鸣，对作家精湛的艺术手法赞不绝口。

简 · 奥斯汀是英国浪漫主义时期最重要的现实主义小说家之一。她继承和发展了 18 世纪英国现实主义传统，为 19 世纪英国现实主义小说的繁荣做了铺垫。作家生前获得的高度评价主要来自司各特爵士、柯勒律治、骚塞等人，摄政王乔治也很喜欢读她的小说。然而总体而言，她的小说在当时并未得到应有评价。1869年，奥斯汀的侄子詹姆斯·爱德华·奥斯汀-利(*James Edward Austen-Leigh*)出版的《奥斯汀回忆录》(*A Memoir of Jane Austen*)，把这位可敬的作家介绍给广大民众。20世纪以来，奥斯汀的作品越来越受欢迎，已被学术界公认为伟大的英国作家。

Pride and Prejudice

【题解】

早在1796年，奥斯汀便开始写作此书，次年完稿，取名“第一印象”(*First Impressions*)，但无人肯出版此书。直到1813年，此书经过彻底改写，题为《傲慢与偏见》，才得以出版，并大获成功。

故事情节围绕隆邦的贝涅特一家展开。贝涅特夫妇有五个女儿，皆待字闺中。贝涅特夫人一生的主要愿望便是为女儿们觅得美满姻缘。故事开始时，隆邦附近的耐得菲尔德庄园被年轻富有的单身汉查尔斯·宾利租下，他和好友菲茨威廉·达西的到来引起邻近家庭的广泛关注。宾利对贝涅特家的大女儿简一见倾心，但二女儿伊丽莎白却不喜欢达西的傲慢态度，达西也视伊丽莎白为浅薄女流之辈，不加理睬，后由于种种原因伊丽莎白和达西之间成见愈深。但经过许多事后，两人都觉察到了自己的傲慢与偏见。一次伊丽莎白随同舅父母途经达西庄园时受到达西的热情接待。达西的魅力和体面深深地打动了伊丽莎白。两人冰释前嫌，有情人终成眷属。

下文选自小说第一、二章。在小说开头，奥斯汀寥寥数语便生动地勾勒出贝涅特夫妇的人物形象。小说的开场白所取得的反讽效果也一直为人们津津乐道。

From Pride and Prejudice

Chapter 1

It is a truth universally acknowledged, that a single man in possession of a good fortune must be in want of a wife.

However little known the feelings or views of such a man may be on his first entering a neighbourhood, this truth is so well fixed in the minds of the surrounding families, that he is considered as the rightful property of some one or other of their daughters.

“My dear Mr. Bennet,” said his lady to him one day, “have you heard that Netherfield Park is let at last?”

Mr. Bennet replied that he had not.

"But it is," returned she; "for Mrs. Long[1] has just been here, and she told me all about it."

Mr. Bennet made no answer.

"Do not you want to know who has taken it?" cried his wife impatiently.

"You want to tell me, and I have no objection to hearing it."

This was invitation enough.

"Why, my dear, you must know, Mrs. Long says that Netherfield is taken by a young man of large fortune from the north of England; that he came down on Monday in a chaise and four[2] to see the place, and was so much delighted with it that he agreed with Mr. Morris[3] immediately; that he is to take possession before Michaelmas, and some of his servants are to be in the house by the end of next week."

"What is his name?"

"Bingley."

"Is he married or single?"

"Oh! single, my dear, to be sure! A single man of large fortune; four or five thousand a year. What a fine thing for our girls!"

"How so? how can it affect them?"

"My dear Mr. Bennet," replied his wife, "how can you be so tiresome! You must know that I am thinking of his marrying one of them."

"Is that his design in settling here?"

"Design! nonsense, how can you talk so! But it is very likely that he may fall in love with one of them, and therefore you must visit him as soon as he comes."

"I see no occasion for that. You and the girls may go, or you may send them by themselves, which perhaps will be still better; for as you are as handsome as any of them, Mr. Bingley might like you the best of the party."

"My dear, you flatter me. I certainly have had my share of beauty, but I do not pretend to be any thing extraordinary now. When a woman has five grown up daughters, she ought to give over thinking of her own beauty."

"In such cases, a woman has not often much beauty to think of."

"But, my dear, you must indeed go and see Mr. Bingley when he comes into the neighbourhood."

"It is more than I engage for, I assure you."

"But consider your daughters. Only think what an establishment it would be for one of them. Sir William and Lady Lucas[4] are determined to go, merely on that account, for in general, you know they visit no new comers. Indeed you must go, for it will be impossible for us to visit him, if you do not[5]."

"You are over-scrupulous, surely. I dare say Mr. Bingley will be very glad to see you; and I will send a few lines by you to assure him of my hearty consent to his marrying which ever he chuses[6] of the girls; though I must throw in a good word for my little Lizzy."

"I desire you will do no such thing. Lizzy is not a bit better than the others; and I am sure she is not half so handsome as Jane, nor half so good humoured as Lydia. But you are always giving her the preference."

"They have none of them much to recommend them," replied he; "they are all silly and ignorant like other girls; but Lizzy has something more of quickness than her sisters."

"Mr. Bennet, how can you abuse your own children in such a way? You take delight in vexing me. You have no compassion on my poor nerves."

"You mistake me, my dear. I have a high respect for your nerves. They are my old friends. I have heard you mention them with consideration these twenty years at least."

"Ah! you do not know what I suffer."

"But I hope you will get over it, and live to see many young men of four thousand a year come into the neighbourhood."

"It will be no use to us, if twenty such should come, since you will not visit them."

"Depend upon it, my dear, that when there are twenty I will visit them all."

Mr. Bennet was so odd a mixture of quick parts[7], sarcastic humour, reserve, and caprice, that the experience of three and twenty years had been insufficient to make his wife understand his character. Her mind was less difficult to develop[8]. She was a woman of mean understanding, little information, and uncertain temper. When she was discontented, she fancied herself nervous. The business of her life was to get her daughters married; its solace was visiting and news.

Chapter 2

Mr Bennet was among the earliest of those who waited on[9] Mr. Bingley. He had always intended to visit him, though to the last always assuring his wife that he should not go; and till the evening after the visit was paid, she had no knowledge of it. It was then disclosed in the following manner. Observing his second daughter employed in trimming a hat, he suddenly addressed her with, "I hope Mr. Bingley will like it, Lizzy."

"We are not in a way to know what Mr. Bingley likes," said her mother resentfully, "since we are not to visit."

"But you forget, mama," said Elizabeth, "that we shall meet him at the assemblies[10], and that Mrs. Long has promised to introduce him."

"I do not believe Mrs. Long will do any such thing. She has two nieces of her own. She is a selfish, hypocritical woman, and I have no opinion of her."

"No more have I," said Mr. Bennet; "and I am glad to find that you do not depend on her serving you."

Mrs. Bennet deigned not to make any reply; but unable to contain herself, began scolding one of her daughters.

"Don't keep coughing so, Kitty[11], for heaven's sake ! Have a little compassion on my nerves. You tear them to pieces."

"Kitty has no discretion in her coughs," said her father; "she times them ill."

"I do not cough for my own amusement," replied Kitty fretfully. "When is your next ball to be, Lizzy?"

"To-morrow fortnight[12]."

"Aye, so it is," cried her mother, "and Mrs. Long does not come back till the day before; so it will be impossible for her to introduce him, for she will not know him herself."

"Then, my dear, you may have the advantage of your friend, and introduce Mr. Bingley to her."

"Impossible, Mr. Bennet, impossible, when I am not acquainted with him myself; how can you be so teazing?"

"I honour your circumspection. A fortnight's acquaintance is certainly very little. One cannot know what a man really is by the end of a fortnight. But if we do not venture, somebody else will[13]; and after all, Mrs. Long and her nieces must stand their chance; and therefore, as she will think it an act of kindness, if you decline the office[14], I will take it on myself."

The girls stared at their father. Mrs. Bennet said only, "Nonsense, nonsense!"

"What can be the meaning of that emphatic exclamation?" cried he. "Do you consider the forms of introduction, and the stress that is laid on them, as nonsense? I cannot quite agree with you there. What say you, Mary?[15] for you are a young lady of deep reflection I know, and read great books, and make extracts."

Mary wished to say something very sensible, but knew not how.

"While Mary is adjusting her ideas," he continued, "let us return to Mr. Bingley."

"I am sick of Mr. Bingley." cried his wife.

"I am sorry to hear that; but why did not you tell me so before? If I had known as much this morning, I certainly would not have called on him. It is very unlucky; but as I have actually paid the visit, we cannot escape the acquaintance now."

The astonishment of the ladies was just what he wished; that of Mrs. Bennet perhaps surpassing the rest; though when the first tumult of joy was over, she began to declare that it was what she had expected all the while.

"How good it was in you, my dear Mr. Bennet! But I knew I should persuade you at last. I was sure you loved your girls too well to neglect such an acquaintance. Well, how pleased I am! And it is such a good joke, too, that you should have gone this morning, and never said a word about it till now."

"Now, Kitty, you may cough as much as you chuse," said Mr. Bennet; and, as he spoke, he left the room, fatigued with the raptures of his wife.

"What an excellent father you have, girls," said she, when the door was shut. "I do not know how you will ever make him amends for his kindness; or me either, for that matter. At our time of life, it is not so pleasant I can tell you, to be making new acquaintance every day; but for your sakes, we would do any thing. Lydia, my love, though you are the youngest, I dare say Mr. Bingley will dance with you at the next ball."

"Oh!" said Lydia stoutly, "I am not afraid; for though I am the youngest, I'm the tallest."

The rest of the evening was spent in conjecturing how soon he would return Mr. Bennet's visit, and determining when they should ask him to dinner.

【注解】

1. Mrs. Long: 贝涅特家的邻居。
2. a chaise and four: 四匹马拉的车。
3. Mr. Morris: 房地产经纪人。
4. Sir William and Lady Lucas: 当地较有名望的贵族。"Sir" 和 "Lady" 分别是男女贵族的头衔。
5. Indeed you must go . . . if you do not: 根据当时的习俗，有新的人家搬来居住，需由男性家长先去拜访，女眷方能与之交往。
6. chuses, 相当于 chooses。

7. quick parts: 敏捷。
8. develop: 此处意为理解。
9. waited on: 拜访。
10. the assemblies: 舞会。
11. Kitty: 贝涅特家四女儿。
12. To-morrow fortnight: 明天起两周后。
13. if we do not venture, somebody else will: 假如我们不愿意把宾利先生介绍给郎夫人，别人也会介绍的。
14. office: 帮忙。
15. Mary: 贝涅特家的三女儿。

【思考题】

1. The opening sentence of this novel is probably one of the most famous first sentences found in fiction. What has this sentence to do with the tone of the whole novel? What are the implied meanings of this sentence?
2. In these two chapters, what methods does the author use to portray the characters of Mr. and Mrs. Bennet?
3. How is the theme "marriage is important to individual and society" displayed through various types of marriages and reasons behind them?

解读举例

1. 奥斯汀的小说经常被指责缺乏激情、肤浅、冷漠。《简·爱》的作者夏洛蒂·勃朗特曾说：简·奥斯汀对激情一无所知，她只不过表现了温文尔雅的英国人的生活表象，而没有去探究他们暴风骤雨般的内心世界。

2. 奥斯汀在其小说中成功描写了自己所熟悉的东西，这就是小说家的首要任务。与她同时代的著名小说家司各特对奥斯汀推崇备至："那位小姐有一种描述日常生活中的人物及其情感，以及梳理各种错综复杂关系的天赋，对我而言这是我平生所见最了不起的。"

作者简介

Mary Shelley

1797—1851

玛丽·雪莱出生于英国。她的父母同为18世纪著名的政界人士：母亲是女性主义运动的先驱、教育家和作家玛丽·沃尔斯通克拉夫特(Mary Wollstonecraft, 1759—1797)，父亲是哲学家、政论家威廉·葛德汶。

玛丽从未接受过正规教育，但父亲允许她进入家里藏书丰富的私人图书馆广泛阅读，并鼓励她要做一个有创造性的人。与此同时，玛丽的家里常常是文人墨客聚集的地方，比如著名的浪漫主义诗人威廉·华兹华斯、塞缪尔·柯勒律治等。他们之间的交谈使玛丽受益匪浅，为她日后的创作奠定了一定基础。玛丽一生都非常崇拜她的母亲，虽然母亲在她出生10天后即离世，但母亲的行为和成就对她日后创作产生了深远影响。1814年5月玛丽结识了年轻诗人珀西·雪莱。雪莱当时已经成家，却很快为玛丽非凡的容貌、举止和才智所折服。两个月后，他们不顾众人反对，私奔离开英国。1816年5月，玛丽和雪莱去瑞士日内瓦湖度夏，与诗人乔治·拜伦毗邻。6月中旬，连续的大雨使他们无法外出游玩，为了消磨时光，他们轮番朗读德国鬼故事。拜伦提议大家各写一篇神怪小说。几位男士都无法终篇，玛丽却越写越认真，1817年当她离开瑞士时，手稿已经写完。一年后小说问世，旋即成为畅销书，在伦敦引起轰动。这就是著名的长篇小说《弗兰肯斯坦—现代普罗米修斯的故事》(*Frankenstein; or, The Modern Prometheus*, 1818)，简称《弗兰肯斯坦》。

《弗兰肯斯坦》这部作品既有浪漫气氛，又有深切的人文关怀，更有令人毛骨悚然的恐怖元素，故此也被人誉为“有史以来最伟大的恐怖作品之一”。对于只有20岁的玛丽来说，这是一个非凡的成就。可以说，这部作品为玛丽赢得了极大的声誉。

经历了瑞士田园般的生活之后，玛丽的生活被阴影笼罩。先是她同父异母的姐姐离家出走并自杀，之后雪莱的前妻又投水自尽。残酷的命运给玛丽造成一次次毁灭性打击，她的孩子接二连三地夭折。1822年7月，29岁的雪莱遭遇暴风雨淹死在海里。雪莱死后留下不少尚未发表的作品，玛丽为亡夫编印遗作，相继出版了《雪莱诗遗作》和《雪莱诗集》。

孤独的玛丽后来又陆续创作出一些作品，其中最著名的是长篇科幻小说《最后一个人》(*The Last Man*, 1826)。在这部作品中，人类集体毁灭，只剩下最后一人。1851年2月1日，玛丽去世。1891年，人们把玛丽的部分短篇遗作结集出版，题为《玛丽·雪莱故事集》。

除了《弗兰肯斯坦》和《最后一个人》之外，玛丽·雪莱还写过另外四部长篇小说，但影响力都不及前两部。这四部小说分别是以 14 世纪意大利宫廷为背景的传奇小说《瓦尔帕格》(*Valperga*，1823)，两部爱情小说《劳德尔》(*Lodore*，1835)和《福尔克纳》(*Faulkner*，1836)，以及具有自传性质的小说《玛希尔德》(*Mathilde*，1959)。《玛希尔德》虽然早在 1819 年就开始动笔，但直到玛丽·雪莱去世后一百多年的 1959 年才正式出版。

Frankenstein; or, The Modern Prometheus

【题解】

《弗兰肯斯坦—现代普罗米修斯的故事》的创作灵感可能来自以下两件事。一次，玛丽·雪莱曾听到她丈夫雪莱和拜伦对当时著名的电力科学实验进行讨论，即电流能否让死去的物体复活。这一点给她带来了灵感，因为小说的主人公维克多·弗兰肯斯坦正是利用电流激活了他所创造的怪物。第二件事是某个夜晚玛丽·雪莱曾做过一场噩梦，梦见一位苍白的、学者模样的人亲手组装的一个物体复活了，做出几乎与人一样的动作。玛丽马上想到这个使她感到惊愕的画面一定也会震慑众多的读者。于是，这一小说应运而生。

《弗兰肯斯坦》主要讲述了日内瓦青年维克多·弗兰肯斯坦的故事：他是一位年轻的科学家，在德国一所大学学习自然科学，无意中发现了“不经过上帝之手”制造人类的方法，于是便收集来人和动物尸体的各种部分，拼成人形，并赋予它生命，制造出了一个体型巨大、丑陋无比的怪物。这个怪物具有超自然的力量，但因外貌丑陋而被世人无情地视作异类加以捕杀。它虽有人类的情感，却永远不能拥有人类的正常生活，因此感到绝望，尤其仇恨给了它生命的弗兰肯斯坦，于是便开始报复。它杀死了所有弗兰肯斯坦爱的人，包括他的弟弟和朋友，还在新婚之夜杀死了他的妻子。弗兰肯斯坦痛恨这个怪物，决心把它消灭。他追到北极，反而为怪物所害，而这个怪物也消失在冰天雪地之中。

下文选自《弗兰肯斯坦》的第二章，主要描写了维克多·弗兰肯斯坦的个性特征与兴趣爱好，以及他与青梅竹马的伊丽莎白和同窗好友亨利的不同之处。

From Frankenstein or, The Modern Prometheus

Chapter 2

We were brought up together; there was not quite a year difference in our ages. I need not say that we were strangers to any species of disunion or dispute. Harmony was the soul of our companionship, and the diversity and contrast that subsisted in our characters drew us nearer together. Elizabeth was of a calmer and more concentrated disposition; but, with all my ardour, I was capable of a more intense application and was more deeply smitten with the thirst for knowledge. She busied herself with following the aerial creations of the poets; and in the majestic and wondrous scenes which surrounded our Swiss home—the sublime shapes of the mountains, the changes of the seasons, tempest and calm, the silence of winter, and the life and turbulence of our Alpine summers—she found ample scope for admiration and delight. While my companion contemplated with a serious and satisfied spirit the magnificent appearances of things, I delighted in investigating their causes. The world was to me a secret which I desired to divine. Curiosity, earnest research to learn the hidden laws of nature, gladness akin to rapture, as they were unfolded to me, are among the earliest sensations I can remember.

On the birth of a second son, my junior by seven years, my parents gave up entirely their wandering life and fixed themselves in their native country. We possessed a house in Geneva, and a campagne[1] on Belrive[2], the eastern shore of the lake, at the distance of rather more than a league from the city. We resided principally in the latter, and the lives of my parents were passed in considerable seclusion. It was my temper to avoid a crowd and to attach myself fervently to a few. I was indifferent, therefore, to my school-fellows in general; but I united myself in the bonds of the closest friendship to one among them. Henry Clerval was the son of a merchant of Geneva. He was a boy of singular talent and fancy. He loved enterprise, hardship, and even danger for its own sake. He was deeply read in books of chivalry and romance. He composed heroic songs and began to write many a tale of enchantment and knightly adventure. He tried to make us act plays and to enter into masquerades.

No human being could have passed a happier childhood than myself. My parents were possessed by the very spirit of kindness and indulgence. We felt that they were not the tyrants to rule our lot according to their caprice, but the agents and creators of all the many delights which we enjoyed. When I mingled with other families I distinctly discerned how peculiarly fortunate my lot was, and gratitude assisted the development of filial love.

My temper was sometimes violent, and my passions vehement; but by some law in my temperature[3] they were turned not towards childish pursuits but to an eager desire to learn, and not to learn all things indiscriminately. I confess that neither the structure of languages, nor the code of governments, nor the politics of various states possessed attractions for me. It was the secrets of heaven and earth that I desired to learn; and whether it was the outward substance of things or the inner spirit of nature and the mysterious soul of man that occupied me, still my inquiries were directed to the metaphysical, or in its highest sense, the physical secrets of the world.

Meanwhile Clerval occupied himself, so to speak, with the moral relations of things. The busy stage of life, the virtues of heroes, and the actions of men were his theme; and his hope and his dream was to become one among those whose names are recorded in story as the gallant and adventurous benefactors of our species. The saintly soul of Elizabeth shone like a shrine-dedicated lamp in our peaceful home. Her sympathy was ours; her smile, her soft voice, the sweet glance of her celestial eyes, were ever there to bless and animate us. She was the living spirit of love to soften and attract; I might have become sullen in my study, through the ardour of my nature, but that she was there to subdue me to a semblance of her own gentleness. And Clerval—could aught ill entrench on the noble spirit of Clerval? Yet he might not have been so perfectly humane, so thoughtful in his generosity, so full of kindness and tenderness amidst his passion for adventurous exploit, had she not unfolded to him the real loveliness of beneficence and made the doing good the end and aim of his soaring ambition.

I feel exquisite pleasure in dwelling on the recollections of childhood, before misfortune had tainted my mind and changed its bright visions of extensive usefulness into gloomy and narrow reflections upon self. Besides, in drawing the picture of my early days, I also record those events which led, by insensible steps, to my after tale of misery, for when I would account to myself for the birth of that passion which afterward ruled my destiny I find it arise, like a mountain river, from ignoble and almost forgotten sources; but, swelling as it proceeded, it became the torrent which, in its course, has swept away all my hopes and joys.

Natural philosophy is the genius that has regulated my fate; I desire, therefore, in this narration, to state those facts which led to my predilection for that science. When I was thirteen years of age we all went on a party of pleasure to the baths near Thonon[4]; the inclemency of the weather obliged us to remain a day confined to the inn. In this house I chanced to find a volume of the works of Cornelius Agrippa[5]. I opened it with apathy; the theory which he attempts to demonstrate and the wonderful facts which he relates soon changed this feeling into enthusiasm. A new light seemed to dawn upon my mind, and bounding with joy, I communicated my discovery to my father. My father looked carelessly at the title page of my book and said, "Ah! Cornelius Agrippa! My dear Victor, do not waste your time upon this; it is sad trash."

If, instead of this remark, my father had taken the pains to explain to me that the principles of Agrippa had been entirely exploded and that a modern system of science had been introduced which possessed much greater powers than the ancient, because the powers of the latter were chimerical, while those of the former were real and practical, under such circumstances I should certainly have thrown Agrippa aside and have contented my imagination, warmed as it was, by returning with greater ardour to my former studies. It is even possible that the train of my ideas would never have received the fatal impulse that led to my ruin. But the cursory glance my father had taken of my volume by no means assured me that he was acquainted with its contents, and I continued to read with the greatest avidity.

When I returned home my first care was to procure the whole works of this author, and afterwards of Paracelsus[6] and Albertus Magnus[7]. I read and studied the wild fancies of these writers with delight; they appeared to me treasures known to few besides myself. I have described myself as always having been imbued with a fervent longing to penetrate the secrets of nature. In spite of the intense labour and wonderful discoveries of modern philosophers, I always came from my studies discontented and unsatisfied. Sir Isaac Newton is said to have avowed that he felt like a child picking up shells beside the great and unexplored ocean of truth. Those of his successors in each branch of natural philosophy with whom I was acquainted appeared even to my boy's apprehensions as tyros engaged in the same pursuit.

The untaught peasant beheld the elements around him and was acquainted with their practical uses. The most learned philosopher knew little more. He had partially unveiled the face of Nature, but her immortal lineaments were still a wonder and a mystery. He might dissect, anatomize, and give names; but, not to speak of a final cause, causes in their secondary and tertiary grades were utterly unknown to him. I had gazed upon the fortifications and impediments that seemed to keep human beings from entering the citadel of nature, and rashly and ignorantly I had repined.

But here were books, and here were men who had penetrated deeper and knew more. I took their word for all that they averred, and I became their disciple. It may appear strange that such should arise in the eighteenth century; but while I followed the routine of education in the schools of Geneva, I was, to a great degree, self-taught with regard to my favourite studies. My father was not scientific, and I was left to struggle with a child's blindness, added to a student's thirst for knowledge. Under the guidance of my new preceptors I entered with the greatest diligence into the search of the philosopher's stone and the elixir of life; but the latter soon obtained my undivided attention. Wealth was an inferior object, but what glory would attend the discovery if I could banish disease from the human frame and render man invulnerable to any but a violent death!

Nor were these my only visions. The raising of ghosts or devils was a promise liberally accorded by my favourite authors, the fulfillment of which I most eagerly sought; and if my incantations were always unsuccessful, I attributed the failure rather to my own inexperience and mistake than to a want of skill or fidelity in my instructors. And thus for a time I was occupied by exploded systems, mingling, like an unadept, a thousand contradictory theories and floundering desperately in a very slough of multifarious knowledge, guided by an ardent imagination and childish reasoning, till an accident again changed the current of my ideas.

When I was about fifteen years old we had retired to our house near Belrive, when we witnessed a most violent and terrible thunderstorm. It advanced from behind the mountains of Jura, and the thunder burst at once with frightful loudness from various quarters of the heavens. I remained, while the storm lasted, watching its progress with curiosity and delight. As I stood at the door, on a sudden I beheld a stream of fire issue from an old and beautiful oak which stood about twenty yards from our house; and so soon as the dazzling light vanished, the oak had disappeared, and nothing remained but a blasted stump. When we visited it the next morning, we found the tree shattered in a singular manner. It was not splintered by the shock, but entirely reduced to thin ribbons of wood. I never beheld anything so utterly destroyed.

Before this I was not unacquainted with the more obvious laws of electricity. On this occasion a man[8] of great research in natural philosophy was with us, and excited by this catastrophe, he entered on the explanation of a theory which he had formed on the subject of electricity and galvanism, which was at once new and astonishing to me. All that he said threw greatly into the shade Cornelius Agrippa, Albertus Magnus, and Paracelsus, the lords of my imagination; but by some fatality the overthrow of these men disinclined me to pursue my accustomed studies. It seemed to me as if nothing would or could ever be known. All that had so long engaged my attention suddenly grew despicable. By one of those caprices of the mind which we are perhaps most subject to in early youth, I at once gave up my former occupations, set down natural history and all its progeny as a deformed and abortive creation, and entertained the greatest disdain for a would-be science which could never even step within the threshold of real knowledge. In this mood of mind I betook myself to the mathematics and the branches of study appertaining to that science as being built upon secure foundations, and so worthy of my consideration.

Thus strangely are our souls constructed, and by such slight ligaments are we bound to prosperity or ruin. When I look back, it seems to me as if this almost miraculous change of inclination and will was the immediate suggestion of the guardian angel of my life—the last effort made by the spirit of preservation to avert the storm that was even then hanging in the stars and ready to envelop me. Her victory was announced by an unusual tranquility and gladness of soul which followed the relinquishing of my ancient and latterly tormenting studies. It was thus that I was to be taught to associate evil with their prosecution, happiness with their disregard. It was a strong effort of the spirit of good, but it was ineffectual. Destiny was too potent, and her immutable laws had decreed my utter and terrible destruction.

【注解】

1. campagne: 乡间别墅。
2. Belrive: 又作 Bellerive, 贝尔里韦湖畔，位于日内瓦湖西南岸。
3. temperature: 性格，性情。
4. Thonon: 托农，法国的一座城市，位于日内瓦湖南岸。
5. Cornelius Agrippa: 科尼利厄斯·阿格里帕 (1486—1535)，查理五世的宫廷秘书，法国神秘学家和哲学家。
6. Paracelsus: 帕拉塞尔瑟斯 (1493—1541)，瑞士医生，炼金术士。
7. Albertus Magus: 阿尔伯图斯·马格努斯 (1193—1280)，亚里士多德学派的哲学家。
8. a man: 这个人指的是 Erasmus Darwin (1731—1802)，他认为电流能使死去的物体复活，并进行过相关实验。

【思考题】

1. How do you understand the subtitle of the novel? Do you think it is proper? Why or why not?
2. What is the true motive behind Victor's creation?
3. Victor attributes his tragic fate to his relentless search for knowledge. Do you think this is the true cause of his suffering? Why or why not?
4. Man is a social animal and it is a general conception about his basic behavioural pattern that he loves to live in society with other human beings. How is the tragedy of major characters of the novel read from the perspective of family, society and isolation?

解读举例

1. 小说主人公维克多·弗兰肯斯坦是一个典型的 18 世纪的科学家的形象。他对科学非常执着认真。他坚持不懈、一丝不苟的态度，打破砂锅问到底的钻研精神是启蒙运动时期多数人的真实写照。通过对这一人物的塑造，玛丽·雪莱再现并颂扬了她当时所处的那个时代。

2. 作者通过小说主人公维克多·弗兰肯斯坦的悲剧表达了对科学无止境发展的忧虑。玛丽·雪莱并没有颂扬 18 世纪这一科技大发展的时代，而是透过这种对科学的盲目崇拜，对技术无休止的探求，揭示出人类社会所潜藏的危机。弗兰肯斯坦是 18 世纪许多人的缩影，一味盲目追求科学，无视自然规律，把自己的意志强加于自然之上，企图掌控生命创造之力来为自己的私利服务，这是典型的人类中心主义的行为。小说可被看作一个生态批评文本。评论家克洛伯尔指出，这是有关科技摧毁整个人类之可能性的第一次文学描写。贝特认为，《弗兰肯斯坦》这部对“违反自然规律”进行批判的作品，对人类正确认识当代科技发展的潜在危险，具有特别重大的意义。

3. 小说主人公维克多·弗兰肯斯坦所创造的怪物丑陋、恐怖，让人畏惧，这个怪物实际上是主人公贪婪、私欲的外在表现形式。与其说弗兰肯斯坦最终葬送在自己创造的怪物手里，不如说他是被自己的贪婪、私欲所害。玛丽·雪莱借助弗兰肯斯坦这一人物向读者揭示了一个普遍真理：一个人不能被自己的贪婪和欲望所左右，否则最终只能自毁前程。

English Literature of the Victorian Age

1832–1901

维多利亚时代是英国综合实力迅猛发展的时期。英国的经济实力空前强大，势力范围迅速扩张。从殖民地掠夺的财富源源不断地流入英国，这也是许多维多利亚时代文学作品的背景。从《简·爱》(*Jane Eyre*, 1847) 中女主人公意外继承叔叔在马地拉给她留下的两万镑遗产，到《远大前程》(*Great Expectations*, 1860—1861) 中失意的匹普去埃及经营茶叶，到《名利场》(*Vanity Fair*, 1847—1848) 中的利蓓卡第一次略施小计就勾引到了从印度回国的财主乔瑟夫，人们不难看出，当时去殖民地赚钱是英国人民公认有效的"生财之道"。总之，这是一个充满了机会的时代，是一个能让人梦想"远大前程"的自信的年代。有评论家认为维多利亚的黄金时代像伊甸园，另一些评论家则认为它像地狱。一般来说，为研究方便，维多利亚时代被文史家们分成三个阶段：维多利亚早期 (1832—1848)、维多利亚中期 (1848—1870) 和维多利亚晚期 (1870—1901)。

维多利亚早期也常被称为"多事之秋"(A Time of Troubles)。经济上的繁荣并不能阻止阶级矛盾的产生。就在新兴资产阶级奇迹般地暴富起来时，劳动者却不得不在残酷的压迫下过着穷困的生活。这一时期反抗压迫、争取民主选举权的运动蓬勃发展，在宪章派 (The Chartist) 诗人的作品中得到忠实反映，具有代表性的有欧内斯特·琼斯 (Ernest Jones, 1819—1869) 的《民主之歌》(*The Songs of Democracy*, 1856)。散文家托马斯·卡莱尔 (Thomas Carlyle, 1795—1881) 的《法国大革命》(*The French Revolution*，1837) 和《过去与现在》(*Past and Present*，1843)，小说家伊丽莎白·盖斯凯尔 (Elizabeth Gaskell, 1810—1865) 的《北方与南方》(*North and South*, 1855) 都在一定程度上揭示了拜金主义和市侩主义对人类道德的腐蚀，而查尔斯·狄更斯 (Charles Dickens, 1812—1870) 在他早期的小说中更是不遗余力地反映了英国私有制社会的阴暗面。

维多利亚中期正好处于相对稳定的 19 世纪五六十年代，科学技术飞速发展，天文、地理和生物学等学科的新成果大大扩展了人类的眼界。这一时期被称为"经济繁荣和宗教分歧的时期"(Economic Prosperity and Religious Controversy)。达尔文的《物种起源》(*The Origin of Species*, 1859) 提出的进化论打破了上帝造物的唯心史观，给传统信仰以猛烈的冲击，人们不得不重新认识自己并再次定位。英国国教的势力衰减，新教派林立，福音派吸引了大批小生产者，知识界的"牛津运动"(The Oxford Movement) 或"高教会派"(High Church) 运动也激烈展开，引起了强烈的反响，甚至使天主教势力抬头。尽管勤奋和富有责任感仍为这一时期的主要价值取向，但全社会都在经历着一场信仰危机。许多文人学者对英国状况深感忧虑。狄更斯等一大批作家继续对维多利亚社会的弊端进行批判。最激烈的一位莫过于约翰·罗斯金 (John Ruskin, 1819—1900)，他的《威尼斯之石》(*The Stones of Venice*, 1851—

1853) 预言了维多利亚工商业文明的灾难，在《直至最后》(*Unto the Last*, 1862) 中则对自由竞争的经济法进行了无情攻击。安东尼・特罗洛普 (Anthony Trollope, 1815—1882) 的小说则相对客观。教育家兼批评家马修・阿诺德 (Matthew Arnold, 1822—1888) 在他的著名论著《文化与无政府状态》(*Culture and Anarchy*, 1869) 中，批判对物质的迷信，提倡文化和精神价值。他对英国社会状况的反思代表了有识之士面对新现实的焦虑和危机感。尽管这个时期存在许多问题，但它仍然是一个繁荣的时期。因为它不仅为英国创造了惊人的物质财富，同时也是各种文学体裁，尤其是长篇小说发展的黄金时代。

维多利亚后期，大英帝国由盛转衰 (Decay of Victorian Values)。英国的霸主地位受到美国和德国挑战，英国加紧对殖民地的掠夺。资本输出和海外扩张造成国内工农业的萧条和萎缩。19 世纪 70 年代末 80 年代初的经济危机进一步加剧了贫富分化，维多利亚王朝推崇的社会道德规范和价值观念纷纷开始瓦解，到 19 世纪 90 年代几乎崩溃。历史学家杨格曾概括说：“当我们注视 80 年代在新思潮和旧观念的旋涡中挣扎，试图寻找一个立足点的时候，我们就产生了茫然、不协调和无所适从的感觉。”这种感觉不仅影响着人们的行为，也反映在当时的文学作品里。斯威夫特之后最重要的讽刺家萨缪尔・巴特勒 (Samuel Butler, 1835—1902) 的自传性小说《众生之道》(*The Way of All Flesh*, 1903) 尖锐讽刺了维多利亚式的家庭生活，特别是小说中暴君似的自以为是的父亲。如果说巴特勒的公开叛逆还不够成熟，唯美主义理论家和创始人瓦尔特・佩特 (Walter Pater, 1839—1894) 和他的追随者们则更为直接地指明了问题。他们宣布父辈们的追求都是无意义的，“我们的问题没有答案，我们唯一可做的就是尽情享受美和短暂的时光。”19 世纪 90 年代的艺术家们非常清醒地知道自己生活在一个伟大世纪的尽头，常常故意摆出一副“世纪终点”(fin de siècle) 姿态。这一时期的诗歌和散文表现出一种故作消沉、带着倦容的矫揉造作和对新的表现形式的追寻，以重新吊起读者的胃口。乔治・摩尔 (George Moore, 1852—1933) 和麦克斯・比尔博姆 (Max Beerbohm, 1872—1956) 的散文及恩斯特・道森 (Ernest Dowson, 1867—1900) 的诗歌都反映出这些特点。《大卫・科波菲尔》(*David Copperfield*, 1849—1850) 中的主人公大卫曾自我总结：“我一直是十分认真的。”四十五年后，奥斯卡・王尔德 (Oscar Wilde, 1854—1900) 在《认真的重要》(*The Importance of Being Earnest*, 1895) 中把“认真”一词变成了一个双关语，一个颠覆了整个维多利亚早期价值观的玩笑。

维多利亚时代文学的一个重要特点是多样化 (diversity)，即多种文学体裁的繁荣。实际上，多样化体现了维多利亚作家的独立性和对文学经验的渴望。面对不断扩大的读者群，作家们几乎都是带着强烈的责任感进行写作，去把握和反映这个令人惊心动魄的时代。诗人们在继续使用一些传统表现形式的同时，也在不断地实验新的、不同寻常的表现形式。最突出的莫过于叙事诗歌艺术的发展了。在小说有力的竞争面前，诗歌也开始寻求以韵文讲故事的新方法，追求史诗般的效果。像阿尔弗雷德·丁尼生 (Alfred, Lord Tennyson, 1809—1892) 的《公主》(*The Princess*, 1847)、《摩德》(*Maud*, 1855)，罗伯特·勃朗宁 (Robert Browning, 1812—1889) 的《环与书》(*The Ring and the Book*, 1868—1869) 就是长篇叙事诗的杰出代表。获得"桂冠诗人"称号的丁尼生抒情、叙事技巧圆熟，勃朗宁尤其擅长用口语描绘人物的内心世界。这个时期还出现了倡导诗歌要重返意大利文艺复兴前、朴素纯真的前拉斐尔派诗人，其代表人物是但丁·加白利·罗塞蒂 (Dante G. Rossetti, 1828—1882) 和威廉·莫里斯 (William Morris, 1834—1896)。一些小说家兼诗人，如乔治·梅瑞狄斯 (George Meredith, 1828—1909) 和艾米莉·勃朗特 (Emily Brontë, 1818—1848) 也尝试用诗歌表达小说中的故事和情感。梅瑞狄斯的《现代爱情》(*Modern Love*, 1862) 堪称描绘破碎的婚姻和情人间对立情绪的经典。

维多利亚时代的散文也成就斐然，这一时期也出现了许多著名的散文家：托马斯·卡莱尔、约翰·亨利·纽曼 (John Henry Newman, 1801—1890)、约翰·斯图亚特·穆勒 (John Stuart Mill, 1806—1873)、约翰·罗斯金、马修·阿诺德、托马斯·亨利·赫胥黎 (Thomas Henry Huxley, 1825—1895) 和瓦尔特·佩特等。他们主要的作品，如卡莱尔的《法国大革命》《过去与现在》，纽曼的《自辩》(*Apologia Pro Vita Sua*, 1864)，穆勒的《论自由》(*On Liberty,* 1859)，罗斯金的《威尼斯之石》，阿诺德的《文化与无政府状态》《批评文集》(*Essays in Criticism*, 1865—1888)，赫胥黎的《人在自然界的位置》(*Evidence as to Man's Place in Nature*, 1863)，佩特的《文艺复兴历史研究》(*Studies in the History of the Renaissance*, 1873) 等，都因独具的风格与魅力被载入英国文学史册。佩特在《风格》(*Style*, 1888) 一文中指出散文是一门特殊的、恰好适合现代世界的艺术，它更适于反映现代生活"混乱的多样性和复杂性"。散文家们对这一时代作出各种各样的反应，以不同的风格在混乱中寻求秩序。卡莱尔在《论英雄、英雄崇拜和历史上的英雄业绩》("On Heroes, Hero-Worship, and the Heroic in History", 1841) 中非常强调作家的责任，他的写作追求一种预言家的效果，而罗斯金更是事事都发表独到的见解，散文的内容涉及宗教、政治、经济、美学及现实生活的各个方面，说理方式也各不相同。穆勒和赫胥黎依靠思路清晰的逻辑推理，模仿18世纪散文家崇尚的理智、明快的文风，作品不带浪漫主义的感情色彩。卡莱尔和罗斯金则更靠近17世纪的文风，他们所谓的复调风格对读者的眼睛和耳朵都有一种感染力，以生动的综合效果打动读者的心弦。

维多利亚时代是一个几乎人人读小说的时代。由于受清教道德标准的约束，在维多利亚早期和中期的文学作品中仍存在一定程度的内容禁忌。维多利亚早期、中期的小说家们在“大众读者口味的期待下，在中产阶级道德的禁锢和出版形式（分期连载）的限制下创造了伟大的艺术，在精神上孕育了一代又一代的人们。”许多评论家认为：“从奥斯汀理性的嘲讽到司各特浪漫情怀的历史透视，从勃朗特姐妹奔放的想象到盖斯凯尔忠实朴素的描摹，从狄更斯的夸张与象征到萨克雷、艾略特的心理分析。总之，从狄更斯到艾略特的一代小说家谱写了英国小说史上最辉煌的一页”。

换言之，自从狄更斯在维多利亚女王即位的同年发表第一部小说起，小说领域里就新人辈出，争奇斗艳。19 世纪 40 年代出现了勃朗特姐妹的《简 · 爱》和《呼啸山庄》(*Wuthering Heights*, 1847)，19 世纪 50 年代威廉 · 麦克皮斯 · 萨克雷 (William Makepeace Thackeray, 1811—1863) 以其《名利场》向魅力经久不衰的狄更斯提出挑战，19 世纪 60 年代特罗洛普成为描绘维多利亚中期社会现实的“肖像画大师”，19 世纪 70 年代乔治·艾略特 (George Eliot, 1819—1880) 发表了她的传世之作《米德尔马契》(*Middlemarch*, 1871—1872)，19 世纪 80 年代《自私自利的人》(*The Egoist*, 1879) 的作者梅瑞狄斯和巴特勒开始受到广泛关注，19 世纪 90 年代托马斯 · 哈代 (Thomas Hardy, 1840—1928) 的一系列富有悲剧色彩的“威塞克斯”小说为维多利亚时代的小说画上了一个圆满的句号。当然，梅瑞狄斯、哈代和巴特勒生活在新旧交替的转折时期，他们的创作在内容和风格上与维多利亚中期的小说家们相比，有很大不同，也有很大创新。梅瑞狄斯的小说以喜剧讽刺手法见长，是最先涉及婚外恋和妇女解放问题的作家之一。他还善于使用典故和隐喻，善于对人物进行心理分析。巴特勒的小说偏重对维多利亚时代的宗教和家庭进行犀利的批判，他的《埃瑞璜》(*Erewhon*, 1872) 是一部讽刺社会传统的反乌托邦小说，采取颠倒和夸张的讽刺手法，埃瑞璜这一名字就来自“乌有乡”(nowhere) 一词的倒写。哈代的小说带有浓厚的乡土气息和宿命色彩，实际上这正表达了作家对工业化所造成的喧嚣和丑恶都市生活的一种反抗。他善于使用象征手法和心理描写，既继承了现实主义小说的优秀传统，又表现出一个现代作家的艺术创新。他的小说揭示社会的伪善和不公，为小人物的灾难和不幸鸣冤，然而又透射出无奈和迷惘。

毋庸置疑，维多利亚时代是英国小说发展的黄金时代。文学的繁荣也折射出这个时代的人文精神，即人们对 19 世纪不断扩展的生活画面作出了热切而积极的反应。一般认为，维多利亚时代戏剧的文学成就不能和同时期的诗歌、散文和小说相比。我们必须把剧本创作和剧院演出分开来看。维多利亚中期伦敦的剧院多如牛毛，当时看戏就像现在看电视一样普遍，但是，在众多的剧作中几乎没什么有长久价值的作品，一般都流于情节剧和传奇剧的形式，在观众中收获廉价的笑声和眼泪。直到 19 世纪 90 年代才开始出现富有生气的剧作，即王尔德和乔治·伯纳德·萧伯纳 (George Bernard Shaw, 1856—1950) 的杰作。

维多利亚时代的文学艺术之所以伟大，首先在于它对一个千变万化的世界的艺术把握和真实反映。在这个时期先后出现的文学流派有以琼斯为代表的宪章派诗歌、以狄更斯为领袖的批判现实主义小说、以罗塞蒂为旗手的前拉斐尔派诗歌、以莫里斯为代表的"乌托邦"小说、以罗伯特·路易斯·史蒂文森 (Robert Louis Stevenson, 1850—1894) 为代表的新浪漫主义小说和以王尔德为首的唯美主义文学，它们都在英国文学史上写下了浓墨重彩的篇章。

Alfred, Lord Tennyson

1809—1892

阿尔弗雷德·丁尼生出生在林肯郡 (Lincoinshire) 一个文化气氛浓郁的牧师家庭。父亲乔治·丁尼生博览群书，能诗会画，母亲亦钟爱诗歌。在这样的家庭气氛的熏陶下，丁尼生从小就对诗歌创作产生了浓厚的兴趣，8 岁开始写诗，14 岁时创作了一部 6000 余行的史诗和一部无韵诗剧。1827 年，18 岁的丁尼生发表了他和两位哥哥合作的处女作《兄弟诗集》(*Poems by Two Brothers*)，其中多为丁尼生所作。21 岁时丁尼生又发表了独立完成的《抒情诗集》(*Poems, Chiefly Lyrical*, 1830)。这些早期诗歌虽然过于追求形式与技巧的效果而失之自然，有时甚至显得十分稚嫩，但也充分表现了丁尼生在诗歌方面的天赋，其中《玛丽安娜》("Mariana")、《追思天方夜谭》("Recollections of the Arabian Nights") 等写得尤为出色。1842 年，丁尼生创作发表了两卷本的《诗集》(*Poems*)，确立了他在英国诗坛上的地位。

两卷本《诗集》的第一卷为《抒情诗集》中部分经过修改后的优秀作品，如《夏洛特女郎》("The Lady of Shalott")、《食落拓枣者》("The Lotos Eaters") 等；第二卷则收录了丁尼生在 1832 年至 1842 年间创作的新诗，其中十分著名的有《尤利西斯》("Ulysses")、《提托诺斯》("Tithonus")、《洛克斯利庄园》("Locksley Hall") 等。除了这些以古希腊、古罗马神话为题材的诗歌外，两卷本《诗集》中还有一些抒情短诗也写得相当出色，如《溅吧，溅吧，溅吧》("Break, Break, Break") 和《圣阿格尼斯前夜》("St. Agnes' Eve") 等。

1832 年的《抒情诗集》和 1842 年的两卷本《诗集》代表了丁尼生诗歌创作的第一时期。五年后，丁尼生发表了他的第一部叙事长诗《公主》，开始了他第二时期的创作。在这一时期，丁尼生一共创作了三部叙事长诗和一部悼亡诗集，标志着他诗歌创作生涯的鼎盛期。1850 年发表的《悼念集》(*In Memoriam*)，由 700 个四行诗节组成，分为 133 首，不仅是英国文学史上最长的，也是和弥尔顿的《黎西达斯》，雪莱的《阿道尼斯》齐名的最伟大的挽诗之一，其诗体被称为悼念诗体。《悼念集》发表的同年，丁尼生继任华兹华斯被授予"桂冠诗人"的称号。

1855 年，丁尼生发表了他的第二部叙事长诗《摩德》。这是一部由许多韵律不一的抒情短诗组成的单人剧 (monodrama)。诗人通过青年之口谴责了当时道德沦丧、世风日下的社会现实。1859 年，丁尼生在自己 50 周岁那年发表了以亚瑟王和圆桌骑士的故事为情节的《国王诗歌》(*Idylls of the King*)，获得了多数读者的好评，但也受到了当时一些著名评论家，如李·亨特、约翰·斯特林 (John Sterling, 1806—1844) 等人的批评。

《公主》《悼念集》《摩德》和《国王诗歌》四部长诗代表着丁尼生诗歌创作的鼎盛时期。此后，丁尼生的文学创作进入了最后一个阶段，其创作兴趣和重点也从诗歌转移到戏剧。从 1875 年的《玛丽女王》(*Queen Mary*) 到 1892 年的《看林人》(*The Foresters*) 这十七年间，丁尼生陆续创作了 7 部剧作。除了《猎鹰》(*The Falcon*, 1884) 在伦敦的圣詹姆士剧院小获成功外，丁尼生的其他 6 部剧作几乎都是在舞台上匆匆过场，然后便销声匿迹。作为一位舞台剧作家，丁尼生是不成功的。然而在这一时期，丁尼生也创作了一些优秀的叙事长诗，其中最著名的是无韵诗《伊诺克·阿登》(*Enoch Arden*，1864)。在这部长诗中，丁尼生一反以往创作叙事长诗采用古代或贵族题材的惯例，取材民间，贴近生活，讲述老百姓的故事，表现普通人的情感，因此在发售的当天上午即销出 16000 余册，一时洛阳纸贵，好评如潮。丁尼生也因此获得了“人民诗人”(the Poet of the People) 的美誉。

1884 年丁尼生在先后两次推辞后终于接受了女王封予的“男爵”头衔，成为英国历史上进入贵族院的唯一一位诗人。1892 年 10 月 6 日，丁尼生与世长辞，安葬在伦敦西敏寺的诗人角。

Ulysses

【题解】

尤利西斯是荷马史诗《奥德赛》中的英雄。“尤利西斯”是《奥德塞》中“奥德修斯”的拉丁文名。在特洛伊战争中，他巧施木马计，攻下了特洛伊城，随后胜利回国。但是丁尼生笔下的尤利西斯还有一个更重要的来源，即但丁《神曲·地狱篇》第 26 歌。根据但丁的描写，尤利西斯虽然回到伊萨卡重登王位，却不甘庸碌，渴望再度出海西征。尽管此时已鬓发斑白，但他追求知识、探索未知世界的雄心依然不减。然而丁尼生的尤利西斯又不是但丁式的尤利西斯，因为但丁笔下的尤利西斯虽渴望出征，却常常因远离家人而受到良心的自责。丁尼生笔下的尤利西斯则把外出冒险去征服未知世界当成生活的最终目标。他豪迈地宣称：“我不能歇下而不去远行，我要把 / 生命之酒喝个点滴不剩”，追求知识必须“像追求正在下坠的星星”。

尤利西斯的冒险精神与探索情结实际反映了丁尼生 1834 年创作这首诗时的心

态。当时正值挚友哈勒姆去世不久，巨大的悲痛促使丁尼生拿起笔写下了这首激情满怀的诗篇，通过表现尤利西斯对出征的渴求倾诉了自己决心抛弃一切去探索世界、与生活抗争的冲动。在和同代作家詹姆士·谢尔顿·诺尔斯 (James Sheridan Knowles, 1784—1862) 的一次谈话中，他曾明确表示《尤利西斯》在很大程度上表现了他自己当时的心境：一方面，哈勒姆的去世摧毁了他的世界；但另一方面，他仍将在生活中不断奋斗，直至生命终结。由此可见，尤利西斯的追求也正是丁尼生本人的追求。

《尤利西斯》是一首以无韵体写成的戏剧独白 (dramatic monologue)，其风格严峻、朴实，是丁尼生早期诗作中比较成功的一篇。

Ulysses

It little profits that an idle king[1],
By this still hearth, among these barren crags,
Matched with an aged wife, I mete and dole[2]
Unequal laws[3] unto a savage race,
That hoard, and sleep, and feed, and know not me.

I cannot rest from travel; I will drink
Life to the lees[4]. All times I have enjoyed
Greatly, have suffered greatly, both with those
That loved me, and alone; on shore, and when
Through scudding drifts[5] the rainy Hyades[6]
Vexed the dim sea. I am become a name[7];
For always roaming with a hungry heart
Much have I seen and known—cities of men
And manners, climates, councils, governments,
Myself not least[8], but honored of them all—
And drunk delight of battle with my peers,
Far on the ringing plains of windy Troy[9].
I am a part of all that I have met;
Yet all experience is an arch wherethrough
Gleams that untraveled world whose margin fades

Forever and forever when I move.
How dull it is to pause, to make an end,
To rust unburnished, not to shine in use!
As though to breathe were life! Life piled on life
Were all too little, and of one to me
Little remains[10]; but every hour is saved
From that eternal silence, something more,
A bringer of new things; and vile it were
For some three suns[11] to store and hoard myself,
And this gray spirit[12] yearning in desire
To follow knowledge like a sinking star,
Beyond the utmost bound of human thought.

This is my son, mine own Telemachus[13],
To whom I leave the scepter and the isle[14]—
Well-loved of me, discerning to fulfill
This labor[15], by slow prudence to make mild
A rugged people, and through soft degrees
Subdue them to the useful and the good.
Most blameless is he, centered in the sphere
Of common duties, decent not to fail
In offices of tenderness, and pay
Meet adoration to my household gods,
When I am gone. He works his work, I mine.

There lies the port; the vessel puffs her sail;
There gloom the dark, broad seas. My mariners,
Souls that have toiled, and wrought, and thought with me—
That ever with a frolic welcome took
The thunder and the sunshine, and opposed
Free hearts, free foreheads[16]—you and I are old;
Old age hath yet his honor and his toil.
Death closes all; but something ere the end,

Some work of noble note, may yet be done,
Not unbecoming men that strove with Gods[17].
The lights begin to twinkle from the rocks;
The long day wanes; the slow moon climbs; the deep
Moans round with many voices. Come, my friends,
'Tis not too late to seek a newer world.
Push off, and sitting well in order smite
The sounding furrows[18]; for my purpose holds
To sail beyond the sunset, and the baths
Of all the western stars[19], until I die.
It may be that the gulfs will wash us down;
It may be we shall touch the Happy Isles[20],
And see the great Achilles[21], whom we knew.
Though much is taken, much abides[22]; and though
We are not now that strength which in old days
Moved earth and heaven, that which we are[23], we are—
One equal temper of heroic hearts,
Made weak by time and fate, but strong in will
To strive, to seek, to find, and not to yield.

【注解】

1. an idle king: 即 Ithaca 国王尤利西斯。
2. mete and dole: 相当于 measure and give out, "mete" 为 measure 的古语形式。
3. Unequal laws: 不公正的法律。这里的意思是由于他的臣民只知道吃、睡，因此不配享有公正的法律。另一种观点认为 unequal laws 的意思是褒奖与惩罚 (rewards and punishments)。
4. to the lees: 我要把生命之酒喝个点滴不剩，"lees" 作残渣解。
5. scudding drifts: 阵阵的雨雾。
6. the rainy Hyades: 毕宿星团，位于金牛座 (Taurus) 中，由两百多颗星星组成。Hyades 在希腊语中意思是下雨天，因为毕宿星团升起时就预示要下雨，故诗中有 "the rainy Hyades" 一说。
7. I am become a name: 有两种解释，一是说由于多年在外，我只不过名义上在此而已；二是说我多年在外闯荡，已获得了名声。
8. Myself not least: 我不是个无名之辈。
9. Troy: 此处指特洛伊战场。
10. Life piled on life . . . Little remains: 一个人活上几世也不嫌多，何况我只有一次生命，此时也余日无多了。

11. three suns: 相当于 three years。
12. gray spirit: 年迈的心灵。因尤利西斯年事已高，故用 "gray" 一词。
13. Telemachus: 尤利西斯的儿子，尤利西斯回国时他已长大成人，可以独自治理国家。
14. the isle: Ithaca。
15. This labor: 这项重任，即指下文所说的 "to make mild /A rugged people" 等。
16. opposed/Free hearts, free foreheads: opposed with free hearts，以开朗的心胸，自由的头脑抗争。
17. strove with Gods: 与诸神较量。这里的诸神指的是当初帮助特洛伊人抗击希腊联军的众神。"strive" 作 struggle 或 compete 解。
18. smite . . . / The sounding furrows: 划出哗哗作响的桨迹。
19. the baths/Of all the western stars: 古希腊人认为，地球是一个圆形的平面，四周则是大洋 (the baths)，星星坠落时都没入水中。
20. the Happy Isles: 古希腊人心目中的极乐世界，荷马将其放在非洲西海岸外的大西洋中。据说有德之人死后均可前往居住。
21. Achilles: 阿喀琉斯，著名的希腊英雄，在特洛伊战争中立下赫赫战功，后被帕里斯 (Paris) 一箭射中脚后跟而死。他死后，他的武器被授予尤利西斯。
22. Though much is taken, much abides: 尽管已耗去了许多，但仍有不少精力。另一种解释是尽管已知道了许多，但仍有不少新事物值得我们去探索。
23. that which we are: 这里的 that 指下行 "One equal temper of heroic hearts"。

【思考题】

1. What kind of life has Ulysses now on the Island of Ithaca? What was his life like in the past, before he returned home from the Trojan War? What is Ulysses' attitude toward life?
2. What do you think of Ulysses' desire to abdicate his duties as the king of Ithaca? Is he being irresponsible? Defend your answer.
3. When Ulysses says in line 43, "He works his work, I mine," what does he mean?
4. At the end of the poem, Ulysses decides not to yield. Yield to what?
5. What are the similarities and differences between Ulysses and the Chinese figure Kuafu, who dies by chasing the sun?

解读举例

1. 古希腊神话中的尤利西斯在丁尼生诗中象征着永远在探索的人类。诗的三个部分表现了主角对往日辉煌的回忆，和对自己的王位后继有人感到放心，并激励人们去奋斗、探索、发现。

2. 《尤利西斯》表现了尤利西斯本人对逝去岁月的怀恋，对继续游历的幻想和对死亡的渴求。在诗的第一、二部分，尤利西斯表达了对现实的不满，但又无法重现往日的光荣，因此在第三部分，他幻想着自己去探索一个“更新的世界”(a newer world)——死亡。

Crossing the Bar

【题解】

1889 年，80 岁高龄的丁尼生在乘船横渡索伦海峡 (The Solent Channel) 时写下了这首脍炙人口的小诗《过沙洲》。诗中，作者用隐喻的手法生动地表达了自己对死亡的渴求，因为通过死亡，作者不仅可以获得永久的安宁，还可以面见自己的领航人。尽管《过沙洲》并不是丁尼生的绝笔，但他生前曾要求后人在编纂自己的诗集时将此诗作为压卷之作放在最后。

Crossing the Bar[1]

Sunset and evening star,
And one clear call for me!
And may there be no moaning of the bar,
When I put out to sea,

But such a tide as moving seems asleep,
Too full for sound and foam,
When that[2] which drew from out the boundless deep
Turn again home.

Twilight and evening bell,
And after that the dark!
And may there be no sadness of farewell,
When I embark;

For though from out our bourne[3] of Time and Place

The flood may bear me far,
I hope to see my Pilot[4] face to face
When I have crossed the bar.

【注解】

1. Bar: 沙洲，即河道或港口泥沙淤积处，涨潮时沙洲没入水中，退潮时可部分裸露出来。这种沙洲往往会阻碍船只的顺利通行，因此在诗中常常被喻为“生死关口”。
2. that: 指上文中的“tide”，也指人的灵魂。
3. bourne: 相当于 boundary。
4. Pilot: 上帝。

【思考题】

1. What overall mood and atmosphere does Tennyson create in this poem? How do the images of sunset, evening star, the tide and the sea, etc. contribute to this mood and atmosphere?
2. Instead of saying death directly, Tennyson uses a metaphor. What is the metaphor? How effective is it used?
3. What is Tennyson's attitude towards death?

Robert Browning
1812—1889

作者简介

罗伯特·勃朗宁出生于伦敦郊外一个银行职员家庭。父亲博览群书，爱好文学，藏书六千余册，且多为音乐、文学、艺术类。在这样一个文学气氛浓郁的家庭中，勃朗宁自幼就喜爱上了文学艺术，据说他 5 岁开始作诗，12 岁便集诗成册，取名《杂凑集》(*Incondita*)，其中只有两首保留了下来。1833 年，21 岁的勃朗宁以匿名形式发表了第一部诗集《波琳》(*Pauline*)，因诗中流露出来的“强烈、颓废的自我意识”而受到哲学家约翰·斯图亚特·穆勒的尖锐批评，促使勃朗宁在后来的创作中摈弃了主观的创作方法，以尽可能客观地表现生活体验。1835 年发表的戏剧诗《巴拉塞尔士》(*Paracelsus*) 受到了评论界的好评，勃朗宁也因此结识了当时文学界的一些名人，如传记作家约翰·福斯特 (John

Forster, 1812—1876)、散文作家卡莱尔、诗人丁尼生、小说家狄更斯等。

从 1837 年到 1847 年的十年间，勃朗宁遵从演员马克莱地 (W. C. Macready, 1793—1873) 的劝告，专心致力于戏剧创作，并于 1837 年推出了他创作的第一部诗剧《斯特拉福》(*Strafford*)。该剧在伦敦大剧院仅公演了四天。尽管勃朗宁的戏剧创作并不成功，但他把创作戏剧对白的经验运用到诗歌创作中，创造出一种“戏剧独白”(dramatic monologue) 的诗歌形式。用勃朗宁自己的话说，戏剧独白就是让各种想象中的人物自由地发表各种言论，而这些想象中的人物常常以历史或绘画作品的主人公为原形，向某个听众发表自己的想法，倾诉自己的心声。1842 年勃朗宁发表了第一个戏剧独白集《戏剧抒情诗》(*Dramatis Lyrics*)，标志着他的诗歌创作开始走向成熟。

1845 年，勃朗宁结识了女诗人伊丽莎白·芭莱特 (Elizabeth Barrett,1806—1861)。尽管后者比他年长 6 岁，且患有残疾，但并不能阻止勃朗宁坠入情网，于是他们不顾芭莱特父亲的反对，于 1846 年秋私下结婚，并私奔到意大利比萨，后移居欧洲文艺复兴的发源地佛罗伦萨，直至 1861 年勃朗宁夫人去世为止。这一时期是勃朗宁诗歌创作的重要时期。正是在这一时期，勃朗宁创作了他最具代表性的一部诗集《男男女女》(*Men and Women*, 1855)。1861 年勃朗宁夫人去世，勃朗宁回到伦敦，开始创作另一部戏剧独白诗集《戏剧人物》(*Dramatis Personae*，1864)。1868 至 1869 年，勃朗宁以连载的形式发表了自己最庞大的一部作品《环与书》。这是一部长达 12 卷、共 21000 行的无韵诗，系根据一本记载 17 世纪罗马一次凶杀审判过程的旧书改编而成，读起来像是一本维多利亚时代的小说，但其多视角的叙述手法又预示了现代小说的创作技巧。《环与书》的出版确立了勃朗宁在 19 世纪英国诗坛上的重要地位。此后的二十年间，勃朗宁又创作发表了《巴劳斯钦历险记》(*Balaustion's Adventure*, 1871) 等 15 部作品。1889 年，72 岁的勃朗宁卒于意大利水城威尼斯，遗体运回国内，葬于西敏寺。

勃朗宁对英国诗歌的最大贡献是他的戏剧独白诗体。虽然丁尼生等人也曾多次用过这一诗歌体裁，但将这一形式发展完善的是勃朗宁。勃朗宁早年深受拜伦、雪莱等浪漫主义诗人的影响，但他的戏剧独白诗则主要吸收了莎剧独白的特点。在语言风格方面，勃朗宁效法玄学派诗人多恩，摈弃圆润、和谐、优美的传统诗歌风格，大量采用口语体，其音韵节奏也常常佶屈聱牙，生硬刺耳，招来许多批评。美国哈佛大学教授桑塔雅那曾斥勃朗宁为一个“笨拙的野蛮人”(a clumsy barbarian)。然而勃朗宁独特的诗歌创作方法与风格对 20 世纪诗歌创作产生了重大影响。这主要表面在两个方面：首先，勃朗宁的主要诗作运用戏剧独白的形式，着重刻画了人物的内心世界；其次，他的诗歌着重挖掘语言内涵，运用多重叙述，客观地表现人物思想与主题。所有这些都影响到了20世纪以庞德、艾略特等人为代表的现代派诗歌的创作。与维多利亚时代的桂冠诗人丁尼生相比，勃朗宁的诗歌成就与名声可能要逊色得多，但他对现代诗歌的影响却是任何一位维多利亚诗人所无法比拟的。

My Last Duchess

【题解】

《我已故的公爵夫人》是勃朗宁早期创作的戏剧独白，也是他最为人熟知的一首作品。该诗根据意大利费拉拉公爵阿方索二世(Alfonso Ⅱ, Duke of Ferrara)生活中一个真实事件改编而成。费拉拉公爵是意大利文艺复兴时期的一位权势人物，他的第一任妻子在婚后不到三年便离开人世，公爵开始考虑再婚。在本诗中，公爵一边领媒人观看自己前妻的肖像，一边谈论自己与公爵夫人的婚姻生活。通过公爵的戏剧独白，读者得以了解他前妻的品性为人。

如同勃朗宁的多数戏剧独白诗，《我已故的公爵夫人》用简单易懂的口语体写成，但由于说话人的叙述不可靠，因此诗中简明的语言极具讽刺意味。

My Last Duchess

Ferrara[1]

That's my last Duchess painted on the wall,
Looking as if she were alive. I call
That piece a wonder, now: Fra Pandolf's[2] hands
Worked busily a day, and there she stands.
Will't please you sit and look at her? I said
"Fra Pandolf" by design, for never read
Strangers like you that pictured countenance,
The depth and passion of its earnest glance,
But to myself they turned (since none puts by
The curtain I have drawn for you, but I)
And seemed as they would ask me, if they durst,
How such a glance came there; so, not the first
Are you to turn and ask thus. Sir, 'twas not

Her husband's presence only, called that spot
Of joy into the Duchess' cheek; perhaps
Fra Pandolf chanced to say, "Her mantle laps
Over my lady's wrist too much," or "Paint
Must never hope to reproduce the faint
Half flush that dies along her throat." Such stuff
Was courtesy, she thought, and cause enough
For calling up that spot of joy. She had
A heart—how shall I say?—too soon made glad,
Too easily impressed; she liked whate'er
She looked on, and her looks went everywhere.
Sir, 'twas all one! My favour[3] at her breast,
The dropping of the daylight in the West,
The bough of cherries some officious[4] fool
Broke in the orchard for her, the white mule
She rode with round the terrace—all and each[5]
Would draw from her alike the approving speech,
Or blush, at least. She thanked men—good! but thanked
Somehow—I know not how—as if she ranked
My gift of a nine-hundred-years-old name
With anybody's gift. Who'd stoop to blame
This sort of trifling? Even had you skill
In speech—which I have not—to make your will
Quite clear to such an one, and say, "Just this
Or that in you disgusts me; here you miss,
Or there exceed the mark"—and if she let
Herself be lessoned so, nor plainly set
Her wits to yours, forsooth[6], and made excuse
—E'en then would be some stooping; and I choose
Never to stoop. Oh, sir, she smiled, no doubt,
Whene'er I passed her; but who passed without
Much the same smile? This grew; I gave commands;
Then all smiles stopped together. There she stands

As if alive[7]. Will 't please you rise? We'll meet
The company below, then. I repeat,
The Count[8] your master's known munificence
Is ample warrant that no just pretense
Of mine for dowry will be disallowed;
Though his fair daughter's self, as I avowed
At starting, is my object. Nay, we'll go
Together down[9], sir. Notice Neptune[10], though,
Taming a sea horse, thought a rarity,
Which Claus of Innsbruck[11] cast in bronze for me!

【注解】

1. Ferrara: 意大利文艺复兴时期的一座名城。
2. Fra Pandolf: 传说中意大利文艺复兴时期的一位修士画家。"Fra" 意为 brother。
3. favour: 相当于 ornament。
4. officious: 过分殷勤的。
5. all and each: 指上文中的 "My favor" "officious fool" "white mule"。
6. forsooth: 相当于 indeed，多用于讽刺或反语中的插入语。
7. I gave commands . . . as if alive: 这几行是否暗示公爵谋害了公爵夫人？与勃朗宁同时代的 Hiram Corsom 教授曾就这个问题请教勃朗宁，诗人沉吟片刻肯定地说："Yes, I meant that the commands were that she should be put to death."。但诗人随即又说："Or he might have had her shut up in a convent."。这说明诗人本人也不能肯定公爵夫人到底出了什么事。
8. The Count: 相当于 Count of Tyrol， 他的侄女将嫁给公爵为妻。
9. Nay, we'll go/Together down: 出于礼貌，媒人走在了公爵后面，因此公爵请他一起走，以示尊重。
10. Neptune: 尼普顿，罗马神话中的海神。下楼前，公爵让媒人顺便看一眼海神尼普顿的铜像。
11. Claus of Innsbruck: 传说中的雕塑家。据说 Count of Tyrol 的首府就在 Innsbruck。

【思考题】

1. To whom is the Duke speaking? What is the occasion? Are the Duke's remarks about his last Duchess a digression, or do they have some relation to the business at hand?
2. Characterize the Duke as much as you can. How does your characterization differ from the Duke's opinion of himself? What is the irony?
3. What passages in the Duke's monologue suggest that he is an intelligent, cultivated Renaissance nobleman? What passages suggest that he is egotistical, tyrannical, and ruthless?

4. Why was the Duke dissatisfied with his last Duchess? What opinion do you derive from the Duchess's personality, and how does it differ from the Duke's opinion?
5. What can we infer from lines 45–46 about the Duchess's fate? Why do you think Browning suggests this fate so indirectly and ambiguously?
6. At the end of the poem, the Duke asks the envoy to notice another work of art, a bronze sculpture showing "Neptune . . . /Taming a sea horse . . . " (lines 54–55). What does this work of art suggest about the theme of the poem as a whole?

解读举例

1. 《我已故的公爵夫人》中的公爵虽贵为王侯，却是个缺乏人性的暴君。他思想肤浅，心胸狭窄，无端猜忌公爵夫人，甚至不惜诉诸暴力，一个最好的证据便是他对媒人说的悄悄话。而公爵夫人却是一个可爱、活泼、天真的女人，其唯一过错便是向每一个对她好的人报以感激的微笑。

2. 《我已故的公爵夫人》中的公爵虽贵为王侯，也免不了遭人误解。公爵实际为人谦和，富有人情味，这从他对媒人的尊重就可以看出。此外，虽然他说自己不善言辞，实际却举止高雅，不失君子风度。而公爵夫人却看不到自己丈夫的这些高贵品行，与别人眉来眼去，搔首弄姿，因此她的结局是咎由自取。

Home Thoughts, From Abroad

【题解】

尽管这首诗题为“异国思故乡”，实际却创作于1845年，当时勃朗宁与伊丽莎白·芭蕾特还未离开英国。诗中，勃朗宁情真意切地描写了一位远在他乡的英国人在春天来临之际，触景生情，深深思念祖国的情景。此外，该诗还是一幅优美的英国乡村风景画。

Home Thoughts, from Abroad

Oh, to be in England[1]
Now that April's there,

And whoever wakes in England
Sees, some morning, unaware,
That the lowest boughs and the brushwood sheaf[2]
Round the elm tree bole are in tiny leaf,
While the chaffinch sings on the orchard bough
In England—now!

And after April, when May follows,
And the whitethroat builds, and all the swallows!
Hark, where my blossomed pear tree in the hedge
Leans to the field and scatters on the clover
Blossoms and dewdrops—at the bent spray's edge—
That's the wise thrush; he sings each song twice over,
Lest you should think he never could recapture
The first fine careless rapture!
And though the fields look rough with hoary dew,
All will be gay when noontide wakes anew
The buttercups, the little children's dower
—Far brighter than this gaudy melon flower[3]!

【注解】

1. Oh, to be in England: 这是一个表达强烈愿望的虚拟语气，意思是"哦，现在要在英国该多好啊！"
2. brushwood sheaf: 这里的brushwood sheaf及后面的"elm tree"(line 6)、"chaffinch"(line 7)、"whitethroat"(line 10)等都是英国乡村常见的植物与飞鸟。
3. melon flower: 生长于欧洲南部亚热带地区的花，此处喻指意大利。

【思考题】

1. It is often true that we do not appreciate the beauty of places we are familiar with until we are away from them. Does this seem the case with the speaker in this poem?
2. Can you list several Chinese Poems that describe homesickness? What are differences between them and this poem?
3. Browning makes a contrast between the "buttercups" and the "gaudy melon flower" at the end of the poem. What is his intention?

Charles Dickens
1812—1870

作者简介

查尔斯·狄更斯出生于英国朴次茅斯市外的一个海港小镇。父亲约翰·狄更斯供职于海军部，每年有几百英镑的收入，但因其挥霍无度，家庭常陷于拮据境地。狄更斯从小病弱，但酷爱读书，从父亲的藏书中读到很多优秀文学作品。9 岁时狄更斯全家迁往伦敦。不久，因父亲偿不起债务入狱，全家也随之迁入债务人监狱。年仅 11 岁的狄更斯被送进一家鞋油作坊做工。家庭的变故把幼小的狄更斯抛进了社会的底层，他开始亲身体验穷人悲惨、贫困的生活。后来，他父亲意外地得到一笔不大的遗产，还债出狱，狄更斯也进入学校读书。这一段辛酸的经历在他心灵上留下了难以磨灭的印记。15 岁时，由于家庭经济紧张，狄更斯辍学到一家律师事务所当缮写员，在业余时间学会了速记，并经常去大英博物馆读书，后又当过法庭速记员。19 岁时，他成为一名记者，专门采写法律界的新闻，也因此接触到各色人物，体验到人情世态的虚伪、贫富的悬殊、法律的黑暗和官场的腐败。这些经历为他日后的文学创作积累了丰富的素材，也极大地影响了他的政治观点。

1833 年狄更斯发表了第一篇讽刺幽默短文，以后经常在报纸杂志上发表特写、短篇故事和描写性散文，1836 年他把这些作品收集出版，即《博兹特写集》(*Sketches by Boz*, 1836)。同年他与出版商的女儿凯瑟琳·霍加斯结婚。1836 年至 1837 年间，狄更斯的第一部长篇作品《匹克威克外传》(*Pickwick Papers*) 连载出版，获得很高声誉。1842 年，狄更斯访问了美国。半年的游历使他对美国的民主和自由大失所望，回国后发表了两部小说，讽刺美国社会中贪污腐化、种族歧视、金钱万能等种种丑恶现象。1846 年狄更斯创办了进步报纸《每日邮报》。狄更斯一生不知疲倦地写作，精力过人，多才多艺，但晚年积劳成疾，于 1870 年 6 月 9 日猝然离世，葬于伦敦西敏寺的诗人角。

狄更斯一生共写有十九部长篇小说、两部礼记和一部儿童英国诗，以及大量中短篇小说、散文、书信和演说词，其创作大致可分为三个时期。第一时期为 1833 年至 1841 年，主要作品有幽默辛辣的《匹克威克外传》，描写孤儿生活的《雾都孤儿》(*Oliver Twist*, 1837—1839)，揭露教育制度黑暗的《尼古拉斯·尼克贝尔》(*Nicholas Nickleby*, 1838—1839)，反映小私有者悲惨命运的《老古玩店》(*The Old Curiosity*

Shop, 1840—1841)，以及以英国发生的"戈登暴乱"为题材的历史小说《巴纳比·拉奇》(*Barnaby Rudge*, 1841)。在这些作品中，作者对资本主义的阴暗面加以揭露和讽刺，但对社会的批判较为温和，他认为罪恶的根源往往归于个别坏人，而法律是正义的维护者和执行者。这一时期的作品还存在着结构松散、描写冗长等缺点。

1842 年至 1850 年是他创作的第二时期。这个时期的作品除了狄更斯访美后写的《游美札记》(*American Notes*, 1842) 和《马丁·朱述尔唯特》(*Martin Chuzzlewit*, 1843—1844) 外，还有《圣诞故事集》(*Christmas Tales*, 1843—1848)、《董贝父子》(*Dombey and Son*, 1846—1848) 和《大卫·科波菲尔》。此时狄更斯开始把批判对准金钱统治和唯利是图等资产阶级痼疾，人物形象也更具社会意义。在艺术手法上，该时期的作品注重故事的完整性，人物语言也更个性化。

1851 年至 1870 年是狄更斯创作的第三时期，也是最后一个时期。他将笔锋指向资本主义社会的要害之处，批判的深度和广度都超过了以前的作品。此时期作品包括《荒凉山庄》(*Bleak House*, 1852—1853)、《艰难时事》(*Hard Times*, 1854)、《小杜丽》(*Little Dorrit*, 1855—1857)、《双城记》(*A Tale of Two Cities*, 1859)、《远大前程》(*Great Expectations*, 1860—1861) 等。这一时期的小说悲剧色彩更为浓厚，讽刺也更为尖刻，幽默则有所减弱，"快乐的结局"也不再那么快乐。在技巧上，晚期小说比前期连贯，情节和主题的关系更为密切，常用贯穿全书的形象或象征来表现小说的主题。

David Copperfield

【题解】

《大卫·科波菲尔》是狄更斯的自传体小说，书中大量描写了作者的亲身经历。在小说序言里，狄更斯写道："在我所有的著作中，我最喜爱这一部……正如许多溺爱子女的父母，我在内心深处有一个宠爱的孩子，他的名字就是'大卫·科波菲尔'。"小说以孤儿大卫·科波菲尔的成长和遭遇为主要线索，通过主人公的自述，展开丰富有趣的情节。

大卫是个遗腹子，年轻而软弱的母亲改嫁富商摩德斯通先生 (Mr. Murdstone)，从此母子俩受尽摩德斯通及他的姐姐摩德斯通小姐的欺凌。大卫被送进了寄宿学校，母亲在家终日受气，抑郁而死。之后，年仅 10 岁的大卫被送到伦敦一家啤酒作坊当童工，寄居在穷跑街的密考伯先生 (Micawber) 家中。他不堪忍受当童工的劳累和屈辱，逃出伦敦，投奔从未见过面的有钱的姨婆 (Betsey Trotwood)，在她供养之下读书成人，并且靠着自己努力逐渐在创作上取得成就，开始走上成名的道路。他与律师的女儿、美丽的朵拉 (Dora) 结了婚，但是特质上的差异让两人很难得到真正的幸福。娇弱的朵拉不幸早亡。在此前后，大卫的周围也发生了一系列变故。最后大卫与少年时代的朋友、善良聪慧的艾妮斯 (Agnes) 结婚，获得了真正的幸福。

小说的第十一章讲述了年幼的大卫初到伦敦当童工的经历，描述了大卫与密考伯这位可怜、可笑又可爱的人物初次会面的情景及这一家人的境遇。

From David Copperfield

Chapter 11
I Begin My Life on My Own Account, and Don't Like It
(excerpt)

No words can express the secret agony of my soul as I sunk into this companionship; compared these henceforth every-day associates with those of my happier childhood—not to say with Steerforth, Traddles, and the rest of those boys; and felt my hopes of growing up to be a learned and distinguished man, crushed in my bosom. The deep remembrance of the sense I had, of being utterly without hope now; of the shame I felt in my position; of the misery it was to my young heart to believe that day by day what I had learned, and thought, and delighted in, and raised my fancy and my emulation up by, would pass away from me, little by little, never to be brought back any more; cannot be written. As often as Mick Walker[1] went away in the course of that forenoon, I mingled my tears with the water in which I was washing the bottles; and sobbed as if there were a flaw in my own breast, and it were in danger of bursting.

The counting-house clock was at half past twelve, and there was general preparation for going away to dinner, when Mr. Quinion[2] tapped at the counting-house window, and beckoned to me to go in. I went in, and found there a stoutish, middle-aged person, in a brown surtout[3] and black tights and shoes, with no more hair upon his head (which was a large one, and very shining) than there is upon an egg,—and with a very extensive face, which he turned full upon me. His clothes were shabby, but he had an imposing shirt-collar on. He carried a jaunty sort of a stick, with a large pair of rusty tassels to it; and a quizzing-glass hung outside his coat—for ornament, I afterwards found, as he very seldom looked through it, and couldn't see anything when he did.

"This," said Mr. Quinion, in allusion to myself, "is he."

"This," said the stranger, with a certain condescending roll in his voice, and a certain indescribable air of doing something genteel, which impressed me very much, "is Master Copperfield. I hope I see you well, sir?"

I said I was very well, and hoped he was. I was sufficiently ill at ease, Heaven knows; but it was not in my nature to complain much at that time of my life, so I said I was very well, and hoped he was.

"I am," said the stranger, "thank Heaven, quite well. I have received a letter from Mr. Murdstone, in which he mentions that he would desire me to receive into an apartment in the rear of my house, which is at present unoccupied—and is, in short, to be let as a—in short," said the stranger, with a smile and in a burst of confidence, "as a bedroom—the young beginner whom I have now the pleasure to—" and the stranger waved his hand, and settled his chin in his shirt-collar.

"This is Mr. Micawber," said Mr. Quinion to me.

"Ahem!" said the stranger, "that is my name."

"Mr. Micawber," said Mr. Quinion, "is known to Mr. Murdstone. He takes orders for us on commission,[4] when he can get any. He has been written to by Mr. Murdstone, on the subject of your lodgings, and he will receive you as a lodger."

"My address," said Mr. Micawber, "is Windsor Terrace[5], City Road. I—in short," said Mr. Micawber, with the same genteel air, and in another burst of confidence—"I live there."

I made him a bow.

"Under the impression," said Mr. Micawber, "that your peregrinations in this metropolis[6] have not as yet been extensive, and that you might have some difficulty in penetrating the arcana of the Modern Babylon[7] in the direction of the City Road—in short," said Mr. Micawber, in another burst of confidence, "that you might lose yourself—I shall be happy to call this evening, and install you in the knowledge of the nearest way."

I thanked him with all my heart, for it was friendly in him to offer to take that trouble.

"At what hour," said Mr. Micawber, "Shall I—"

"At about eight," said Mr. Quinion.

"At about eight," said Mr. Micawber. "I beg to wish you good day, Mr. Quinion. I will intrude no longer."

So he put on his hat, and went out with his cane under his arm: very upright, and humming a tune when he was clear of the counting house.

Mr. Quinion then formally engaged me to be as useful as I could in the warehouse of Murdstone and Grinby, at a salary, I think, of six shillings a week. I am not clear whether it was six or seven. I am inclined to believe, from my uncertainty on this head, that it was six at first and seven afterwards. He paid me a week down (from his own pocket, I believe), and I gave Mealy sixpence out of it to get my trunk carried to Windsor Terrace at night: it being too heavy for my strength, small as it was. I paid sixpence more for my dinner, which was a meat pie and a turn at a neighboring pump[8]; and passed the hour which was allowed for that meal, in walking about the streets.

At the appointed time in the evening, Mr. Micawber reappeared. I washed my hands and face, to do the greater honor to his gentility, and we walked to our house, as I suppose I must now call it, together; Mr. Micawber impressing the names of streets, and the shapes of corner houses upon me, as we went along, that I might find my way back, easily, in the morning.

Arrived at his house in Windsor Terrace (which I noticed was shabby like himself, but also, like himself, made all the show it could), he presented me to Mrs. Micawber, a thin and faded lady, not at all young, who was sitting in the parlor (the first floor was altogether unfurnished, and the blinds were kept down to delude the neighbours), with a baby at her breast. This baby was one of twins; and I may remark here that I hardly ever, in all my experience of the family, saw both the twins detached from Mrs. Micawber at the same time. One of them was always taking refreshment.

There were two other children; Master Micawber, aged about four, and Miss Micawber, aged about three. These and a dark-complexioned young woman, with a habit of snorting, who was servant to the family, and informed me, before half an hour had expired, that she was "a Orfling[9]," and came from Saint Luke's workhouse[10], in the neighbourhood, completed the establishment. My room was at the top of the house, at the back: a close chamber; stencilled all over with an ornament which my young imagination represented as a blue muffin; and very scantily furnished.

"I never thought," said Mrs. Micawber, when she came up, twin and all, to show me the apartment, and sat down to take breath, "before I was married, when I lived with papa and mama, that I should ever find it necessary to take a lodger. But Mr. Micawber being in difficulties, all considerations of private feeling must give way."

I said: "Yes, ma'am."

"Mr. Micawber's difficulties are almost overwhelming just at present," said Mrs.

Micawber; "and whether it is possible to bring him through them, I don't know. When I lived at home with papa and mama, I really should have hardly understood what the word meant, in the sense in which I now employ it, but experientia[11] does it—as papa used to say."

I cannot satisfy myself whether she told me that Mr. Micawber had been an officer in the Marines, or whether I have imagined it. I only know that I believe to this hour that he was in the Marines once upon a time, without knowing why. He was a sort of town traveller for a number of miscellaneous houses, now; but made little or nothing of it, I am afraid.

"If Mr. Micawber's creditors will not give him time," said Mrs. Micawber, "they must take the consequences; and the sooner they bring it to an issue the better. Blood cannot be obtained from a stone, neither can anything on account be obtained at present (not to mention law expenses) from Mr. Micawber."

I never can quite understand whether my precocious self-dependence confused Mrs. Micawber in reference to my age, or whether she was so full of the subject that she would have talked about it to the very twins if there had been nobody else to communicate with, but this was the strain in which she began, and she went on accordingly all the time I knew her.

Poor Mrs.Micawber! She said she had tried to exert herself; and so, I have no doubt, she had. The center of the street-door was perfectly covered with a great brass-plate, on which was engraved "Mrs. Micawber's Boarding Establishment for Young Ladies": but I never found that any young lady had ever been to school there; or that any young lady ever came, or proposed to come; or that the least preparation was ever made to receive any young lady. The only visitors I ever saw or heard of, were creditors. They used to come at all hours, and some of them were quite ferocious. One dirty-faced man, I think he was a boot-maker, used to edge himself into the passage as early as seven o'clock in the morning, and call up the stairs to Mr. Micawber—"Come! You ain't out yet, you know. Pay us, will you? Don't hide, you know: that's mean. I wouldn't be mean if I was you. Pay us, will you? You just pay us, d'ye hear? Come!" Receiving no answer to these taunts, he would mount in his wrath to the words "swindlers" and "robbers"; and these being ineffectual too, would sometimes go to the extremity of crossing the street, and roaring up at the windows of the second floor, where he knew Mr. Micawber was. At these times, Mr. Micawber would be transported with grief and mortification, even to the length (as I was once made aware by a scream from his wife) of making motions at himself with a razor; but within half an hour afterwards, he would polish up his shoes with extraordinary pains, and go out, humming a tune with a greater air of gentility than ever. Mrs Micawber was quite as elastic. I have known her to be thrown into fainting fits by the king's taxes at three o'clock, and to eat lamb chops, breaded, and drink warm ale (paid for with two teaspoons that had gone to the pawnbroker's) at four. On one occasion, when an execution[12] had just been put in, coming home through some chance as early as six o'clock, I saw her lying (of course with a twin) under the grate in a swoon, with her hair all torn about her face; but I never knew her more cheerful than she was, that very same night, over a veal-cutlet before the kitchen fire, telling me stories about her papa and mama, and the company they used to keep.

In this house, and with this family, I passed my leisure time. My own exclusive breakfast of a penny loaf and a pennyworth of milk, I provided myself. I kept another small loaf, and a modicum of cheese, on a particular shelf of a particular cupboard, to make my supper on when I came back at night. This made a hole in the six or seven shillings, I know well; and I was out at the warehouse all day, and had to support myself on that money all the week. From Monday morning until Saturday night, I had no advice, no counsel, no encouragement, no consolation, no assistance, no support, of any kind, from any one, that I can call to mind, as I hope to go to heaven! . . .

Mr. Micawber's difficulties were an addition to the distressed state of my mind. In my forlorn state I became quite attached to the family, and used to walk about, busy with Mrs. Micawber's calculations of ways and means, and heavy with the weight of Mr. Micawber's debts. On a Saturday night, which was my grand treat,—partly because it was a great thing to walk home with six or seven shillings in my pocket, looking into the shops and thinking what such a sum would buy, and partly because I went home early,—Mrs. Micawber would make the most heart-rending confidences to me; also on a Sunday morning, when I mixed the portion of tea or coffee I had bought over-night, in a little shaving-pot, and sat late at my breakfast. It was nothing at all unusual for Mr. Micawber to sob violently at the beginning of one of these Saturday night conversations, and sing about Jack's delight being his lovely Nan[13], towards the end of it. I have known him come home to supper with a flood of tears, and a declaration that nothing was now left but a jail; and go to bed making a calculation of the expense of putting bow-windows to the house, "in case anything turned up," which was his favorite expression. And Mrs. Micawber was just the same.

A curious equality of friendship, originating, I suppose, in our respective circumstances, sprung up between me and these people, notwithstanding the ludicrous disparity in our years. But I never allowed myself to be prevailed upon to accept any invitation to eat and drink with them out of their stock (knowing that they got on badly with the butcher and baker, and had often not too much for themselves), until Mrs. Micawber took me into her entire confidence. This she did one evening as Follows:

"Master Copperfield," said Mrs. Micawber, "I make no stranger of you, and therefore do not hesitate to say that Mr. Micawber's difficulties are coming to a crisis."

It made me very miserable to hear it, and I looked at Mrs. Micawber's red eyes with the utmost sympathy.

"With the exception of the heel of a Dutch cheese—which is not adapted to the wants of a young family—" said Mrs. Micawber, "there is really not a scrap of anything in the larder. I was accustomed to speak of the larder when I lived with papa and mama, and I use the word almost unconsciously. What I mean to express, is, that there is nothing to eat in the house."

"Dear me!" I said, in great concern.

I had two or three shillings of my week's money in my pocket—from which I presume that it must have been on a Wednesday night when we held this conversation—and I hastily produced them, and with heartfelt emotion begged Mrs. Micawber to accept of them as a loan. But that lady, kissing me, and making me put them back in my pocket, replied that she couldn't think of it.

"No, my dear Master Copperfield," said she, "far be it from my thoughts! But you have a discretion beyond your years, and can render me another kind of service, if you will; and a service I will thankfully accept of."

I begged Mrs. Micawber to name it.

"I have parted with the plate myself," said Mrs. Micawber, "Six tea, two salt, and a pair of sugars,[14] I have at different times borrowed money on, in secret, with my own hands. But the twins are a great tie; and to me, with my recollections of papa and mama, these transactions are very painful. There are still a few trifles that we could part with. Mr. Micawber's feelings would never allow him to dispose of them; and Clickett"—this was the girl from the workhouse—"being of a vulgar mind, would take painful liberties if so much confidence was reposed in her. Master Copperfield, if I might ask you"—

I understood Mrs. Micawber now, and begged her to make use of me to any extent. I began to dispose of the more portable articles of property that very evening; and went out on a similar expedition almost every morning, before I went to Murdstone and Grinby's.

【注解】

1. Mick Walker: 大卫在 Murdstone and Grinby 啤酒作坊的工友。
2. Mr. Quinion: 小说中 Murdstone and Grinby 公司经营酒业的经纪人。
3. surtout: 一种袖子肥大的外套。
4. He takes orders for us on commission: 他替我们承揽订货，赚取佣金。
5. Windsor Terrace: 一排楼房的名称。英国城市中成排的住宅常以 terrace 为名。
6. your peregrinations in this metropolis: 你在这大都市里的游历。
7. penetrating the arcana of the Modern Babylon: 穿过这现代巴比伦城的迷宫。
8. a turn at a neighbouring pump: 在就近的酒店里喝上一杯。"pump"此处指汲取啤酒的桶，转指酒店。"a turn" 意为开一次龙头，即要一杯啤酒。
9. "a Orfling": 孤儿。orphan 在未受过教育的人的口语里变了形，就成了 orfling。
10. Saint Luke's workhouse: 圣路加贫民习艺所。workhouse 是英国资产阶级残酷剥削失去生活依靠的贫民的场所，根据 1843 年的《济贫法》而设，被称为"穷人的巴士底狱"(The Poor Man's Bastille)。
11. experientia: 相当于 experience，经验，这里用拉丁文以示典雅。
12. execution: 因还不起债而被没收部分家产，以拍卖抵债。
13. Jack's delight being his lovely Nan: 当时的一首流行歌曲。
14. Six tea, two salt, and a pair of sugars: 六把茶匙、两把盐匙和一把糖夹子。

【思考题】

1. Dickens is a master at creating comic and unforgettable characters, for instance, Mr. and Mrs. Micawber. How does Dickens portray Mr. Micawber in this chapter? What qualities of his character strike you most?
2. Why does the novel employ the first point of view? What are its merits and demerits?
3. Comment on the author's language. What is the level of speech, literary or colloquial? What characteristics impress you most?
4. Is child labor a unique phenomenon created by the system of capitalism? Please comment on the relationship between child labor and capitalism.

【简评】

狄更斯是英国批判现实主义的创始人和杰出代表。他善于描写儿童心理，用儿童的眼光去观察周围世界的景象，使小说更为亲切可信。他善于刻画形形色色的人物，总能从他们的容貌、举止、言语中找到充分表露其性格的特征，使他们的形象既夸张又逼真。他还是个幽默大师，总是用乐观的情绪来感染读者，又会用幽默来冲淡和回避现实社会的尖锐矛盾。狄更斯多方面的才能在《大卫·科波菲尔》这部作品里得到了充分的表现。

狄更斯笔下的人物，如密考伯夫妇等大都没有明显的性格发展变化，因而被认为是“扁形”人物或“只有二度空间”的人物。然而狄更斯为他的人物提供了一个非常典型的活动环境，这个环境中的一切都带有浓缩和夸张的特征。典型环境与人物性格的契合使狄更斯塑造的人物形象给人留下深刻的印象。

Charlotte Brontë
1816—1855

作者简介

夏洛蒂·勃朗特出生于英国北部约克郡的偏远村庄桑顿。父亲佩特里克·勃朗特博览群书，喜爱文学。夏洛蒂母亲早逝，八岁时同几个姐妹一起被送进一所为牧师之女开设的慈善学校。那里恶劣的生活条件过早地夺去了夏洛蒂两个姐姐的生命。勃朗特先生把夏洛蒂和妹妹艾米莉领回家，让她们与其他子女一起在家中念书，并亲自授课。孩子们天资聪颖，都对文学有着浓厚的兴趣。他们广泛阅读，自编手抄本刊物，共同写出许多关于安格里安王朝和冈多尔岛国的精彩故事。

1831年夏洛蒂被送往伍勒女士 (Miss Wooler) 开办的寄宿学校学习，成绩优秀。1835年她应邀重返此校当老师，并把妹妹艾米莉和安妮作为学生带在身边。她曾把几篇诗稿寄给桂冠诗人骚塞以求指教，得到的却是对妇女从事文学创作的轻蔑指责。她没有气馁，坚持写作。夏洛蒂曾两次任家庭教师。为了能自己办学，1842年2月夏洛蒂和艾米莉在姨母的赞助下去布鲁塞尔一所寄宿学校学习德语和法语，年底因姨母病危返回英国。次年夏洛蒂只身返回布鲁塞尔任英语教师，并爱上了学识渊博却早有妻室的校长黑格先生，任教期满便毅然回国。

夏洛蒂偶然发现艾米莉和安妮都在悄悄写诗，在她的倡议下，1846年三姐妹自费出版了化名诗集《柯勒、埃利斯和阿克顿·贝尔诗集》(*Poems by Currer, Ellis and Acton Bell*)。诗集虽然受到冷遇，却给她们带来精神上的安慰，正如夏洛蒂所说：“失败没有压垮我们，仅仅为了成功而奋斗本身就给人生以极大乐趣。”三姐妹开始写小说。夏洛蒂的第一部小说《教师》(*Professor*, 1857) 是根据她在布鲁塞尔的经历写成的，遭到出版商的拒绝，直到她去世之后才出版。1847 年 10 月，夏洛蒂的小说《简·爱》出版，因其题材新颖、感情真挚，立刻受到读者和多数批评家的欢迎。同年 12 月，艾米莉的小说《呼啸山庄》和安妮的小说《艾格尼丝·格雷》(*Agnes Grey*) 出版，但没有引起多大注意。1848 年，不幸接踵而来：夏洛蒂的弟弟布兰威尔首先病故，不久艾米莉和安妮也相继因肺病去世。1848 年 8 月，夏洛蒂完成小说《谢利》(*Shirley*, 1849)，出版后又获得成功。1853 年，她的最后一部小说《维莱特》(*Villette*) 问世，与此同时，她致力于两个妹妹的诗歌和小说的整理和再版工作，并写了回忆她们的文章。

1854 年，夏洛蒂与父亲的助理牧师阿瑟·贝尔·尼科尔斯 (Arthur Bell Nicholls, 1817—1906) 结婚，次年在怀孕期间染病逝世。

Jane Eyre

【题解】

《简·爱》是夏洛蒂的成名作，也是她的代表作。故事发生在 19 世纪中叶英国的一个乡村小镇。主人公简·爱是个失去双亲的孤女，被舅舅收养，寄人篱下，受到舅母和表兄、表姐的虐待，后被送进孤儿院式的慈善学校。艰辛的学校生活不仅教给了简知识，也培养了她的反抗意识。毕业后，简来到桑菲尔德庄园主罗切斯特先生家里担任家庭教师。罗切斯特被简细腻丰富的精神世界和不趋炎附势的可贵品质深深吸引；而简也在同罗切斯特的接触中窥视到他内心的痛苦，发现了与自己的精神相契合的思想，于是两人不顾地位差异相爱。就在他们举行婚礼的那天，罗切斯特早有妻室的秘密被人揭穿。原来，一直被囚禁在阁楼上的疯女人就是他的妻子，于是简毅然离开罗切斯特。在经历了流浪的种种艰辛后，饥寒交迫的简被牧师里弗斯兄妹救起，并意外地发现里弗斯兄妹是她的表亲。简的叔父在海外去世后给她留下一笔遗产，简慷慨地将其与表兄妹们平分。她的高尚品质吸引了里弗斯牧师，他向简求婚，并请求简跟他去印度传教。但是简的内心始终燃烧着对罗切斯特的爱情，她拒绝了里弗斯的请求，又重新回到罗切斯特身边。这时的桑菲尔德庄园已被疯女人放火烧掉。疯女人葬身火海，罗切斯特救她未成反被烧伤，双目失明。简并不在乎这些，和罗切斯特终成眷属。

下文选自小说第二卷第八章。该章以细腻的笔触描述了简的独立意识和追求平等的强烈愿望。

From Jane Eyre

Volume 2, Chapter 8

A splendid Midsummer shone over England: skies so pure, suns so radiant as were then seen in long succession, seldom favour, even singly, our wave-girt land[1]. It was as if a band of Italian days had come from the South, like a flock of glorious passenger birds, and lighted to rest them on the cliffs of Albion[2]. The hay was all got in; the fields round Thornfield[3] were green and shorn; the roads white and baked; the trees were in their dark prime; hedge and wood, full-leaved and deeply tinted, contrasted well with the sunny hue of the cleared meadows between.

On Midsummer-eve[4], Adele[5], weary with gathering wild strawberries in Hay-Lane half the day, had gone to bed with the sun. I watched her drop asleep, and when I left her I sought the garden.

It was now the sweetest hour of the twenty-four:—"Day its fervid fires had wasted[6]," and dew fell cool on panting plain and scorched summit. Where the sun had gone down in simple state—pure of the pomp of clouds—spread a solemn purple, burning with the light of red jewel and furnace flame at one point, on one hill-peak, and extending high and wide, soft and still softer, over half heaven. The east had its own charm of fine, deep blue, and its own modest gem, a rising and solitary star: soon it would boast the moon; but she was yet beneath the horizon.

I walked awhile on the pavement; but a subtle, well-known scent—that of a cigar—stole from some window; I saw the library casement open a handbreadth; I knew I might be watched thence; so I went apart into the orchard. No nook in the grounds more sheltered and more Eden-like; it was full of trees, it bloomed with flowers: a very high wall shut it out from the court, on one side; on the other, a beech avenue screened it from the lawn. At the bottom was a sunk fence, its sole separation from lonely fields: a winding walk, bordered with laurels and terminating in a giant horse-chestnut, circled at the base by a seat, led down to the fence. Here one could wander unseen. While such honey-dew fell, such silence reigned, such gloaming gathered, I felt as if I could haunt such shade for ever; but in threading the flower and fruit-parterres at the upper part of the enclosure, enticed there by the light the now-rising moon casts on this more open quarter, my step is stayed—not by sound, not by sight, but once more by a warning fragrance.

Sweet-briar and southern-wood, jasmine, pink, and rose have long been yielding their evening sacrifice of incense: this new scent is neither of shrub nor flower; it is—I know it well—it is Mr. Rochester's cigar. I look round and I listen. I see trees laden with ripening fruit. I hear a nightingale warbling in a wood half a mile off; no moving form is visible, no coming step audible; but that perfume increases: I must flee. I make for the wicket[7] leading to the shrubbery, and I see Mr. Rochester entering. I step aside into the ivy recess; he will not stay long: he will soon return whence he came, and if I sit still he will never see me.

But no—eventide[8] is as pleasant to him as to me, and this antique garden as attractive; and he strolls on, now lifting the gooseberry-tree branches to look at the fruit, large as plums, with which they are laden; now taking a ripe cherry from the wall; now stopping towards a knot of flowers, either to inhale their fragrance or to admire the dew-beads on their petals. A great moth goes humming by me; it alights on a plant at Mr. Rochester's foot: he sees it, and bends to examine it.

"Now, he has his back towards me," thought I, "and he is occupied too; perhaps, if I walk softly, I can slip away unnoticed."

I strode on an edging of turf that the crackle of the pebbly gravel might not betray me: he was standing among the beds at a yard or two distant from where I had to pass; the moth apparently engaged him. "I shall get by very well," I meditated. As I crossed his shadow, thrown long over the garden by the moon, not yet risen high, he said quietly without turning:—

"Jane, come and look at this fellow."

I had made no noise: he had not eyes behind—could his shadow feel? I started at first, and then I approached him.

"Look at his wings," said he, "he reminds me rather of a West Indian insect; one does not often see so large and gay a night-rover in England: there! he is flown."

The moth roamed away; I was sheepishly retreating also: but Mr. Rochester followed me, and when we reached the wicket, he said:—

"Turn back: on so lovely a night it is a shame to sit in the house; and surely no one can wish to go to bed while sunset is thus at meeting with moonrise."

It is one of my faults, that though my tongue is sometimes prompt enough at an answer, there are times when it sadly fails me in framing an excuse; and always the lapse occurs at some crisis, when a facile word or plausible pretext is specially wanted to get me out of painful embarrassment. I did not like to walk at this hour alone with Mr. Rochester in the shadowy orchard; but I could not find a reason to allege for leaving him. I followed with lagging step, and thoughts busily bent on discovering a means of extrication; but he himself looked so composed and so grave also, I became ashamed of feeling any confusion: the evil—if evil existent or prospective there was—seemed to lie with me only; his mind was unconscious and quiet.

"Jane," he recommenced, as we entered the laurel-walk, and slowly strayed down in the direction of the sunk fence and the horse-chestnut, "Thornfield is a pleasant place in summer, is it not?"

"Yes, sir."

"You must have become in some degree attached to the house,—you, who have an eye for natural beauties, and a good deal of the organ of Adhesiveness[9]?"

"I am attached to it, indeed."

"And, though I don't comprehend how it is, I perceive you have acquired a degree of regard for that foolish little child Adele, too; and even for simple dame Fairfax[10]?"

"Yes, sir; in different ways, I have an affection for both."

"And would be sorry to part with them?"

"Yes."

"Pity!" he said, and sighed and paused. "It is always the way of events in this life," he continued presently: "no sooner have you got settled in a pleasant resting-place, than a voice calls out to you to rise and move on, for the hour of repose is expired."

"Must I move on, sir?" I asked. "Must I leave Thornfield?"

"I believe you must, Jane. I am sorry Janet, but I believe indeed you must." This was a blow: but I did not let it prostrate me.

"Well, sir, I shall be ready when the order to march comes."

"It is come now—I must give it to-night."

"Then you are going to be married, sir?"

"Ex-act-ly—pre-cise-ly: with your usual acuteness, you have hit the nail straight on the head."

"Soon, sir?"

"Very soon, my—that is, Miss Eyre: and you'll remember, Jane, the first time I, or Rumour, plainly intimated to you that it was my intention to put my old bachelor's neck into the sacred noose, to enter into the holy estate of matrimony—to take Miss Ingram to my bosom, in short, (she's an extensive armful: but that's not to the point—one can't have too much of such a very excellent thing as my beautiful Blanche): well, as I was saying—

listen to me Jane! You're not turning your head to look after more moths, are you? That was only a lady-clock, child, 'flying away home.' I wish to remind you that it was you who first said to me, with that discretion I respect in you—with that foresight, prudence, and humility which befit your responsible and dependent position—that in case I married Miss Ingarm, both you and little Adele had better trot forthwith. I pass over the sort of slur conveyed in this suggestion on the character of my beloved; indeed, when you are far away, Janet, I'll try to forget it: I shall notice only its wisdom; which is such that I have made it my law of action Adele must go to school; and you, Miss Eyre, must get a new situation."

"Yes, sir, I will advertise immediately: and meantime, I suppose—" I was going to say, "I suppose I may stay here, till I find another shelter to betake myself to;" but I stopped, feeling it would not do to risk a long sentence, for my voice was not quite under command.

"In about a month I hope to be a bridegroom," continued Mr. Rochester; "and in the interim, I shall myself look out for employment and an asylum for you."

"Thank you, sir; I am sorry to give—"

"Oh—no need to apologize! I consider that when a dependant does her duty as well as you have done yours, she has a sort of claim upon her employer for any little assistance he can conveniently render her; indeed I have already, through my future mother-in-law, heard of a place that I think will suit: it is to undertake the education of the five daughters of Mrs. Dionysius O'Gall of Bitternutt Lodge, Connaught, Ireland. You'll like Ireland, I think: they're such warm-hearted people there, they say."

"It is a long way off, sir."

"No matter—a girl of your sense will not object to the voyage or the distance."

"Not the voyage, but the distance: and then the sea is a barrier—"

"From what, Jane?"

"From England; and from Thornfield: and—"

"Well?"

"From you, sir."

I said this almost involuntarily; and with as little sanction of free will, my tears gushed out. I did not cry so as to be heard, however; I avoided sobbing. The thought of Mrs. O'Gall and Bitternutt Lodge struck cold to my heart; and colder the thought of all the brine and foam, destined, as it seemed, to rush between me and the master, at whose side

I now walked; and coldest the remembrance of the wider ocean—wealth, caste, custom intervened between me and what I naturally and inevitably loved.

"It is a long way," I again said.

"It is, to be sure; and when you get to Bitternutt Lodge, Connaught, Ireland, I shall never see you again, Jane: that's morally certain. I never go over to Ireland, not having myself much of a fancy for the country. We have been good friends, Jane, have we not?"

"Yes, sir."

"And when friends are on the eve of separation, they like to spend the little time that remains to them close to each other. Come—we'll talk over the voyage and the parting quietly, half an hour or so, while the stars enter into their shining life up in heaven yonder: here is the chestnut tree; here is the bench at its old roots. Come, we will sit there in peace to-night, though we should never more be destined to sit there together." He seated me and himself.

"It is a long way to Ireland, Janet, and I am sorry to send my little friend on such weary travels: but if I can't do better, how is it to be helped? Are you anything akin to me, do you think, Jane?"

I could risk no sort of answer by this time: my heart was full.

"Because," he said, "I sometimes have a queer feeling with regard to you—especially when you are near me, as now: it is as if I had a string somewhere under my left ribs[11], tightly and inextricably knotted to a similar string situated in the corresponding quarter of your little frame. And if that boisterous channel, and two hundred miles or so of land come broad between us, I am afraid that cord of communion will be snaped; and then I've a nervous notion I should take to bleeding inwardly. As for you,—you'd forget me."

"That I never should, sir: you know—" impossible to proceed.

"Jane, do you hear that nightingale singing in the wood?—Listen!"

In listening, I sobbed convulsively; for I could repress what I endured no longer: I was obliged to yield; and I was shaken from head to foot with acute distress. When I did speak, it was only to express an impetuous wish that I had never been born, or never come to Thornfield.

"Because you are sorry to leave it?"

The vehemence of emotion, stirred by grief and love within me, was claiming mastery, and struggling for full sway; and asserting a right to predominate: to overcome, to live, rise, and reign at last; yes,—and to speak.

"I grieve to leave Thornfield: I love Thornfield:—I love it, because I have lived in it a full and delightful life,—momentarily at least. I have not been trampled on. I have not been petrified I have not been buried with inferior minds, and excluded from every glimpse of communion with what is bright, and energetic, and high. I have talked, face to face, with what I reverence; with what I delight in,—with an original, a vigorous, an expanded mind. I have known you, Mr. Rochester; and it strikes me with terror and anguish to feel I absolutely must be torn from you for ever. I see the necessity of departure; and it is like looking on the necessity of death."

"Where do you see the necessity?" he asked, suddenly.

"Where? You, sir, have placed it before me."

"In what shape?"

"In the shape of Miss Ingram; a noble and beautiful woman,—your bride."

"My bride! What bride? I have no bride!"

"But you will have."

"Yes;—I will!—I will" He set his teeth.

"Then I must go:—you have said it yourself."

"No: you must stay! I swear it—and the oath shall be kept."

"I tell you I must go!" I retorted, roused to something like passion. "Do you think I can stay to become nothing to you? Do you think I am an automaton?—a machine without feelings? and can bear to have my morsel of bread snatched from my lips, and my drop of living water dashed from my cup? Do you think, because I am poor, obscure, plain, and little, I am soulless and heartless?—You think wrong!—I have as much soul as you,—and full as much heart! And if God had gifted me with some beauty, and much wealth, I should have made it as hard for you to leave me, as it is now for me to leave you. I am not talking to you now through the medium of custom, conventionalities, nor even of mortal flesh:—it is my spirit that addresses your spirit; just as if both had passed through the grave, and we stood at god's feet, equal,—as we are!"

"As we are!" repeated Mr. Rochester—"so," he added, enclosing me in his arms, gathering me to his breast, pressing his lips on my lips: "so, Jane!"

"Yes, so, sir," I rejoined: "and yet not so; for you are a married man—to as good as a married man, and wed to one inferior to you—to one with whom you have no sympathy—whom I do not believe you truly love; for I have seen and heard you sneer at her. I would scorn such a union; therefore I am better than you—let me go!"

"Where, Jane? To Ireland?"

"Yes—to Ireland. I have spoken my mind, and can go anywhere now."

"Jane, be still; don't struggle so, like a wild, frantic bird that is rending its own plumage in its desperation."

"I am no bird; and no net ensnares me: I am a free human being with an independent will; which I now exert to leave you."

Another effort set me at liberty, and I stood erect before him.

"And your will shall decide your destiny," he said: "I offer you my hand, my heart, and a share of all my possessions."

"You play a farce, which I merely laugh at."

"I ask you to pass through life at my side—to be my second self, and best earthly companion."

"For that fate you have already made your choice, and must abide by it."

"Jane, be still a few moments; you are over-excited: I will be still too."

A waft of wind came sweeping down the laurel-walk, and trembled through the boughs of the chestnut: it wandered away—away—to an indefinite distance—it died. The nightingale's song was then the only voice of the hour: in listening to it, I again wept. Mr. Rochester sat quiet, looking at me gently and seriously. Some time passed before he spoke; he at last said:—

"Come to my side, Jane, and let us explain, and understand one another."

"I will never again come to your side: I am torn away now, and cannot return."

"But, Jane, I summon you as my wife: it is you only I intend to marry."

I was silent: I thought he mocked me.

"Come, Jane—come hither."

"Your bride stands between us."

He rose, and with a stride reached me.

"My bride is here," he said, again drawing me to him, "because my equal is here, and my likeness. Jane, will you marry me?"

Still I did not answer; and still I writhed myself from his grasp: for I was still incredulous.

"Do you doubt me, Jane?"

"Entirely."

"You have no faith in me?"

"Not a whit."

"Am I a liar in your eyes?" he asked passionately. "Little sceptic, you shall be convinced. What love have I for Miss Ingram? None: and that you know. What love has she for me? None; as I have taken pains to prove: I caused a rumour to reach her that my fortune was not a third of what was supposed, and after that I presented myself to see the result: it was coldness both from her and her mother. I would not—I could not—marry Miss Ingram. You—you strange—you almost unearthly thing!—I love as my own flesh. You—poor and obscure, and small and plain as you are—I entreat to accept me as a husband."

"What, me!" I ejaculated: beginning in his earnestness—and especially in his incivility—to credit his sincerity; "me, who have not a friend in the world but you—if you are my friend: not a shilling but what you have given me?"

"You, Jane. I must have you for my own—entirely my own. Will you be mine? Say yes, quickly."

"Mr. Rochester, let me look at your face: turn to the moonlight."

"Why?"

"Because I want to read your countenance: turn!"

"There: you will find it scarcely more legible than a crumpled, scratched page. Read on: only make haste, for I suffer."

His face was very much agitated and very much flushed, and there were strong workings in the features, and strange gleams in the eyes.

"Oh, Jane, you torture me!" he exclaimed. "With that searching and yet faithful and generous look, you torture me!"

"How can I do that? If you are true, and your offer real, my only feelings to you must be gratitude and devotion—they cannot torture."

"Gratitude!" he ejaculated; and added wildly—"Jane, accept me quickly. Say, Edward—give me my name—Edward, I will marry you."

"Are you in earnest?—Do you truly love me?—Do you sincerely wish me to be your wife?"

"I do; and if an oath is necessary to satisfy you, I swear it."

"Then, sir, I will marry you."

"Edward—my little wife!"

"Dear Edward!"

"Come to me—come to me entirely now," said he; and added, in his deepest tone, speaking in my ear as his cheek was laid on mine, "Make my happiness—I will make yours."

"God, pardon me!" he subjoined ere long [12]; "and man, meddle not with me[13]: I have her, and will hold her."

"There is no one to meddle, sir. I have no kindred to interfere."

"No—that is the best of it," he said. And if I had loved him less I should have thought his accent and look of exultation savage: but, sitting by him, roused from the nightmare of parting—called to the paradise of union—I thought only of the bliss given me to drink in so abundant a flow. Again and again he said, "Are you happy, Jane?" And again and again I answered, "Yes." After which he murmured, "It will atone—it will atone. Have I not found her friendless, and cold, and comfortless? Will I not guard, and cherish, and solace her? Is there not love in my heart, and constancy in my resolves? It will expiate at God's tribunal. I know my Maker sanctions what I do. For the world's judgment—I wash my hands thereof[14]. For man's opinion—I defy it."

But what had befallen the night? The moon was not yet set, and we were all in shadow: I could scarcely see my master's face, near as I was. And what ailed the chestnut tree? it writhed and groaned; while wind roared in the laurel walk, and came sweeping over us.

"We must go in," said Mr. Rochester: "the weather changes. I could have sat with thee till morning, Jane."

"And so," thought I, "could I with you." I should have said so, perhaps, but a livid, vivid spark leapt out of a cloud at which I was looking, and there was a crack, a crash, and a close rattling peal; and I thought only of hiding my dazzled eyes against Mr. Rochester's shoulder. The rain rushed down. He hurried me up the walk, through the grounds, and into the house; but we were quite wet before we could pass the threshold. He was taking off my shawl in the hall, and shaking the water out of my loosened hair, when Mrs. Fairfax emerged from her room. I did not observe her at first, nor did Mr. Rochester. The lamp was lit. The clock was on the stroke of twelve.

"Hasten to take off your wet things," said he; "and before you go, good-night—good-night, my darling!"

He kissed me repeatedly. When I looked up, on leaving his arms, there stood the widow, pale, grave, and amazed. I only smiled at her, and ran up stairs. "Explanation will do for another time," thought I. Still, when I reached my chamber, I felt a pang at the idea she should even temporarily misconstrue what she had seen. But joy soon effaced every other feeling; and loud as the wind blew, near and deep as the thunder crashed, fierce and frequent as the lightning gleamed, cataract—like as the rain fell during a storm of two hours, duration, I experienced no fear, and little awe. Mr. Rochester came thrice to my door in the course of it, to ask if I was safe and tranquil: and that was comfort, that was strength for anything.

Before I left my bed in the morning, little Adele came running in to tell me that the great horse-chestnut at the bottom of the orchard had been struck by lightning in the night, and half of it split away.

【注解】

1. wave-girt land: 波涛环绕的地方，即英格兰。
2. the cliffs of Albion: 阿尔比恩的悬崖。"Albion"是英格兰或不列颠的诗名。
3. Thornfield: 罗切斯特先生的桑菲尔德庄园。
4. Midsummer-eve: 指施洗约翰节，在 6 月 24 日。
5. Adele: 阿黛勒，罗切斯特先生收养的弃婴，法国歌女的私生女。
6. Day its fervid fires had wasted: 白天已将它炽热的火耗尽。出自苏格兰诗人托马斯·坎贝尔 (Thomas Campbell，1777—1844) 的诗《土耳其女士》("The Turkish Lady") 第五、六行：Day her sultry fires had wasted, Calm and sweet the moonlight rose.
7. wicket: 小门。
8. eventide: 黄昏。
9. a good deal of the organ of Adhcsiveness: 依恋器官特别发达。
10. dame Fairfax: 菲尔费克斯太太，罗切斯特先生的女管家。
11. a string somewhere under my left ribs: 暗指《旧约・创世纪》中亚当和夏娃的故事。
12. ere long: 相当于 before long，不久。
13. and man, meddle not with me: 不要让人来干涉我。此处隐含着罗切斯特的不安，他早有妻室。
14. I wash my hands thereof: 我从此不管。

【思考题】

1. Charlotte Brontë was one of the first women novelists to employ the theme of the "independent" woman. Throughout the novel, Jane Eyre is seen as a woman struggling against social structures to define herself on her own terms. Discuss how the female sensibility is expressed in this chapter.
2. How does Mr. Rochester treat Jane in this chapter? What aspects in Jane's character attract him most?

【简评】

按照维多利亚时代妇女的行为规范，简·爱有两大过失：①向一个男人主动表达自己的爱；②拒绝另一个男人的求婚。当时有一种评价说《简·爱》的作者如果是一个女人，那她“也是一个非女性化的女人”。作者遭此非议的主要原因在于她充分而大胆地描写了女人的“偏见、观念和激情”。从女性主义角度来看，《简·爱》远远超出了自己的时代，真正在文学中确立妇女的独立意识。它不仅控诉了当时男性的压迫，歌颂了女性的优越，而且还真实地反映了女性的天然情感，弗吉尼亚·伍尔夫曾赞扬它“勇敢、真诚、紧紧扣住女人的感受”。

Emily Brontë
1818—1848

作者简介

艾米莉·勃朗特生于英国北部约克郡的山村桑顿。她是夏洛蒂·勃朗特的妹妹，但是性格与姐姐很不相同。她孤僻、内向，喜欢动物，热爱家乡的哈沃斯荒原，常常独自一人牵着爱犬在荒原上漫游。1835 年艾米莉跟随夏洛蒂前往伍勒女士的寄宿学校学习，不到一年便返回。艾米莉也当过家庭教师，但为期很短。艾米莉很早就开始写诗。她的一些诗歌记述了童年与姐妹、弟弟所做的文学游戏中冈多尔岛国的故事，收录在《冈多尔诗集》(*Gondal Poems*) 中。其中的《怀念》(“Remembrance”, 1846) 是一首优美动人的挽歌，以凄凉哀婉的格调表达了主人公对情人的深切怀念。其他的诗歌也都感情真挚，想象丰富，极有个性。1846 年，勃朗特三姐妹自费出版诗集《柯勒、埃利斯和阿克顿·贝尔诗集》。“埃利斯”即艾米莉的化名。1847 年，艾米莉唯一的一部小说《呼啸山庄》出版。《呼啸山庄》在当时并没有引起世人注意，现在却被评论家们称为维多利亚时代一部独具特色的伟大作品。艾米莉终身未嫁，却凭借一颗敏感、热烈的心描绘出一个感人肺腑的爱情复仇故事。1848 年 12 月，艾米莉病逝。

Wuthering Heights

【题解】

《呼啸山庄》的故事发生在英国北部约克郡偏僻荒原上一座终日狂风呼啸的山庄。呼啸山庄的主人恩肖先生从利物浦领回一个无家可归的弃儿，给他取名希斯克利夫，并待他如同亲生，却引起儿子辛德雷的强烈不满和嫉妒，而女儿凯瑟琳与这个皮肤黝黑、一身野气的孩子很快成了形影相随的伙伴。恩肖死后，希斯克利夫失去了保护，辛德雷少爷待他如同奴仆，并禁止妹妹与其玩耍。凯瑟琳与希斯克利夫孩提时的友谊在不知不觉中已发展成真挚的爱情。相似的个性、相同的生活趣味和反抗目标，使他们互以对方的生存作为自己存在的条件，但是在等级分明的社会里，凯瑟琳却难以嫁给希斯克利夫。当她作出天真的决定，答应嫁给画眉山庄的阔少——温文尔雅的林顿时，希斯克利夫突然失踪了。当晚凯瑟琳站在狂风暴雨中大哭了一夜，重病一场，为日后的精神崩溃埋下隐患。三年后希斯克利夫重新出现，已变成一个富人，他对凯瑟琳的爱一如既往，但又夹杂着恨与仇的苦涩情感。此时已是林顿夫人的凯瑟琳面对猜忌的丈夫和自己日夜思念的精神恋人，内心再度掀起狂烈的风暴，痛苦万分，不久死于难产，留下与林顿生的女儿小凯蒂。希斯克利夫在痛苦中近乎疯狂地一步步将复仇进行到底。他靠赌博夺走了辛德雷的全部财产，成了呼啸山庄的主人。他还虐待辛德雷的儿子哈里顿，将他的野蛮和无知当作自己最大的快乐。他引诱林顿的妹妹伊莎贝拉并娶她为妻，十几年之后，又强迫小凯蒂嫁给自己病恹恹的儿子，以夺取他所仇恨的画眉山庄。复仇的目的完全达到了，希斯克利夫依然无法医治心灵的创伤。他变得精神恍惚，用绝食的方式自杀，死后葬在凯瑟琳的身旁。而小凯蒂和哈里顿在经历了暴风雨似的摧残之后，他们之间萌发了纯真的爱情。

下文所选内容为小说第十五章，描绘了希斯克利夫与凯瑟琳最后一次见面的感人场景。

From Wuthering Heights

Chapter 15

Another week over, and I[1] am so many days nearer health and spring! I have now heard all my neighbour's[2] history, at different sittings[3], as the housekeeper[4] could spare time from more important occupations. I'll continue it in her own words, only a little condensed. She is, on the whole, a very fair narrator, and I don't think I could improve her style.

In the evening, she said—the evening of my visit to the Heights[5]—I knew, as well as if I saw him, that Mr. Heathcliff was about the place[6]; and I shunned going out, because I still carried his letter[7] in my pocket, and didn't want to be threatened or teased any more. I had made up my mind not to give it till my master went somewhere, as I could not guess how its receipt would affect Catherine. The consequence was that it did not reach her before the lapse of three days. The fourth was Sunday, and I brought it into her room after the family were gone to church. There was a man servant left to keep the house with me, and we generally made a practice of locking the doors during the hours of service[8]; but on that occasion the weather was so warm and pleasant that I set them wide open, and, to fulfill my engagement[9], as I knew who would be coming, I told my companion that the mistress wished very much for some oranges, and he must run over to the village and get a few, to be paid for on the morrow. He departed, and I went upstairs.

Mrs. Linton sat in a loose, white dress, with a light shawl over her shoulders, in the recess of the open window as usual. Her thick, long hair had been partly removed[10] at the beginning of her illness, and now she wore it simply combed in its natural tresses over her temples and neck. Her appearance was altered, as I had told Heathcliff; but when she was calm there seemed unearthly beauty in the change. The flash of her eyes had been succeeded by a dreamy and melancholy softness; they no longer gave the impression of looking at the objects around her; they appeared always to gaze beyond, and far beyond—you would have said out of this world. Then the paleness of her face—its haggard aspect having vanished as she recovered flesh—and the peculiar expression arising from her mental state, though painfully suggestive of their causes, added to the touching interest which she awakened[11], and—invariable to me, I know, and to any person who saw her, I should think—refuted more tangible proofs of convalescence, and stamped her as one doomed to decay.

A book lay spread on the sill before her, and the scarcely perceptible wind fluttered its leaves at intervals. I believe Linton had laid it there, for she never endeavoured to divert herself with reading or occupation of any kind, and he would spend many an hour in trying to entice her attention to some subject which had formerly been her amusement. She was conscious of his aim, and in her better moods endured his efforts placidly, only showing their uselessness by now and then suppressing a wearied sigh, and checking him at last with the saddest of smiles and kisses. At other times, she would turn petulantly away, and hide her face in her hands, or even push him off angrily; and then he took care to let her alone, for he was certain of doing no good.

Gimmerton chapel[12] bells were still ringing, and the full, mellow flow of the beck in the valley came soothingly on the ear. It was a sweet substitute for the yet absent murmur of the summer foliage which drowned that music about the Grange when the trees were in leaf. At Wuthering Heights it always sounded on quiet days following a great thaw or a season of steady rain. And of Wuthering Heights Catherine was thinking as she listened—that is, if she thought or listened at all; but she had the vague, distant look I mentioned before, which expressed no recognition of material things either by ear or eye.

"There's a letter for you, Mrs. Linton," I said, gently inserting it in one hand that rested on her knee. "You must read it immediately, because it wants an answer. Shall I break the seal?" "Yes," she answered, without altering the direction of her eyes. I opened it; it was very short. "Now," I continued, "read it." She drew away her hand, and let it fall. I replaced it in her lap, and stood waiting till it should please her to glance down; but that movement was so long delayed that at last I resumed,—

"Must I read it, ma'am? It is from Mr. Heathcliff."

There was a start and a troubled gleam of recollection, and a struggle to arrange her ideas. She lifted the letter, and seemed to peruse it, and when she came to the signature she sighed; yet still I found she had not gathered its import, for, upon my desiring to hear her reply, she merely pointed to the name and gazed at me with mournful and questioning eagerness.

"Well, he wishes to see you," said I, guessing her need of an interpreter. "He's in the garden by this time, and impatient to know what answer I shall bring."

As I spoke I observed a large dog lying on the sunny grass beneath raise its ears as if about to bark, and then, smoothing them back, announce, by a wag of the tail, that some one approached whom it did not consider a stranger. Mrs. Linton bent forward and listened breathlessly. The minute after a step traversed the hall. The open house was too tempting for Heathcliff to resist walking in. Most likely he supposed that I was inclined to shirk my promise, and so resolved to trust to his own audacity. With straining eagerness Catherine gazed towards the entrance of her chamber. He did not hit the right room directly. She motioned me to admit him, but he found it out ere I could reach the door, and in a stride or two was at her side, and had her grasped in his arms.

He neither spoke nor loosed his hold for some five minutes, during which period he bestowed more kisses than ever he gave in his life before, I dare say; but then my mistress had kissed him first, and I plainly saw that he could hardly bear, for downright agony, to look into her face. The same conviction had stricken him as me, from the instant he beheld her, that there was no prospect of ultimate recovery there; she was fated, sure to die.

"O Cathy! O my life! how can I bear it?" was the first sentence he uttered, in a tone that did not seek to disguise his despair. And now he stared at her so earnestly that I thought the very intensity of his gaze would bring tears into his eyes; but they burned with anguish—they did not melt.

"What now?" said Catherine, leaning back and returning his look with a suddenly clouded brow. Her humour was a mere vane for constantly varying caprices. "You and Edgar have broken my heart, Heathcliff! And you both come to bewail the deed to me, as if you were the people to be pitied! I shall not pity you, not I. You have killed me—and thriven on it, I think. How many years do you mean to live after I am gone?"

Heathcliff had knelt on one knee to embrace her. He attempted to rise, but she seized his hair and kept him down.

"I wish I could hold you," she continued bitterly, "till we were both dead! I shouldn't care what you suffered. I care nothing for your sufferings. Why shouldn't you suffer? I do! Will you forget me? Will you be happy when I am in the earth? Will you say twenty years hence, 'That's the grave of Catherine Earnshaw. I loved her long ago, and was wretched to lose her: but it is past. I've loved many others since. My children are dearer to me than she was, and at death I shall not rejoice that I am going to her; I shall be sorry that I must leave them!' Will you say so, Heathcliff?"

"Don't torture me till I'm as mad as yourself," cried he, wrenching his head free and grinding his teeth.

The two, to a cool spectator, made a strange and fearful picture. Well might Catherine deem that heaven would be a land of exile to her, unless with her mortal body she cast away her mortal character also. Her present countenance had a wild vindictiveness in its white cheek, and a bloodless lip and scintillating eye; and she retained in her closed fingers a portion of the locks she had been grasping. As to her companion, while raising himself with one hand, he had taken her arm with the other, and so inadequate was his stock of gentleness to the requirements of her condition that on his letting go I saw four distinct impressions left blue in the colourless skin.

"Are you possessed with a devil," he pursued savagely, "to talk in that manner to me when you are dying? Do you reflect that all those words will be branded in my memory, and eating deeper eternally after you have left me? You know you lie to say I have killed you; and, Catherine, you know that I could as soon forget you as my existence[13]! Is it not sufficient for your infernal selfishness that, while you are at peace, I shall writhe in the torments of hell?"

"I shall not be at peace," moaned Catherine, recalled to a sense of physical weakness by the violent, unequal throbbing of her heart, which beat visibly and audibly under this excess of agitation. She said nothing further till the paroxysm was over, then she continued more kindly,—

"I'm not wishing you greater torment than I have, Heathcliff. I only wish us never to be parted; and should a word of mine distress you hereafter, think I feel the same distress underground, and for my own sake forgive me! Come here and kneel down again. You never harmed me in your life. Nay, if you nurse anger, that will be worse to remember than my harsh words. Won't you come here again? Do!"

Heathcliff went to the back of her chair and leant over, but not so far as to let her see his face, which was livid with emotion. She bent round to look at him. He would not permit it. Turning abruptly, he walked to the fire-place, where he stood, silent with his back towards us. Mrs. Linton's glance followed him suspiciously. Every movement woke a new sentiment in her. After a pause and a prolonged gaze she resumed, addressing me in accents of indignant disappointment,—

"Oh, you see, Nelly, he would not relent a moment to keep me out of the grave. That is how I'm loved! Well, never mind. That is not my Heathcliff. I shall love mine yet, and take him with me; he's in my soul. And," added she musingly, "the thing that irks me most is this shattered prison[14], after all. I'm tired of being enclosed here. I'm wearying to escape into that glorious world, and to be always there—not seeing it dimly through tears, and yearning for it through the walls of an aching heart, but really with it and in it. Nelly, you think you are better and more fortunate than I, in full health and strength. You are sorry for me. Very soon that will be altered. I shall be sorry for you. I shall be incomparably beyond and above you all. I wonder he won't be near me!" She went on to herself. "I thought he wished it. Heathcliff dear, you should not be sullen now. Do come to me, Heathcliff."

In her eagerness she rose and supported herself on the arm of the chair. At that earnest appeal he turned to her, looking absolutely desperate. His eyes, wide and wet, at last flashed fiercely on her; his breast heaved convulsively. An instant they held asunder[15], and then how they met I hardly saw, but Catherine made a spring, and he caught her, and they were locked in an embrace from which I thought my mistress would never be released alive—in fact, to my eyes, she seemed directly insensible. He flung himself into the nearest seat, and on my approaching hurriedly to ascertain if she had fainted, he gnashed at me and foamed like a mad dog, and gathered her to him with greedy jealousy. I did not feel as if I were in the company of a creature of my own species. It appeared that he would not understand, though I spoke to him, so I stood off and held my tongue in great perplexity.

A movement of Catherine's relieved me a little presently. She put up her hand to clasp his neck, and bring her cheek to his as he held her; while he, in return, covering her with frantic caresses, said wildly,—

"You teach me how cruel you've been—cruel and false. Why did you despise me? Why did you betray your own heart, Cathy? I have not one word of comfort. You deserve this. You have killed yourself[16]. Yes, you may kiss me, and cry, and wring out my kisses and tears; they'll blight you—they'll damn you. You loved me; then what right had you to leave me? What right—answer me—for the poor fancy you felt for Linton? Because misery, and degradation, and death, and nothing that God or Satan could inflict would have parted us, you, of your own will, did it. I have not broken your heart—you have broken it; and in breaking it you have broken mine. So much the worse for me that I am strong. Do I want to live? What kind of living will it be when you—O God! Would you like to live with your soul in the grave?"

"Let me alone! Let me alone!" sobbed Catherine. "If I've done wrong, I'm dying for it. It is enough! You left me too; but I won't upbraid you. I forgive you. Forgive me."

"It is hard to forgive, and to look at those eyes, and feel those wasted hands," he answered. "Kiss me again, and don't let me see your eyes. I forgive what you have done to me. I love my murderer—but yours[17]! How can I?"

They were silent—their faces hid against each other, and washed by each other's tears. At least, I suppose the weeping was on both sides, as it seemed Heathcliff could weep on a great occasion like this.

I grew very uncomfortable, meanwhile, for the afternoon wore fast away, the man whom I had sent off returned from his errand, and I could distinguish by the shine of the westering sun up the valley a concourse thickening outside Gimmerton chapel porch.

"Service is over," I announced. "My master will be here in half an hour."

Heathcliff groaned a curse, and strained Catherine closer. She never moved.

Ere long I perceived a group of the servants passing up the road towards the kitchen wing. Mr. Linton was not far behind. He opened the gate himself, and sauntered slowly up, probably enjoying the lovely afternoon that breathed as soft as summer.

"Now he is here," I exclaimed. "for Heaven's sake hurry down! You'll not meet any one on the front stairs. Do be quick, and stay among the trees till he is fairly in."

"I must go, Cathy," said Heathcliff, seeking to extricate himself from his companion's arms. "But if I live I'll see you again before you are asleep. I won't stay five yards from your window."

"You must not go!" she answered, holding him as firmly as her strength allowed. "You shall not, I tell you."

"For one hour," he pleaded earnestly.

"Not for one minute," she replied.

"I must—Linton will be up immediately," persisted the alarmed intruder. He would have risen and unfixed her fingers by the act; she clung fast, gasping. There was mad resolution in her face.

"No!" she shrieked. "Oh, don't, don't go. It is the last time! Edgar will not hurt us. Heathcliff, I shall die! I shall die!"

"Damn the fool! There he is," cried Heathcliff, sinking back into his seat. "Hush, my darling! Hush, hush, Catherine! I'll stay. If he shot me so, I'd expire with a blessing on my lips."

And there they were fast again. I heard my master mounting the stairs. The cold sweat ran from my forehead; I was horrified.

"Are you going to listen to her ravings?" I said, passionately. "She does not know what she says. Will you ruin her, because she has not wit to help herself? Get up! You could be free instantly. That is the most diabolical deed that ever you did. We are all done for, master, mistress, and servant."

I wrung my hands and cried out, and Mr. Linton hastened his step at the noise. In the midst of my agitation I was sincerely glad to observe that Catherine's arms had fallen relaxed, and her head hung down.

"She's fainted or dead," I thought; "so much the better. Far better that she should be dead than lingering a burden and a misery-maker to all about her."

Edgar sprang to his unbidden guest, blanched with astonishment and rage. What he meant to do I cannot tell. However, the other stopped all demonstrations at once by placing the lifeless-looking form in his arms.

"Look there!" he said. "Unless you be a fiend, help her first: then you shall speak to me!"

He walked into the parlour and sat down. Mr. Linton summoned me, and with great difficulty, and after resorting to many means, we managed to restore her to sensation; but she was all bewildered. She sighed, and moaned, and knew nobody. Edgar, in his anxiety for her, forgot her hated friend. I did not. I went at the earliest opportunity and besought him to depart, affirming that Catherine was better, and he should hear from me in the morning how she passed the night.

"I shall not refuse to go out of doors," he answered; "but I shall stay in the garden; and, Nelly, mind you keep your word to-morrow. I shall be under those larch trees. Mind! or I pay another visit, whether Linton be in or not."

He sent a rapid glance through the half-open door of the chamber, and, ascertaining that what I stated was apparently true, delivered the house of his luckless presence.

【注解】

1. I: 此处是指洛克伍德先生，希斯克利夫在画眉山庄的租客。
2. my neighbour: 指希斯克利夫先生。
3. at different sittings: 在不同的谈话中。
4. the housekeeper: 已故凯瑟琳的女仆耐莉，现画眉山庄的管家，下文故事的叙述者。
5. my visit to the Heights: 指耐莉去呼啸山庄的那天。
6. Mr. Heathcliff was about the place: 希斯克利夫先生就躲在画眉山庄附近。
7. his letter: 希斯克利夫托耐莉交给凯瑟琳的信。
8. service: 做礼拜。
9. to fulfil my engagement: 完成送信和安排两人见面的任务。
10. partly removed: 剪去了一部分。
11. added to the touching interest which she awakened: 使她格外令人怜恤。
12. Gimmerton chapel: 画眉山庄附近的一座小教堂。
13. I could as soon forget you as my existence: 我无法忘记你就像无法忘记自己的存在。
14. this shattered prison: 指自己的身体这具躯壳。
15. they held asunder: 他们各站一方。
16. You have killed yourself: 指凯瑟琳决定嫁给林顿，害了她自己。
17. yours=your murderer，与前文的 "my murderer" 均指凯瑟琳。

【思考题】

1. What might be the causes for the tragic ending of the love between Heathcliff and Catherine?
2. In this chapter, how do you understand Heathcliff's words to Catherine, "You deserve this. You have killed yourself"? Try to analyze Catherine's character.
3. Discuss the novel's narrative structure. In whose voice are the events narrated in this chapter?

解读举例

1. 《呼啸山庄》并非一个单纯的爱情复仇故事。通过因地位悬殊而酿成的爱情悲剧及主人公的复仇，作品反映了当时英国社会尖锐的阶级矛盾，鞭笞了英国资产阶级社会的势利、虚伪和种种不公平现象。《呼啸山庄》的故事实际是通过艾米莉的眼睛表现了工业区汹涌澎湃的社会斗争。

2. 《呼啸山庄》是一部追求个性解放的小说。它以充满想象的艺术形式表现了个人精神上的压力、紧张和冲突。

3. 《呼啸山庄》体现了自然界两种力量的矛盾和冲突。一种属于风平浪静的世界，另一种则属于狂风暴雨的世界。这两种世界分别象征“文明”与“野蛮”两种社会。凯瑟琳、希斯克利夫是暴风雨世界的孩子，与林顿属于不同的世界，因此矛盾是无法调和的。

4. 《呼啸山庄》是一部带有神秘色彩的小说。超自然的爱是贯穿全书的主题，无论是凯瑟琳还是艾米莉·勃朗特都在执着地追求一种精神上的团聚与回归。爱情是一种超越物质的精神力量，只有从肉体和生活的枷锁中解放出来，才能达到与宇宙统一的境界。

作者简介

George Eliot
1819—1880

乔治·艾略特原名玛丽·安·埃文斯 (Mary Ann Evans)，出生于英国沃里克郡的乡村。父亲为农庄经理人。她幼年时期曾先后在两所宗教色彩浓厚的寄宿学校读书，笃信福音教，通晓法文、德文、意大利文、拉丁文等多种语言。1836年母亲去世，她辍学为父亲管家。1841年随父亲迁往考文垂，结识了自由思想家查尔斯·布雷 (Charles Bray, 1811—1884)，同时受《基督教起源的调查》(*An Inquiry Concerning the Origin of Christianity*, 1838) 一书的影响，声明与宗教决裂，不再进教堂。但她仍然深切理解和同情一切虔诚的宗教感情，这一思想反映在她后来的许多作品中。1844年，艾略特参与翻译施特劳斯的《耶稣传》(*Life of Jesus, Critically Examined*)，该译作于1846年出版，在思想界产生很大影响。艾略特因此而名噪一时，从此开始了文学生涯。1850年她开始担任《威斯敏斯特评论》(*Westminster Review*) 的副编辑，认识了哲学家兼剧评家乔治·亨利·刘易斯 (George Henry Lewes, 1817—1878)。艾略特和刘易斯志趣相投，他们共同生活了二十四年。1854年，她翻译了费尔巴哈的《基督教的本质》(*Essence of Christianity*)，后来又翻译过斯宾诺莎的《伦理学》(*Ethics*)，并为《威斯敏斯特评论》撰写了大量的专栏文章，所写的书评包含了她对现实主义小说的认识和以此为基础形成的理论，这些文章后来都结集出版。

1856年，在刘易斯的鼓励下，艾略特开始小说创作，写了3部回忆早年家乡生活的中篇小说，1858年结集成《教区生活场景》(*Scenes of Clerical Life*)，首次以"乔治·艾略特"的名字出版。她开始在创作中实践自己的小说理论，忠实于表现平凡人物的生活，唤起人们的同情，在现实主义小说传统中别开生面，引起文学界的普遍重视。

艾略特一生共创作7部长篇小说。她的小说创作一般被分为前后两期。前期小说描写19世纪初期单纯质朴的乡村生活；后期小说内容复杂，以重大的历史、政治、社会事件为题材。但她的创作思想前后一致，作品具有哲理性，富有幽默感。

在1859至1861年期间，她创作和出版了3部长篇小说，均得到极大好评。它们分别是《亚当·比德》(*Adam Bede*, 1859)、《弗洛斯河上的磨坊》(*The Mill on the Floss*, 1860) 和《织工马南》(*Silas Marner*, 1861)。

1861 年，乔治·艾略特在游览佛罗伦萨时决定以 15 世纪意大利宗教改革为背景写一部历史小说，后以“罗慕拉”(Romola) 为题于 1862 至 1863 年出版，但读者和评论界对它的反应远不及她的其他小说。她后来创作了以英国 1832 年选举中的动乱为背景的政治小说《激进分子菲利克斯·霍尔特》(*Felix Holt*: *The Radical*, 1867) 和以英国政治改革为背景的巨著《米德尔马契》(*Middlemarch*, 1871—1872)。《米德尔马契》被普遍认为是艾略特的代表作，小说围绕两个想为社会造福的青年在婚姻、事业上的失败，勾勒了一幅英国地方生活的画面。这部小说得到众多评论家的大力推崇，如美国小说家和评论家亨利·詹姆斯 (Henry James, 1843—1916) 称其为“英国传统小说发展的极限”，而弗吉尼亚·伍尔夫 (Virginia Woolf, 1882—1941) 则称之为“一部为数不多的写给成年人的英国小说”。《丹尼尔·德隆达》(*Daniel Deronda*, 1876) 则是艾略特唯一一部描写当代生活，并以英国都市和欧洲大陆为背景的小说。艾略特的其他作品还包括诗剧《西班牙吉卜赛人》(*The Spanish Gypsy*, 1868) 及一些诗与散文。

1878 年刘易斯病逝。1880 年 5 月艾略特与约翰·克罗斯 (John Cross, 1840—1924) 正式结婚，1880 年 12 月 22 日于伦敦逝世。

艾略特是 19 世纪维多利亚时代最杰出的现实主义小说家之一。艾略特的小说中常有大段的议论，但并不给人以抽象说教的印象，这主要是因为她笔下的人物并不公式化。她非常重视对人物活动的环境进行详细描写，笔下人物大多有比较复杂的性格，而且性格的发展及人物的思想动机、行为和效果的分析都有可靠的心理和社会依据，所以人物形象逼真，其所处的环境也真实典型。她细腻的心理分析影响了许多后来作家，如哈代、亨利·詹姆斯、D. H. 劳伦斯 (D. H. Lawrence, 1885—1930) 和马塞尔·普鲁斯特 (Marcel Proust, 1871—1922) 等。

Silas Marner

【题解】

《织工马南》是艾略特的早期作品之一。故事发生在 18 世纪的英国。麻纱织布工人马南被亲密好友诬告，无辜背上偷窃罪名，因而被当地的教会逐出教区，迁至外郡，居住于一间小茅舍中，因孤独逐渐变成一名守财奴，每晚以数金币为乐。十五年后的一天夜里，他辛辛苦苦积攒的金币被当地乡绅的儿子邓斯顿所偷，而几天后一名孤女意外地爬到他的寒舍，从此马南的命运发生了神奇的变化，爱心在他已枯萎的生命中开花结果。他独自抚养孤女爱碧长大，父女建立了深厚的感情，马南与周围邻居的关系也因此恢复正常。十几年后，爱碧长大成人，嫁给同村一个朴实能干的小伙子。而邓斯顿的遗骨被发现于抽干水的石灰坑里，金币重见天日。这时当地最有地位、最富有的人，乡绅的另一个儿子戈德弗雷，终于受到良心的谴责，承认爱碧是当时与他秘密结婚的妻子所生。因后来的妻子不能生育，戈德弗雷欲认领爱碧，并指定她为遗产继承人，但爱碧不愿离开养父马南，甘愿放弃财富与地位。马南终于在晚年获得幸福。

小说的第十四章讲述了马南独自抚养爱碧的艰辛和乐趣。从他下定决心那天开始，爱碧成了连接他和外界的纽带，他与其他村民的关系逐渐发生微妙的变化，在村民心目中的形象也发生了变化。本章详细描述了父女之间的亲密感情及村民的朴实善良。

Silas Marner

Chapter 14

. . .

Baby was christened, the rector deciding that a double baptism was the lesser risk to incur; and on this occasion Silas, making himself as clean and tidy as he could, appeared for the first time within the church, and shared in the observances held sacred by his neighbours. He was quite unable, by means of anything he heard or saw, to identify the Raveloe religion with his old faith; if he could at any time in his previous life have done so, it must have been by the aid of a strong feeling ready to vibrate with sympathy, rather than by a comparison of phrases and ideas; and now for long years that feeling had been dormant. He had no distinct idea about the baptism and the churchgoing, except that Dolly[1] had said it was for the good of the child; and in this way, as the weeks grew to months, the child created fresh and fresh links between his life and the lives from which he had hitherto shrunk continually into narrower isolation. Unlike the gold which needed nothing, and must be worshipped in close-locked solitude—which was hidden away from the daylight, was deaf to the song of birds, and started to no human tones—Eppie was a creature of endless claims and ever-growing desires, seeking and loving sunshine, and living sounds, and living movements; making trial of everything, with trust in new joy, and stirring the human kindness in all eyes that looked on her. The gold had kept his thoughts in an ever-repeated circle, leading to nothing beyond itself; but Eppie was an object compacted of changes and hopes that forced his thoughts onward and carried them far away from their old eager pacing towards the same blank limit—carried them away to the new things that would come with the coming years, when Eppie would have learned to understand how her father Silas cared for her, and made him look for images of that time in the ties and charities that bound together the families of his neighbours. The gold had asked that he should sit weaving longer and longer, deafened and blinded more and more to all things except the monotony of his loom and the repetition of his web; but Eppie called him away from his weaving, and made him think all its pauses a holiday, reawakening his senses with her fresh life, even to the old winter flies that came crawling forth in the early spring sunshine, and warming him into joy because she had joy.

And when the sunshine grew strong and lasting, so that the buttercups were thick in the meadows, Silas might be seen in the sunny midday, or in the late afternoon when the shadows were lengthening under the hedgerows, strolling out with uncovered head to carry Eppie beyond the Stone-pits to where the flowers grew, till they reached some favourite bank where he could sit down; while Eppie toddled to pluck the flowers, and make remarks to the winged things that murmured happily above the bright petals, calling, "Dad-dad's" attention continually by bringing him the flowers. Then she would turn her ear to some sudden bird-note, and Silas learned to please her by making signs of hushed stillness, that they might listen for the note to come again; so that when it came, she set up her small back and laughed with gurgling triumph. Sitting on the banks in this way, Silas began to look for the once familiar herbs again; and as the leaves, with their unchanged outlinc and markings, lay on his palm, there was a sense of crowding remembrances from which he turned away timidly, taking refuge in Eppie's little world, that lay lightly on his enfeebled spirit.

As the child's mind was growing into knowledge, his mind was growing into memory; as her life unfolded, his soul, long stupefied in a cold, narrow prison, was unfolding too, and trembling gradually into full consciousness.

It was an influence which must gather force with every new year. The tones that stirred Silas's heart grew articulate, and called for more distinct answers; shapes and sounds grew clearer for Eppie's eyes and ears, and there was more that "Dad-dad" was imperatively required to notice and account for. Also, by the time Eppie was three years old, she developed a fine capacity for mischief, and for devising ingenious ways of being troublesome, which found much exercise not only for Silas's patience, but for his watchfulness and penetration. Sorely was poor Silas puzzled on such occasions by the incompatible demands of love Dolly Winthrop told him that punishment was good for Eppie; and that, as for rearing a child without making it tingle a little in soft and safe places now and then, it was not to be done.

"To be sure, there's another thing you might do, Master Marner," added Dolly meditatively: "you might shut her up once i' the coal-hole. That was what I did wi' Aaron[2], for I was that silly wi' the youngest lad as I could never bear to smack him. Not as I could find i' my heart to let him stay i' the coal hole more nor a minute, but it was enough to colly him all over, so as he must be new washed and dressed, and it was as good as a rod to him—that was. But I put it upo' your conscience, Master Marner, as there's one of 'em you must choose—ayther smacking or the coal-hole—else she'll get so masterful there'll be no holding her."

Silas was impressed with the melancholy truth of this last remark; but his force of mind failed before the only two penal methods open to him, not only because it was painful to him to hurt Eppie, but because he trembled at a moment's contention with her, lest she should love him the less for it. Let even an affectionate Goliath[3] get himself tied to a small tender thing, dreading to hurt it by pulling, and dreading still more to snap the cord, and which of the two, pray, will be master? It was clear that Eppie, with her short toddling steps, must lead father Silas a pretty dance on any fine morning when circumstances favoured mischief.

For example, he had wisely chosen a broad strip of linen as a means of fastening her to his loom when he was busy. It made a broad belt round her waist, and was long enough to allow of her reaching the truckle-bed and sitting down on it, but not long enough for her to attempt any dangerous climbing. One bright summer's morning Silas had been more engrossed than usual in "setting up" a new piece of work—an occasion on which his scissors were in requisition. These scissors, owing to an especial warning of Dolly's, had been kept carefully out of Eppie's reach; but the click of them had had a peculiar attraction for her ear, and watching the results of that click, she had derived the philosophic lesson that the same cause would produce the same effect. Silas had seated himself in his loom, and the noise of weaving had begun. But he had left his scissors on a ledge which Eppie's arm was long enough to reach; and now, like a small mouse, watching her opportunity, she stole quietly from her corner, secured the scissors, and toddled to the bed again, setting up her back as a mode of concealing the fact. She had a distinct intention as to the use of the scissors; and having cut the linen strip in a jagged but effectual manner, in two moments she had run out at the open door, where the sunshine was inviting her, while poor Silas believed her to be a better child than usual. It was not until he happened to need his scissors that the terrible fact burst upon him: Eppie had run out by herself—had perhaps fallen into the Stone-pit. Silas, shaken by the worst fear that could have befallen him, rushed out, calling "Eppie!" and ran eagerly about the unenclosed space, exploring the dry cavities into which she might have fallen, and then gazing with questioning dread at the smooth red surface of the water. The cold drops stood on his brow. How long had she been out? There was one hope—that she had crept through the stile and got into the fields, where he habitually took her to stroll. But the grass was high in the meadow, and there was no descrying her if she were there except by a close search that would be a trespass on Mr. Osgood's[4] crop. Still, that misdemeanour must be committed; and poor Silas, after peering all round the hedgerows, traversed the grass, beginning with perturbed vision to see Eppie behind every group of red sorrel, and to see her moving always farther off as he approached. The meadow was searched in vain; and he got over the stile into the next field, looking with dying hope towards a small pond which was now reduced to its summer shallowness, so as to leave a wide margin of good adhesive mud. Here, however, sat Eppie, discoursing cheerfully to her own small boot, which she was using as a bucket to convey the water into a deep hoofmark, while her little naked foot was planted comfortably on a cushion of olive-green mud. A red-headed calf was observing her with alarmed doubt through the opposite hedge.

Here was clearly a case of aberration in a christened child which demanded severe treatment; but Silas, overcome with convulsive joy at finding his treasure again, could do nothing but snatch her up and cover her with half-sobbing kisses. It was not until he had carried her home, and had begun to think of the necessary washing, that he recollected the need that he should punish Eppie and "make her remember." The idea that she might run away again and come to harm gave him unusual resolution, and for the first time he determined to try the coal-hole, a small closet near the hearth.

"Naughty, naughty Eppie," he suddenly began, holding her on his knee, and pointing to her muddy feet and clothes—"naughty to cut with the scissors and run away. Eppie must go into the coal-hole for being naughty. Daddy must put her in the coal-hole."

He half expected that this would be shock enough, and that Eppie would begin to cry. But instead of that she began to shake herself on his knee, as if the proposition opened a pleasing novelty. Seeing that he must proceed to extremities, he put her into the coal-hole and held the door closed, with a trembling sense that he was using a strong measure. For a moment there was silence, but then came a little cry, "Opy, opy!" and Silas let her out again, saying, "Now, Eppie 'ull never be naughty again, else she must go in the coal-hole, a black, naughty place."

The weaving must stand still a long while this morning, for now Eppie must be washed and have clean clothes on; but it was to be hoped that this punishment would have a lasting effect, and save time in future—though perhaps it would have been better if Eppie had cried more.

In half an hour she was clean again, and Silas having turned his back to see what he could do with the linen band, threw it down again, with the reflection that Eppie would be good without fastening for the rest of the morning. He turned round again, and was going to place her in her little chair near the loom, when she peeped out at him with black face and hands again, and said, "Eppie in de toal-hole!"

This total failure of the coal-hole discipline shook Silas's belief in the efficacy of punishment. "She'd take it all for fun," he observed to Dolly, "if I didn't hurt her, and that I can't do, Mrs. Winthrop. If she makes me a bit o' trouble I can bear it. And she's got no tricks but what she'll grow out of."

"Well, that's partly true, Master Marner," said Dolly sympathetically; "and if you can't bring your mind to frighten her off touching things, you must do what you can to keep'em out of her way. That's what I do wi' the pups[5] as the lads are allays a-rearing. They will worry and gnaw, worry and gnaw they will, if it was one's Sunday cap as hung anywhere so as they could drag it. They know no difference, God help 'em; it's the pushing o' the teeth as sets 'em on, that's what it is."

So Eppie was reared without punishment, the burden of her misdeeds being borne vicariously by father Silas. The stone hut was made a soft nest for her, lined with downy patience; and also in the world that lay beyond the stone hut she knew nothing of frowns and denials.

Notwithstanding the difficulty of carrying her and his yarn or linen at the same time, Silas took her with him in most of his journeys to the farmhouses, unwilling to leave her behind at Dolly Winthrop's, who was always ready to take care of her; and little curly-headed Eppie, the weaver's child, became an object of interest at several outlying homesteads, as well as in the village. Hitherto he had been treated very much as if he had been a useful gnome or brownie[6]—a queer and unaccountable creature, who must necessarily be looked at with wondering curiosity and repulsion, and with whom one would be glad to make all greetings and bargains as brief as possible, but who must be dealt with in a propitiatory way, and occasionally have a present of pork or garden stuff to carry home with him, seeing that without him there was no getting the yarn woven. But now Silas met with open smiling faces and cheerful questioning as a person whose satisfactions and difficulties could be understood. Everywhere he must sit a little and talk about the child, and words of interest were always ready for him. "Ah Master Marner, you'll be lucky if she takes the measles soon and easy!" or, "Why, there isn't many lone men 'ud ha' been wishing to take up with a little un like that. But I reckon the weaving makes you handier than men as do outdoor work; you're partly as handy as a woman, for weaving comes next to spinning." Elderly masters and mistresses, seated observantly in large kitchen armchairs, shook their heads over the difficulties attendant on rearing children, felt Eppie's round arms and legs, and pronounced them remarkably firm, and told Silas that if she turned out well (which, however, there was no telling) it would be a fine thing for him to have a steady lass to do for him when he got helpless. Servant maidens were fond of carrying her out to look at the hens and chickens, or to see if any cherries could be shaken down in the orchard; and the small boys and girls approached her slowly, with cautious movement and steady gaze, like little dogs face to face with one of their own kind, till attraction had reached the point at which the soft lips were put out for a kiss. No child was afraid of approaching Silas when Eppie was near him—there was no repulsion around him now, either for young or old; for the little child had come to link him once more with the whole world. There was love between him and the child that blent them into one, and there was love between the child and the world—from men and women with parental looks and tones to the red ladybirds and the round pebbles.

Silas began now to think of Raveloe life entirely in relation to Eppie—she must have everything that was a good in Raveloe; and he listened docilely, that he might come to understand better what this life was, from which for fifteen years he had stood aloof as from a strange thing, wherewith he could have no communion; as some man who has a precious plant, to which he would give a nurturing home in a new soil, thinks of the rain, and the sunshine, and all influences in relation to his nursling, and asks industriously for all knowledge that will help him to satisfy the wants of the searching roots, or to guard leaf and bud from invading harm. The disposition to hoard had been utterly crushed at the very first by the loss of his long-stored gold. The coins he earned afterwards seemed as irrelevant as stones brought to complete a house suddenly buried by an earthquake; the sense of bereavement was too heavy upon him for the old thrill of satisfaction to arise again at the touch of the newly-earned coin. And now something had come to replace his hoard which gave a growing purpose to the earnings, drawing his hope and joy continually onward beyond the money.

In old days there were angels who came and took men by the hand and led them away from the city of destruction. We see no white-winged angels now. But yet men are led away from threatening destruction: a hand is put into theirs which leads them forth gently towards a calm and bright land, so that they look no more backward; and the hand may be a little child's.

【注解】

1. Dolly: 马南在拉维罗村的好心邻居多莉。
2. Aaron: 小说中多莉的小儿子，爱碧后来的丈夫。
3. Goliath:《圣经》里被大卫杀死的巨人。
4. Mr. Osgood: 拉维罗村的村民。
5. pups: 相当于 puppies，小狗。
6. gnome or brownie: “gnome” 为土地神，宝藏守护神；“brownie” 为棕神，传说中夜间帮人做家务的精灵。

【思考题】

1. *Silas Marner is* frequently referred to as a “fairy tale.” What fairy tale elements does it have? Does the label fit?
2. In Eliot’s novels, there are many commentaries from the author. Do you think the novel would be more effective if Eliot did not make any comments about the story?
3. Comment on the author’s language. What is the level of speech, literary or colloquial? What characteristics impress you most?

解读举例

1. 《织工马南》是艾略特最后一部反映乡村生活的小说。在这部小说中，艾略特把现代工业社会的虚伪价值观与正在消失的英国古老乡村的价值观并置，把城市与自然对立，给读者提供了“美好英格兰”的生活图景。在这里，人们拥有朴实的情感，对生活、宗教都有自己质朴的理解。他们坦诚、宽容，包容一切。在这里，金钱不是衡量万物的标准，也没有工业社会中常见的疏离和异化等现象。

2. 《织工马南》宣扬了朴素的“善有善报，恶有恶报”的道理。品行恶劣的邓斯顿葬身石灰坑，自私胆怯的戈德弗雷热爱孩子却得不到亲生女儿的爱，而善良的马南历经磨难之后终于能享受天伦之乐，这种结局体现了艾略特对“诗性正义”的理解。

3. 《织工马南》试图阐释爱的拯救意义，以前的马南以积攒金币为乐，收养爱碧之后，他逐渐改变，走出孤立，与他人建立纯洁自然的人际关系。对他人的爱最终证明比对金钱的爱更能为人类带来快乐和幸福。

English Literature in the Twentieth Century

1900–1945

20世纪是英国国际地位不断下降的一个世纪。19世纪下半叶，大英帝国的国力在维多利亚时代达到鼎盛。然而，进入20世纪，第一次世界大战动摇了英国的霸主地位，第二次世界大战使英国彻底失去往日的辉煌。战争的创伤、经济的衰退、国际地位的下降，使20世纪上半叶的英国文学呈现新的特点。

20世纪初，英国文学一方面继承了维多利亚时代的现实主义传统，另一方面则努力摆脱当时的道德观和维多利亚时代文学的说教倾向。第一次世界大战前，英国文学对维多利亚时代的背离更多体现在作品所展现的情绪和思想上；第一次世界大战后，现实主义文学受到现代主义文学的挑战，英国作家开始在形式和主题方面对文学进行变革。

一战前，许多作家发扬现实主义的创作手法，非常关注人的生存环境，生动描述处于转型时期的英国社会。哈代在20世纪虽已放弃小说而转向诗歌创作，但他在19世纪末发表的《德伯家的苔丝》(*Tess of the d'Urbervilles*, 1891) 和《无名的裘德》(*Jude the Obscure*, 1896) 刻画了现代工业文明中人的漂泊、孤独和异化，已经触及20世纪现代文学中的核心主题。1901至1910年间，以阿诺德·贝内特 (Arnold Bennet, 1867—1931)、约翰·高尔斯华绥 (John Galsworthy, 1867—1931) 和赫伯特·乔治·威尔斯 (Herbert George Wells, 1866—1946) 为代表的爱德华时代作家继承了现实主义传统。贝内特深受法国自然主义的影响，在《老妇谭》(*The Old Wives' Tale*, 1908) 中描写了世纪之交英国小镇的现实生活，表现了在时间的流逝和冷漠的生活中，人的无助和徒劳。高尔斯华绥在《福尔赛世家》(*The Forsyte Saga*, 1922) 等作品中以现实主义手法，形象地刻画了走向没落的贵族阶级，描述了英国中产阶级的生活，虽略带讽刺，但不乏同情。威尔斯则在《时间机器》(*The Time Machine*, 1895)、《隐身人》(*The Invisible Man*, 1897) 等作品中运用科幻小说的形式，描述了一个社会和政治的乌托邦，批评了现代社会。此外，鲁德亚德·吉卜林 (Rudyard Kipling, 1865—1936) 的作品具有强烈的殖民主义色彩，表现了不同文化之间的冲突与融合。在具有自传色彩的小说《人性的枷锁》(*Of Human Bondage*, 1915) 中，威廉·萨默塞特·毛姆 (William Somerset Maugham, 1874—1965) 探讨了人性和束缚人发展的各种因素，涉及孤独、异化等现代主义文学的常见主题。

萧伯纳在戏剧方面取得了令人瞩目的成就。他发扬了以亨利克·易卜生 (Henrik Ibsen, 1828—1906) 为代表的欧洲新现实主义社会问题剧的戏剧艺术，通过大量剧作探索英国现实社会，揭示各类社会问题，并对这些问题进行深入剖析和批判，语言诙谐、对白幽默，吸引了众多读者和观众，振兴了20世纪上半叶的英国戏剧，并于1925年获得诺贝尔文学奖。19世纪末20世纪初的爱尔兰民族运动也引发了爱尔兰文艺复兴。爱尔兰文艺复兴的突出成就表现在戏剧方面。威廉·巴特勒·叶芝 (William

Butler Yeats, 1865—1939)、格雷戈里夫人 (Lady Gregory, 1852—1932)、爱德华·马丁 (Edward Martyn, 1859—1923) 等人共同创立了爱尔兰文学剧院和爱尔兰民族戏剧社，为叶芝、约翰·米林顿·辛格 (John Millington Synge, 1871—1909) 和肖恩·奥凯西 (Sean O'Casey, 1880—1964) 等剧作家的创作和其作品的演出提供了良好的环境。

英国现代主义文学在这一时期取得了辉煌的成就。作为现代主义小说的先驱，亨利·詹姆斯[①]在《小说的艺术》(*The Art of Fiction*，1888) 中强调了小说作为一种艺术形式的地位。他关注小说的叙述视角，认为应运用意识中心 (the center of consciousness)，对人物心理进行细致刻画，故而也成为心理现实主义的代表作家。同时，詹姆斯关注人性中的邪恶，对其他英国现代主义作家产生了重要影响。约瑟夫·康拉德 (Joseph Conrad，1857—1924) 在作品中经常运用多重视角来表现人与社会的冲突，力图展现人与自我及现代文明与原始本能的冲突，体现了英国文学从现实主义向现代主义过渡期间的一些特点。

1910 年 12 月，伦敦举办了第一次后印象主义画展，标志着艺术从表现人物的外部生活环境向人物内心和个人情感的转变。女作家伍尔夫甚至指出人性从此开始变化。随后发生的一系列重大事件给英国人的传统价值观带来巨大冲击。一战中英国损失惨重，大英帝国的霸主地位开始动摇；20 世纪 30 年代的资本主义世界经济危机和随后爆发的第二次世界大战，导致西方传统价值观念崩塌，西方社会呈现出如诗人艾略特所说的“荒原”状态。原本理性、有序的社会不复存在，取而代之的是混乱与迷惘。现代主义作家对西方文化和文明深感失望，对之进行了严厉批判。他们在作品中刻画了人们在现代社会中感受到的孤独、彷徨、压抑、悲观和焦虑，表达了对人类生存现状的忧思。因此，现代主义文学最重要的主题是异化与焦虑。现实主义作品侧重描写人物的外部生活环境，现代主义作品则专注于展现人物的自我意识。现实主义作品讲究有逻辑的叙述，而现代主义作品则努力抓住稍纵即逝的感受。因此，现代主义文学表现出内倾和非理性的特点，进行形式上的实验，采取了诸如意识流、内心独白、时空倒错、多重叙事视角等新的创作手法。

20 世纪 20 年代是英国现代主义文学发展的鼎盛时期。詹姆斯·乔伊斯 (James Joyce, 1882—1941) 在多部作品中表现了人们精神上的麻木和瘫痪。伍尔夫认为小说家的职责是呈现并阐释“易变、未知和无限的人类精神”，她的作品着重表现日常生活给人的精神和灵魂带来的冲击。乔伊斯和伍尔夫将意识流手法发展到一个新的高度，把人物支离破碎的主观意识生动地呈现在读者面前。D. H. 劳伦斯则关注工业

① 詹姆斯一直是美国作家，只是在去世前一年 (1915) 才转入英国籍，故将詹姆斯收入《新编美国文学选读》中。

文明对人类本能和情感的压抑和歪曲，试图通过回归原始自然来寻找出路。爱德华·摩根·福斯特 (Edward Morgen Forster, 1879—1970) 的创作手法相对传统，在《印度之行》(*A Passage to India*, 1924) 中表现了英国在印度殖民时期不同文化之间的冲突，探讨了人与人之间沟通与理解的意义。

尽管现代主义文学取得了傲人的成果，但它并不被普通读者所接受。20 世纪 30 年代，随着现代主义文学的式微，传统的现实主义文学重新抬头，政治与宗教再次成为作家关注的焦点。很多作家不再对道德冷漠视之，而是对社会进行无情的讽刺和批判。阿道司·伦纳德·赫胥黎 (Aldous Leonard Huxley, 1894—1963) 用科幻小说的形式表达了对一战后社会的失望；约翰·博因顿·普里斯特利 (John Boynton Priestley, 1894—1984) 在戏剧和小说中讽刺了当时社会混乱的道德观；伊夫林·沃 (Evelyn Waugh, 1903—1966) 的作品讽刺了社会中存在的各种腐败现象和一些人甘愿醉生梦死的颓废生活状态；被称为“天主教作家”的格林厄姆·格林 (Graham Greene, 1904—1991) 在众多小说中描写了人的自然天性与刻板宗教的冲突。20 世纪 30 至 40 年代，通俗小说与严肃小说的分野更加明显。阿加莎·克里斯蒂 (Agatha Christie, 1890—1976) 的侦探小说和罗伯特·格雷夫斯 (Robert Graves, 1895—1985) 的历史小说都拥有大量读者。

20 世纪上半叶，英国诗歌也开始转向现代主义。哈代在放弃小说创作后，全心投入诗歌创作，在 1898 年至 1928 年间共出版 8 部诗集，创作了长篇诗剧《列王》(*The Dynasts*, 1904) 和大量抒情诗歌，既描写乡村和自然，也反思战争、人性和死亡，其独特的诗体、格律和语言也影响了罗伯特·弗洛斯特 (Robert Frost，1874—1963)、威斯坦·休·奥登 (Wystan Hugh Auden, 1907—1973)、菲利普·拉金 (Philip Larkin, 1922—1985) 等众多英美诗人。T. S. 艾略特 (T. S. Eliot, 1888—1965) 则将现代主义诗歌带向高峰。《荒原》(*The Waste Land*, 1922) 描述了西方社会普遍存在的精神枯竭现象和生存危机，并指出，现代社会犹如一片缺乏信仰、丧失道德的荒原。诗作一经发表，就奠定了现代文学的基调。叶芝不仅是推动爱尔兰戏剧复兴的重要人物，他创作的诗歌也推动了爱尔兰民族文化的发展。在创作中，他大量运用爱尔兰的神话和民间传说，努力在诗作中体现爱尔兰诗歌的独特传统，取得了杰出成就，并于 1923 年获得诺贝尔文学奖。奥登在诗歌的形式与主题方面进行了大量探索，既追随哈代的诗风，也接受现代主义的一些影响，成为 20 世纪 30 年代最有影响力的诗人。迪伦·托马斯 (Dylan Thomas, 1914—1953) 是 20 世纪 40 年代英国诗坛的大家。他的诗歌注重抒情，情感浓烈，从细微的感觉去探索生与死的意义，继承了威尔士吟游诗人关注自然和历史的传统，引领了这一时期英国诗歌的新浪漫主义潮流。

Thomas Hardy
1840—1928

托马斯·哈代是跨世纪的文学巨擘，在小说和诗歌创作方面都成绩斐然。他是英国文学史上一个承上启下的作家。一方面，他继承了传统的现实主义创作手法；另一方面，他对劳伦斯等英国现代主义作家产生了巨大影响。

哈代生于多塞特郡的一个石匠之家。他的父母虽然出身低微，却颇有修养，非常重视教育，支持哈代学习。哈代的父亲主要以修缮教堂为生，天生喜爱器乐，常参加教堂的唱诗班和乡间节日的庆祝活动。儿时的哈代也随父亲参与乡间传统的丰收庆典和狂欢，这些活动给哈代留下了深刻影响，并在他的小说中得到了充分的描述和展现。哈代从十六岁开始一直坚持自学法语、德语、拉丁语和希腊语。二十一岁时，哈代来到伦敦，接触到了更广阔的社会。在伦敦的六年期间，哈代感受到上流社会的虚伪与阴暗，观察到繁华都市下隐藏的丑陋和肮脏，这一切使他对故乡恬静的生活、宁静的田野、善良平和的人们有了更深的感情，也使他在以后的创作中总是将文明与原始、都市与自然对立。

哈代最初创作的是诗歌，却屡遭退稿。他便另辟蹊径，开始用笔讲述英格兰西南部的乡村生活，并于 1868 年完成第一部小说《穷汉与贵妇》(*The Poor Man and the Lady*)，但没有出版社愿意出版，小说现已遗失。除此之外，哈代一生共创作发表 14 部小说，大都发生在一个被称为威塞克斯 (Wessex) 的地方，这是以他的故乡多塞特郡为蓝本臆造的一个地方，具有典型的英格兰乡村风情。哈代笔下的威塞克斯代表着英国传统的生活方式和道德观念。他的人物只有顺应了这片古老土地上的习俗和道德才能获得温馨的爱情和宁静的幸福。那些渴望轰轰烈烈的爱情、向往狂热又充满激情的现代生活的人物最终都走向了死亡，因为他们的行为违背了威塞克斯自然原始的生活规则，他们最终无力摆脱古老而神秘的威塞克斯土地，一切努力都是徒劳。

哈代把自己的小说分为三类。第一类是“罗曼史和幻想”(Romances and Fantasies)，第二类是“爱情与阴谋故事”(Novels of Ingenuity)，第三类是“性格与环境小说”(Novels of Character and Environment)。第三类小说大多为悲剧，包含了哈代最主要的作品，如《在绿荫下》(*Under the Greenwood Tree*, 1872)、《远离尘嚣》(*Far from the Madding Crowd*, 1874)、《还乡》(*The Return of the Native*, 1878)、《卡斯特

桥市长》(*The Mayor of Casterbridge*, 1886)、《林地居民》(*The Woodlanders*, 1887)、《德伯家的苔丝》(*Tess of the d'Urbervilles*, 1891) 和《无名的裘德》(*Jude the Obscure*, 1896)。哈代笔下的悲剧是由性格与环境的冲突造成的。人物由于性格与环境格格不入，想摆脱环境的控制，最终却都受到环境的惩罚。哈代认为，"诗人和小说家的任务是表现隐蔽在伟大事物下的悲惨和隐蔽在悲惨事物下的伟大。"因此，在哈代的作品中，小人物反抗环境、反抗命运的徒劳举动又蕴含了一种悲壮的震撼力。在最后一部小说《无名的裘德》中，哈代以他超前的目光对社会和宗教进行了深刻的批判，描述了他理想的人生观、爱情观和婚姻观。然而，由于当时社会的不理解和严厉批评，哈代在完成该作品后便停止小说创作，转向了诗歌。

哈代一生著述丰富。他创造的威塞克斯生动展现了 19 世纪英国农村的面貌，赞扬了农民的淳朴、天真、热情和对爱情的忠贞，同时也表现了现代文明对天然的农村生活带来的影响和冲击。哈代通常被认为是悲剧作家，他笔下的人物难以摆脱命运和环境的捉弄与摆布，而生命中过多的巧合又似乎使人物的努力和奋斗都化为乌有。他在创作中多采用现实主义手法，但他更注重人物的心理和精神世界，而不是物质世界，因为他认为人的精神生活在某种意义上比物质生活更重要。哈代的小说情节曲折，引人入胜，语言优美，富有诗意，对自然的描写有很强的象征性，往往给读者以极大的震撼。尽管生前褒贬不一，但哈代是 19 世纪和 20 世纪之交的文学史上当之无愧的文学巨人。

Tess of the d'Urbervilles

【题解】

在《德伯家的苔丝》中，贫家姑娘苔丝到富"亲戚"亚雷·德伯家帮工，却被其奸污并致怀孕。她毅然离开德伯家，生下一子，不久夭折。她随后到一家牛奶场挤奶，遇到安玑·克莱，与之相爱。在新婚之夜，当苔丝向安玑坦白过去时，并不纯洁的安玑却因此责备苔丝，并离家出走，抛下痛苦万分的苔丝。由于生活所迫，苔丝被迫沦为亚雷·德伯的情妇。安玑在巴西反省自责，意识到错怪了苔丝，便回到英国找她，希望能获得她的原谅。苔丝在绝望中杀死了亚雷，与安玑逃走，但最后被处死。

哈代通过苔丝的悲惨遭遇表达了对社会的谴责。小说的副标题是"一个纯洁的女人"。哈代把一个两度"失身"的女子称为纯洁的女人，对保守虚伪的维多利亚时代道德法则提出了严厉的批评，进行了辛辣的讽刺。小说中的其他人物代表了维多利亚社会中的方方面面。亚雷·德伯在污辱了苔丝以后，却又摇身一变，成了宗教的卫道士，道貌岸然地声称要“拯救”苔丝，实际上却使她陷入更深的痛苦。哈代在这里无情地嘲讽了基督教的伪善。安玑·克莱一方面代表着具有新思想的知识分子，与出身贫寒的苔丝相恋成婚，另一方面却又难以摆脱旧有的道德贞操观的束缚，他的犹豫最终将苔丝推入了绝望的深渊。在故事的结尾，苔丝将妹妹托付给安玑，表明哈代还是肯定了安玑的进步性，他虽然也曾犹豫不决，但最终还是摒弃了陈规旧律，拥抱了苔丝。

下文选自《德伯家的苔丝》第五十八章。苔丝杀死亚雷后，与安玑逃到一所无人居住的空房子，度过了一生中最幸福的五天，直到被警察逮捕。

From Tess of the d'Urbervilles[1]

Chapter 58

The night was strangely solemn and still. In the small hours she whispered to him the whole story of how he had walked in his sleep with her in his arms across the Froom stream, at the imminent risk of both their lives, and laid her down in the stone coffin at the ruined abbey. He had never known of that till now.

"Why didn't you tell me next day?" he said. "It might have prevented much misunderstanding and woe."

"Don't think of what's past!" said she. "I am not going to think outside of now. Why should we! Who knows what to-morrow has in store?"

But it apparently had no sorrow. The morning was wet and foggy, and Clare, rightly informed that the caretaker only opened the windows on fine days, ventured to creep out of their chamber and explore the house, leaving Tess asleep. There was no food on the premises, but there was water, and he took advantage of the fog to emerge from the mansion and fetch tea, bread, and butter from a shop in a little place two miles beyond, as also a small tin kettle and spirit-lamp, that they might get fire without smoke. His re-entry awoke her; and they breakfasted on what he had brought.

They were indisposed to stir abroad, and the day passed, and the night following, and the next, and next; till, almost without their being aware, five days had slipped by in absolute seclusion, not a sight or sound of a human being disturbing their peacefulness, such as it was. The changes of the weather were their only events, the birds of the New Forest their only company. By tacit consent they hardly once spoke of any incident of the past subsequent to their wedding-day. The gloomy intervening time seemed to sink into chaos, over which the present and prior times closed as if it never had been. Whenever he suggested that they should leave their shelter, and go forwards towards Southampton or London, she showed a strange unwillingness to move.

"Why should we put an end to all that's sweet and lovely!" she deprecated. "What must come will come." And, looking through the shutter-chink: "All is trouble outside there; inside here content."

He peeped out also. It was quite true; within was affection, union, error forgiven: outside was the inexorable.

"And—and," she said, pressing her cheek against his; "I fear that what you think of me now may not last. I do not wish to outlive your present feeling for me. I would rather not. I would rather be dead and buried when the time comes for you to despise me, so that it may never be known to me that you despised me."

"I cannot ever despise you."

"I also hope that. But considering what my life has been, I cannot see why any man should, sooner or later, be able to help despising me . . . . How wickedly mad I was! Yet formerly I never could bear to hurt a fly or a worm, and the sight of a bird in a cage used often to make me cry."

They remained yet another day. In the night the dull sky cleared, and the result was that the old caretaker at the cottage awoke early. The brilliant sunrise made her unusually brisk; she decided to open the contiguous mansion immediately, and to air it thoroughly on such a day. Thus it occurred that, having arrived and opened the lower rooms before six o'clock, she ascended to the bedchambers, and was about to turn the handle of the one wherein they lay. At that moment she fancied she could hear the breathing of persons within. Her slippers and her antiquity had rendered her progress a noiseless one so far, and she made for instant retreat; then, deeming that her hearing might have deceived her, she turned anew to the door and softly tried the handle. The lock was out of order, but a piece of furniture had been moved forward on the inside, which prevented her opening the door more than an inch or two. A stream of morning light through the shutter-chink fell upon the faces of the pair, wrapped in profound slumber, Tess's lips being parted like a half-opened flower near his cheek. The caretaker was so struck with their innocent appearance, and with the elegance of Tess's gown hanging across a chair, her silk stockings beside it, the pretty parasol, and the other habits in which she bad arrived because she had none else, that her first indignation at the effrontery of tramps and vagabonds gave way to a momentary sentimentality over this genteel elopement, as it seemed. She closed the door, and withdrew as softly as she had come, to go and consult with her neighbours on the odd discovery.

Not more than a minute had elapsed after her withdrawal when Tess woke, and then Clare. Both had a sense that something had disturbed them, though they could not say what; and the uneasy feeling which it engendered grew stronger. As soon as he was dressed he narrowly scanned the lawn through the two or three inches of shutter-chink.

"I think we will leave at once," said he. "It is a fine day. And I cannot help fancying somebody is about the house. At any rate, the woman will be sure to come to-day."

She passively assented, and putting the room in order they took up the few articles that belonged to them, and departed noiselessly. When they had got into the Forest she turned to take a last look at the house.

"Ah, happy house—good-bye!" she said. "My life can only be a question of a few weeks. Why should we not have stayed there?"

"Don't say it, Tess! We shall soon get out of this district altogether. We'll continue our course as we've begun it, and keep straight north. Nobody will think of looking for us there. We shall be looked for at the Wessex ports if we are sought at all. When we are in the north we will get to a port and away."

Having thus persuaded her the plan was pursued, and they kept a bee line northward. Their long repose at the manor-house lent them walking power now; and towards mid-day they found that they were approaching the steepled city of Melchester, which lay directly in their way. He decided to rest her in a clump of trees during the afternoon, and push onward under cover of darkness. At dusk Clare purchased food as usual, and their night march began, the boundary between Upper and Mid-Wessex being crossed about eight o'clock.

To walk across country without much regard to roads was not new to Tess, and she showed her old agility in the performance. The intercepting city, ancient Melchester, they were obliged to pass through in order to take advantage of the town bridge for crossing a large river that obstructed them. It was about midnight when they went along the deserted streets, lighted fitfully by the few lamps, keeping off the pavement that it might not echo their footsteps. The graceful pile of cathedral architecture rose dimly on their left hand, but it was lost upon them now. Once out of the town they followed the turnpike-road, which after a few miles plunged across an open plain.

Though the sky was dense with cloud a diffused light from some fragment of a moon had hitherto helped them a little. But the moon had now sunk, the clouds seemed to settle almost on their heads, and the night grew as dark as a cave. However, they found their way along, keeping as much on the turf as possible that their tread might not resound, which it was easy to do, there being no hedge or fence of any kind. All around was open loneliness and black solitude, over which a stiff breeze blew.

They had proceeded thus gropingly two or three miles further when on a sudden Clare became conscious of some vast erection close in his front, rising sheer from the grass. They had almost struck themselves against it.

"What monstrous place is this?" said Angel.

"It hums," said she. "Hearken!"

He listened. The wind, playing upon the edifice, produced a booming tune, like the note of some gigantic one-stringed harp. No other sound came from it, and lifting his hand and advancing a step or two, Clare felt the vertical surface of the structure. It seemed to be of solid stone, without joint or moulding. Carrying his fingers onward he found that what he had come in contact with was a colossal rectangular pillar; by stretching out his left hand he could feel a similar one adjoining. At an indefinite height overhead something made the black sky blacker, which had the semblance of a vast architrave uniting the pillars horizontally. They carefully entered beneath and between; the surfaces echoed their soft rustle; but they seemed to be still out of doors. The place was roofless. Tess drew her breath fearfully, and Angel, perplexed, said—"What can it be?"

Feeling sideways they encountered another tower-like pillar, square and uncompromising as the first; beyond it another and another. The place was all doors and pillars, some connected above by continuous architraves.

"A very Temple of the Winds," he said.

The next pillar was isolated; others composed a trilithon; others were prostrate, their flanks forming a causeway wide enough for a carriage; and it was soon obvious that they made up a forest of monoliths grouped upon the grassy expanse of the plain. The couple advanced further into this pavilion of the night till they stood in its midst.

"It is Stonehenge[2]!" said Clare.

"The heathen temple, you mean?"

"Yes. Older than the centuries; older than the d'Urbervilles! Well, what shall we do, darling? We may find shelter further on." But Tess, really tired by this time, flung herself upon an oblong slab that lay close at hand, and was sheltered from the wind by a pillar. Owing to the action of the sun during the preceding day the stone was warm and dry, in comforting contrast to the rough and chill grass around, which had damped her skirts and shoes.

"I don't want to go any further, Angel," she said stretching out her hand for his. "Can't we bide here?"

"I fear not. This spot is visible for miles by day, although it does not seem so now."

"One of my mother's people was a shepherd hereabouts, now I think of it. And you used to say at Talbothays that I was a heathen. So now I am at home."

He knelt down beside her outstretched form, and put his lips upon hers.

"Sleepy are you, dear? I think you are lying on an altar."

"I like very much to be here," she murmured. "It is so solemn and lonely—after my great happiness—with nothing but the sky above my face. It seems as if there were no folk in the world but we two; and I wish there were not—except 'Liza-Lu."

Clare thought she might as well rest here till it should get a little lighter, and he flung his overcoat upon her, and sat down by her side.

"Angel, if anything happens to me, will you watch over 'Liza-Lu for my sake?" she asked, when they had listened a long time to the wind among the pillars.

"I will."

"She is so good and simple and pure. O, Angel—I wish you would marry her if you lose me, as you will do shortly. O, if you would!"

"If I lose you I lose all! And she is my sister-in-law."

"That's nothing, dearest. People marry sister-in-laws continually about Marlott; and 'Liza Lu is so gentle and sweet, and she is growing so beautiful. O I could share you with her willingly when we are spirits! If you would train her and teach her, Angel, and bring her up for your own self! . . . She has all the best of me without the bad of me; and if she were to become yours it would almost seem as if death had not divided us . . . . Well, I have said it. I won't mention it again."

She ceased, and he fell into thought. In the far north-east sky he could see between the pillars a level streak of light. The uniform concavity of black cloud was lifting bodily like the lid of a pot, letting in at the earth's edge the coming day, against which the towering monoliths and trilithons began to be blackly defined.

"Did they sacrifice to God here?" asked she.

"No," said he.

"Who to?"

"I believe to the sun. That lofty stone set away by itself is in the direction of the sun, which will presently rise behind it."

"This reminds me, dear," she said. "You remember you never would interfere with any belief of mine before we were married? But I knew your mind all the same, and I thought as you thought—not from any reasons of my own, but because you thought so. Tell me now, Angel, do you think we shall meet again after we are dead? I want to know."

He kissed her to avoid a reply at such a time.

"O, Angel—I fear that means no!" said she, with a suppressed sob. "And I wanted so to see you again—so much, so much! What—not even you and I, Angel, who love each other so well?"

Like a greater than himself[3], to the critical question at the critical time he did not answer; and they were again silent. In a minute or two her breathing became more regular, her clasp of his hand relaxed, and she fell asleep. The band of silver paleness along the east horizon made even the distant parts of the Great Plain appear dark and near; and the whole enormous landscape bore that impress of reserve, taciturnity, and hesitation which is usual just before day. The eastward pillars and their architraves stood up blackly against the light, and the great flame-shaped Sun-stone beyond them; and the Stone of Sacrifice midway. Presently the night wind died out, and the quivering little pools in the cup-like hollows of the stones lay still. At the same time something seemed to move on the verge of the dip eastward—a mere dot. It was the head of a man approaching them from the hollow beyond the Sun-stone. Clare wished they had gone onward, but in the circumstances decided to remain quiet. The figure came straight towards the circle of pillars in which they were.

He heard something behind him, the brush of feet. Turning, he saw over the prostrate columns another figure; then before he was aware, another was at hand on the right, under a trilithon, and another on the left. The dawn shone full on the front of the man westward, and Clare could discern from this that he was tall, and walked as if trained. They all closed in with evident purpose. Her story then was true! Springing to his feet, he looked around for a weapon, loose stone, means of escape, anything. By this time the nearest man was upon him.

"It is no use, sir," he said. "There are sixteen of us on the Plain, and the whole country is reared."

"Let her finish her sleep!" he implored in a whisper of the men as they gathered round.

When they saw where she lay, which they had not done till then, they showed no objection, and stood watching her, as still as the pillars around. He went to the stone and bent over her, holding one poor little hand; her breathing now was quick and small, like that of a lesser creature than a woman. All waited in the growing light, their faces and hands as if they were silvered, the remainder of their figures dark, the stones glistening green-gray, the Plain still a mass of shade. Soon the light was strong, and a ray shone upon her unconscious form, peering under her eyelids and waking her.

"What is it, Angel?" she said, starting up. "Have they come for me?"

"Yes, dearest," he said. "They have come."

"It is as it should be," she murmured. "Angel, I am almost glad—yes, glad! This happiness could not have lasted. It was too much. I have had enough; and now I shall not live for you to despise me!" She stood up, shook herself, and went forward, neither of the men having moved.

"I am ready," she said quietly.

【注解】

1. d'Urbervilles："d" 是法语 de 的缩写，相当于英语的 of。在欧洲封建社会中，人们把 de 放在贵族的封地地名之前来表示贵族的姓氏，后来这种带有 de 的姓氏就被认为是贵族。
2. Stonehenge: 巨石阵，英国南部索尔兹伯里附近一组立着的石群。
3. a greater than himself: "a greater" 指耶稣基督。

【思考题】

1. How does Tess feel about their five-day stay in the old mansion? Is she eager to leave and reach a safe place? Why or why not?
2. How is Tess discovered by others? What is her response when she is arrested?
3. Hardy rarely questions public morality openly in *Tess of the d'Urbervilles*. Nevertheless, there is a powerful critique of the social principles that were dominant in Tess's time. Find some examples to show Hardy's criticism of the Victorian morality.

【简评】

在以往的作品中，哈代多把人物的悲剧归因于个人性格，而在《德伯家的苔丝》里，哈代把笔触指向社会制度和传统的陈规陋习，指出苔丝的悲剧是由社会造成的。由于社会制度造成的巨大贫富差距，大量农民破产，年仅16岁的苔丝才被迫去德伯家认亲戚、做帮工。在失身之后，当时的社会不会去追究富有的亚雷的责任，不甘心做他人玩物的苔丝毅然离开德伯家。而后，在安玑与苔丝的爱情上，尽管安玑也曾去过妓院，却因无法接受苔丝曾经失身的现实而远走他乡，这也体现了维多利亚时代社会对男性与女性的区别对待。苔丝一方面在精神上承受着巨大的痛苦和压力，另一方面在物质生活上也面临着前所未有的危机。在全家人衣食无着的情况下，她才同意与德伯同居。因此，苔丝的悲惨遭遇是当时社会许多妇女共同命运的写照。苔丝这个人物之所以光彩照人，正是因为她对社会的不断反抗。她在第一次失身后，并没有安于当亚雷的情妇；在她的婴儿濒临死亡时，她不顾宗教礼仪，自己为他施洗；安玑从巴西回来找她，绝望中的苔丝杀死了一手造成她悲惨命运的亚雷，使她的反抗达到高潮；最后，尽管当时的法律禁止与亡妻的姐妹结婚，她仍然将妹妹托付给安玑。苔丝最终被处以死刑，那在风中默默招展的黑旗给人以极强的震撼。

George Bernard Shaw

1856—1950

作者简介

萧伯纳出生于爱尔兰都柏林，但一生的大部分时间在伦敦度过，是著名的剧作家和社会活动家。他生于一个没落的“上流社会”家庭，从小爱读书，十五岁时成为一家房地产公司的小职员，一年后提升为出纳。这份工作使他对贫民窟的生活有所了解。1876年他辞去工作，来到伦敦。1879至1883年间他接连写了5本小说，但都不成功。1882年，受亨利·乔治 (Henry George, 1839—1897) 及其著作《进步与贫困》(*Progress and Poverty*, 1879) 的影响，萧伯纳开始对政治经济学产生兴趣。马克思的《资本论》更加深了他对社会现实的认识。1884年，他加入费边社 (Fabian Society)，经常在街头、公园演说。直到老年，他一直是积极的社会活动家。

对社会问题的关注直接影响了萧伯纳的戏剧创作。他反对19世纪末流行的迎合观众口味、虚假浪漫、不触及社会根本的戏剧，也反对“为艺术而艺术”的唯美主义创作主张。他创作戏剧的目的是要探讨某些严肃的社会问题，并启发观众思考。他对社会问题剧的先驱、挪威剧作家易卜生推崇备至，写了《易卜生主义之精髓》(*The Quintessence of Ibsenism*, 1891) 一书。其早期剧作，《鳏夫的房产》(*Widowers' Houses*, 1892) 描写了贫民区房主的狡诈与贪婪；《华伦夫人的职业》(*Mrs. Warren's Profession*, 1893) 则通过出身低贱的华伦夫人与她受过高等教育的女儿之间的冲突，揭露上流社会那些所谓体面人的肮脏本质。随后，萧伯纳创作发表了《武器与人》(*Arms and the Man*, 1894) 和《康蒂妲》(*Candida*, 1897)，讽刺了传统戏剧对爱情和战争所进行的虚假美化。1897 年发表的《魔鬼的门徒》(*The Devil's Disciple*) 讽刺了利用宗教压制他人的做法。

萧伯纳最重要的戏剧均创作于 20 世纪初叶。《人与超人》(*Man and Superman*, 1905) 是第一部被萧伯纳称为讨论剧 (The Drama of Ideas, or the Discussion Play) 的哲理剧。通过象征"生命力"的安对泰纳的不懈追求，作者探讨了人类优生与创造超人的本能。另一部重要的讨论剧《巴巴拉少校》(*Major Barbara*, 1905) 则大胆地阐述了"贫穷即是罪恶"的观点。《医生的窘境》(*The Doctor's Dilemma*, 1906) 讨论了职业道德的问题。《皮格马利翁》(Pygmalion, 1913) 抨击了当时英国腐朽保守的等级意识，《伤心之家》(*Heartbreak House*, 1920) 是萧伯纳最得意的一部作品，通过强烈的象征手法表现了一战前欧洲的虚假、无聊、困惑等问题。结构庞大的《回到麦修色拉》(*Back to Methuselah*, 1922) 赋予《圣经·旧约》以新的解释。1925 年，萧伯纳以其唯一一部悲剧《圣女贞德》(*St. Joan*, 1923) 获得了当年度诺贝尔文学奖。他创作后期的重要作品包括政治讽刺剧《苹果车》(*The Apple Cart*, 1929) 和《真相毕露》(*Too True to Be Good*, 1932)。

萧伯纳的作品数量惊人 (共 51 部剧作)，多数主题严肃，语言优美，涉及面广，其中即使是严肃的说教也读来生动有力。在戏剧创作手法上，萧伯纳也有颇多创新，如运用长篇前言、后记、狂想曲式的梦境描写等。通过在"新戏剧" (The New Drama) 领域的大胆实践，萧伯纳有力地推动了英国戏剧的复兴。有人认为，萧伯纳在英国戏剧史上的地位仅次于莎士比亚。

Pygmalion

【题解】

《皮格马利翁》是萧伯纳很受广大观众喜爱的喜剧。皮格马利翁是希腊神话中著名的雕塑家，在工作中爱上了自己雕刻的美女像。在他的请求下，爱神阿佛洛狄忒赋予了雕像生命。剧中语音学家希金斯的"实验"与皮格马利翁的经历有相似之处：他用6个月的时间将一位满口伦敦土语的卖花女训练成一位谈吐高雅、举止端庄、足以与任何一位贵妇人相媲美的"上等女人"。不同的是希金斯教授并没有对他的"杰作"产生爱情。

下文为《皮格马利翁》第二幕的一个片段。

From Pygmalion

Act 2 (excerpt)

. . .

The flower girl[1] *enters in state. She has a hat with three ostrich feathers, orange, sky-blue, and red. She has a nearly clean apron and the shoddy coat has been tidied a little. The pathos of this deplorable figure, with its innocent vanity and consequential air, touches Pickering*[2]*, who has already straightened himself in the presence of Mrs Pearce*[3]*. But as to Higgins*[4]*, the only distinction he makes between men and women is that when he is neither bullying nor exclaiming to the heavens against some featherweight cross, he coaxes women as a child coaxes its nurse when it wants to get anything out of her.*

HIGGINS (*brusquely, recognizing her with unconcealed disappointment, and at once, babylike, making an intolerable grievance of it*) Why, this is the girl I jotted down last night. She's no use: I've got all the records I want of the Lisson Grove lingo; and I'm not going to waste another cylinder on it. (*To the girl*) Be off with you: I don't want you.

THE FLOWER GIRL. Dont you be so saucy. You aint heard what I come for yet. *(To Mrs Pearce, who is waiting at the door for further instructions) Did you tell him I come in a taxi?*

MRS PEARCE. Nonsense, girl! What do you think a gentleman like Mr Higgins cares what you came in?

THE FLOWER GIRL. Oh, we are so proud![5] He aint above giving lessons, not him: I heard him say so. Well, I ain't come here to ask for any compliment; and if my money's not good enough I can go elsewhere.

HIGGINS. Good enough for what?

THE FLOWER GIRL. Good enough for y-oo[6]. Now you know, dont you? I'm come to have lessons, I am. And to pay for em t-oo: make no mistake.

HIGGINS (*stupent*) Well!!! (*Recovering his breath with a gasp*) What do you expect me to say to you?

THE FLOWER GIRL. Well, if you was a gentleman, you might ask me to sit down, I think. Don't I tell you[7] I'm bringing you business?

HIGGINS. Pickering: shall we ask this baggage to sit down, or shall we throw her out of the window?

THE FLOWER GIRL (*running away in terror to the piano, where she turns at bay*) Ah-ah-oh-ow-ow-ow-oo! (*Wounded and whimpering*) I won't be called a baggage when I've offered to pay like any lady. *Motionless, the two men stare at her from the other side of the room, amazed.*

PICKERING (*gently*) But what is it you want?

THE FLOWER GIRL. I want to be a lady in a flower shop stead of sellin at the corner of Tottenham Court Road[8]. But they won't take me unless I can talk more genteel. He said he could teach me. Well, here I am ready to pay him—not asking any favor—and he treats me zif I was dirt.

MRS PEARCE. How can you be such a foolish ignorant girl as to think you could afford to pay Mr Higgins?

THE FLOWER GIRL. Why shouldnt I? I know what lessons costs as well as you do; and I'm ready to pay.

HIGGINS. How much?

THE FLOWER GIRL (*coming back to him, triumphant*) Now you're talking! I thought you'd come off it when you saw a chance of getting back a bit of what you chucked at me last night. (*Confidentially*) You'd had a drop in[9], hadn't you?

HIGGINS (*peremptorily*) Sit down.

THE FLOWER GIRL. Oh, if you're going to make a compliment of it—

HIGGINS (*thundering at her*) Sit down.

MRS PEARCE (severely) Sit down, girl. Do as you're told.

THE FLOWER GIRL. AH-ah-ah-ow-ow-oo! (*She stands, half rebellious, half-bewildered*).

PICKERING (*very courteous*) Wont you sit down? (*He places the stray chair near the hearthrug between himself and Higgins*).

LIZA (coyly) Don't mind if I do. (*She sits down. Pickering returns to the hearthrug*).

HIGGINS. What's your name?

THE FLOWER GIRL. Liza Doolittle.

HIGGINS (*declaiming gravely*)

Eliza, Elizabeth, Betsy and Bess,
They went to the woods to get a bird's nes':

PICKERING. They found a nest with four eggs in it:

HIGGINS. They took one apiece, and left three in it.

They laugh heartily at their own fun.

LIZA. Oh, don't be silly.

MRS PEARCE (*placing herself behind Eliza's chair*) You mustn't speak to the gentleman like that.

LIZA. Well, why won't he speak sensible to me?

HIGGINS. Come back to business. How much do you propose to pay me for the lessons?

LIZA. Oh, I know what's right. A lady friend of mine gets French lessons for eighteenpence an hour from a real French gentleman. Well, you wouldn't have the face to ask me the same for teaching me my own language as you would for French; so I won't give more than a shilling. Take it or leave it.

HIGGINS (*walking up and down the room, rattling his keys and his cash in his pockets*) You know, Pickering, if you consider a shilling, not as a simple shilling, but as a percentage of this girl's income, it works out as fully equivalent to sixty or seventy guineas from a millionaire.

PICKERING. How so?

HIGGINS. Figure it out. A millionaire has about £150 a day. She earns about half-a-crown.

LIZA (*haughtily*) Who told you I only—

HIGGINS (*continuing*) She offers me two-fifths of her day's income for a lesson. Two-fifths of a millionaire's income for a day would be somewhere about £60. It's handsome. By George, it's enormous! It's the biggest offer I ever had.

LIZA (*rising, terrified*) Sixty pounds. What are you talking about? I never offered you sixty pounds. Where would I get—

HIGGINS. Hold you tongue.

LIZA (*weeping*) But I aint got sixty pounds. Oh—

MRS PEARCE. Dont cry, you silly girl. Sit down. Nobody is going to touch your money.

HIGGINS. Somebody is going to touch you, with a broomstick, if you don't stop snivelling. Sit down.

LIZA (*obeying slowly*) Ah-ah-ah-ow-oo-o! One would think you was my father.

HIGGINS. If I decide to teach you, I'll be worse than two fathers to you. Here (*he offers her his silk handkerchief*)!

LIZA. Whats this for?

HIGGINS. To wipe your eyes. To wipe any part of your face that feels moist. Remember: that's your handkerchief; and that's your sleeve. Don't mistake the one for the other if you wish to become a lady in a shop.

Liza, utterly bewildered, stares helplessly at him.

MRS PEARCE. It's no use talking to her like that, Mr Higgins: she doesn't understand you. Besides, you're quite wrong: she does'nt do it that way at all (*she takes the handkerchief*).

LIZA (*snatching it*) Here! You give me that handkerchief. He gev it to me, not to you.

PICKERING (*laughing*) He did. I think it must be regarded as her property, Mrs Pearce.

MRS PEARCE (*resigning herself*) Serve you right, Mr Higgins.

PICKERING. Higgins: I'm interested. What about the ambassador's garden party? I'll say you're the greatest teacher alive if you make that good. I'll bet you all the expenses of the experiment you can't do it. And I'll pay for the lessons.

LIZA. Oh, you are real good. Thank you, Captain.

HIGGINS (*tempted, looking at her*) It's almost irresistible. She's so deliciously low—so horribly dirty—

LIZA (*protesting extremely*) Ah-ah-ah-ah-ow-ow-oo-oo!!! I ain't dirty: I washed my face and hands afore I come, I did.

PICKERING. You're certainly not going to turn her head with flattery, Higgins.

MRS PEARCE (*uneasy*) Oh, don't say that, sir: there's more ways than one of turning a girl's head; and nobody can do it better than Mr Higgins, though he may not always mean it. I do hope, sir, you won't encourage him to do anything foolish.

HIGGINS (*becoming excited as the idea grows on him*) What is life but a series of inspired follies? The difficulty is to find them to do. Never lose a chance: it doesn't come every day. I shall make a duchess of this draggletailed guttersnipe.

LIZA (*strongly deprecating this view of her*) Ah-ah-ah-ow-ow-oo!

HIGGINS (*carried away*) Yes: in six months—in three if she has a good ear and a quick tongue—I'll take her anywhere and pass her off as anything. We'll start today: now!

this moment! Take her away and clean her, Mrs Pearce. Monkey Brand[10], if it won't come off any other way. Is there a good fire in the kitchen?

MRS PEARCE (*protesting*) Yes; but—

HIGGINS (*storming on*) Take all her clothes off and burn them. Ring up Whiteley[11] or somebody for new ones. Wrap her up in brown paper til they come.

LIZA. You're no gentleman, you're not, to talk of such things. I'm a good girl, I am; and I know what the like of you are, I do.

HIGGINS. We want none of your Lisson Grove prudery here, young woman. You've got to learn to behave like a duchess. Take her away, Mrs Pearce. If she gives you any trouble, wallop her.

LIZA (*springing up and running between Pickering and Mrs Pearce for protection*) No! I'll call the police, I will.

MRS PEARCE. But I've no place to put her.

HIGGINS. Put her in the dustbin.

LIZA. Ah-ah-ah-ow-ow-oo!

PICKERING. Oh come, Higgins! be reasonable.

MRS PEARCE (*resolutely*) You must be reasonable, Mr Higgins: really you must. You can't walk over everybody like this.

Higgins, thus scolded, subsides. The hurricane is succeeded by a zephyr of amiable surprise.

HIGGINS (*with professional exquisiteness of modulation*) I walk over everybody! My dear Mrs Pearce, my dear Pickering, I never had the slightest intention of walking over anyone. All I propose is that we should be kind to this poor girl. We must help her to prepare and fit herself for her new station in life. If I did not express myself clearly it was because I did not wish to hurt her delicacy, or yours.

Liza, reassured, steals back to her chair.

MRS PEARCE (*to Pickering*) Well, did you ever hear anything like that, sir?

PICKERING (*laughing heartily*) Never, Mrs Pearce: never.

HIGGINS (*patiently*) What's the matter?

MRS PEARCE. Well, the matter is, sir, that you can't take a girl up like that as if you were picking up a pebble on the beach.

HIGGINS. Why not?

MRS PEARCE. Why not! But you don't know anything about her. What about her parents? She may be married.

LIZA. Garn!

HIGGINS. There! As the girl very properly says, Garn! Married indeed! Don't you know that a woman of that class looks a worn out drudge of fifty a year after she's married?

LIZA. Whoo'd marry me?

HIGGINS (*suddenly resorting to the most thrillingly beautiful low tones in his best elocutionary style*) By George, Eliza, the streets will be strewn with the bodies of men shooting themselves for your sake before I've done with you.

MRS PEARCE. Nonsense, sir. You mustn't talk like that to her.

LIZA (*rising and squaring herself determinedly*) I'm goinga way. He's off his chump, he is. I don't want no balmies[12] teaching me.

HIGGINS (*wounded in his tenderest point by her insensibility to his elocution*) Oh, indeed! I'm mad, am I? Very well, Mrs Pearce: you needn't order the new clothes for her. Throw her out.

LIZA (*whimpering*) Nah-ow. You got no right to touch me.

MRS PEARCE. You see now what comes of being saucy. (*Indicating the door*) This way, please.

LIZA (*almost in tears*) I didn't want no clothes. I wouldn't have taken them (*she throws away the handkerchief*). I can buy my own clothes.

HIGGINS (*deftly retrieving the handkerchief and intercepting her on her reluctant way to the door*) You're an ungrateful wicked girl. This is my return for offering to take you out of the gutter and dress you beautifully and make a lady of you.

MRS PEARCE. Stop, Mr Higgins. I wont allow it. It's you that are wicked. Go home to your parents, girl; and tell them to take better care of you.

LIZA. I ain't got no parents. They told me I was big enough to earn my own living and turned me out.

MRS PEARCE. Where's you mother?

LIZA. I ain't got no mother. Her that turned me out was my sixth stepmother. But I done without them. And I'm a good girl, I am.

HIGGINS. Very well, then, what on earth is all this fuss about? The girl doesn't belong to anybody—is no use to anybody but me. (*He goes to Mrs Pearce and begins coaxing*). You can adopt her, Mrs Pearce: I'm sure a daughter would be a great amusement to you. Now don't make any more fuss. Take her downstairs; and—

MRS PEARCE. But what's to become of her? Is she to be paid anything? Do be sensible, sir.

HIGGINS. Oh, pay her whatever is necessary; put it down in the housekeeping book. (*Impatiently*) What on earth will she want with money? She'll have her food and her clothes. She'll only drink if you give her money.

LIZA (*turning on him*) Oh you are a brute. It's a lie: nobody ever saw the sign of liquor on me. (To Pickering) Oh, sir: you're a gentleman: don't let him speak to me like that.

PICKERING (*in good-humored remonstrance*) Does it occur to you, Higgins, that the girl has some feelings?

HIGGINS (*looking critically at her*) Oh no, I don't think so. Not any feelings that we need bother about. (*Cheerily*) Have you, Eliza?

LIZA. I got my feelings same as anyone else.

HIGGINS (*to Pickering, reflectively*) You see the difficulty?

PICKERING. Eh, What difficulty?

HIGGINS. To get her to talk grammar. The mere pronunciation is easy enough.

LIZA. I don't want to talk grammar. I want to talk like a lady in a flower-shop.

MRS PEARCE. Will you please keep to the point, Mr Higgins. I want to know on what terms the girl is to be here. Is she to have any wages? And what is to become of her when you've finished your teaching? You must look ahead a little.

HIGGINS (*impatiently*) What's to become of her if I leave her in the gutter? Tell me that, Mrs Pearce.

MRS PEARCE. That's her own business, not yours, Mr Higgins.

HIGGINS. Well, when I've done with her, we can throw her back into the gutter; and then it will be her own business again; so that's all right.

LIZA. Oh, you've no feeling heart in you: you don't care for nothing but yourself. (*She rises and takes the floor resolutely*). Here! I've had enough of this. I'm going (*making for the door*). You ought to be ashamed of yourself, you ought.

HIGGINS (*snatching a chocolate cream from the piano, his eyes suddenly beginning to twinkle with mischief*) Have some chocolates, Eliza.

LIZA (*halting, tempted*) How do I know what might be in them? I've heard of girls being drugged by the like of you.

Higgins whips out his penknife; cuts a chocolate in two; puts one half into his mouth and bolts it; and offers her the other half.

HIGGINS. Pledge of good faith, Eliza. I eat one half: you eat the other. (*Liza opens her mouth to retort: he pops the half chocolate into it*). You shall have boxes of them, barrels of them, every day. You shall live on them. Eh?

LIZA (*who has disposed of the chocolate after being nearly choked by it*) I wouldn't have ate it, only I'm too ladylike to take it out of my mouth.

HIGGINS. Listen, Eliza. I think you said you came in a taxi.

LIZA. Well, what if I did? I've as good a right to take a taxi as anyone else.

HIGGINS. You have, Eliza; and in future you shall have as many taxis as you want. You shall go up and down and round the town in a taxi every day. Think of that, Eliza.

MRS PEARCE. Mr Higgins: you're tempting the girl. It's not right. She should think of the future.

HIGGINS. At her age! Nonsense! Time enough to think of the future when you hav'nt any future to think of. No, Eliza: do as this lady does; think of other people's futures; but never think of your own. Think of chocolates, and taxis, and gold, and diamonds.

LIZA. No: I don't want no gold and no diamonds. I'm a good girl, I am. (*She sits down again, with an attempt at dignity*).

HIGGINS. You shall remain so, Eliza, under the care of Mrs Pearce. And you shall marry an officer in the Guards, with a beautiful moustache: the son of a marquis, who will disinherit him for marrying you, but will relent when he sees your beauty and goodness—

PICKERING. Excuse me, Higgins; but I really must interfere. Mrs Pearce is quite right. If this girl is to put herself in your hands for six months for an experiment in teaching, she must understand thoroughly what she's doing.

HIGGINS. How can she? She's incapable of understanding anything. Besides, do any of us understand what we are doing? If we did, would we ever do it?

PICKERING. Very clever, Higgins; but not to the present point. (*To Eliza*) Miss Doolittle—

LIZA (*overwhelmed*) Ah-ah-ow-oo!

HIGGINS. There! That's all you'll get out of Eliza. Ah-ah-ow-oo! No use explaining. As a military man you ought to know that. Give her her orders: that's enough for her. Eliza: you are to live here for the next six months, learning how to speak beautifully, like a lady in a florist's shop. If you're good and do whatever you're told, you shall sleep in a proper bedroom, and have lots to eat, and money to buy chocolates and take rides in taxis. If you're naughty and idle you will sleep in the back kitchen among the black beetles, and be walloped by Mrs Pearce with a broomstick. At the end of six months you shall go to Buckingham Palace in a carriage, beautifully dressed. If the King finds out you're not a lady, you will be taken by the police to the Tower of London[13], where your head will be cut off as a warning to other presumptuous flower girls. If you are not found out, you shall have a present of seven-and-sixpence to start life with as a lady in a shop. If you refuse this offer you will be a most ungrateful wicked girl; and the angels will weep for you. (*To Pickering*) Now are you satisfied, Pickering? (*To Mrs Pearce*) Can I put it more plainly and fairly, Mrs Pearce?

MRS PEARCE (*patiently*) I think you'd better let me speak to the girl properly in private. I don't know that I can take charge of her or consent to the arrangement at all. Of course I know you don't mean her any harm; but when you get what you call interested in people's accents, you never think or care what may happen to them or you. Come with me, Eliza.

HIGGINS. That's all right. Thank you, Mrs Pearce. Bundle her off to the bathroom.

LIZA (*rising reluctantly and suspiciously*) You're a great bully, you are. I won't stay here if I don't like. I won't let nobody wallop me. I never asked to go to Bucknam Palace, I did'nt. I was never in trouble with the police, not me. I'm a good girl—

MRS PEARCE. Don't answer back, girl. You don't understand the gentleman. Come with me. (*She leads the way to the door, and holds it open for Eliza*).

LIZA (*as she goes out*) Well, what I say is right. I won't go near the King, not if I'm going to have my head cut off. If I'd known what I was letting myself in for, I wouldn't have come here. I always been a good girl; and I never offered to say a word to him; and I don't owe him nothing; and I don't care; and I won't be put upon; and I have my feelings the same as anyone else—*Mrs Pearce shuts the door; and Eliza's plaints are no longer audible.*

【注解】

1. The flower girl: 在第一幕中卖花女莉莎与希金斯相遇，后者答应纠正她的语音，第二幕开始时即为卖花女前来希金斯府上要求上语音课。
2. Pickering: 即 Colonel Pickering, 剧中的印地语学者，《口语梵文》的作者。
3. Mrs Pearce：希金斯的女管家。
4. Higgins: 剧中的语音学家，教授。

5. we are so proud: 不规范的口语表达方式，正确的应是 I am。
6. y-oo: 伦敦东区土语中 you 的发音。这类土语还包括 t-oo (too)，ah-ah-oh-ow-ow-oo (Oh!), stead of (instead of), sellin (selling), zif (as if), gev (gave), afore (before), whood (who would), nah-ow (no) 等。
7. Don't I tell you: 应为 Didn't I tell you。莉莎的伦敦土语不仅发音不规范，许多表达方式也不符合语法规则。下文中类似的情况有"I done without them"（省略助动词）、"I don't want no gold and no diamonds"（"no"应为 any），等等。
8. Tottenham Court Road: 伦敦最繁华的商业街，街上的家具店比较有名。
9. had a drop in: 醉醺醺的。
10. Monkey Brand: 一种去污粉。
11. Whiteley: 伦敦一家较大的百货商店。
12. balmies: balmy 在英国俚语中有"疯狂的，古怪的"等意思。该词被莉莎用作名词，指"疯狂的人，古怪的人"。
13. the Tower of London: 伦敦塔，曾为王宫和监狱。

【思考题】

1. What is Liza's reason for wanting lessons in speaking? What has caused Higgins to change his attitude and finally to take her as a student?
2. In their attitudes toward Liza, Colonel Pickering forms a contrast to Higgins. What are their differences? What can be discerned about their characters from these differences?
3. Liza is a girl with strong feelings of self-esteem. What examples can you find from the text?

【简评】

与萧伯纳其他较严肃的戏剧一样，该剧也讽刺了中产阶级的虚伪，探讨了诸如"上等人"与"下等人"之间的区别、"灰姑娘"变成"上等人"后该如何生活等社会问题。通过将莉莎从"下等人"训练成为一名"上等人"的实验，萧伯纳试图表明社会衡量一个人不能仅停留在外表，否则得出的印象必定是主观、肤浅的。该剧与一般风尚喜剧 (comedy of manners) 的不同之处不仅在于它严肃的主题，还在于它对卖花女、清洁工的真实描写，以及对莉莎心理转变过程的细致刻画。全剧气氛轻松，对话诙谐机智且不乏讽刺，人物个性鲜明，对希金斯和莉莎的描写尤为出色，充分显示出萧伯纳卓越的喜剧天赋。

Joseph Conrad

1857—1924

作者简介

约瑟夫·康拉德原籍波兰，波兰语姓名约瑟夫·特奥多尔·康拉德·科热尼奥夫斯基 (Józef Teoder Konrad Korzeniowski)，出生于波兰南部的别尔季切夫。当时，他的祖国正处于沙俄统治之下。父母均属乡绅阶层，父亲热衷文学与政治。1862 年，他的父亲因参加波兰独立运动被沙皇政府流放到俄罗斯北部的沃洛格达，五岁的康拉德跟随父母一起来到了流放地。颠沛流离的生活使他的父母相继在流放中死去，康拉德由舅父抚养成人。康拉德十四岁时立志当一名水手。1874 年，康拉德从波兰到法国马赛当海员，开始了他长达二十余年的航海生涯。他先后担任过二副、大副和船长，到过东南亚、非洲、南美等地，目睹了远离本土的西方人在各种极端考验面前所展现出的人品风貌。康拉德的小说大都取材于这段生活中的真实经历或见闻。1878 年，康拉德第一次航行到英国，1886 年加入英国国籍，同时将其波兰语姓名简化为约瑟夫·康拉德。他以惊人的速度学习并掌握了英语。1889 年，康拉德开始创作小说。1895 年，康拉德出版了他的第一部长篇小说《奥尔迈耶的愚蠢》(*Almayer's Folly*)。1898 年，康拉德结束海上生活，定居英国，专门从事小说创作。他一共写了 13 部长篇小说，38 篇中短篇小说和 2 卷回忆录，其中比较著名的有长篇小说《“白水仙”号上的黑家伙》(*The Nigger of the "Narcissus"*, 1897)、《吉姆老爷》(*Lord Jim*, 1900)、《诺斯特罗莫》(*Nostromo*, 1904)、《间谍》(*The Secret Agent*, 1907)、《机缘》(*Chance*, 1912)、《胜利》(*Victory*, 1915) 及中篇小说《青春》(*Youth*, 1902) 和《黑暗的心》(*Heart of Darkness*, 1902) 等。

康拉德在英国文学史上占有相当重要的地位。他的创作处于英国现实主义小说衰落、现代主义小说崛起的过渡阶段，作品兼有现实主义和浪漫主义色彩，又具有现代主义的某些特征。他使用的多重声音 (multiple voice) 和多层次的叙述结构使他的小说具有更为丰富的哲理内涵。庄重、典雅的语言和诗一般的小说意境给他的作品增添了不少魅力。康拉德还受到当时流行的印象主义艺术影响，他的小说创造性地融汇了印象主义的艺术技法，营造了一种似真似幻、扑朔迷离的氛围。康拉德对极端处境中人物的人格进行了探索，揭示了人类善恶双重性的本质，小说多带有悲观、神秘主义色彩，因而显得凄婉深沉，发人深省。康拉德在他的小说中无情抨击了殖民主义的罪恶，表达了他对生活在社会底层的被压迫者的同情。康拉德在漫长的创作生涯中一直孜孜不倦，给世人留下了宝贵的精神财富。

Heart of Darkness

【题解】

康拉德早就萌发了游历非洲的热望。1890 年 5 月 15 日，康拉德启程前往刚果，历经磨难，同年 9 月 24 日返回英国。这次旅行使他看到了真正的非洲。康拉德以他在刚果的经历为素材，创作出他最著名的中篇小说《黑暗的心》。

《黑暗的心》记录了一位名叫马洛的水手所讲的冒险故事，这个故事涉及他的亲身经历，具有异域风光、恐怖冒险、阴谋、伏击、悬念、神秘等冒险小说的特征。马洛被一家殖民公司雇为船长，乘一条汽船沿非洲西岸来到刚果河口，逆流而上，深入非洲中心到达公司设在非洲的总站。他的任务是营救一位生命垂危的贸易站代理人库尔茨。库尔茨原来是个倍受文明熏陶、充满理想主义的非凡人物，但在常驻非洲、进行象牙交易期间，变成了残酷压榨当地黑人的恶魔。途中，马洛听到关于库尔茨的种种传说，对他产生了极大的好奇心，千方百计想见到他。当他终于见到库尔茨时，库尔茨已经生命垂危，死前连呼“恐怖！恐怖！”马洛回到欧洲，将库尔茨的遗物交给他的未婚妻，并谎称库尔茨临终时念叨着未婚妻的名字。

这里选的是小说的开篇。小说以倒叙的形式展开。在苍茫的暮色中，历尽沧桑的水手马洛向其他船员讲述他如何鬼使神差地到达非洲，沿刚果河逆流而上到达总站的所见所闻，嘲讽了“文明”白人的愚昧、无知、贪婪、残暴和荒谬，对黑人的非人遭遇寄予同情，鞭挞了罪恶的殖民统治。

From Heart of Darkness

Part 1

The *Nellie*, a cruising yawl, swung to her anchor without a flutter of the sails, and was at rest. The flood had made[1], the wind was nearly calm, and being bound down the river, the only thing for it was to come to and wait for the turn of the tide.

The sea-reach of the Thames stretched before us like the beginning of an interminable waterway. In the offing the sea and the sky were welded together without a joint, and in the luminous space the tanned sails of the barges drifting up with the tide seemed to stand still in red clusters of canvas sharply peaked, with gleams of varnished sprits. A haze rested on the low shores that ran out to sea in vanishing flatness. The air was dark above Gravesend[2], and farther back still seemed condensed into a mournful gloom, brooding motionless over the biggest, and the greatest, town on earth.

The Director of Companies was our captain and our host. We four affectionately watched his back as he stood in the bows looking to seaward. On the whole river there was nothing that looked half so nautical. He resembled a pilot, which to a seaman is trustworthiness personified. It was difficult to realize his work was not out there in the luminous estuary, but behind him, within the brooding gloom.

Between us there was, as I have already said somewhere, the bond of the sea. Besides holding our hearts together through long periods of separation, it had the effect of making us tolerant of each other's yarns—and even convictions. The Lawyer—the best of old fellows—had, because of his many years and many virtues, the only cushion on deck, and was lying on the only rug. The Accountant had brought out already a box of dominoes[3], and was toying architecturally with the bones. Marlow sat cross-legged right aft, leaning against the mizzenmast. He had sunken cheeks, a yellow complexion, a straight back, an ascetic aspect, and, with his arms dropped, the palms of hands outwards, resembled an idol. The director, satisfied the anchor had good hold, made his way aft and sat down amongst us. We exchanged a few words lazily. Afterwards there was silence on board the yacht. For some reason or other we did not begin that game of dominoes. We felt meditative, and fit for nothing but placid staring. The day was ending in a serenity of still and exquisite brilliance. The water shone pacifically; the sky, without a speck, was a benign immensity of unstained light; the very mist on the Essex marsh was like a gauzy and radiant fabric, hung from the wooded rises inland, and draping the low shores in diaphanous folds. Only the gloom to the west, brooding over the upper reaches, became more sombre every minute, as if angered by the approach of the sun.

And at last, in its curved and imperceptible fall, the sun sank low, and from glowing white changed to a dull red without rays and without heat, as if about to go out suddenly, stricken to death by the touch of that gloom brooding over a crowd of men.

Forthwith a change came over the waters, and the serenity became less brilliant but more profound. The old river in its broad reach rested unruffled at the decline of day, after ages of good service done to the race that peopled its banks, spread out in the tranquil dignity of a waterway leading to the uttermost ends of the earth. We looked at the venerable stream not in the vivid flush of a short day that comes and departs for ever, but in the August light of abiding memories. And indeed nothing is easier for a man who has, as the phrase goes, "followed the sea" with reverence and affection, than to evoke the great spirit of the past upon the lower reaches of the Thames. The tidal current runs to and fro in its unceasing service, crowded with memories of men and ships it had borne to the rest of home or to the battles of the sea. It had known and served all the men of whom the nation is proud, from Sir Francis Drake[4] to Sir John Franklin[5], knights all, titled and untitled—the great knights-errant of the sea. It had borne all the ships whose names are like jewels flashing in the night of time, from the *Golden Hind* returning with her round flanks full of treasure, to be visited by the Queen's Highness and thus pass out of the gigantic tale, to the *Erebus* and *Terror*, bound on other conquests—and that never returned. It had known the ships and the men. They had sailed from Deptford, from Greenwich, from Erith[6]—the adventurers and the settlers; kings, ships and the ships of men on The Change[7]; captains, admirals, the dark "interlopers" of the Eastern trade[8], and the commissioned "generals" of East India fleets. Hunters for gold or pursuers of fame, they all had gone out on that stream, bearing the sword, and often the torch, messengers of the might within the land, bearers of a spark from the sacred fire. What greatness had not floated on the ebb of that river into the mystery of an unknown earth! . . . The dreams of men, the seed of commonwealths, the germs of empires.

The sun set; the dusk fell on the stream, and lights began to appear along the shore. The Chapman lighthouse, a three-legged thing erect on a mud-flat, shone strongly. Lights of ships moved in the fairway—a great stir of lights going up and going down. And farther west on the upper reaches the place of the monstrous town was still marked ominously on the sky, a brooding gloom in sunshine, a lurid glare under the stars.

"And this also," said Marlow suddenly, "has been one of the dark places of the earth."

He was the only man of us who still "followed the sea." The worst that could be said of him was that he did not represent his class. He was a seaman, but he was a wanderer, too, while most seamen lead, if one may so express it, a sedentary life. Their minds are of the stay-at-home order, and their home is always with them—the ship; and so is their country—the sea. One ship is very much like another, and the sea is always the same. In the immutability of their surroundings the foreign shores, the foreign faces, the changing immensity of life, glide past, veiled not by a sense of mystery but by a slightly disdainful ignorance; for there is nothing mysterious to a seaman unless it be the sea itself, which is the mistress of his existence and as inscrutable as Destiny. For the rest, after his hours of work, a casual stroll or a casual spree on shore suffices to unfold for him the secret of a whole continent, and generally he finds the secret not worth knowing. The yarns of seamen have a direct simplicity, the whole meaning of which lies within the shell of a cracked nut. But Marlow was not typical (if his propensity to spin yarns be excepted), and to him the meaning of an episode was not inside like a kernel but outside, enveloping the tale which brought it out only as a glow brings out a haze, in the likeness of one of these misty halos that sometimes are made visible by the spectral illuminination of moonshine.

His remark did not seem at all surprising. It was just like Marlow. It was accepted in silence. No one took the trouble to grunt even; and presently he said, very slow—

"I was thinking of very old times, when the Romans first came here, nineteen hundred years ago-the other day . . . Light came out of this river since—you say Knights? Yes; but it is like a running blaze on a plain, like a flash of lightning in the clouds. We live in the flicker—may it last as long as the old earth keeps rolling! But darkness was here yesterday. Imagine the feelings of a commander of a fine—what d'ye call 'em?—trireme[9] in the Mediterranean, ordered suddenly to the north; run overland across the Gauls[10] in a hurry; put in charge of one of these craft the legionaries—a wonderful lot of handy men they must have been, too—used to build, apparently by the hundred, in a month or two, if we may believe what we read. Imagine him here—the very end of the world, a sea the colour of lead, a sky the colour of smoke, a kind of ship about as rigid as a concertina—and going up this river with stores, or orders, or what you like. Sand-banks, marshes, forests, savages,—precious little to eat fit for a civilized man, nothing but Thames water to drink. No Falernian wine here, no going ashore. Here and there a military camp lost in a wilderness, like a needle in a bundle of hay—cold, fog, tempests, disease, exile, and death—death skulking in the air, in the water, in the bush. They must have been dying like flies here. Oh, yes—he did it. Did it very well, too, no doubt, and without thinking much about it either, except afterwards to brag of what he had gone through in his time, perhaps. They were men enough to face the darkness. And perhaps he was cheered by keeping his eye on a chance of promotion to the fleet at Ravenna by and by, if he had good friends in Rome and survived the awful climate. Or think of a decent young citizen in a toga—perhaps too much dice, you know—coming out here in the train of some prefect, or tax gatherer, or trader even, to mend his fortunes. Land in a swamp, march through the woods, and in some inland post feel the savagery, the utter savagery, had closed round him—all that mysterious life of the wilderness that stirs in the forest, in the jungles, in the hearts of wild men. There's no initiation either into such mysteries. He has to live in the midst of the incomprehensible, which is also detestable. And it has a fascination, too, that goes to work upon him. The fascination of the abomination—you know, imagine the growing regrets, the longing to escape, the powerless disgust, the surrender, the hate."

He paused.

"Mind," he began again, lifting one arm from the elbow, the palm of the hand outwards, so that, with his legs folded before him, he had the pose of a Buddha preaching in European clothes and without a lotus-flower—"Mind, none of us would feel exactly like this. What saves us is efficiency—the devotion to efficiency. But these chaps were not much account, really. They were no colonists; their administration was merely a squeeze, and nothing more, I suspect. They were conquerors, and for that you want only brute force—nothing to boast of, when you have it, since your strength is just an accident arising from the weakness of others. They grabbed what they could get for the sake of what was to be got. It was just robbery with violence, aggravated murder on a great scale, and men going at it blind—as is very proper for those who tackle a darkness. The conquest of the earth, which mostly means the taking it away from those who have a different complexion or slightly flatter noses than ourselves, is not a pretty thing when you look into it too much. What redeems it is the idea only[11]. An idea at the back of it; not a sentimental pretence but an idea; and an unselfish belief in the idea—something you can set up, and bow down before, and offer a sacrifice to . . . ."

He broke off. Flames glided in the river, small green flames, red flames, white flames, pursuing, overtaking, joining, crossing each other—then separating slowly or hastily. The traffic of the great city went on in the deepening night upon the sleepless river. We looked on, waiting patiently—there was nothing else to do till the end of the flood; but it was only after a long silence, when he said, in a hesitating voice, "I suppose you fellows remember I did once turn fresh-water sailor for a bit," that we knew we were fated, before the ebb began to run, to hear about one of Marlow's inconclusive experiences.

"I don't want to bother you much with what happened to me personally," He began, showing in this remark the weakness of many tellers of tales who seem so often unaware of what their audience would best like to hear; "yet to understand the effect of it on me you ought to know how I got out there, what I saw, how I went up that river to the place where

I first met the poor chap. It was the farthest point of navigation and the culminating point of my experience. It seemed somehow to throw a kind of light on everything about me—and into my thoughts. It was sombre enough, too—and pitiful—not extraordinary in any way—not very clear either. No, not very clear. And yet it seemed to throw a kind of light.

"I had then, as you remember, just returned to London after a lot of Indian Ocean, Pacific, China Seas—a regular dose of the East[12]—six years or so, and I was loafing about, hindering you fellows in your work and invading your homes, just as though I had got a heavenly mission to civilize you. It was very fine for a time, but after a bit I did get tired of resting. Then I began to look for a ship—I should think the hardest work on earth. But the ships wouldn't even look at me. And I got tired of that game, too.

"Now when I was a little chap I had a passion for maps. I would look for hours at South America, or Africa, or Australia, and lose myself in all the glories of exploration. At that time there were many blank spaces on the earth, and when I saw one that looked particularly inviting on a map (but they all look that) I would put my finger on it and say, 'When I grow up I will go there,' The North Pole was one of these places, I remember. Well, I haven't been there yet, and shall not try now. The glamour's off. Other places were scattered about the Equator, and in every sort of latitude all over the two hemispheres. I have been in some of them, and . . . well, we won't talk about that. But there was one yet—the biggest, the most blank, so to speak—that I had a hankering after.

"True, by this time it was not a blank space any more. It had got filled since my boyhood with rivers and lakes and names. It had ceased to be a blank space of delightful mystery—a white patch for a boy to dream gloriously over. It had become a place of darkness. But there was in it one river especially, a mighty big river, that you could see on the map, resembling an immense snake uncoiled, with its head in the sea, its body at rest curving afar over a vast country, and its tail lost in the depths of the land. And as I looked at the map of it in a shop-window, it fascinated me as a snake would be a bird—a silly little bird. Then I remembered there was a big concern, a Company for trade on that river. Dash it all! I thought to myself, they can't trade without using some kind of craft on that lot of fresh water—steamboats! Why shouldn't I try to get charge of one? I went on along Fleet Street[13], but could not shake off the idea. The snake had charmed me.

"You understand it was a Continental concern, that Trading society[14]; but I have a lot of relations living on the Continent, because it's cheap and not so nasty as it looks, they say.

"I am sorry to own I began to worry them. This was already a fresh departure for me[15]. I was not used to get things that way, you know. I always went my own road and on my own legs where I had a mind to go. I wouldn't have believed it of myself; but, then—you see—I felt somehow I must get there by hook or by crook. So I worried them. The men said 'My dear fellow,'and did nothing. Then—would you believe it?—I tried the women. I, Charlie Marlow, set the women to work—to get a job. Heavens! Well, you see, the notion drove me. I had an aunt, a dear enthusiastic soul. She wrote: 'It will be delightful. I am ready to do anything, anything for you. It is a glorious idea. I know the wife of a very high personage in the Administration, and also a man who has lots of influence with,' etc. She was determined to make no end of fuss to get me appointed skipper of a river steamboat, if such was my fancy.

"I got my appointment—of course; and I got it very quick. It appears the Company had received news that one of their captains had been killed in a scuffle with the natives. This was my chance, and it made me the more anxious to go. It was only months and months afterwards, when I made the attempt to recover what was left of the body, that I heard the original quarrel arose from a misunderstanding about some hens. Yes, two black hens. Fresleven—that was the fellow's name, a Dane—thought himself wronged somehow in the bargain, so he went ashore and started to hammer the chief of the village with a stick. Oh, it didn't surprise me in the least to hear this, and at the same time to be told that Fresleven was the gentlest, quietest creature that ever walked on two legs. No doubt he was; but he had been a couple of years already out there engaged in the noble cause, you know, and he probably felt the need at last of asserting his self-respect in some way. Therefore he whacked the old nigger mercilessly, while a big crowd of his people watched him, thunderstruck, till some man—I was told the chief's son—in desperation at hearing the old chap yell, made a tentative jab with a spear at the white man—and of course it went quite easy between the shoulder-blades. Then the whole population cleared into the forest, expecting all kinds of calamities to happen, while, on the other hand, the steamer Fresleven commanded left also in a bad panic, in charge of the engineer, I believe. Afterwards nobody seemed to trouble much about Fresleven's remains, till I got out and stepped into his shoes. I couldn't let it rest, though; but when an opportunity offered at last to meet my predecessor, the grass growing through his ribs was tall enough to hide his bones. They were all there. The supernatural being had not been touched after he fell. And the village was deserted, the huts gaped black, rotting, all askew within the fallen enclosures. A calamity had come to it, sure enough. The people had vanished. Mad terror had scattered them, men, women, and children, through the bush, and they had never returned. What became of the hens I don't know either. I should think the cause of progress got them, anyhow. However, through this glorious affair I got my appointment, before I had fairly begun to hope for it.

"I flew around like mad to get ready, and before forty-eight hours I was crossing the Channel to show myself to my employers, and sign the contract. In a very few hours I arrived in a city that always makes me think of a whited sepulchre. Prejudice no doubt. I had no difficulty in finding the Company's offices. It was the biggest thing in the town, and everybody I met was full of it. They were going to run an over-sea empire, and make no end of coin by trade.

"A narrow and deserted street in deep shadow, high houses, innumerable windows with venetian blinds, a dead silence, grass sprouting between the stones, imposing carriage archways right and left, immense double doors standing ponderously ajar. I slipped through one of these cracks, went up a swept and ungarnished staircase, as arid as a desert, and opened the first door I came to. Two women, one fat and the other slim, sat on straw-bottomed chairs, knitting black wool. The slim one got up and walked straight at me—still knitting with downcast eyes—and only just as I began to think of getting out of her way, as you would for a somnambulist, stood still, and looked up. Her dress was as plain as an umbrella-cover, and she turned round without a word and preceded me into a waiting-room. I gave my name, and looked about. Deal table in the middle, plain chairs all round the walls, on one end a large shining map, marked with all the colours of a rainbow. There was a vast amount of red—good to see at any time, because one knows that some real work is done in there, a deuce of a lot of blue, a little green, smears of orange, and, on the East Coast, a purple patch, to show where the jolly pioneers of progress drink the jolly lager-beer. However, I wasn't going into any of these. I was going into the yellow. Dead in the centre. And the river was there—fascinating—deadly—like a snake. Ough! A door opened, a white-haired secretarial head, but wearing a compassionate expression, appeared, and a skinny forefinger beckoned me into the sanctuary. Its light was dim, and a heavy writing-desk squatted in the middle. From behind that structure came out an impression of pale plumpness in a frock-coat. The great man himself. He was five feet six, I should judge, and had his grip on the handle-end of ever so many millions. He shook hands, I fancy, murmured vaguely, was satisfied with my French. *Bon voyage*[16].

"In about forty-five seconds I found myself again in the waiting-room with the compassionate secretary, who, full of desolation and sympathy, made me sign some document. I believe I undertook amongst other things not to disclose any trade secrets. Well, I am not going to.

"I began to feel slightly uneasy. You know I am not used to such ceremonies, and there was something ominous in the atmosphere. It was just as though I had been let into some conspiracy—I don't know—something not quite right; and I was glad to get out. In the outer room the two women knitted black wool feverishly. People were arriving, and the younger one was walking back and forth introducing them. The old one sat on her chair. Her flat cloth slippers were propped up on a foot-warmer, and a cat reposed on her lap. She wore a starched white affair on her head, had a wart on one cheek, and silver-rimmed spectacles hung on the tip of her nose. She glanced at me above the glasses. The swift and indifferent placidity of that look troubled me. Two youths with foolish and cheery countenances were being piloted over, and she threw at them the same quick glance of unconcerned wisdom. She seemed to know all about them and about me, too. An eerie feeling came over me. She seemed uncanny and fateful. Often far away there I thought of these two, guarding the door of Darkness, knitting black wool as for a warm pall, one introducing, introducing continuously to the unknown, the other scrutinizing the cheery and foolish faces with unconcerned old eyes. *Ave*[17]! Old knitter of black wool. *Morituri te Salutant*[18]. Not many of those she looked at ever saw her again—not half, by a long way.

"There was yet a visit to the doctor. 'A simple formality,' assured me the secretary, with an air of taking an immense part in all my sorrows. Accordingly a young chap wearing his hat over the left eyebrow, some clerk I suppose—there must have been clerks in the business, though the house was as still as a house in a city of the dead—came from somewhere up-stairs, and led me forth. He was shabby and careless, with ink-stains on the sleeves of his jacket, and his cravat was large and billowy, under a chin shaped like the toe of an old boot. It was a little too early for the doctor, so I proposed a drink, and thereupon he developed a vein of joviality. As we sat over our vermouths he glorified the Company's business, and by and by I expressed casually my surprise at him not going out there. He became very cool and collected all at once. 'I am not such a fool as I look, quoth Plato to his disciples,' he said sententiously, emptied his glass with great resolution, and we rose.

"The old doctor felt my pulse, evidently thinking of something else the while. 'Good, good for there,' he mumbled, and then with a certain eagerness asked me whether I would let him measure my head. Rather surprised, I said Yes, when he produced a thing like calipers and got the dimensions back and front and every way, taking notes carefully. He was an unshaven little man in a threadbare coat like a gaberdine, with his feet in slippers, and I thought him a harmless fool. 'I always ask leave, in the interests of science, to measure the crania of those going out there,' he said. 'And when they come back, too?' I asked. 'Oh, I never see them,' he remarked; 'and, moreover, the changes take place inside, you know.' He smiled, as if at some quiet joke. 'So you are going out there. Famous. Interesting, too.' He gave me a searching glance, and made another note. 'Ever any madness in your family?' he asked, in a matter-of-fact tone. I felt very annoyed. 'Is that question in the interests of science, too?' 'It would be.' he said, without taking notice of my irritation, 'interesting for science to watch the mental changes of individuals, on the spot, but . . . ' 'Are you an alienist?[19] ' I interrupted. 'Every doctor should be—a little,' answered that original, imperturbably. 'I have a little theory which you messieurs who go out there must help me to prove. This is my share in the advantages my country shall reap from the possession of such a magnificent dependency. The mere wealth I leave to others. Pardon my questions, but you are the first Englishman coming under my observation . . .' I hastened to assure him I was not in the least typical. 'If I were,' said I, 'I wouldn't be talking like this with you.' 'What you say is rather profound, and probably erroneous,' he said, with a laugh. 'Avoid irritation more than exposure to the sun. Adieu. How do you English say, eh? Good-bye. Ah! Good-bye. Adieu. In the tropics one must before everything keep calm.' . . . He lifted a warning forefinger . . . . '*Du calme, du calme. Adieu.*' . . .

【注解】

1. The flood had made: 根据上下文可知此句意为“潮水开始上涨”。
2. Gravesend: 格雷弗森德，地名，在伦敦附近。
3. dominoes: 多米诺骨牌，一种游戏。
4. Sir Francis Drake: 弗朗西斯·德雷克爵士驾驶金鹿号，听命于伊丽莎白一世，为英国雄霸海上立下汗马功劳。
5. Sir John Franklin: 约翰·弗兰克林爵士于 1845 年率领一只探险队，驾驶埃里巴斯和特罗号，寻找“西北航道”。但 1848 年冬天，船上人员全部遇难。
6. from Deptford . . . Erith: "Deptford" "Greenwich" "Erith" 指德特福、格林威治、埃瑞斯，是位于伦敦和格雷弗森德的三个海港城市。
7. The Change: 指伦敦的股票交易所。
8. the dark "interlopers" of the Eastern Trade: 去东方做买卖、无行船执照的走私犯。

9. trireme: 三层桨座的战舰。
10. the Gauls: 指法国北部的高卢区。
11. What redeems it is the idea only: 倘若能够给这种做法正名的话，只有依靠所谓看法不同的托词了。
12. a regular dose of the East: 作者用暗喻的手法，幽默地表达出“这是一次例行的东方之行”。
13. Fleet Street: 伦敦的一条街，也是新闻业的代名词。
14. You understand it was a Continental concern, that Trading Society: 你们知道那是大陆上的一家商号，一家大贸易公司。
15. This was already a fresh departure for me: 根据上下文，此句意为“这对我来说，像是变成了另一个人”。
16. Bon Voyage: 法语，意为“一路顺风”。
17. Ave: 拉丁语，意为“万福”。
18. Morituri te Salutant: 拉丁语，意为“死神向你致敬”。
19. an alienist: (旧用法) 精神病学家。

【思考题】

1. What is the tone of Conrad when he describes the people going out on the Thames to remote parts of the world? What is the “monstrous town,” or the “brooding gloom”?
2. What does the narrator mean when he says that to Marlow “the meaning of an episode was not inside like a kernel but outside, enveloping the tale which brought it out only as a glow brings out a haze . . . ”?
3. Pick out the phrases and words that have satirical or symbolic overtones in the selection, and explain them.
4. Marlow as a narrator also appears in Conrad’s other novels. Comment on the advantages of using such a narrator for the novelist.
5. The Nigerian writer Chinua Achebe claims that *Heart of Darkness* is an “offensive and deplorable book” that “set[s] Africa up as a foil to Europe, as a place of negations at once remote and vaguely familiar, in comparison with which Europe’s own state of spiritual grace will be manifest.” Do you agree with Achebe? Why or why not?

【简评】

《黑暗的心》包含多个层次。首先，它是用浪漫主义手法写成的一篇异域历险故事。其次，它用现实主义手法对帝国主义殖民政策进行批判。再次，它用印象主义手法揭示文明与原始的对立。最后，它用象征主义手法表现了人心的黑暗。马洛从欧洲走向非洲，是从文明走向原始，是深入人性的潜意识认识人在剥去文明外衣后的“伊德”(Id)，发现人本质上的善恶二重性。小说的标题在一定程度上暗示了主题。

在一个层次上，它指刚果的自然地理及其居民的肤色，表示了一种原始的“黑色”。在另一个层次上，它指殖民者在刚果的罪恶活动，暗示这些“光明的使者”实际上有一颗“黑暗的心”。黑与白的本义与它们代表的意义互为颠倒，彼此对立，具有嘲讽意味。

William Butler Yeats
1865—1939

作者简介

威廉·巴特勒·叶芝，爱尔兰诗人、戏剧家和批评家，出生于都柏林一个新教家庭，其父是著名肖像画家。五岁时，全家迁居伦敦。1884 年叶芝进入都柏林艺术学校学习画画，但因其志在写作，不久便离开学校，专注于诗歌创作。1885 年叶芝开始出版诗作，1887 年返回伦敦，结识唯美主义作家王尔德、莫里斯、欧内斯特·道生 (Ernest Dowson, 1867—1900) 等人，并着手编辑威廉·布莱克的诗集，其创作也深受布莱克的影响。

1894 年叶芝访问巴黎，开始了解法国近代诗人，而在他的朋友、英国诗人兼批评家亚瑟·西蒙斯 (Arthur Symons, 1865—1945) 的影响下，他对象征诗派也有了深刻了解。唯美主义和象征主义对叶芝早期的创作很有影响。叶芝早年曾参加爱尔兰独立运动，但后来脱离政治运动，专心于文学创作，认为这是唤起爱尔兰民族意识、求得民族独立的有效途径。1896 年他结识爱尔兰戏剧家格雷戈里夫人，并于 1904 年与她在都柏林共同创办阿比剧团 (The Abbey Theatre)。叶芝亲自管理阿比剧团，创作了许多剧本，包括《时漏》(*The Hour Glass*, 1903)、《理想的国土》(*The Land of Heart's Desire*, 1894)、《黛德尔》(*Dedidre*, 1907) 等。1911 年，叶芝随阿比剧团去美国巡回演出，结识美国当代诗人庞德，两人互有影响。此前，叶芝曾于 1889 年遇见演员莫德·龚因 (Maud Gonne, 1866—1953)。龚因也是爱尔兰独立运动的积极参与者。叶芝狂热地爱上了她，并为她写下了不少优美的诗章，下文所选的《当你老了》("When You Are Old") 就是其中较为著名的一首。

叶芝的诗歌创作可分为三个时期。早期作品多取材于神话，带有神秘主义色彩，一方面继承了当时爱尔兰民间的相信魔法、幻术的传统，另一方面也受斯宾塞、雪莱及布莱克的影响。这一时期的作品主要有《世间玫瑰》("The Rose of the World", 1892)、《伊尼斯弗里湖岛》("The Lake Isle of Innisfree", 1890)、《梦想仙境的人》

("The Man Who Dreamed of Faeryland", 1891)、《戈尔王的疯狂》("The Madness of King Goll", 1889) 等。

之后，受爱尔兰民族主义及德国哲学家尼采的影响，叶芝的诗歌开始追求一种更简洁、更大众化的风格，多以政治和个人心理为题材，内容朴实，形象趋于具体，文字亦较前简练，不再追求一种“非人格的美”(impersonal beauty)。叶芝这一时期的创作成就主要体现在《在那七片树林里》(*In the Seven Woods*, 1903)、《绿盔及其他》(*The Green Helmet and Other Poems*, 1910) 及《责任》(*Responsibilities*, 1914) 中。

创办阿比剧团的经历，时事的动荡，以及庞德和艾略特创作和评论的影响，促使叶芝再一次对自己的创作风格进行调整，在追求文辞缜密、雅俗共赏的基础上，加入某些“空灵”的成分，力图创建一个天人合一的神秘主义和象征主义体系，以求宇宙观和艺术创作的统一。在他的散文作品《幻象》(*A Vision*, 1925/1937) 及 1938 年出版的三卷本《自传》(*Autobiographies*) 中，叶芝阐述了这一体系。这一体系的建立不仅仅是出于哲学和神学的需要，更多的是为了满足叶芝艺术创作的要求。《第二次降临》("The Second Coming", 1919) 和《驶向拜占庭》("Sailing to Byzantium", 1928) 两诗对此都有所反映。叶芝这一时期的主要诗作均收录于《塔》(*The Tower*, 1928) 及《盘旋的楼梯》(*The Winding Stair*, 1929) 中。

叶芝认为创造性的想象可以升华个人的经验，他的诗歌具有独特的魅力和超乎现实主义的感情深度。艾略特曾这样评论叶芝，他是“当代最伟大的诗人，在英语中自无疑问，在我看来也是任何语言中最伟大的诗人。”因其在文学创作中的巨大成就，叶芝于 1923 年获得诺贝尔文学奖。

When You Are Old

【题解】

此诗为叶芝 1891 年为他的恋人龚因所写，系受法国 16 世纪诗人龙沙的一首十四行诗的启发而作。龙沙的这首十四行诗没有题目，开头一行为“Quand vouz sevez bien vieille, an soir, à la chandelle”（当你年老时，夜晚秉烛而坐），与叶芝《当你老了》的起句十分相近，但两诗结尾相去甚远。叶芝的诗虽短，但感情浓烈而含蓄，明显带有斯宾塞和雪莱等人所代表的浪漫主义传统色彩，充分表达了诗人对龚因真挚、脱俗的感情。

When You Are Old

When you are old and grey and full of sleep,
And nodding by the fire, take down this book[1],
And slowly read, and dream of the soft look
Your eyes had once, and of their shadows deep[2];

How many loved your moments of glad grace[3],
And loved your beauty with love false or true,
But one man loved the pilgrim soul in you[4],
And loved the sorrows of your changing face[5];

And bending down beside the glowing bars[6],
Murmur, a little sadly, how love fled
And paced upon the mountains overhead
And hid his face amid a crowd of stars.

【注解】

1. And hodding . . . this book: 此句中“the fire”指壁炉的炉火；“this book”指叶芝写给莫德的诗信。
2. and of their shadows deep: “their”指眼睛；“shadows deep”指眼光深沉清澈。
3. your moments of glad grace: 你欢乐时刻的魅力。这里所写的“glad grace”与下一行所提到的“beauty”（美貌）均为世俗所爱慕的表面、肤浅的东西，与叶芝说他所爱的“the pilgrim soul in you”和“sorrows of your changing face”形成鲜明对比。
4. But one man loved the pilgrim soul in you: 此行为诗人自指。“pilgrim”是宗教的朝圣者，“pilgrim soul”指龚因对爱尔兰民族独立的追求如同朝圣者一般虔诚。
5. the sorrows of your changing face: “sorrows”泛指严肃深沉的感情，而“changing face”则是指常变的、动态的美，均相对第六行中外表的、静态的美貌 (beauty) 而言。
6. the glowing bars: 指被炉火映照着的壁炉铁箅。

【思考题】

1. The poet does not directly state how much he loves the actress now, but pictures a scene in the far future when she is old. Do you think the method is effective? Why?
2. What is the meaning or purpose of the last stanza? What figures of speech are used here, and what is the message the pictures convey to you in the last several lines?
3. How does the poet contrast his love for her with the love of others?

The Lake Isle of Innisfree

【题解】

此诗是叶芝著名的抒情诗之一，是他在 19 世纪后期盛行于英国的前拉斐尔派 (Pre-Raphaelites) 的影响下创作的作品。伊尼斯弗里是爱尔兰西部斯莱戈 (Sligo) 附近吉尔湖 (Lough Gill) 的一个小岛。斯莱戈是叶芝青年时代居住过的地方。在他的自传里，叶芝对创作这首诗的情况有如下记载："我仍然保存着十几岁时在斯莱戈就有的想法，想仿效梭罗。……一天我怀着浓厚的乡思走过舰队街 (Fleet Street)，忽然听见细细的滴水声，看见一家商店橱窗里装饰着一股小喷泉，喷出的水顶着一只小球，使它不断在空中旋转，不落下来，这使我想起了湖水。凭这一时的回想，我写出《伊尼斯弗里湖岛》这首诗。这是我第一首具有自己音调的抒情诗。我开始灵活运用音律以避免繁缛的修辞和人们随之习惯发出的感慨。但当时我还只是模糊地，而不是经常地意识到，为了达到这个目的，我应当只使用普通的句子结构。如果是晚几年的话，我就不会在第一行里使用'arise and go'这种陈旧的说法，也不会在最后一节里用上倒装句法了。"

《伊尼斯弗里湖岛》一诗结构紧凑，语言流畅，富有韵律感，表达了诗人渴望回归自然，过一种古老、纯朴、隐士般生活的愿望。

The Lake Isle of Innisfree

I will arise and go now[1], and go to Innisfree,
And a small cabin build there, of clay and wattles made[2];
Nine bean-rows will I have there, a hive for the honey-bee,
And live alone in the bee-loud glade[3].

And I shall have some peace there, for peace comes dropping slow[4],
Dropping from the veils of the morning to where the cricket sings[5];
There midnight's all a glimmer, and noon a purple glow,
And evening full of the linnet's wings[6].

I will arise and go now, for always night and day,
I hear lake water lapping with low sounds by the shore;

While I stand on the roadway, or on the pavements grey,
I hear it in the deep heart's core.

【注解】

1. I will arise and go now: 这一句和《圣经》的语言类似，所以叶芝在自传中说它是“陈旧”的语言。
2. of clay and wattles made: 指小屋是用树枝柳条敷上泥土制成的。
3. the bee-loud glade: “glade” 指树林中的空旷地，“bee-loud” 指蜜蜂的嗡嗡声不绝于耳。
4. peace comes dropping slow: 闲适安静的境界 (peace) 是点滴聚成 (comes dropping slow)，即慢慢形成的。
5. Dropping from . . . sings: “the veils of the morning” 指清晨的薄薄烟雾。“where the cricket sings” 则是以对比手法，用有声的蟋蟀来衬托静寂的气氛，与英国浪漫主义诗人济慈的十四行诗 “On the Grasshopper and the Cricket” 中的描写有异曲同工之妙。
6. full of the linnet's wings: 指红雀 (linnet) 四处飞舞。

【思考题】

1. Read the poem aloud, and determine its meter and rhyme. What are the effects of these musical elements?
2. What do “roadway” and “pavements gray” in line 11 stand for? What is the meaning of the last two lines?
3. What does Innisfree symbolize in the poem?

James Joyce
1882—1941

作者简介

詹姆斯·乔伊斯出生于爱尔兰都柏林，其父约翰·乔伊斯为都柏林税务官，收入丰厚。1891年，乔伊斯的父亲因政治原因被解职，又不善持家，从此家道中落，依靠典押和借债度日。乔伊斯六岁时进入天主教耶稣会办的学校学习，由于才智出众、成绩优秀而年年获奖。天主教学校宗教教育十分严格，乔伊斯却逐渐认识到宗教只是一种精神枷锁，并拒绝担任圣职。1898年，乔伊斯进入皇家大学都柏林学院攻读语言学，博览群书，掌握多种外语，对文学产生了浓厚的兴趣。他认为爱尔兰的狭隘闭塞只会扼杀他的文学生命，因此下定决心，弃家离国。1902年获学士学位之后，乔伊斯前往巴黎，依靠写书评和教英语为生，常常食不果腹。他在这一时期的书评和美学笔记后来被汇编成《詹姆斯·乔伊斯评论文集》(*Critical Writings*)，于1959年出版。1903年4月，乔伊斯因其母病危回国。母亲的亡故带给他沉重的精神打击。正像《一个青年艺术家的肖像》(*A Portrait of the Artist as a Young Man*, 1916) 里所描绘的那样，他常常一个人在孤独的夜里徘徊于都柏林的街头。

1904年发生的两件事在乔伊斯一生中占据了非常重要的位置。头件大事是开始写小说《英雄斯蒂芬》(*Stephen Hero*, 1904)，后改写成《一个青年艺术家的肖像》。另一件大事是同年6月16日，乔伊斯结识了将要与他患难与共、终生相伴的女友娜拉·巴纳克。他后来把这一天定为巨著《尤利西斯》(*Ulysses,* 1922) 的故事发生日，从而使这一天成为西方文学界的一个重要节日——布卢姆 (Bloom) 日。乔伊斯携娜拉赴意大利港口城市的里雅斯特，后几经辗转，颠沛流离，直到1920年应庞德之邀方在巴黎定居。尽管生活拮据，发表作品困难重重，乔伊斯还是完成了《都柏林人》(*Dubliners*, 1914) 和《一个青年艺术家的肖像》的创作，并从1914年开始创作《尤利西斯》，于1921年完成。从三十五岁开始，乔伊斯疾病缠身，1923年创作最后一部作品时，不得不用口授的形式。

乔伊斯也曾涉足诗歌和戏剧领域。他从十五六岁时就开始写诗歌或素描小品，但大多没有保存。1900年发表易卜生剧评，得到易卜生本人的赞赏。1907年，乔伊斯创作发表了诗集《室内乐》(*Chamber Music*)，1918年发表了唯一一部剧本《流亡》(*Exile*)。乔伊斯在小说方面成就最高，却历尽坎坷。第一部短篇小说集《都柏林人》遭到多个出版商的冷遇，等待了整整八年才得以问世，然而其客观冷静、细致入微的笔法和对社会毫不留情的批判给读者留下了深刻的印象，反映出乔伊斯绝不粉饰人生的艺术品质。第二部小说《一个青年艺术家的肖像》是一部半自传性小说，它采用自由联想、内心独白等意识流创作手法，表现了青年艺术家斯蒂芬在心理与艺术方面的成长历程。第三部作品《尤利西斯》是《一个青年艺术家的肖像》的继续和发展。作者大量运用意识流技巧，成功描绘了布卢姆这一人物的内心世界，反映出作者在人物描写上的深度和广度。《尤利西斯》被誉为西方文学中意识流小说的经典之作。乔伊斯的最后一部作品《芬尼根守灵夜》(*Finnegans Wake*, 1939) 历时14个寒暑，他在创作过程中字斟句酌，有时一段文字要改写14次以上。作品中描写的梦情节复杂、多变，极具象征意义。此外作者还采用多种语言风格、各种各样的新字和多层次的结构，使得这部绝笔之作深奥难懂。

乔伊斯是一个勤奋的天才，也是一个孤独的叛逆者，在"自我放逐"中追求艺术的完美。他对人性的洞察和直率的描述，对语言的体会和掌握，以及在写作技巧方面的创新与探索，都对西方20世纪的文学发展产生了巨大的影响。

Eveline

【题解】

《伊芙琳》是乔伊斯短篇小说集《都柏林人》中的第四篇。《都柏林人》创作于1904至1907年之间，共有15个短篇，《伊芙琳》一篇最直接地表现了都柏林青年人瘫痪的精神状态。女主人公的生活单调、乏味，其父生性暴躁。她认识了一个叫弗兰克的外国水手，两人在私下里来往。弗兰克策划让她随船与自己私奔，经过激烈的思想斗争后伊芙琳决定外逃。“逃跑！她必须逃跑！弗兰克会拯救她，会给她带来生活，甚至爱情。”但就在轮船启航前，她动摇、害怕了，发现自己没有勇气奔向梦寐以求的自由。心灵的瘫痪终于使她的理想和追求破灭流产。

Eveline

She sat at the window watching the evening invade the avenue. Her head was leaned against the window curtains and in her nostrils was the odour of dusty cretonne. She was tired.

Few people passed. The man out of the last house passed on his way home; she heard his footsteps clacking along the concrete pavement and afterwards crunching on the cinder path before the new red houses. One time there used to be a field in which they used to play every evening with other people's children. Then a man from Belfast bought the field and built houses in it—not like their little brown houses[1], but bright brick houses with shining roofs. The children of the avenue used to play together in that field—the Devines, the Waters, the Dunns, little Keogh the cripple, she and her brothers and sisters. Ernest, however, never played: he was too grown up. Her father used often to hunt them in out of the field with his blackthorn stick[2]; but usually little Keogh used to keep nix[3] and call out when he saw her father coming. Still they seemed to have been rather happy then. Her father was not so bad then; and besides, her mother was alive. That was a long time ago; she and her brothers and sisters were all grown up; her mother was dead. Tizzie Dunn was dead, too, and the Waters had gone back to England. Everything changed. Now she was going to go away like the others, to leave her home.

Home! She looked round the room, reviewing all its familiar objects which she had dusted once a week for so many years, wondering where on earth all the dust came from. Perhaps she would never see again those familiar objects from which she had never dreamed of being divided. And yet during all those years she had never found out the name of the priest whose yellowing photograph hung on the wall above the broken harmonium beside the coloured print of the promises made to Blessed Margaret Mary Alacoque[4]. He had been a school friend of her father. Whenever he showed the photograph to a visitor her father used to pass it with a casual word:

—He is in Melbourne now.

She had consented to go away, to leave her home. Was that wise? She tried to weigh each side of the question. In her home anyway she had shelter and food; she had those whom she had known all her life about her. Of course she had to work hard, both in the house and at business. What would they say of her in the Stores when they found out that she had run away with a fellow? Say she was a fool, perhaps; and her place would be filled up by advertisement. Miss Gavan would be glad. She had always had an edge on her, especially whenever there were people listening.

—Miss Hill, don't you see these ladies are waiting?

—Look lively, Miss Hill, please.

She would not cry many tears at leaving the Stores.

But in her new home, in a distant unknown country, it would not be like that. Then she would be married—she, Eveline. People would treat her with respect then. She would not be treated as her mother had been. Even now, though she was over nineteen, she sometimes felt herself in danger of her father's violence. She knew it was that that had given her the palpitations. When they were growing up he had never gone for her, like he used to go for Harry and Ernest, because she was a girl; but latterly he had begun to threaten her and say what he would do to her only for her dead mother's sake. And now she had nobody to protect her. Ernest was dead and Harry, who was in the church decorating business, was nearly always down somewhere in the country. Besides, the invariable squabble for money on Saturday nights had begun to weary her unspeakably. She always gave her entire wages—seven shillings—and Harry always sent up what he could but the trouble was to get any money from her father. He said she used to squander the money, that she had no head, that he wasn't going to give her his hard-earned money to throw about the streets, and much more, for he was usually fairly bad of a Saturday night. In the end he would give her the money and ask her had she any intention of buying Sunday's dinner. Then she had to rush out as quickly as she could and do her marketing, holding her black leather purse tightly in her hand as she elbowed her way through the crowds and returning home late under her load of provisions. She had hard work to keep the house together and to see that the two young children who had been left to her charge went to school regularly and got their meals regularly. It was hard work—a hard life—but now that she was about to leave it she did not find it a wholly undesirable life.

She was about to explore another life with Frank. Frank was very kind, manly, open-hearted. She was to go away with him by the night-boat to be his wife and to live with him in Buenos Ayres[5] where he had a home waiting for her. How well she remembered the first time she had seen him; he was lodging in a house on the main road where she used to visit. It seemed a few weeks ago. He was standing at the gate, his peaked cap pushed back on his head and his hair tumbled forward over a face of bronze. Then they had come to know each other. He used to meet her outside the Stores every evening and see her home. He took her to see *The Bohemian Girl*[6] and she felt elated as she sat in an unaccustomed part of the theatre with him. He was awfully fond of music and sang a little. People knew that they were courting and, when he sang about the lass that loves a sailor, she always felt pleasantly confused. He used to call her Poppens[7] out of fun. First of all it had been an excitement for her to have a fellow and then she had begun to like him. He had tales of distant countries. He had started as a deck boy at a pound a month on a ship of the Allan Line[8] going out to Canada. He told her the names of the ships he had been on and the names of the different services. He had sailed through the Straits of Magellan[9] and he told her stories of the terrible Patagonians[10]. He had fallen on his feet in Buenos Ayres, he said, and had come over to the old country just for a holiday. Of course, her father had found out the affair and had forbidden her to have anything to say to him.

—I know these sailor chaps, he said.

One day he had quarreled with Frank and after that she had to meet her lover secretly.

The evening deepened in the avenue. The white of two letters in her lap grew indistinct. One was to Harry; the other was to her father. Ernest had been her favourite but she liked Harry too. Her father was becoming old lately, she noticed; he would miss her. Sometimes he could be very nice. Not long before, when she had been laid up for a day, he had read her out a ghost story and made toast for her at the fire. Another day, when their mother was alive, they had all gone for a picnic to the Hill of Howth. She remembered her father putting on her mother's bonnet to make the children laugh.

Her time was running out but she continued to sit by the window, leaning her head against the window curtain, inhaling the odour of dusty cretonne. Down far in the avenue she could hear a street organ playing. She knew the air. Strange that it should come that very night to remind her of the promise to her mother, her promise to keep the home together as long as she could. She remembered the last night of her mother's illness; she was again in the close dark room at the other side of the hall and outside she heard a melancholy air of Italy. The organ-player had been ordered to go away and given sixpence[11]. She remembered her father strutting back into the sickroom saying:

—Damned Italians[12]! Coming over here!

As she mused the pitiful vision of her mother's life laid its spell on the very quick of her being—that life of commonplace sacrifices closing in final craziness. She trembled as she heard again her mother's voice saying constantly with foolish insistence:

—Derevaun Seraun[13]! Derevaun Seraun!

She stood up in a sudden impulse of terror. Escape! She must escape! Frank would save her. He would give her life, perhaps love, too. But she wanted to live. Why should she be unhappy? She had a right to happiness. Frank would take her in his arms, fold her in his arms. He would save her.

She stood among the swaying crowd in the station at the North Wall. He held her hand and she knew that he was speaking to her, saying something about the passage over and over again. The station was full of soldiers with brown baggages. Through the wide doors of the sheds she caught a glimpse of the black mass of the boat, lying in beside the quay wall, with illumined portholes[14]. She answered nothing. She felt her cheek pale and cold and, out of a maze of distress, she prayed to God to direct her, to show her what was her duty. The boat blew a long mournful whistle into the mist. If she went, tomorrow she would be on the sea with Frank, steaming towards Buenos Ayres. Their passage had been booked. Could she still draw back after all he had done for her? Her distress awoke a nausea in her body and she kept moving her lips in silent fervent prayer.

A bell clanged upon her heart. She felt him seize her hand:

—Come!

All the seas of the world tumbled about her heart. He was drawing her into them: he would drown her. She gripped with both hands at the iron railing.

—Come!

No! No! No! It was impossible. Her hands clutched the iron in frenzy. Amid the seas she sent a cry of anguish!

—Eveline! Evvy!

He rushed beyond the barrier and called to her to follow. He was shouted at to go on but he still called to her. She set her white face to him, passive, like a helpless animal. Her eyes gave him no sign of love or farewell or recognition.

【注解】

1. little brown houses: 在《英雄斯蒂芬》里，乔伊斯曾提到过“棕色”的隐含意义：“……棕色的小房屋似乎是爱尔兰瘫痪的化身。”
2. his blackthorn stick: 在爱尔兰的传说中黑刺李 (blackthorn) 是一种不祥的树木，常与暴力和魔法相连。
3. to keep nix: “nix” 相当于 no、nothing 或 watch out。这里意为站岗放哨。
4. the promises made to Blessed Margaret Mary Alacoque: “Blessed Margaret Mary Alacoque” 即圣玛格丽特·玛丽·阿拉柯克，法国修女，以苦修而闻名。
5. Buenos Ayres: 即 Buenos Aires，南美港口，现阿根廷首都布宜诺斯艾利斯。
6. *The Bohemian Girl*: 轻歌剧《波希米亚女郎》。剧中出身贵族的 Arlene 被吉卜赛人绑架，十二年后长成美丽的吉卜赛女郎，后被吉卜赛女王出卖，幸遇分别多年的父亲，重新过上富裕的生活。然而她还是深深地怀念自由不羁的吉卜赛生活。
7. Poppens: 即 Poppet, 一种昵称，类似于“可爱的小人儿”。
8. Allan Line: 阿兰航线。从英国的利物浦出发，途经南美几个港口 (如里约热内卢、布宜诺斯艾利斯等)，绕过合恩角抵达太平洋沿岸的美国和加拿大。
9. Straits of Magellan: 连接太平洋和大西洋的麦哲伦海峡。
10. the terrible Patagonians: 生活在阿根廷南端的部落。
11. sixpence: 六便士。通常小费数目在一到两个便士。
12. Damned Italians: 当时爱尔兰的意大利移民不多，大多以巡回演出为业。
13. Derevaun Seraun: 错误的爱尔兰盖尔语，意为“幸福的结局是痛苦”。另一解释为“歌曲的结尾是疯狂”。
14. portholes: 舷窗。

【思考题】

1. Explain how Joyce reveals the restrictions in Eveline's life. Do you think Eveline has enough reasons to leave her home for a new life?
2. According to Joyce himself, "(a)n epiphany meant a sudden spiritual manifestation, whether in the vulgarity of speech or of gesture or in a memorable phase of the mind itself." What do you think of the last scene of the story? And what is the purpose of the

detailed presentation of Eveline's thoughts throughout the evening?

3. What is revealed of the Dublin society through Eveline's story?

解读举例

1. 《伊芙琳》反映了都柏林社会的黑暗。伊芙琳是所有都柏林女孩的象征，只要一天不挣脱宗教与家庭的枷锁，她们就注定要重复她们母亲的命运，成为父系社会的牺牲品。

2. 《伊芙琳》表现了都柏林人瘫痪的精神状态。伊芙琳并没有被真正剥夺自由，她拥有机会，可她没有勇气和力量去把握机会、获得自由。青年是如此，老年人亦如此。这种心灵的麻木能够扼杀一切希望。

3. 《伊芙琳》表现了人类的生存本能。这种本能使伊芙琳渴望得到爱情和新生活，然而又保护她不受更多的伤害。海洋和东去的航行是逃避、解放和新生的象征，但同时也是危险和死亡的象征。许多单纯的都柏林女孩被外国水手带到利物浦后遭到遗弃，流离失所。这也是伊芙琳过分谨慎的原因之一。

Virginia Woolf
1882—1941

作者简介

弗吉尼亚·伍尔夫是重要的现代主义作家，以描述人物精神世界和关注女性生活的作品闻名于世。她出生于文学世家，父亲莱斯利·斯蒂芬 (Leslie Stephen, 1832—1904) 是著名学者，与亨利·詹姆斯和哈代等当时的文学界名流多有接触。伍尔夫自幼身体羸弱，没有接受过正式的学校教育，但她在父亲的藏书室里阅读了大量作品，聆听了文学前辈的各种见解，耳濡目染，受到了良好的文化熏陶。

1904 年，伍尔夫迁居伦敦的布鲁姆斯伯里 (Bloomsbury)，每周四在寓所举行沙龙，接待文艺学术界人士，该住所遂成为著名的布鲁姆斯伯里文学团体 (Bloomsbury group) 的活动中心。1912 年她与团体成员之一伦纳德·伍尔夫 (Leonard Woolf, 1880—1969) 结婚，1917 年他们共同创立

了霍加斯出版社 (The Hogarth Press)，出版了著名诗人艾略特、短篇小说家凯瑟琳·曼斯菲尔德 (Katherine Mansfield, 1888—1923) 和伍尔夫本人的作品，推动了现代主义在英国的发展。伍尔夫早期的作品《远航》(*A Voyage Out*, 1915) 和《夜与日》(*Night and Day*, 1919) 较为传统。此后她深受乔伊斯意识流和柏格森直觉主义的影响，开始进行大胆创新，先后发表了《达洛维夫人》(*Mrs. Dalloway*, 1925)、《到灯塔去》(*To the Lighthouse*, 1927) 和《海浪》(*The Waves*, 1931) 等作品，确定了她在现代主义小说家中的地位。伍尔夫自幼患有精神疾病。1941 年，伍尔夫预感到自己的疾病可能复发并难以恢复，她最终选择了投河自尽。

伍尔夫笔下的人物通常是平凡的人。她通过描写其内心世界，反映社会现实与人生问题。她认为人的体验在不断流动，作家的责任是捕捉人物内心瞬息万变的感受，淋漓尽致地表现人物复杂的心理变化。她娴熟地运用意识流技巧，在记录人物自我感受和意识变化的同时，生动地刻画人物形象。在创作小说的同时，伍尔夫也写下大量文学评论，收集在两卷本的《普通读者》(*The Common Reader*, 1925, 1932) 内，丰富了对现代主义文学的论述。

伍尔夫还是女性运动的先驱。她的作品特别关注女性的生存状况和精神生活。在《一间自己的房子》(*A Room of One's Own*, 1929) 中，她专门讨论了女性问题，指出女性精神独立的前提是金钱和物质上的独立。只有拥有了自己的房子和收入，女性才能充分发挥自己的创作才能。虽然伍尔夫因在作品中过于强调精神生活而受到一些非议，但她无疑是英国文学史上一名举足轻重的作家。

Mrs. Dalloway

【题解】

《达洛维夫人》是为伍尔夫赢得声誉的第一部成功作品。如乔伊斯的《尤利西斯》，《达洛维夫人》将所有事件压缩在达洛维夫人一天十二个小时的生活之内，记述这段时间里她的内心活动，并通过回忆和现实的交错穿插，概括她一生的重要经历。作品还描写了其他主要人物。一个是她过去的恋人，从印度回来的彼得·沃尔什；另一个是立过战功、现却患严重精神疾病的退伍军士塞普蒂姆斯·华伦·史密斯。

三十年来，克拉莉莎·达洛维日复一日地履行贤妻良母的职责，不免有些寂寞沉闷，生活在一种莫名的疑虑和恐惧之中。彼得·沃尔什从印度回来的第二天便去看望达洛维夫人，并应邀出席当晚举行的晚会。他的思想活动大部分是回想当年在克拉莉莎父母家的情景。他和克拉莉莎彼此相爱，但克拉莉莎却嫁给了理查德·达洛维。在去印度的途中，沃尔什与一个萍水相逢的女子结了婚；而此刻与达洛维夫人相对而坐，却发现他们依然相互爱慕。

小说以不少篇幅描写了史密斯的心情。战争带给他严重的精神创伤，使他失去了情感。妻子带他四处求医，但无济于事，最后他为躲避医生的"骚扰"跳窗自杀。

在达洛维夫人上街买花的同一天，史密斯夫妇也从街上走过，并在公园停留，因此获得了与达洛维夫人同样的见闻。伍尔夫在小说中安排这两条线索，目的是表现"神志清醒的人"和"精神失常的人"在同一时刻观察世界的不同感受。下文所选的是小说开头部分。达洛维夫人为准备晚会上街买花。当她漫步伦敦街头时，思潮汹涌，浮想联翩。作者高超的意识流写作技巧，由此可见一斑。

From Mrs. Dalloway

The Opening Scene: Out for Flowers

Mrs. Dalloway said she would buy the flowers herself.

For Lucy had her work cut out for her[1]. The doors would be taken off their hinges; Rumpelmayer's men[2] were coming. And then, thought Clarissa Dalloway, what a morning—fresh as if issued to children on a beach.

What a lark! What a plunge![3] For so it had always seemed to her, when, with a little squeak of the hinges, which she could hear now, she had burst open the French windows[4] and plunged at Bourton[5] into the open air. How fresh, how calm, stiller than this[6] of course, the air was in the early morning; like the flap of a wave; the kiss of a wave; chill and sharp and yet (for a girl of eighteen as she then was) solemn, feeling as she did, standing there at the open window, that something awful was about to happen; looking at the flowers, at the trees with the smoke winding off them and the rooks rising, falling; standing and looking until Peter Walsh said, "Musing among the vegetables?"—was that it?— "I prefer men to cauliflowers"[7]—was that it? He must have said it at breakfast one morning when she had gone out on to the terrace—Peter Walsh. He would be back from India one of these days, June or July, she forgot which, for his letters were awfully dull; it was his sayings one remembered; his eyes, his pocket-knife[8], his smile, his grumpiness and, when millions of things had utterly vanished—how strange it was!—a few sayings like this about cabbages.

She stiffened a little on the kerb, waiting for Durtnall's van[9] to pass. A charming woman, Scrope Purvis[10] thought her (knowing her as one does know people who live next door to one in Westminster[11]); a touch of the bird about her, of the jay[12], blue-green, light, vivacious, though she was over fifty, and grown very white since her illness. There she perched, never seeing him, waiting to cross, very upright.

For having lived in Westminster—how many years now? over twenty,—one feels even in the midst of the traffic, or waking at night, Clarissa was positive, a particular hush, or solemnity; an indescribable pause; a suspense (but that might be her heart, affected, they said, by influenza) before Big Ben[13] strikes. There! Out it boomed. First a warning, musical; then the hour, irrevocable.[14] The leaden circles[15] dissolved in the air. Such fools we are, she thought, crossing Victoria Street. For Heaven only knows why one loves it so[16], how one sees it so, making it up, building it round one, tumbling it, creating it every moment afresh; but the veriest frumps[17], the most dejected of miseries sitting on doorsteps (drink their downfall) do the same; can't be dealt with, she felt positive, by Acts of Parliament for that very reason: they love life. In people's eyes, in the swing, tramp, and trudge[18]; in the bellow and the uproar; the carriages, motor cars, omnibuses, vans, sandwich men shuffling and swinging; brass bands; barrel organs; in the triumph and the jingle and the strange high singing of some aeroplane overhead was what she loved; life; London; this moment of June.

For it was the middle of June. The War[19] was over, except for some one like Mrs. Foxcroft at the Embassy last night eating her heart out[20] because that nice boy was killed and now the old Manor House[21] must go to a cousin; or Lady Bexborough who opened a bazaar, they said, with the telegram in her hand, John, her favourite, killed; but it was over; thank Heaven—over. It was June. The King and Queen were at the Palace. And everywhere, though it was still so early, there was a beating, a stirring of galloping ponies, tapping of cricket bats; Lords, Ascot, Ranelagh[22] and all the rest of it; wrapped in the soft mesh of the grey-blue morning air, which, as the day wore on, would unwind them, and set down on their lawns and pitches the bouncing ponies, whose forefeet just struck the ground and up they sprung, the whirling young men, and laughing girls in their transparent muslins who, even now, after dancing all night, were taking their absurd woolly dogs for a run; and even now, at this hour, discreet old dowagers were shooting out in their motor cars on errands of mystery; and the shopkeepers were fidgeting in their windows with their paste[23] and diamonds, their lovely old sea-green brooches in eighteenth-century settings to tempt Americans (but one must economise, not buy things rashly for Elizabeth[24]), and she, too, loving it as she did with an absurd and faithful passion, being part of it, since her people were courtiers once in the time of the Georges[25], she, too, was going that very night to kindle and illuminate; to give her party. But how strange, on entering the Park[26], the silence; the mist; the hum; the slow-swimming happy ducks; the pouched birds waddling; and who should be coming along with his back against the Government buildings, most appropriately, carrying a despatch box stamped with the Royal Arms[27], who but Hugh Whitbread[28]; her old friend Hugh—the admirable Hugh!

"Good-morning to you, Clarissa!" said Hugh, rather extravagantly[29], for they had known each other as children. "Where are you off to?"

"I love walking in London," said Mrs. Dalloway. "Really it's better than walking in the country."

They had just come up—unfortunately—to see doctors. Other people came to see pictures; go to the opera; take their daughters out[30]; the Whitbreads came "to see doctors." Times without number Clarissa had visited Evelyn Whitbread in a nursing home. Was Evelyn ill again? Evelyn was a good deal out of sorts, said Hugh, intimating[31] by a kind of pout or swell of his very well-covered, manly, extremely handsome, perfectly upholstered body (he was almost too well dressed always, but presumably had to be, with his little job at Court) that his wife had some internal ailment, nothing serious, which, as an old friend, Clarissa Dalloway would quite understand without requiring him to specify. Ah yes, she did of course; what a nuisance; and felt very sisterly and oddly conscious at the same time of her hat. Not the right hat for the early morning, was that it? For Hugh always made her feel, as he bustled on, raising his hat rather extravagantly and assuring her that she might be a girl of eighteen, and of course he was coming to her party to-night, Evelyn absolutely insisted, only a little late he might be after the party at the Palace to which he had to take one of Jim's boys,—she always felt a little skimpy[32] beside Hugh; schoolgirlish; but attached to him, partly from having known him always, but she did think him a good sort in his own way, though Richard[33] was nearly driven mad by him, and as for Peter Walsh, he had never to this day forgiven her for liking him.

She could remember scene after scene at Bourton—Peter furious; Hugh not, of course, his match in any way, but still not a positive imbecile[34] as Peter made out; not a mere barber's block[35]. When his old mother wanted him to give up shooting or to take her to Bath[36] he did it, without a word; he was really unselfish, and as for saying, as Peter did, that he had no heart, no brain, nothing but the manners and breeding of an English gentleman, that was only her dear Peter at his worst; and he could be intolerable; he could be impossible; but adorable to walk with on a morning like this.

(June had drawn out every leaf on the trees. The mothers of Pimlico[37] gave suck to their young. Messages were passing from the Fleet to the Admiralty[38]. Arlington Street and Piccadilly[39] seemed to chafe the very air in the Park and lift its leaves hotly, brilliantly, on waves of that divine vitality which Clarissa loved. To dance, to ride, she had adored all that.)

For they might be parted for hundreds of years, she and Peter; she never wrote a letter and his were dry sticks[40]; but suddenly it would come over her, If he were with me now what would he say?—some days, some sights bringing him back to her calmly, without the old bitterness; which perhaps was the reward of having cared for people; they came back in the middle of St. James's Park on a fine morning—indeed they did. But Peter—however beautiful the day might be, and the trees and the grass, and the little girl in pink—Peter never saw a thing of all that. He would put on his spectacles, if she told him to; he would look. It was the state of the world that interested him[41]; Wagner[42], Pope's[43] poetry, people's characters eternally, and the defects of her own soul. How he scolded her! How they argued! She would marry a Prime Minister and stand at the top of a staircase; the perfect hostess he called her (she had cried over it in her bedroom), she had the makings of the perfect hostess[44], he said.

So she would still find herself arguing in St. James's Park, still making out that she had been right—and she had too—not to marry him. For in marriage a little licence[45], a little independence there must be between people living together day in day out in the same house; which Richard gave her, and she him. (Where was he this morning for instance? Some committee, she never asked what.) But with Peter everything had to be shared; everything gone into. And it was intolerable, and when it came to that scene in the little garden by the fountain, she had to break with him or they would have been destroyed, both of them ruined, she was convinced; though she had borne about with her for years like an arrow sticking in her heart the grief, the anguish; and then the horror of the moment when some one told her at a concert that he had married a woman met on the boat going to India! Never should she forget all that! Cold, heartless, a prude, he called her. Never could she understand how he cared. But those Indian women did presumably—silly, pretty, flimsy nincompoops[46]. And she wasted her pity. For he was quite happy, he assured her—perfectly happy, though he had never done a thing that they talked of; his whole life had been a failure. It made her angry still.

She had reached the Park gates. She stood for a moment, looking at the omnibuses in Piccadilly.

She would not say of any one in the world now that they were this or were that. She felt very young; at the same time unspeakably aged. She sliced like a knife through everything; at the same time was outside, looking on.[47] She had a perpetual sense, as she watched the taxi cabs, of being out, out, far out to sea and alone; she always had the feeling that it was very, very dangerous to live even one day. Not that she thought herself clever, or much out of the ordinary. How she had got through life on the few twigs of knowledge Fräulein Daniels[48] gave them she could not think. She knew nothing; no language, no history; she scarcely read a book now, except memoirs in bed; and yet to her it was absolutely absorbing; all this; the cabs passing; and she would not say of Peter, she would not say of herself, I am this, I am that.

Her only gift was knowing people almost by instinct, she thought, walking on. If you put her in a room with some one, up went her back like a cat's; or she purred. Devonshire House, Bath House[49], the house with the china cockatoo, she had seen them all lit up once; and remembered Sylvia, Fred, Sally Seton[50]—such hosts of people; and dancing all night; and the waggons plodding past to market; and driving home across the Park. She remembered once throwing a shilling into the Serpentine[51]. But every one remembered; what she loved was this, here, now, in front of her; the fat lady in the cab. Did it matter then, she asked herself, walking towards Bond Street[52], did it matter that she must inevitably cease completely; all this must go on without her; did she resent it; or did it not become consoling to believe that death ended absolutely? But that somehow in the streets of London, on the ebb and flow of things, here, there, she survived, Peter survived, lived in each other, she being part, she was positive, of the trees at home; of the house there, ugly, rambling all to bits and pieces as it was; part of people she had never met; being laid out like a mist between the people she knew best, who lifted her on their branches as she had seen the trees lift the mist, but it spread ever so far, her life, herself. But what was she dreaming as she looked into Hatchards' shop window? What was she trying to recover? What image of white dawn in the country, as she read in the book spread open:

Fear no more the heat o' the sun
Nor the furious winter's rages.[53]

This late age of the world's experience[54] had bred in them all, all men and women, a well of tears. Tears and sorrows; courage and endurance; a perfectly upright and stoical bearing. Think, for example, of the woman she admired most, Lady Bexborough, opening the bazaar.

There were *Jorrocks' Jaunts and Jollities*; there were *Soapy Sponge* and *Mrs. Asquith's Memoirs* and *Big Game Shooting in Nigeria*, all spread open.[55] Ever so many books there were; but none that seemed exactly right to take to Evelyn Whitbread in her nursing home. Nothing that would serve to amuse her and make that indescribably dried-up little woman look, as Clarissa came in, just for a moment cordial; before they settled down for the usual interminable talk of women's ailments. How much she wanted it—that people should look pleased as she came in, Clarissa thought and turned and walked back towards Bond Street, annoyed, because it was silly to have other reasons for doing things. Much rather would she have been one of those people like Richard who did things for themselves, whereas, she thought, waiting to cross, half the time she did things not simply, not for themselves; but to make people think this or that; perfect idiocy she knew (and now the policeman held up his hand[56]) for no one was ever for a second taken in. Oh if she could have had her life over again! she thought, stepping on to the pavement, could have looked even differently!

She would have been, in the first place, dark like Lady Bexborough, with a skin of crumpled leather and beautiful eyes. She would have been, like Lady Bexborough, slow and stately; rather large; interested in politics like a man; with a country house; very dignified, very sincere. Instead of which she had a narrow pea-stick figure; a ridiculous little face, beaked like a bird's. That she held herself well was true; and had nice hands and feet; and dressed well, considering that she spent little. But often now this body she wore (she stopped to look at a Dutch picture), this body, with all its capacities, seemed nothing—nothing at all. She had the oddest sense of being herself invisible; unseen; unknown; there being no more marrying, no more having of children now, but only this astonishing and rather solemn progress with the rest of them, up Bond Street, this being Mrs. Dalloway; not even Clarissa any more; this being Mrs. Richard Dalloway.

Bond Street fascinated her; Bond Street early in the morning in the season; its flags flying; its shops; no splash; no glitter; one roll of tweed in the shop where her father had bought his suits for fifty years; a few pearls; salmon on an iceblock.

"That is all," she said, looking at the fishmonger's. "That is all," she repeated, pausing for a moment at the window of a glove shop where, before the War, you could buy almost perfect gloves. And her old Uncle William used to say a lady is known by her shoes and her gloves. He had turned on his bed[57] one morning in the middle of the War. He had said, "I have had enough." Gloves and shoes; she had a passion for gloves; but her own daughter, her Elizabeth, cared not a straw for either of them.

Not a straw, she thought, going on up Bond Street to a shop where they kept flowers for her when she gave a party. Elizabeth really cared for her dog most of all. The whole house this morning smelt of tar. Still, better poor Grizzle than Miss Kilman[58]; better distemper and tar and all the rest of it than sitting mewed in a stuffy bedroom with a prayer book! Better anything, she was inclined to say. But it might be only a phase, as Richard said, such as all girls go through. It might be falling in love. But why with Miss Kilman? who had been badly treated of course; one must make allowances for that, and Richard said she was very able, had a really historical mind. Anyhow they were inseparable, and Elizabeth, her own daughter, went to Communion[59]; and how she dressed, how she treated people who came to lunch she did not care a bit, it being her experience that the religious ecstasy made people callous (so did causes); dulled their feelings, for Miss Kilman would do anything for the Russians, starved herself for the Austrians[60], but in private inflicted positive torture, so insensitive was she, dressed in a green mackintosh coat. Year in year out she wore that coat; she perspired; she was never in the room five minutes without making you feel her superiority, your inferiority; how poor she was; how rich you were; how she lived in a slum without a cushion or a bed or a rug or whatever it might be, all her soul rusted with that grievance sticking in it, her dismissal from school during the War—poor embittered unfortunate creature! For it was not her one hated but the idea of her, which undoubtedly had gathered in to itself a great deal that was not Miss Kilman; had become one of those spectres with which one battles in the night; one of those spectres who stand astride us and suck up half our life-blood, dominators and tyrants; for no doubt with another throw of the dice, had the black been uppermost and not the white[61], she would have loved Miss Kilman! But not in this world. No.

It rasped her, though, to have stirring about in her this brutal monster[62]! to hear twigs cracking and feel hooves planted down in the depths of that leaf-encumbered forest, the soul; never to be content quite, or quite secure, for at any moment the brute would be stirring, this hatred, which, especially since her illness, had power to make her feel scraped, hurt in her spine; gave her physical pain, and made all pleasure in beauty, in friendship, in being well, in being loved and making her home delightful rock, quiver, and bend as if indeed there were a monster grubbing at the roots, as if the whole panoply of content were nothing but self love! this hatred!

Nonsense, nonsense! She cried to herself, pushing through the swing doors of Mulberry's the florists.

She advanced, light, tall, very upright, to be greeted at once by button-faced Miss Pym[63], whose hands were always bright red, as if they had been stood in cold water with the flowers.

There were flowers: delphiniums, sweet peas, bunches of lilac; and carnations, masses of carnations. There were roses; there were irises. Ah yes—so she breathed in the earthy garden sweet smell as she stood talking to Miss Pym who owed her help, and thought her kind, for kind she had been years ago; very kind, but she looked older, this year, turning her head from side to side among the irises and roses and nodding tufts of lilac with her eyes half closed, snuffing in, after the street uproar, the delicious scent, the exquisite coolness. And then, opening her eyes, how fresh like frilled linen clean from a laundry laid in wicker trays the roses looked; and dark and prim the red carnations, holding their heads up; and all the sweet peas spreading in their bowls, tinged violet, snow white, pale—as if it were the evening and girls in muslin frocks came out to pick sweet peas and roses after the superb summer's day, with its almost blue-black sky, its delphiniums, its carnations, its arum lilies was over; and it was the moment between six and seven when every flower—roses, carnations, irises, lilac—glows; white, violet, red, deep orange; every flower seems to burn by itself, softly, purely in the misty beds; and how she loved the grey-white moths spinning in and out, over the cherry pie, over the evening primroses!

And as she began to go with Miss Pym from jar to jar, choosing, nonsense, nonsense, she said to herself, more and more gently, as if this beauty, this scent, this colour, and Miss Pym liking her, trusting her, were a wave which she let flow over her and surmount that hatred, that monster, surmount it all; and it lifted her up and up when—oh! a pistol shot[64] in the street outside!

"Dear, those motor cars," said Miss Pym, going to the window to look, and coming back and smiling apologetically with her hands full of sweet peas, as if those motor cars, those tyres of motor cars, were all her fault.

【注解】

1. Lucy had her work cut out for her: 露西的活儿已经给她安排好了。露西是达洛维夫人家的女佣。
2. Rumpelmayer's men: Rumpelmayer 营造公司的工人。Rumpelmayer 是一家房屋修造商的名称，

将派人来卸掉冬季用的门窗。

3. What a lark! What a plunge!: 多么畅快！投入清晨新鲜的空气中是多么令人欣喜！这两句惊叹语均为达洛维夫人的内心感受。以下一长段内心独白是她对三十年前一个同样明媚的初夏早晨的回忆。
4. French windows: 落地长窗。
5. Bourton: 达洛维少女时代父母家所在地。
6. than this: “this” 指伦敦街头。
7. “Musing among the vegetables? . . . I prefer men to cauliflowers”: 你怎么在草丛里想入非非？……我宁可与人结伴而不愿与花椰菜交朋友。这里的 “vegetables” 泛指上文所说的 “trees” “flowers” 等植物。彼得这句话的意思是，克拉莉莎对花草树木特别敏感，而他则对人的世界更有兴趣。这是他对克拉莉莎的第一句尖刻的评论。
8. his pocket-knife: 彼得心情紧张时常取出小折刀修剪指甲。
9. Durtnall’s van: 某商号的运货车。
10. Scrope Purvis: 据下文推断，是达洛维夫人的邻居，两人路遇。这一段是从她的角度或观点来看达洛维夫人。
11. Westminster: 英国议院所在地。
12. jay: 一种欧洲鸟类，羽毛鲜艳，常发出“唧唧”的叫声。
13. Big Ben: 大本钟，伦敦标志性建筑，它的钟声是物理时间的标志，与达洛维夫人意识活动所依据的“心理”时间相对。
14. First a warning . . . irrevocable: 这里描写的是听者的主观反应。第一响只是一种警告，尚且悦耳，然后是一声声报时的钟声，使人产生时不再来的感觉。
15. leaden circles: 沉闷的音浪。
16. why one loves it so: 这里的 “it” 所指并不十分明确，从上文看它可能是指钟声 (boom)，从下文看它是指生活 (they love life)，二者可能通过“时间” (time) 相联系。
17. the veriest frumps: 那些衣着最邋遢的女人。veriest 是 very 的最高级，意为 the highest possible。
18. in the swing, tramp, and trudge: “swing”“tramp” 和 “trudge” 这三个词指述的是三种不同的走路姿态，即脚步轻快、脚步沉重和步履艰难。它们与下文的一连串名词都是达洛维夫人漫步街头时的所见所闻和对周围事物的感受。
19. The War: 指第一次世界大战。
20. eating her heart out: 忧伤过度。
21. the old Manor House: 指英国绅士家族的豪宅大院。这句话的意思是，由于 Mrs Foxcroft 的儿子死于战争，她的财产 (包括 Manor House) 便只能由她的最近亲属 (一位表亲) 来继承。
22. Lords, Ascot, Ranelagh: 此处 “Lords” 是指伦敦一处著名的板球场地，“Ascot” 是一处著名的赛马场，“Ranelagh” 也许也是一处赛马场。
23. paste: 一种玻璃似的物质，用来制造人造钻石。
24. Elizabeth: 达洛维夫人的女儿。与女儿在感情和心理上的隔阂是她的一块心病。
25. her people were courtiers . . . of the Georges: 她的家族在乔治王朝时代当过廷臣。
26. Park: 指圣詹姆斯公园 (St. James Park)。
27. a dispatch box stamped with the Royal Arms: 盖有皇家纹章的公文递送箱。

28. Hugh Whitbread: 达洛维夫人年轻时的朋友，在法院当差 (with his little job at Court)。下文的 Evelyn Whitbread 是他的妻子，因患精神病而住在疗养院。
29. extravagantly: 过分地。
30. take their daughters out: 指女儿成年时把她们带出家门，引进社交界。
31. intimating: 此处 intimate 用作动词，意为"清楚地表明，显示"。
32. skimpy: 微感不足的。
33. Richard: 即 Richard Dalloway, 达洛维夫人的丈夫，保守的下议院议员。
34. imbecile: 软弱愚蠢的人。
35. barber's block: 理发师的帽楦，用木制成，有"愚蠢"的含义。
36. Bath: 英国一市镇，以温泉闻名。
37. Pimlico: 伦敦西南一地区。
38. from the Fleet to the Admiralty: "the Fleet" 即舰队街，报馆集中地。"Admiralty" 即海军部。
39. Piccadilly: 皮卡迪利大街，伦敦繁华区。
40. dry sticks: 枯燥无味的。
41. It was the state of the world that interested him: 他所感兴趣的是世间百态，对应上文所说的"I prefer men to cauliflowers."。
42. Wagner: 即德国作曲家、剧作家瓦格纳。
43. Pope: 即英国诗人蒲伯。
44. she had the making of the perfect hostess: 她有条件成为出色的主妇。此语的意思是克拉莉莎有操持家务的能力而缺乏浪漫的幻想。这是彼得对年轻的克拉莉莎第二句尖刻的评论。
45. licence: 这里意为自由。
46. flimsy nincompoops: 轻薄的糊涂人。
47. She sliced . . . looking on: 她能像利刃一样插入一切事物的里面，同时却又置身其外，冷眼旁观。这是达洛维夫人对自己处境的感受和写照。她身处伦敦熙熙攘攘的闹市，却又感到与世疏远，隐隐流露出孤独感和失落感，甚至还有一种危机感。
48. Fräulein Daniels: 丹尼尔斯小姐，达洛维夫人少年时的德籍家庭女教师。"Fräulein" 为德语，相当于英文中的 Miss。
49. Devonshire House, Bath House: 伦敦著名古屋。
50. Sylvia, Fred, Sally Seton: 达洛维夫人早年的亲友。
51. the Serpentine: 伦敦海德公园附近的小湖。
52. Bond Street: 邦德街，伦敦繁华的商业大街。
53. Fear no more . . . winter's rages: 出自莎士比亚创作晚期的剧本《辛白林》(*Cymbeline*, 1609) 中两个弟兄之歌。
54. This late age of the world's experience: 最近几年的生活，尤指第一次世界大战的苦难经历。
55. There were . . . all spread open: 句中 *Jorrock's Jaunts and Jollities*, *Soapy Sponge*, *Mrs. Asquith's Memoirs* 和 *Big Game Shooting in Nigeria* 均为 20 世纪 20 年代的流行读物。
56. and now the policeman held up his hand: 警察举手禁止行人通过。
57. turned on his bed: 在床上死去。
58. better poor Grizzle than Miss Kilman: "poor Grizzle" 是达洛维夫人的女儿伊丽莎白的爱犬；"Miss

Kilman"是伊丽莎白的家庭教师基尔曼小姐。

59. Communion: 圣餐，基督教的主要仪式之一。
60. starved herself for the Austrians: 愿为奥地利人挨饿。基尔曼小姐命运多舛，生命中唯一的幸福时光是在德国度过的，对之有感情，因而也对与德国关系密切的奥地利有特别情感。
61. with another throw . . . not the white: 如果再掷一次骰子，上面是黑点而不是白点。此语的意思是"如果她的命运不是现在这样的话"，与上文"if she could have had her life over again"意义相同。
62. this brutal monster: 此处为比喻，承上文而言是指达洛维夫人对女儿的教师基尔曼小姐的怨恨；推而广之，则是指她的孤独感和恐惧感。它们像粗暴的恶魔，潜伏在她灵魂深处，折磨着她的心灵。
63. Miss Pym: 花店的女主人。
64. a pistol shot: 指街上突然传来的一声巨响，实际并不是手枪声，而是汽车发动机回火发出的爆裂声。

【思考题】

1. What are the general feelings of Mrs. Dalloway about her life and her marriage? Find evidences in the excerpt to support your point.
2. How do you think about the relationship between Mrs. Dalloway and her daughter? Why do you think so?
3. Do you think Clarissa and Peter Walsh loved each other? What do you think are the reasons for their separation?
4. What do you suppose are the reasons for Mrs. Dalloway's dislike for Miss Kilman?

【简评】

作为一名现代主义作家，伍尔夫强调现代文学要表现作家的主观感受，深入揭示人的内心世界，而以上选文正反映了她为"揭示内心最深处火焰的闪光"所作的努力。达洛维夫人为准备晚上的聚会而上街买花。当她漫步街头，各种思绪便像流云一般飘荡，往返于过去的经验和现实的感受之间。作者纯熟地运用意识流写作技巧，细致描绘了达洛维内心深处的活动，从想到需要把自家的门拆下，到年轻时的情人、自身的优缺点、一生的抉择；从回想女儿到回想丈夫，回想女儿的历史教师，以及其他许许多多熟识的人。这些思绪并不按时间顺序排列，而是由街头的所见所闻不断引发，具有一定的任意性。意识之流以强大的力量将达洛维夫人一生不同阶段的经历聚合在一个短暂的时间内，并延伸到广阔的空间。因此，在有限的时间和空间里，读者得以窥视主人公当时复杂的心理变化，也看到了她一生的生活轨迹。

Wystan Hugh Auden
1907—1973

作者简介

威斯坦·休·奥登，美籍英国诗人，出生于约克郡一个较为殷实的家庭，父亲祖籍冰岛，父母从事医学工作。1925年奥登进入牛津大学学习，专攻文学，毕业后赴德学习德国文学，1930年回国，任中学教师达五年之久。20世纪30年代后期，奥登投身政治和社会活动，同时从事创作。1937年前往西班牙支持反法西斯斗争，给政府军当过担架队员和救护车驾驶员。1938年，奥登与英国小说家克里斯多夫·衣修午德(Christopher Isherwood, 1904—1986)结伴来到中国，并合著了《战地行纪》(*Journey to a War*, 1939)，对处于抗日烽火之中的中国人民表示同情。次年奥登与衣修午德一起移居美国，1946年加入美国籍，在美国执教多年。1956年，奥登重返英国，被聘为牛津大学诗学教授(1956—1960)。

奥登的创作可分为三个时期。早期(1927—1932)作品内容广泛，题材来自冰岛萨加古英诗、英国公学故事，以及马克思、弗洛伊德和其他哲学家的著作。技巧上先后受到哈代、杰拉尔德·曼利·霍普金斯(Gerard Manley Hopkins, 1844—1889)、艾略特、叶芝等人的影响，但又颇多创新，影响甚广，成为以牛津大学文艺青年为首的"奥登一代"的代言人。代表作品有《诗集》(*Poems*, 1930)、《雄辩家》(*The Orators*, 1932)等。受20世纪30年代西方经济大衰退等因素的影响，奥登渐趋激进。中期(1933—1939)作品针砭资本主义社会的弊端，对当时的工业停滞、大批工人失业等社会与经济问题均有所反映。主要作品有《看吧，陌生人》(*Look, Strangers!*, 1936)，以及与衣修午德合写的三部诗剧《皮下之狗》(*The Dog Beneath the Skin*, 1935)、《攀登》(*The Ascent*, 1936)和《在边界上》(*On the Frontier*, 1938)。这一时期奥登还写了不少散文、书评和报告文学，其中最著名的有1937年到西班牙短暂旅行后写的《西班牙》(*Spain*, 1937)及上文提到的《战地行纪》。移居美国后，奥登进入创作后期(1939—1973)，他接受克尔恺郭尔和尼布尔的思想，作品弥漫着浓郁的宗教色彩，表达了对当时西方社会的悲观看法。代表作品有长诗《海与镜》(*The Sea and the Mirror*, 1945)、《忧虑时代》(*The Age of Anxiety*, 1947)、《暂时》(*For the Time Being*, 1944)、《阿喀琉斯之盾》(*The Shield of Achilles*, 1955)、《屋子内外》(*About the House*, 1965)、《无墙之城》(*City without Walls*, 1969)等。此外，奥登还著有散文评论集《染工之手》(*The Dyer's Hand*, 1963)及《次要的世界》(*Secondary Worlds*, 1968)。

奥登的诗歌充满活力，富于变化，多有创新，在诗歌的形式与格律上进行了多种卓有成效的尝试。他思想敏锐、活跃，诗艺精巧，曾有不止一个评论家将他与英国桂冠诗人德莱顿相提并论。

Musée des Beaux Arts

【题解】

此诗作于1938年，标题为法语，意为“美术博物馆”(Museum of Fine Arts)，此处特指比利时布鲁塞尔的美术博物馆。奥登曾在此博物馆内见到画家勃鲁盖尔的一幅名为《伊卡洛斯》(*Icarus*)的作品。在希腊神话中，伊卡洛斯与其父迪达鲁斯(Dedalus)双双以蜡翼粘身飞离囚禁他们的小岛，但伊卡洛斯不听其父的警告，飞得太高，离太阳过近，以至蜡翅被阳光融化，坠海而死。勃鲁盖尔的画表现了伊卡洛斯坠海的场面。在画的一角，伊卡洛斯的双腿正没入海中，而画面其余的大部分却似乎与此毫无关系，海上的船只和岸上犁田的农民仍在有条不紊地进行他们的工作，好像根本没有注意这桩事。奥登认为，和其他古典美术大师一样，勃鲁盖尔对这一场景的处理是别有深意的。在他看来，苦难甚至牺牲，都是个人的事，与他人无关；而且灾难的发生往往莫名其妙、不以人的意志为转移，所以其他人也不必因此而打乱他们正常的生活。

Musée des Beaux Arts

About suffering they were never wrong,
The Old Masters: how well they understood
Its human position; how it takes place
While someone else is eating or opening a window or just walking dully along;
How, when the aged are reverently, passionately waiting
For the miraculous birth, there always must be
Children who did not specially want it to happen, skating
On a pond at the edge of the wood:
They never forgot
That even the dreadful martyrdom must run its course
Anyhow in a corner, some untidy spot

Where the dogs go on with their doggy life and the torturer's horse
Scratches its innocent behind on a tree.[1]

In Brueghel's[2] Icarus, for instance: how everything turns away
Quite leisurely from the disaster; the plowman may
Have heard the splash, the forsaken[3] cry,
But for him it was not an important failure; the sun shone
As it had to on the white legs disappearing into the green
Water; and the expensive delicate ship that must have seen
Something amazing, a boy falling out of the sky,
Had somewhere to get to and sailed calmly on.

【注解】

1. 第一节中，作者可能是在描述勃鲁盖尔的另外两幅作品——《对无辜者的屠杀》(*The Massacre of the Innocents*) 和《伯利恒的户口调查》(*The Numbering at Bethlehem*)。
2. Brueghel: 指 Pieter Brueghel (the Elder), 尼德兰画家，善画农村景色，反映农民生活和社会风俗，主要作品有《农民的婚礼》《盲人的寓言》等。
3. forsaken: 悲惨的，被抛弃的。

【思考题】

1. Auden describes Bruegel's several paintings in the poem. How do these various details characterize the ordinary world?
2. What suggests that Auden is writing about the modern world as well as that of the past?
3. What do Auden and "The Old Masters" suggest about the significance and experience of human suffering?
4. Pay attention to the variations in length of Auden's lines and the irregular rhyme scheme. What do you suppose are the reasons for such variations?

In Memory of W. B. Yeats

【题解】

此诗创作于 1939 年，表达了奥登对爱尔兰诗人叶芝的敬仰。奥登对叶芝去世的那一天印象深刻，认为会有成千上万的人记住这位爱尔兰诗人和他去世的这一天。他把叶芝和他的出生地爱尔兰联系在一起进行评论，确信叶芝的诗歌将会长久地流传下去，即使在欧洲最黑暗的日子也能给读者带来欢乐。

该诗于 1940 年首次发表时，奥登仍在一定程度上受第一次世界大战后欧洲左翼运动的影响。而在他于 1966 年出版的《短诗结集 1927—1957》(*Collected Shorted Poems 1927—1957*) 中，该诗提到吉卜林和克洛岱尔的三节被删去。本文所选为未删节的原诗。

In Memory of W. B. Yeats

I

He disappeared in the dead of winter[1]:
The brooks were frozen, the airports almost deserted,
And snow disfigured the public statues;
The mercury sank in the mouth of the dying day.
O all the instruments agree[2]
The day of his death was a dark cold day.

Far from his illness
The wolves ran on through the evergreen forests,
The peasant river was untempted by the fashionable quays;
By mourning tongues
The death of the poet was kept from his poems.

But for him it was his last afternoon as himself,
An afternoon of nurses and rumours;
The provinces of his body revolted,
The squares of his mind were empty,
Silence invaded the suburbs,
The current of his feeling failed; he became his admirers.

Now he is scattered among a hundred cities
And wholly given over to unfamiliar affections[3],

To find his happiness in another kind of wood[4]
And be punished under a foreign code of conscience.
The words of a dead man
Are modified in the guts of the living.

But in the importance and noise of to-morrow
When the brokers are roaring like beasts on the floor of the Bourse[5],
And the poor have the sufferings to which they are fairly accustomed,
And each in the cell of himself is almost convinced of his freedom,
A few thousand will think of this day
As one thinks of a day when one did something slightly unusual.
What instruments we have agree
The day of his death was dark cold day.

II

You were silly like us; your gift survived it all:
The parish of rich women, physical decay,
Yourself. Mad Ireland hurt you into poetry.
Now Ireland has her madness and her weather still,
For poetry makes nothing happen: it survives
In the valley of its making where executives
Would never want to tamper, flows on south
From ranches of isolation and the busy griefs,
Raw towns that we believe and die in; it survives,
A way of happening, a mouth.

III

Earth, receive an honoured guest;
William Yeats is laid to rest.
Let the Irish vessel lie
Emptied of its poetry.

Time that is intolerant
Of the brave and innocent,
And indifferent in a week

To a beautiful physique,

Worships language and forgives
Everyone by whom it lives;
Pardons cowardice, conceit,
Lays its honours at their feet.

Time that with this strange excuse
Pardoned Kipling and his views[6],
And will pardon Paul Claudel[7],
Pardons him for writing well.[8]

In the nightmare of the dark
All the dogs of Europe bark,
And the living nations wait,
Each sequestered in its hate;

Intellectual disgrace
Stares from every human face,
And the seas of pity lie
Locked and frozen in each eye.

Follow poet, follow right
To the bottom of the night.
With your unconstraining voice
Still persuade us to rejoice;

With the farming of a verse
Make a vineyard of the curse,
Sing of human unsuccess
In a rapture of distress;

In the deserts of the heart

Let the healing fountain start,
In the prison of his days
Teach the free man how to praise.

【注解】

1. in the dead of winter: 在冬天最寒冷的时节。
2. O all the instruments agree: 所有的乐器都奏着同样的曲调来哀悼诗人之死。此句后被奥登改为"What instruments we have agree"。
3. wholly given over to unfamiliar affections: 他（叶芝）的情感完全属于那些与他并无私交的人。
4. To find his happiness in another kind of wood: 此处奥登可能是在借用但丁在《神曲·地狱篇》中的诗句："在我生命旅程的中途，在一处找不到直路的黑暗森林中，我找到了我自己。"(In the middle of the journey of our life I came to myself within a dark wood where the straight way was lost.)
5. the Bourse: 股票交易所。
6. Pardoned Kipling and his views: "Kipling"即吉卜林，英国小说家、诗人，作品表现大英帝国所谓的扩张精神，有"帝国主义诗人"之称。1940时的奥登对他持反对态度。
7. Paul Claudel: 即保尔·克洛岱尔(1868—1955), 法国外交官、诗人、剧作家，作品表现对天主教的信仰及肉体与灵魂的冲突，政治上右倾，有剧作《给玛丽报信》《缎子鞋》及诗作《五大颂歌》等。
8. Time that is intolerant . . . Pardons him for writing well: 这三节在《短诗结集1927—1957》中被奥登删去。

【思考题】

1. "Mad Ireland hurt you into Poetry." According to Auden, what is the relationship between Yeats and Ireland? And what are the motives for Yeats' poetry?
2. Does Auden believe that Yeats' poetry succeeded in exerting any healthful effect upon Ireland? What are the evidences?
3. Make a summary of the meaning of each of the three stanzas.

解读举例

1. 奥登在诗歌中回溯了叶芝逝世当天的情形，从肉体的衰朽和精神的永恒两个角度展开叙述，深切缅怀这位伟大的诗人，高度赞扬他的文学成就和留下的精神遗产。

2. 奥登在诗歌中流露出一种不安的情绪，这或许跟他感知到了弥漫在欧洲上空的战争阴云有关。奥登意识到西方世界在一战之后再次面临着崩溃和陷入战争浩劫的危险。他用挽歌的笔调描写自己对叶芝的哀悼，同时掺杂了对黑暗现实的愤慨和忧虑，使诗歌呈现出一种阴郁的基调。

3. 这是一首具有现代派气息的诗歌，语气冷峻，意象奇崛。奥登并没有过度美化叶芝的个人形象，叶芝的去世被叙述为大自然中的一个普通事件，并不神圣，叶芝本人也并不完美，他“像你我一样愚笨”，可是他的文学才华和品格使他成为值得敬仰的人。

4. 奥登相信诗歌和文学的治愈力量，它们在平凡的日子里给人慰藉，在黑暗和苦难中给人温暖与希望。奥登在悼念叶芝的同时，也在赞扬诗歌精神的不朽。

Contemporary English Literature

1945–

小说家及文学评论家马尔科姆·布雷德伯里 (Malcolm Bradbury, 1932—2000) 曾指出，二战后的英国文学经历了双重危机：世界的危机（Crisis of the World) 和文字的危机 (Crisis of the Word)。两次世界大战导致世界动荡不安，原有世界秩序崩塌，各种社会运动频发，作家们开始深度思考有关"人类存在"的问题。此外，传统的语言价值观开始遭到质疑和颠覆，这也体现出英国作家对人文精神危机的关注与反思。因此，英国文学一方面延续现实主义的传统手法，另一方面则又开始了对后现代主义的探索与实验。

二战后，表现日常生活、历史和政治现实的现实主义英国文学蓬勃发展。乔治·奥威尔 (George Orwell，1903—1950) 以创作政治寓言闻名。他的《动物农庄》(*Animal Farm*, 1945) 和《1984》(*1984*, 1949) 成为反乌托邦文学的重要著作。威廉·戈尔丁 (William Golding，1911—1993) 的代表作《蝇王》(*Lord of the Flies*，1954) 富有寓言色彩，深刻揭示了人性的邪恶和黑暗，而他也于 1983 年荣获诺贝尔文学奖。

20 世纪 50 年代，一批青年作家在英国文坛崛起。这些作家被称为愤怒的青年 (The Angry Young Men)，他们大都延续了现实主义的写作传统，其笔下的主人公出身低微却又渴望跻身上流社会，但传统观念中的等级差异使他们的愿望难以实现，因而对社会极为不满和愤怒。这一时期的代表作品有约翰·奥斯本 (John Osborne，1929—1994) 的戏剧《愤怒的回顾》(*Look Back in Anger*，1956)，金斯利·艾米斯 (Kingsley Amis，1922—1995) 的小说《幸运的吉姆》(*Lucky Jim*，1954)，约翰·韦恩 (John Wain，1925—1994) 的《每况愈下》(*Hurry on Down*，1953)，艾伦·西利托 (Alan Sillitoe，1928—2010) 的《长跑运动员的孤独》("The Loneliness of the Long Distance Runner"，1959) 等。

这一时期的英国文学，尤其是英国戏剧明显体现出存在主义哲学思想。存在主义作品虽然多描述荒诞的社会、沮丧的人们、精神的丧失、自我的分裂及存在的虚无，但人道主义的回归和对终极理想的追求仍然是这类作品的主题。塞缪尔·贝克特 (Samuel Beckett，1906—1989) 的两幕剧《等待戈多》(*Waiting for Godot*，1952) 被誉为 20 世纪荒诞派戏剧的第一剧。作品通过无聊漫长的等待，描述了二战后人们苦闷、孤独的生活，反映了人类的生存危机和精神危机。贝克特也因此获得 1969 年的诺贝尔文学奖。在荒诞派戏剧方面取得巨大成就的还有哈罗德·品特 (Harold Pinter，1930—2008)，他善于通过日常小事表现当代人的生活困境，成为 20 世纪后半叶最优秀的戏剧家。2005 年，因"揭示了日常闲谈中的危机，强行打开了压抑的封闭空间"，品特被授予诺贝尔文学奖。

二战后的后现代理论思潮对英国文学产生了深远的影响。现代主义与后现代主义都背离了 19 世纪的现实主义，在叙事和人物塑造中运用碎片式的写作手法，注重描写人物的内心意识和主观精神。然而，现代主义文学将碎片、分裂与主观性视为存在的危机，可以通过人的努力来化解；后现代主义则认为人在这种危机和混乱面前无能为力，根本不可能找到理性和秩序。20 世纪 60 年代，英国文坛出现了许多实验小说，这些作品在创作上有了大胆的革新。约翰・福尔斯 (John Fowles，1926—2005) 在《法国中尉的女人》(*The French Lieutenant's Woman*，1969) 中强调作品的虚构性，既戏仿维多利亚时代的现实主义写法，又对之进行颠覆，作家本人也作为人物出现在作品之中。安格斯・威尔逊 (Angus Wilson，1913—1991) 在政治寓言小说《动物园里的老头》(*The Old Man at the Zoo*，1961) 中，将动物园视为人类社会的缩影，探讨了人性的恶。

在诗歌方面，二战后是菲利普・拉金 (Philip Larkin，1922—1985) 和泰德・休斯 (Ted Hughes，1930—1998) 独领风骚的时代。以拉金为首的运动派 (The Movement) 诗人在 20 世纪 50 年代崛起，强调用理性的结构与质朴的语言真实地反映社会现实。拉金擅长运用日常中的常见意象来抒发情绪，其语言明了、质朴易懂。休斯并没有追随运动派的风格，而是在诗歌中大量运用动物的意象来探讨人与自然的关系。

二战后英国还涌现了一批杰出的女作家。多丽丝・莱辛 (Doris Lessing，1919—2013) 凭借《金色笔记》(*The Golden Notebook*，1962) 获得 2007 年的诺贝尔文学奖。该小说的主人公是一名女作家，她在黑、红、黄、蓝四个不同颜色的笔记本上对自己不同的生活侧面进行心理剖析，最后试图在金色笔记中达到统一和谐，探讨了人格分裂和女性自由等话题。此外，艾丽丝・默多克 (Iris Murdoch，1919—1999)、穆里尔・斯帕克 (Muriel Spark，1918—2006)、玛格丽特・德拉布尔 (Margaret Drabble，1939—) 等女作家都从女性的视角描述了当代女性的生活，为英国文坛增添了一道亮丽的风景。

20 世纪 80 年代和 90 年代涌现的新一代作家继承了后现代主义创新的风格，同时也注重作品的可读性，创作了一批新潮的实验小说。马丁・艾米斯 (Martin Amis，1949—2010)、伊恩・麦克尤恩 (Ian McEwan，1948—) 和朱利安・巴恩斯 (Julian Barnes，1946—) 是其中的杰出代表。此外，从海外移民英国的一些少数族裔作家也在英国文坛大放异彩。具有印度血统、出生在特立尼达和多巴哥的 V. S. 奈保尔 (V. S. Naipaul，1932—2018)，以及获 2017 年诺贝尔文学奖的日裔作家石黑一雄 (Kazuo Ishiguro，1954—) 都已步入主流作家的行列，成为英国文坛的生力军。

进入 21 世纪后，英国作家对历史与现实的观照仍然情有独钟。查蒂・史密斯 (Zadie Smith，1975—) 的《白牙》(*White Teeth*，2000) 呈现了后殖民时代多元文化背景下的伦敦生活，包含了不少 20 世纪后半叶英国文学的元素，如后殖民、他者、族裔、身份、都市等。麦克尤恩的长篇小说《赎罪》(*Atonement*，2001) 讲述了一个关于爱情、罪恶和战争的故事，时间跨度有六十年之久，从个人历史的微观层面窥探20世纪的历史图景。希拉里·曼特尔 (Hilary Mantel，1952—) 有关亨利八世权臣克伦威尔的三部曲也是虚实结合的历史小说，前两部作品《狼厅》(*Wolf Hall*，2009) 和《提堂》(*Bring Up the Bodies*, 2012) 均获得布克奖，而第三部作品《镜与光》(*The Mirror & the Light*, 2020) 也获得布克奖提名。苏格兰作家阿莉·史密斯 (Ali Smith，1962—) 的"季节四部曲"也探讨了不少当前社会的热点问题，体现了作者对当下生活现实的关注。

此外，21世纪之后，英国作家更加关注科技发展与生态危机，在作品中对科技发展产生的负面影响进行了反思。大卫·米切尔 (David Mitchell，1969—) 在《云图》(*Cloud Atlas*，2004) 中讲述了6个跨越不同时代（从19世纪到未来世界）的故事，既包含历史元素，又带有科幻色彩。麦克尤恩在小说《星期六》(*Saturday*，2005) 中，探讨了科学与人文之间的冲突与互补。石黑一雄在《莫失莫忘》(*Never Let Me Go*，2005) 中反思了人类滥用科学、悖逆伦理、疏离人文关怀的问题。汤姆·麦卡锡 (Tom McCarthy，1969—) 的《绸缎岛》(*Satin Island*，2015) 则以先锋姿态探讨了数码系统与数据软件对文学创作的影响。麦克尤恩的《我这样的机器》(*Machines Like Me*，2019) 和石黑一雄的《克拉拉与太阳》(*Klara and the Sun*，2021) 也反映出两位作家对科技与生活如何相互影响这一话题的持续关注。

从21世纪的前20年来看，恐怖主义、战争、死亡、经济危机、脱欧、病毒改变了英国社会的发展走向，也成为当下英国文学的关键词。21世纪的英国作家批判继承了英国文学固有的现实主义传统，同时又充分吸纳现代主义、后现代主义的创新精神，继续援用杂糅、戏仿、拼贴和历史拟写等手段，在叙事形式上消解了现实主义与后现代主义、虚构与非虚构等诸多艺术样式之间的对立，在创作主题上也实现了科技与人文、伦理与审美、宗教与世俗、区域化与全球化、通俗文化与政治诉求等众多命题之间的交融。

William Golding

1911—1993

威廉·戈尔丁 1911 年出生于英格兰康沃尔郡一个知识分子家庭。父亲是文法学校的老师，戈尔丁就是在父亲所在的学校完成了中学教育。1930 年，戈尔丁考入牛津大学布拉西诺斯学院学习，入学时所选的专业是自然科学，后转为文学专业。1935 年，戈尔丁大学毕业，一边考教育学证书，一边尝试演员、舞台监督、制片人等工作。1939 年，戈尔丁与安·布克菲尔完婚，并开始在索尔兹伯里的华兹华斯主教学校任教。1940 年 12 月，戈尔丁加入英国皇家海军服役，曾经参与追击德国俾斯麦号战列舰的战斗，也参加了诺曼底登陆。戈尔丁在第二次世界大战中的经历对他的人生观产生了重要的影响，他认识到了战争的残酷，因而对人性的本质和人类的命运产生了质疑。1945 年，戈尔丁回到主教学校任教，教授英文、哲学与古典文学，并利用业余时间不断进行文学创作。

1954 年，戈尔丁发表了小说处女作《蝇王》(*Lord of the Flies*)。《蝇王》描写了一群六岁至十三岁的孩子，他们作为空难事件的幸存者，流落到了一个无人的珊瑚岛。起初他们试图模仿成人，在大孩子拉尔夫的领导下，建立文明社会，但是在缺乏道德约束和监控的情况下，孩子们渐渐聚拢在以暴力为旗帜的杰克的身边，开始自相残杀，将荒岛变成了硝烟四起的杀戮场。《蝇王》表面上叙述的是一群孩子荒岛历险的故事，但是它不能归属儿童文学的范畴，而是一部现代寓言，借助孩子们的遭遇，揭示了隐藏在人性深层的黑暗中心，体现了作者对整个人类文明的普世关照。诚如戈尔丁所言，“邪恶产生于人类自己的内心深处——是人类的恶造成了邪恶的制度，或者改变了最初的情况、改变了原来的发展，是它把美好的事物变成了邪恶、有害的事物。”

《蝇王》出版前曾多次遭各大出版商退稿，他们纷纷抱怨这部刚过百页的作品过于阴暗。小说出版后，却受到了读者的热烈欢迎，成为英国当代小说的经典名作。紧随《蝇王》，1955 年戈尔丁发表了小说《继承者》(*The Inheritors*)。故事的背景设定在旧石器时代，讲述的是在恶劣环境中寻找生存希望的善良的尼安德特人 (Neanderthals，或译为穴居人) 遭遇自私的克罗马努人 (Cro-Magnon)，并为后者取代的故事。小说体现了戈尔丁对人类学的浓厚兴趣，和《蝇王》一样，关心的是人类命运的走向。戈尔丁借这部小说想象史前时代，在人类祖先的身上寻找到了人性邪恶的根源。1956年，戈尔丁发表小说《品契·马丁》(*Pincher Martin*)，这是一部后现代主义风格浓厚的作品。小说详细描写了主人公遇袭坠海后，在海上努力求生时复杂的心理活动。而直到小说结尾，作者才揭示主人公早已死亡的事实，小说中对主人公心理活动的描述其实是死者不愿接受自己已经死去的事实而进行的幻想性建构。

1961年，戈尔丁辞去教职，成为一名专业作家。1964年，他完成了小说《教堂塔尖》(*The Spire*)，讲述了一个中世纪的教士罔顾现实，想要建造一个高达120多米的教堂塔尖以展示上帝的荣光而最终失败的故事。此后，他又发表了小说《黑暗昭昭》(*Darkness Visible*, 1979)、《航程祭典》(*Rites of Passage*, 1980)等。1983年，戈尔丁被授予诺贝尔文学奖。1984年，他完成了以作家为主人公，旨在探讨写作本质的小说《纸人》(*The Paper Men*, 1984)。他后期的小说还包括与《航程祭典》合为三部曲的《近方位》(*Close Quarters*, 1987)和《下面的火》(*Fire Down Below*, 1989)。1993年，戈尔丁因心脏病在英国去世。在他去世两年后，费伯出版社(Faber & Faber)出版了戈尔丁最后一部小说《巧语》(*The Double Tongue*, 1995)。

戈尔丁的小说没有复杂晦涩的语言，也没有跌宕起伏的情节，却有着打动人心、发人深省的力量。戈尔丁的小说哲理性强，探讨了善与恶、文明与野蛮、生存的本能与道德的责任等多重问题。他的作品具有神话或寓言的性质，对人性中隐藏的恶进行了深入挖掘和呈现，传达了作者对20世纪迭起的战争、大国间的冷战、现代性带来的异化、人类文明的倒退等现象的不满和对人类未来命运的忧虑。正如瑞典文学院的诺贝尔奖颁奖词所言，戈尔丁的小说“用明晰的现实主义的叙述艺术和多样的具有普遍意义的神话，阐明了当今世界人类的状况。”

Lord of the Flies

【题解】

小说的标题“蝇王”典出《圣经》。在《圣经》中，蝇王指的是别西卜(Beelzebub，又译为比埃兹巴伯)。这个词源自希伯来语，最早指的是腓力斯人所崇拜的众神之一巴力神。由于它的发音在希伯来文中和“苍蝇之王”一致，因而被简称为“蝇王”。随着基督教的演进，“别西卜”逐渐成了魔王撒旦的另外一个指称。“蝇王”这一标题在小说中有双重深意。首先，“蝇王”这一意象曾经以实体的形式出现在了小说中。孩子们杀死了母猪，将它的头钉在木桩上。猪头腐烂，上面爬满了苍蝇，是名副其实的“苍蝇之王”。更重要的是，“蝇王”因此成为邪恶的代名词。它是孩子们所犯下的第一桩杀戮之罪的结果，暗示了在这群孩子的灵魂深处埋藏着恶的种子。

本文选自小说最后一章"猎手的尖叫"。《蝇王》中，拉尔夫和他的朋友佩吉和西蒙带领一批孩子，负责建造房屋、采集果实、保存火种。他们是文明的化身。而另一批孩子在杰克的领导下，组成捕猎队，负责追踪并捕杀野猪。在杰克的带领下，猎杀游戏升级。杰克将目标瞄准了和自己意见相左的拉尔夫及他的朋友们。捕猎队先在群殴之下杀死了西蒙，又从山上推下巨石，压死了佩吉。年纪较小的孩子们出于恐惧，纷纷依附于杰克。形单影只的拉尔夫被迫踏上了逃亡之旅。"猎手的尖叫"描写的就是孩子们在杰克的领导下，围剿他们曾经的领袖拉尔夫的情景。为了逼出隐藏在树林里的拉尔夫，他们点火烧毁了果树林。整个岛屿都在火焰中战栗，充满热带风光、祥和的珊瑚岛变成了人间炼狱。

From Lord of the Flies

Chapter 12 Cry of the Hunters

Ralph fastened his hands round the chewed spear and his hair fell. Someone was muttering, only a few yards away towards the Castle Rock. He heard a savage say "No!" in a shocked voice; and then there was suppressed laughter. He squatted back on his heels and showed his teeth at the wall of branches. He raised his spear, snarled a little, and waited.

Once more the invisible group sniggered. He heard a curious trickling sound and then a louder crepitation[1] as if someone were unwrapping great sheets of cellophane[2]. A stick snapped and he stifled a cough. Smoke was seeping through the branches in white and yellow wisps, the patch of blue sky over head turned to the colour of a storm cloud, and then the smoke billowed round him.

Someone laughed excitedly, and a voice shouted.

"Smoke!"

He wormed his way through the thicket towards the forest, keeping as far as possible beneath the smoke. Presently he saw open space, and the green leaves of the edge of the thicket. A smallish savage was standing between him and the rest of the forest, a savage striped red and white, and carrying a spear. He was coughing and smearing the paint about his eyes with the back of his hand as he tried to see through the increasing smoke. Ralph launched himself like a cat; stabled, snarling, with the spear, and the savage doubled up. There was a shout from beyond the thicket and then Ralph was running with the swiftness of fear through the undergrowth. He came to a pig-run, followed it for perhaps a hundred yards, and then swerved off. Behind him the ululation[3] swept across the island once more and a single voice shouted three times. He guessed that was the signal to advance and sped away again, till his chest was like fire. Then he flung himself down under a bush and waited for a moment till his breathing steadied. He passed his tongue tentatively over his teeth and lips and heard far off the ululation of the pursuers.

There were many things he could do. He could climb a tree; but that was putting all his eggs in one basket. If he were detected, they had nothing more difficult to do than wait.

If only one had time to think!

Another double cry at the same distance gave him a clue to their plan. Any savage balked in the forest would utter the double shout and hold up the line till he was free again. That way they might hope to keep the cordon[4] unbroken right across the island. Ralph thought of the boar that had broken through them with such ease. If necessary, when the chase came too close, he could charge the cordon while it was still thin, burst through, and run back. But run back where? The cordon would turn and sweep again. Sooner or later he would have to sleep or eat—and then he would awaken with hands clawing at him; and the hunt would become a running down.

What was to be done, then? The tree? Burst the line like a boar? Either way the choice was terrible.

A single cry quickened his heart-beat and, leaping up, he dashed away toward the ocean side and the thick jungle till he was hung up among creepers; he stayed there for a moment with his calves quivering. If only one could have quiet, a long pause, a time to think!

And there again, shrill and inevitable, was the ululation sweeping across the island. At that sound he shied like a horse among the creepers and ran once more till he was panting. He flung himself down by some ferns. The tree, or the charge? He mastered his breathing for a moment, wiped his mouth, and told himself to be calm. Samneric[5] were somewhere in that line, and hating it. Or were they? And supposing, instead of them, he met the chief, or Roger who carried death in his hands?

Ralph pushed back his tangled hair and wiped the sweat out of his best eye. He spoke aloud: "Think."

What was the sensible thing to do?

There was no Piggy to talk sense. There was no solemn assembly for debate nor dignity of the conch.

"Think."

Most, he was beginning to dread the curtain that might waver in his brain, blacking out the sense of danger, making a simpleton of him.

A third idea would be to hide so well that the advancing line would pass without discovering him.

He jerked his head off the ground and listened. There was another noise to attend to now, a deep grumbling noise, as though the forest itself were angry with him, a somber noise across which the ululations were scribbled excruciatingly as on slate. He knew he had heard it before somewhere, but had no time to remember.

Break the line.

A tree.

Hide, and let them pass.

A nearer cry stood him on his feet and immediately he was away again, running fast among thorns and brambles. Suddenly he blundered into the open, found himself again in that open space—and there was the fathom-wide grin of the skull, no longer ridiculing a deep blue patch of sky but jeering up into a blanket of smoke. Then Ralph was running beneath trees, with the grumble of the forest explained. They had smoked him out and set the island on fire.

Hide was better than a tree because you had a chance of breaking the line if you were discovered.

Hide, then.

He wondered if a pig would agree, and grimaced at nothing. Find the deepest thicket, the darkest hole on the island, and creep in. Now, as he ran, he peered about him. Bars and splashes of sunlight flitted over him and sweat made glistening streaks on his dirty body. The cries were far now, and faint.

At last he found what seemed to him the right place, though the decision was desperate. Here, bushes and a wild tangle of creeper made a mat that kept out all the light of the sun. Beneath it was a space, perhaps a foot high, though it was pierced everywhere by parallel and rising stems. If you wormed into the middle of that you would be five yards from the edge, and hidden, unless the savage chose to lie down and look for you; and even then, you would be in darkness—and if the worst happened and he saw you, then you had a chance to burst out at him, fling the whole line out of step and double back.

Cautiously, his stick trailing behind him. Ralph wormed between the rising stems. When he reached the middle of the mat he lay and listened.

The fire was a big one and the drum-roll that he had thought was left so far behind was nearer. Couldn't a fire outrun a galloping horse? He could see the sun-splashed ground over an area of perhaps fifty yards from where he lay, and as he watched, the sunlight in every patch blinked at him. This was so like the curtain that flapped in his brain that for a moment he thought the blinking was inside him. But then the patches blinked more rapidly, dulled and went out, so that he saw that a great heaviness of smoke lay between the island and the sun.

If anyone peered under the bushes and chanced to glimpse human flesh it might be Samneric who would pretend not to see and say nothing. He laid his cheek against the chocolate-colored earth, licked his dry lips and closed his eyes. Under the thicket, the earth was vibrating very slightly; or perhaps there was a sound beneath the obvious thunder of the fire and scribbled ululations that was too low to hear.

Someone cried out. Ralph jerked his cheek off the earth and looked into the dulled light. They must be near now, he thought, and his chest began to thump. Hide, break the line, climb a tree—which was the best after all? The trouble was you only had one chance.

Now the fire was nearer; those volleying shots were great limbs, trunks even, bursting. The fools! The fools! The fire must be almost at the fruit trees—what would they eat tomorrow?

Ralph stirred restlessly in his narrow bed. One chanced nothing! What could they do? Beat him? So what? Kill him? A stick sharpened at both ends.

The cries, suddenly nearer, jerked him up. He could see a striped savage moving hastily out of a green tangle, and coming toward the mat where he hid, a savage who carried a spear. Ralph gripped his fingers into the earth. Be ready now, in case.

Ralph fumbled to hold his spear so that it was point foremost; and now he saw that the stick was sharpened at both ends.

The savage stopped fifteen yards away and uttered his cry.

Perhaps he can hear my heart over the noises of the fire. Don't scream. Get ready.

The savage moved forward so that you could only see him from the waist down. That was the butt of his spear. Now you could see him from the knee down. Don't scream. A herd of pigs came squealing out of the greenery behind the savage and rushed away into the forest. Birds were screaming, mice shrieking, and a little hopping thing came under the mat and cowered.

Five yards away the savage stopped, standing right by the thicket, and cried out. Ralph drew his feet up and crouched. The stake was in his hands, the stake sharpened at both ends, the stake that vibrated so wildly, that grew long, short, light, heavy, light again.

The ululation spread from shore to shore. The savage knelt down by the edge of the thicket, and there were lights flickering in the forest behind him. You could see a knee disturb the mold. Now the other. Two hands. A spear.

A face.

The savage peered into the obscurity beneath the thicket. You could tell that he saw light on this side and on that, but not in the middle—there. In the middle was a blob of dark and the savage wrinkled up his face, trying to decipher the darkness.

The seconds lengthened. Ralph was looking straight into the savage's eyes.

Don't scream.

You'll get back.

Now he's seen you. He's making sure. A stick sharpened.

Ralph screamed, a scream of fright and anger and desperation. His legs straightened, the screams became continuous and foaming. He shot forward, burst the thicket, was in the open, screaming, snarling, bloody. He swung the stake and the savage tumbled over; but there were others coming toward him, crying out. He swerved as a spear flew past and then was silent, running. All at once the lights flickering ahead of him merged together, the roar of the forest rose to thunder and a tall bush directly in his path burst into a great fan-shaped flame. He swung to the right, running desperately fast, with the heat beating on his left side and the fire racing forward like a tide. The ululation rose behind him and spread along, a series of short sharp cries, the sighting call. A brown figure showed up at his right and fell away. They were all running, all crying out madly. He could hear them crashing in the undergrowth and on the left was the hot, bright thunder of the fire. He forgot his wounds, his hunger and thirst, and became fear; hopeless fear on flying feet, rushing through the forest towards the open beach. Spots jumped before his eyes and turned into red circles that expanded quickly till they passed out of sight. Below him, someone's legs were getting tired and the desperate ululation advanced like a jagged fringe of menace and was almost overhead.

He tumbled over a root and the cry that pursued him rose ever higher. He saw a shelter burst into flames and the fire flapped at his right shoulder and there was the glitter of water. Then he was down, rolling over and over in the warm sand, crouching with arm up to ward off, trying to cry for mercy.

He staggered to his feet, tensed for more terrors, and looked up at a huge peaked cap. It was a white-topped cap, and above the green shade of the peak was a crown, an anchor, gold foliage. He saw white drill, epaulettes[6], a revolver, a row of gilt buttons down the front of a uniform.

A naval officer stood on the sand, looking down at Ralph in wary astonishment. On the beach behind him was a cutter, her bows hauled up and held by two ratings. In the stern-sheets another rating held a sub-machine gun.

The ululation faltered and died away.

The officer looked at Ralph doubtfully for a moment, then took his hand away from the butt of the revolver.

"Hullo."

Squirming a little, conscious of his filthy appearance, Ralph answered shyly.

"Hullo."

The officer nodded, as if a question had been answered.

"Are there any adults—any grown—ups with you?"

Dumbly, Ralph shook his head. He turned a half-pace on the sand. A semicircle of little boys, their bodies streaked with coloured clay, sharp sticks in their hands, were standing on the beach making no noise at all.

"Fun and games," said the officer.

The fire reached the coco-nut palms by the beach and swallowed them noisily. A flame, seemingly detached, swung like an acrobat and licked up the palm heads on the platform. The sky was black.

The officer grinned cheerfully at Ralph.

"We saw your smoke. What have you been doing? Having a war or something?"

Ralph nodded.

The officer inspected the little scarecrow[7] in front of him. The kid needed a bath, a hair-cut, a nose-wipe and a great deal of ointment.

"Nobody killed, I hope? And dead bodies?"

"Only two. And they've gone."

The officer leaned down and looked closely at Ralph.

"Two? Killed?"

Ralph nodded again. Behind him, the whole island was shuddering with flame. The officer knew, as a rule, when people were telling the truth. He whistled softly.

Other boys were appearing now, tiny tots some of them, brown, with the distended bellies of small savages. One of them came close to the officer and looked up.

"I'm , I'm—"

But there was no more to come. Percival Wemys Madison sought in his head for an incantation that had faded clean away.

The officer turned back to Ralph.

"We'll take you off. How many of you are there?"

Ralph shook his head. The officer looked past him to the group of painted boys.

"Who's boss here?"

"I am," Ralph said loudly.

A little boy who wore the remains of an extraordinary black cap on his red hair and who carried the remains of a pair of spectacles at his waist, started forward, then changed his mind and stood still.

"We saw your smoke. And you don't know how many of you there are?"

"No, sir."

"I should have thought," said the officer as he visualized the search before him, "I should have thought that a pack of British boys—you're all British aren't you?—would have been able to put up a better show than that—I mean—"

"It was like that at first," said Ralph, "before things—"

He stopped.

"We were together then—"

The officer nodded helpfully.

"I know. Jolly good show. Like the Coral Island."

Ralph looked at him dumbly. For a moment he had a fleeing picture of the strange glamour that had once invested the beaches. But the island was scored up like dead wood—Simon was dead—and Jack had . . . The tears began to flow and sobs shook him. He gave himself up to them now for the first time on the island; great, shuddering spasms of grief that seemed to wrench his whole body. His voice rose under the black smoke before the burning wreckage of the island; and infected by that emotion, the other little boys began to shake and sob too. And in the middle of them, with filthy body, matted hair, and unwiped nose. Ralph wept for the end of innocence, the darkness of man's heart, and the fall through the air of the true, wise friend called Piggy.

The officer, surrounded by these noises, was moved and a little embarrassed. He turned away to give them time to pull themselves together; and waited, allowing his eyes to rest on the trim cruiser in the distance.

【注解】

1. crepitation：噼啪声。文中指孩子们开始放火烧林，树木遇火，噼啪作响。
2. cellophane：玻璃纸。
3. ululation：嚎声，吠声。这里用动物的声音比喻孩子们说话喊叫的声音，暗示他们已经沦为野蛮人，像动物一样捕猎。
4. cordon：封锁线。
5. Samneric：文中指两个人，即Sam和Eric。他们是一对双胞胎，一直形影不离。他们曾经是拉尔夫的追随者，在杰克的暴力胁迫下和其他孩子一起追捕拉尔夫。
6. epaulettes：(军官的)肩章。
7. scarecrow：骨瘦如柴的人，衣衫褴褛的人。

【思考题】

1. Who are the hunters described in this chapter? What are they hunting? Why does Golding describe them as savages?
2. Why does the naval officer come to the island? Does he understand the nature of the hunting against Ralph at first? When he at last learns the truth, how does he respond?
3. In Chapter 12, "Ralph wept for the end of innocence, the darkness of man's heart, and the fall through the air of the true, wise friend called Piggy." How would you understand this sentence?
4. Is there anything similar between the naval officer and the children on the island? If yes, how are they similar?
5. Some critics say that the ending of *Lord of the Flies* is full of irony. Do you agree with this view? Why?

【简评】

《蝇王》中的小岛，没有食人猛兽出没，人却碰到了天敌——人类自己。为了将拉尔夫逼出隐身的丛林，杰克不惜下令放火烧林，将整个小岛变成一片火海。小说对拉尔夫的恐惧进行了极为精细的描写。每一个树丛背后，都可能隐藏着拉尔夫昔日的伙伴，在等待着扑上来用削尖了的梭镖将他杀死。他那张皇失措的心境、孤注一掷的反抗及不顾一切的狂奔，无一不在诉说着恐惧和绝望。不过，令拉尔夫没有想到的是，他竟然获了救。岛上的大火引来了在附近游弋的军舰。不过，救了拉尔夫的海军军官根本无法猜到岛上发生的一切。当他看到拉尔夫和追赶拉尔夫的孩子们，还以为他们在玩追捕的游戏。幸存的拉尔夫不禁失声恸哭："这是他上岛以来第一次尽情地哭；他的整个身子仿佛被巨大的悲痛所扭曲，一阵阵地抽搐着……拉尔夫在为天真的终结哭泣，为人心的黑暗哭泣。"

《蝇王》的结尾是定格式的。人与人之间的迫害达到了顶点——熊熊大火前是两组面对面、已经和野蛮人无异的孩子。脱离了文明社会的束缚，人性之恶扭曲了每一个孩子的面容。这个结尾更有另外的深意：我们可以责备孩子，怪他们携带着人类的原罪，然而，在小说结尾充当救世主的海军军官，又何尝不是一场更大的杀戮游戏中的一分子？当孩子们用自制的投枪相互猎杀时，成人们在用飞机、军舰、炮弹制造大规模的死亡；当孩子们将荒岛变成战场时，成人们在整个世界燃起战火，让无数家庭流离失所。正如戈尔丁自己在采访中所说的："军官在许多方面和那些变成猎人的男孩子没有什么差别。他也是堕落的。他也在猎杀。只是他不知道自己竟然是这样的。"透过《蝇王》，戈尔丁直接批判了以相互争斗、相互残杀为特点的人类社会范式，对文明和人性进行了悲观性的预测。

Doris Lessing
1919—2013

作者简介

多丽丝·莱辛 1919 年出生于波斯(即今天的伊朗)，父亲是一名银行职员。1925 年，莱辛的父母决定到非洲经营农场，莱辛随他们迁居到英属罗得西亚(即今天的津巴布韦)。为了能够让长女莱辛受到严格的教育，莱辛的母亲将她送到了当地的女子教会学校。教会学校严苛的氛围和父母过度的期望使莱辛产生了强烈的叛逆情绪，她十四岁的时候就辍了学。辍学后的莱辛当过保姆、秘书、打字员，尝试过多种职业。1939 年，莱辛嫁给了身为公务员的弗兰克·维斯顿。这场婚姻维持了三年时间，莱辛生下一儿一女，离婚后孩子归父亲抚养。1945 年，莱辛和德国政治活动家戈特弗雷德·莱辛结婚。1949 年，这场婚姻也宣告失败。莱辛带着与戈特弗雷德所生的幼子回到了英国伦敦，终生没有再婚。

早在回到英国前，莱辛就开始了小说创作。回到英国后，她更是全身心投入写作。

1950 年，她出版了第一部长篇小说《青草在歌唱》(*The Grass Is Singing*)。这部小说以撒哈拉以南的非洲为背景，女主人公玛丽·特纳和丈夫在罗得西亚经营着一所农场。农场管理不善，丈夫长期卧病在床，生活极其困窘，玛丽不得不依靠家里的黑人男仆摩西，从他那里寻找慰藉。然而，玛丽和摩西亲密的关系引起了白人邻居们的不满，玛丽开除了摩西，摩西在愤怒中开枪将女主人杀死。《青草在歌唱》揭示了这样一个现实：种族隔离制度不仅为黑人带来了无尽痛苦，身为殖民者的白人其实也是这一制度的牺牲品。这部小说深刻的主题使它一出版就受到了读者的欢迎，批评家纷纷赞誉英国文坛自此又诞生了一颗新星。

《青草在歌唱》的成功坚定了莱辛从事文学创作的决心。1962 年，莱辛完成了小说《金色笔记》。《金色笔记》描写了女主人公安娜·沃尔夫的情爱生活和精神困境。小说的结构十分复杂。莱辛将安娜的现实经历和她对过去的回忆交织在一起，将她的真实生活和她所创作的小说文本交织在一起。小说具有百科全书的特征，透过安娜的故事，折射出 20 世纪 50 年代的风云变幻。南非种族隔离、匈牙利事变等历史事件在作品中均有呈现。这部小说最为精彩的是它对女性内心世界的深入挖掘，以及对女性生存状态的深层次思考。

莱辛在 20 世纪 50 年代和 60 年代的创作多取材自她在非洲的所见所感。除了《青草在歌唱》和《金色笔记》两部作品以外，莱辛还完成了"暴力的孩子"("The Children of Violence") 五部曲，即《玛莎·奎斯特》(*Martha Quest*, 1952)、《良缘》(*A Proper Marriage*, 1954)、《风暴的余波》(*A Ripple from the Storm*, 1958)、《被陆地围住的》(*Landlocked*, 1966) 和《四门之城》(*The Four-Gated City*, 1969)。这一系列作品以一位来自罗得西亚的白人女性的成长历程为主线。自 20 世纪 70 年代开始，莱辛转向科幻小说创作，出版了"南船座中的老人星：档案" (Canopus in Argos: Archives) 系列太空小说，该系列包括《什卡斯塔》(*Re: Colonized Planet Five, Shikasta*, 1979)、《第三、四、五区域间的联姻》(*The Marriage between Zones Three, Four, and Five*, 1980)、《天狼星试验》(*The Sirian Experiments: The Report of Ambien* II*, of the Five*, 1981)、《八号行星代表的产生》(*The Making of the Representative for Planet Eight*, 1982)、《与沃炎帝国多愁善感的使者们有关的文件》(*Documents Relating to the Sentimental Agents in the Volyen Empire*, 1983) 等作品。一些批评家认为莱辛写科幻小说是对才华的浪费，莱辛却认为，"科幻小说是最好的社会小说"。她想象这些遥远星系的外星生物，以外星社会为参照，反思当代社会面临的诸多问题。

进入古稀之年后，莱辛仍然保持着旺盛的创造力。她发表了两卷记述早年生活的自传《在我皮肤的下面》(*Under My Skin*, 1994) 和《影中独行：莱辛自传 1949—

1962》(*Walking in the Shade: Volume Two of My Autobiography, 1949—1962*, 1997)。此外，她还完成了小说《又来了，爱情》(*Love, Again*, 1996)、《最甜蜜的梦》(*The Sweetest Dream*, 2002)、《裂隙》(*The Cleft*, 2007) 等。2007 年，莱辛以八十八岁高龄获得了诺贝尔文学奖。

莱辛是英国文坛少有的多产作家。她的写作生涯长达半个多世纪，作品数量众多、体裁各异、主题丰富。如果要寻找共性，那就是莱辛在作品中刻画了大量勇于追求个性、有着独立思想的女性。也正因为如此，很多人将莱辛与女性主义者画上了等号。不过，莱辛本人却不愿意被贴上女性主义的标签。相比而言，她更愿意通过手中的笔，呈现出女性生活的多样性和两性关系的复杂性。瑞典文学院在颁奖词中，称莱辛是“女性经验的史诗作者，用怀疑的态度、火热的激情和远见，清晰地剖析了一个被割裂的文化。”

The Golden Notebook

【题解】

《金色笔记》的女主人公安娜·沃尔夫是一位作家，《自由女人》是她创作的以自己为原型的作品。她将《自由女人》裁剪成五个部分，在每个部分的空档，穿插上了按照黑、红、黄、蓝顺序排列的个人笔记——黑色笔记记载着她早年的非洲经历，红色笔记有关政治信仰，黄色笔记是一部新小说的草稿，蓝色笔记是私人日记。安娜将生活分门别类，归入不同的笔记。她想通过这种方式，整理自己行将崩溃的混乱精神世界。然而，这种人为的割裂所产生的效果适得其反，复杂的生活无法接受泾渭分明的切分。为此，安娜增补了一个全新的笔记——金色笔记。在这个笔记里，安娜不再区分生活、艺术、政治和感情，实现了内心的释放和平衡。本文节选自《金色笔记》第一章。从小标题可以看出这是主人公安娜所创作的小说《自由女人》的第一部分。该章节描述了安娜和好朋友莫莉在租住的公寓中聊天的场景，勾勒出两位女性人物颇具差异的性格，以及她们作为“自由女性”所面对的生活现状和人生难题。

From The Golden Notebook

Free Women

Chapter 1

Anna meets her friend Molly in the summer of 1957 after a separation

The two women were alone in the London flat.

"The point is," said Anna, as her friend came back from the telephone on the landing, "the point is, that as far as I can see, everything's cracking up."

Molly was a woman much on the telephone. When it rang she had just enquired: "Well, what's the gossip?" Now she said, "That's Richard, and he's coming over. It seems today's his only free moment for the next month. Or so he insists."

"Well I'm not leaving," said Anna.

"No, you stay just where you are."

Molly considered her own appearance—he was wearing trousers and a sweater, both the worse for wear. "He'll have to take me as I come," she concluded, and sat down by the window. "He wouldn't say what it's about—another crisis with Marion, I suppose."

"Didn't he write to you?" asked Anna, cautious.

"Both he and Marion wrote—ever such *bonhomous*[1] letters. Odd, isn't it?"

This *odd, isn't it*? was the characteristic note of the intimate conversations they designated gossip. But having struck the note, Molly swerved off with: "It's no use talking now, because he's coming right over, he says."

"He'll probably go when he sees me here," said Anna, cheerfully, but slightly aggressive. Molly glanced at her, keenly, and said: "Oh, but why?"

It had always been understood that Anna and Richard disliked each other; and before Anna had always left when Richard was expected. Now Molly said: "Actually I think he rather likes you, in his heart of hearts. The point is, he's committed to liking me, on principle—he's such a fool he's always got to either like or dislike someone, so all the dislike he won't admit he has for me gets pushed off on to you."

"It's a pleasure," said Anna. "But do you know something? I discovered while you were away that for a lot of people you and I are practically interchangeable."

"You've only just understood that?" said Molly, triumphant as always when Anna came up with—as far as she was concerned—facts that were self-evident.

In this relationship a balance had been struck early on: Molly was altogether more worldly-wise than Anna who, for her part, had a superiority of talent.

Anna held her own private views. Now she smiled, admitting that she had been very slow.

"When we're so different in every way," said Molly, "it's odd. I suppose because we both live the same kind of life—not getting married and so on. That's all they see."

"Free women," said Anna, wryly. She added, with an anger new to Molly, so that she earned another quick scrutinising glance from her friend: "They still define us in terms of relationships with men, even the best of them."

"Well, we do, don't we?" said Molly, rather tart. "Well, it's awfully hard not to," she amended, hastily, because of the look of surprise Anna now gave her. There was a short pause, during which the women did not look at each other but reflected that a year apart was a long time, even for an old friendship.

Molly said at last, sighing: "Free. Do you know, when I was away, I was thinking about us, and I've decided that we're a completely new type of woman. We must be, surely?"

"There's nothing new under the sun," said Anna, in an attempt at a German accent. Molly, irritated—she spoke half a dozen languages well—said: "There's nothing new under the sun," in a perfect reproduction of a shrewd old woman's voice, German accented.

Anna grimaced, acknowledging failure. She could not learn languages, and was too self-conscious ever to become somebody else: for a moment Molly had even looked like Mother Sugar[2], otherwise Mrs. Marks, to whom both had gone for psycho-analysis. The reservations both had felt about the solemn and painful ritual were expressed by the pet name, "Mother Sugar"; which, as time passed, became a name for much more than a person, and indicated a whole way of looking at life—traditional, rooted, conservative, in spite of its scandalous familiarity with everything amoral. In spite of—that was how Anna and Molly, discussing the ritual, had felt it; recently Anna had been feeling more and more it was because of; and this was one of the things she was looking forward to discussing with her friend.

But now Molly, reacting as she had often done in the past, to the slightest suggestion of a criticism from Anna of Mother Sugar, said quickly: "All the same, she was wonderful, and I was in much too bad a shape to criticise."

"Mother Sugar used to say, 'You're Electra[3],' or 'You're Antigone[4],' and that was the end, as far as she was concerned," said Anna.

"Well, not quite the end," said Molly, wryly insisting on the painful probing hours both had spent.

"Yes," said Anna, unexpectedly insisting, so that Molly, for the third time, looked at her curiously. "Yes. Oh I'm not saying she didn't do me all the good in the world. I'm sure I'd never have coped with what I've had to cope with without her. But all the same . . . I remember quite clearly one afternoon, sitting there—the big room, and the discreet wall lights, and the Buddha and the pictures and the statues."

"Well?" said Molly, now very critical.

Anna, in the face of this unspoken but clear determination not to discuss it, said: "I've been thinking about it all during the last few months . . . now I'd like to talk about it with you. After all, we both went through it, and with the same person . . . "

"Well?"

Anna persisted: "I remember that afternoon, knowing I'd never go back. It was all that damned art all over the place."

Molly drew in her breath, sharp. She said, quickly: "I don't know what you mean." As Anna did not reply, she said, accusing: "And have you written anything since I've been away?"

"No."

"I keep telling you," said Molly, her voice shrill, "I'll never forgive you if you throw that talent away. I mean it. I've done it, and I can't stand watching you—I've messed with painting and dancing and acting and scribbling, and now . . . you're so talented, Anna. Why? I simply don't understand."

"How can I ever say why, when you're always so bitter and accusing?"

Molly even had tears in her eyes, which were fastened in the most painful reproach on her friend. She brought out with difficulty: "At the back of my mind I always thought, well, I'll get married, so it doesn't matter my wasting all the talents I was born with. Until recently I was even dreaming about having more children—yes I know it's idiotic but it's true. And now I'm forty and Tommy's grown up. But the point is, if you're not writing simply because you're thinking about getting married . . . "

"But we both want to get married," said Anna, making it humorous; the tone restored reserve to the conversation; she had understood, with pain, that she was not, after all, going to be able to discuss certain subjects with Molly.

Molly smiled, dryly, gave her friend an acute, bitter look, and said: "All right, but you'll be sorry later."

"*Sorry*," said Anna, laughing, out of surprise. "Molly, why is it you'll never believe other people have the disabilities you have?"

"You were lucky enough to be given one talent, and not four."

"Perhaps my one talent has had as much pressure on it as your four?"

"I can't talk to you in this mood. Shall I make you some tea while we're waiting for Richard?"

"I'd rather have beer or something." She added, provocative: "I've been thinking I might very well take to drink later on."

Molly said, in the older sister's tone Anna had invited: "You shouldn't make jokes, Anna. Not when you see what it does to people—look at Marion. I wonder if she's been drinking while I was away?"

"I can tell you. She has—yes, she came to see me several times."

"She came to see you?"

"That's what I was leading up to, when I said you and I seem to be interchangeable."

Molly tended to be possessive—she showed resentment, as Anna had known she would, as she said: "I suppose you're going to say Richard came to see you too?" Anna nodded; and Molly said, briskly, "I'll get us some beer." She returned from the kitchen with two long cold-beaded glasses, and said: "Well you'd better tell me all about it before Richard comes, hadn't you?"

Richard was Molly's husband; or rather, he had been her husband. Molly was the product of what she referred to as "one of those 'twenties marriages[5]'". Her mother and father had both glittered, but briefly, in the intellectual and bohemian circles that had spun around the great central lights of Huxley[6], Lawrence[7], Joyce[8], etc. Her childhood had been disastrous, since this marriage only lasted a few months. She had married, at the age of eighteen, the son of a friend of her father's. She knew now she had married out of a need for security and even respectability. The boy Tommy was a product of this marriage. Richard at twenty had already been on the way to becoming the very solid businessman he had since proved himself: and Molly and he had stood their incompatibility for not much more than a year. He had then married Marion, and there were three boys. Tommy had remained with Molly. Richard and she, once the business of the divorce was over, became friends again. Later, Marion became her friend. This, then, was the situation to which

Molly often referred as: "It's all very odd, isn't it?"

"Richard came to see me about Tommy," said Anna.

"What? Why?"

"Oh—idiotic! He asked me if I thought it was good for Tommy to spend so much time brooding. I said I thought it was good for everyone to brood, if by that he meant, thinking; and that since Tommy was twenty and grown up it was not for us to interfere anyway."

"Well it isn't good for him," said Molly.

"He asked me if I thought it would be good for Tommy to go off on some trip or other to Germany—a business trip, with him. I told him to ask Tommy, not me. Of course Tommy said no."

"Of course. Well I'm sorry Tommy didn't go."

"But the real reason he came, I think, was because of Marion. But Marion had just been to see me, and had a prior claim so to speak. So I wouldn't discuss Marion at all. I think it's likely he's coming to discuss Marion with you."

Molly was watching Anna closely. "How many times did Richard come?"

"About five or six times."

After a silence, Molly let her anger spurt out with: "It's very odd he seems to expect me almost to control Marion. Why me? Or you? Well, perhaps you'd better go after all. It's going to be difficult if all sorts of complications have been going on while my back was turned."

Anna said firmly: "No, Molly. I didn't ask Richard to come and see me. I didn't ask Marion to come and see me. After all, it's not your fault or mine that we seem to play the same role for people. I said what you would have said—at least, I think so."

There was a note of humorous, even childish pleading in this. But it was deliberate. Molly, the older sister, smiled and said: "Well, all right." She continued to observe Anna narrowly; and Anna was careful to appear unaware of it. She did not want to tell Molly what had happened between her and Richard now; not until she could tell her the whole story of the last miserable year.

"Is Marion drinking badly?"

"Yes, I think she is."

"And she told you all about it?"

"Yes. In detail. And what's odd is, I swear she talked as if I were you—even making slips of the tongue, calling me Molly and so on."

"Well, I don't know," said Molly. "Who would ever have thought? And you and I are different as chalk and cheese."

"Perhaps not so different," said Anna, drily; but Molly laughed in disbelief.

She was a tallish woman, and big-boned, but she appeared slight, and even boyish. This was because of how she did her hair, which was a rough, streaky gold, cut like a boy's; and because of her clothes, for which she had a great natural talent. She took pleasure in the various guises she could use: for instance, being a hoyden[9] in lean trousers and sweaters, and then a siren, her large green eyes made-up, her cheekbones prominent, wearing a dress which made the most of her full breasts.

This was one of the private games she played with life, which Anna envied her; yet in moments of self-rebuke she would tell Anna she was ashamed of herself, she so much enjoyed the different roles: "It's as if I were really different—don't you see? I even feel a different person. And there's something spiteful in it—that man, you know, I told you about him last week—he saw me the first time in my old slacks[10] and my sloppy old jersey[11], and then I rolled into the restaurant, nothing less than a femme fatale[12], and he didn't know how to have me, he couldn't say a word all evening, and I enjoyed it. Well, Anna?"

"But you do enjoy it," Anna would say, laughing.

But Anna was small, thin, dark, brittle, with large black always-on-guard eyes, and a fluffy haircut. She was, on the whole, satisfied with herself, but she was always the same. She envied Molly's capacity to project her own changes of mood. Anna wore neat, delicate clothes, which tended to be either prim, or perhaps a little odd; and relied upon her delicate white hands, and her small, pointed white face to make an impression. But she was shy, unable to assert herself, and, she was convinced, easily overlooked.

When the two women went out together, Anna deliberately effaced herself and played to the dramatic Molly. When they were alone, she tended to take the lead. But this had by no means been true at the beginning of their friendship. Molly, abrupt, straightforward, tactless, had frankly domineered Anna. Slowly, and the offices of Mother Sugar had had a good deal to do with it, Anna learned to stand up for herself. Even now there were moments when she should challenge Molly when she did not. She admitted to herself she was a coward; she would always give in rather than have fights or scenes. A quarrel would lay Anna low for days, whereas Molly thrived on them. She would burst into exuberant tears, say unforgivable things, and have forgotten all about it half a day later. Meanwhile

Anna would be limply recovering in her flat.

That they were both "insecure" and "unrooted", words which dated from the era of Mother Sugar, they both freely acknowledged. But Anna had recently been learning to use these words in a different way, not as something to be apologized for, but as flags or banners for an attitude that amounted to a different philosophy. She had enjoyed fantasies of saying to Molly: We've had the wrong attitude to the whole thing, and it's Mother Sugar's fault—what is this security and balance that's supposed to be so good? What's wrong with living emotionally from hand-to-mouth in a world that's changing as fast as it is?

But now, sitting with Molly talking, as they had so many hundreds of times before, Anna was saying to herself: Why do I always have this awful need to make other people see things as I do? It's childish, why should they? What it amounts to is that I'm scared of being alone in what I feel.

【注解】

1. bonhomous：亲切，愉快。
2. Mother Sugar：“苏格大娘”，指的是莫莉和安娜的心理分析师马科斯太太 (Mrs. Marks)。莫莉和安娜各自有心理创伤，才去看心理医生。她们昵称马科斯太太为“苏格大娘”，是一种幽默的手法，要让这段苦涩的经历有一点甜 (sugar) 的意味。
3. Electra：厄勒克特拉，希腊神话中的人物，有恋父情结。她是阿伽门农与克吕泰墨斯特拉的女儿，为其父报仇而与其弟俄瑞斯特斯联手杀死了他们的母亲和母亲的情夫埃奎斯托斯。
4. Antigone：安提戈涅，希腊神话中的人物俄狄浦斯与伊俄卡斯忒的女儿。她不顾舅父克瑞翁的反对而将自己的哥哥安葬。
5. twenties marriages：那些 20 年代的婚姻。
6. Huxley：即阿道司·伦纳德·赫胥黎，英国著名作家。
7. Lawrence：即英国著名作家 D. H. 劳伦斯。
8. Joyce：即爱尔兰著名作家乔伊斯。
9. hoyden：顽皮的姑娘。
10. slacks：运动裤，宽松长裤。
11. jersey：运动衫，紧身针织套衫。
12. femme fatale：有“红颜祸水”之意。

【思考题】

1. Who is Mother Sugar? What does this image represent?
2. Why does Molly feel unhappy when she finds that her ex-husband Richard and his new wife Marion come to visit Anna?

3. What is Molly's character like? What is Anna's character like?
4. According to Anna, how do men define women? Why are Anna and Molly called "free women"? Are they really free?
5. Which major theme recurs in all the stories of Doris Lessing?

【简评】

“自由女人”一节是《金色笔记》的开篇。这里的自由女人，意有所指，说的是女主人公安娜和她的好友莫莉。安娜是一位单亲母亲，独立抚养着十三岁大的女儿珍妮特。她是一位作家，早年曾经在非洲生活，憎恨种族主义，反对任何形式的压迫和不平等，有着激进的政治观点。莫莉也是一个单亲母亲。她跳过芭蕾，当过画家、记者，演过戏剧，不满足于停留在同一个地方，渴望体验不同形式的生活。无论是安娜还是莫莉的生活方式，都和她们所身处时代的保守气氛格格不入。20 世纪 50 年代，英国曾经出现过反对女性主义运动的逆流，不少男性叫嚣着要求女性恪守本分，回归家庭，成为贤妻良母。安娜和莫莉皆是“离经叛道”者，她们拒绝充当家中的天使、男人的应声虫，她们寻求经济独立，追求个人幸福，充满了理想主义色彩。

不过，在《金色笔记》中，这两个“自由女性”内心深处所渴望的，其实并不是自由，而是爱。节选中，莫莉告诉安娜：“在我的内心深处，我总是想：我会结婚的……最近，我甚至梦想多养几个孩子——是的，我知道这想法很愚蠢，但这是真的。”而安娜也承认：“我们两人都想结婚。”她们期待着能够碰到一个可以理解自己、可以平等交流、愿意真诚付出的男性伴侣。然而，在当时男权至上的社会，这样的愿望近乎幻想。在《金色笔记》的结尾，安娜依然寻寻觅觅，莫莉却放弃了抗争，嫁给了一个商人。《自由女人》这个标题，未尝不是一种反讽。

John Fowles
1926—2005

作者简介

约翰·福尔斯是二战以后英国重要的小说家之一，1926 年出生于英国埃萨克斯的一个小镇，那里的环境相当保守和封闭。从小在各种规矩的压制下长大的福尔斯却因此认识到了自由的可贵，骨子里充满了叛逆精神。1933 年，福尔斯进入贝德福德寄宿学校学习。1940 年，为了躲避第二次世界大战的战火，福尔斯休学一个学期，随家人迁到了英国西部风光秀丽的德文郡。在那里，福尔斯终日沉浸在自然中，身

心得以解放。离开学校后，福尔斯加入英国皇家海军，成为一名中尉军官。退役后，福尔斯进入牛津大学学习法国和德国文学，深受到当时盛行的法国存在主义的影响。1950 年福尔斯以优秀生的身份从牛津新学院毕业后，来到法国和希腊教授英文。虽然这一段在欧洲大陆的生活只有短短三年，福尔斯却认为这段时光彻底拓宽了他的视野："我不再想成为一个英国作家。我想成为一个欧洲作家，那种我称之为'大欧洲'式的作家。"（"大欧洲"是指所有文化底蕴属于欧洲的地区。）1952 年底，福尔斯回到英国，在从事教师职业之余开始了练笔式的写作。1963 年福尔斯出版第一部小说，从此成为一名职业作家，佳作迭出，受到了读者的热烈欢迎。1988 年，福尔斯出现严重的中风症状。自此以后，他虽然还继续写一些随笔、评论，却不得不放弃了他所热爱的小说创作。

福尔斯第一部正式出版的作品是《收藏家》(*The Collector*, 1963，又译为"采蝶人")。这是一部惊险小说。弗雷德里克·克莱拉出身贫寒、性格内向，心理阴暗、畸形。他在生活中唯一的精神寄托就是收集蝴蝶标本。一次中彩使他一夜暴富，于是他便买下了一栋大房子，绑架了出身富裕家庭、在大学学习艺术的米兰达·格雷，把她像蝴蝶标本一样收藏，囚禁在地窖里。米兰达向往自由，不愿意成为弗雷德里克的藏品，最终由于肺炎病死在地窖。小说的叙述分为两个部分：前半部以弗雷德里克·克莱拉为焦点，后半部是米兰达的日记。在这部小说中，读者能看到同一事件不同视角的记录，在双重视角的张力下，福尔斯探讨了自由、权力，以及什么是叙述真实、什么是想象真实等问题。小说中的弗雷德里克固然可鄙，但是他产生乖僻行为的原因则是来自这个社会。

1965 年，福尔斯出版了小说《魔术师》(*The Magus*)。该作品有"成长小说"(bildungsroman) 的痕迹。年轻的尼古拉斯来到一个与世隔绝的希腊小岛，遇到了魔术师康奇斯。通过参与康奇斯所设立的"创世游戏"(godgames)，尼古拉斯对真实的自我中自私丑陋的一面有了一定的认识。早在从希腊回国后，福尔斯就开始动笔构思这部作品。作品涵盖了他对社会、宗教、人性、艺术等抽象问题的探讨。整个小说结构散漫，和《收藏家》的紧凑形成对比。

1967 年发表的《法国中尉的女人》(*The French Lieutenant's Woman*) 确立了福尔斯在战后英国文坛的重要地位。这部小说透过现代人的视角解构维多利亚时代的英国，彰显出维多利亚时代道德观的虚伪。处在向现代社会转型期的男主人公查尔斯在女主人公萨拉的引导下，逐步体会到现代人所特有的孤独感。小说设有数个结局，无论是从技巧、主题还是人物刻画上都富有新意。

1974 年出版的《乌木塔》(*The Ebony Tower*) 是一部短篇小说集。在同名小说《乌木塔》中，身为艺术家的男主人公认识到了自己生活的空洞乏味和艺术上的苍白。描写艺术家的生活同样是福尔斯 1977 年的长篇小说《丹尼尔 · 马丁》(*Daniel Martin*) 的主题。这是一部自传色彩很强的作品。小说以倒叙和插叙等手法打破了传统的自传体小说线性的叙述结构，用拼贴的方式勾勒出马丁的成长和心路历程，为读者展现了 20 世纪现代人的生活长卷，深刻剖析了现代人的生存困境。1982 年出版的《曼蒂莎》(*Mantissa*) 是一部寓言小说。1985 年，福尔斯完成了小说《空想》(*A Maggot*)。小说创造了一个 18 世纪的仿真世界，是历史小说和侦探小说的结合。

虽然读者对福尔斯的了解主要通过他的长篇小说，但福尔斯其实是个多面手，其作品还包括短篇小说、哲学文章、地方志及诗歌等。在福尔斯看来，创作的最高法则就是自由，不应该受到形式和种类的限制。因此，福尔斯的小说常常是历史小说、浪漫小说、侦探小说、悬疑小说、幻想小说的糅合，有很强的故事性。福尔斯除了重视作品的可读性外，还注重在小说技巧上的探索。他的作品具有鲜明的后现代性，大量采用戏仿、多重视角、时空倒错 (anachronism) 等方法，对传统文本所构筑的虚拟真实进行大胆颠覆。在技巧革新的同时，福尔斯并没有将文本彻底解构成一片意义的废墟，而是在其间倾注了大量他对人类终极意义的有益思考，他的作品不仅体现了他高超的艺术技巧，更承载了他对人类的生存困境、现代人的孤独和异化感、存在主义的自由观等问题的独到看法。

The French Lieutenant's Woman

【题解】

作品中“法国中尉的女人”是指女主人公萨拉。她是具有强烈反叛意识的女性。在维多利亚时代虚伪道德至上的社会中，她谎称自己是某个已婚的法国中尉的情妇，故意让这个社会将自己摒弃，以保持个人在行动和灵魂上的自由。男主人公查尔斯出身上流社会，有一定自由思想，对古生物学颇感兴趣。尽管他已经和富商之女欧内斯蒂娜 · 弗里曼订婚，但还是情不自禁地被谜一样的萨拉所吸引。和特立独行的萨拉相爱让他渐渐意识到自己身处的上流社会的虚伪和空虚，也迫使他开始思考什么是人生的意义。然而，萨拉突然消失了。查尔斯于是匆匆赶往伦敦，盼望能够在那里找到萨拉。这里所选的第五十五章描述了查尔斯在赶往伦敦的火车上所发生的事。

From The French Lieutenant's Woman

Chapter 55

Charles arrived at the station in ridiculously good time the next morning; and having gone through the ungentlemanly business of seeing his things loaded into the baggage van and then selected an empty first-class compartment, he sat impatiently waiting for the train to start. Other passengers looked in from time to time, and were rebuffed by that Grogon[1] stare (this compartment is reserved for non-lepers) the English have so easily at command. A whistle sounded, and Charles thought he had won the solitude he craved. But then, at the very last moment, a massively bearded face appeared at his window. The cold stare was met by the even colder stare of a man in a hurry to get aboard.

The late comer muttered a "Pardon me, sir" and made his way to the far end to the compartment. He sat, a man of forty or so, his top hat firmly square, his hands on his knees, regaining his breath. There was something rather aggressively secure about him; he was perhaps not quite a gentleman . . . an ambitious butler (but butlers did not travel first class) or a successful lay preacher-one of the bullying tabernacle kind, a would-be Spurgeon[2], converting souls by scorching them with the cheap rhetoric of eternal damnation. A decidedly unpleasant man, thought Charles, and so typical of the age—and therefore emphatically to be snubbed if he tried to enter into conversation.

As sometimes happens when one stares covertly at people and speculates about them, Charles was caught in the act, and reproved for it. There was a very clear suggestion in the sharp look sideways that Charles should keep his eyes to himself. He hastily directed his gaze outside his window and consoled himself that at least the person shunned intimacy as much as he did.

Very soon the even movement lulled Charles into a douce daydream. London was a large city; but she must soon look for work. He had the time, the resources, the will; a week might pass, two, but then she would stand before him; perhaps yet another address would slip through his letter box. The wheels said it: she-could-not-be-so-cruel, she-could-not-be-so-cruel, she-could-not-be-so-cruel . . . the train passed through the red and green valleys towards Cullompton. Charles saw its church, without knowing where the place was, and soon afterwards closed his eyes. He had slept poorly that previous night.

For a while his traveling companion took no notice of the sleeping Charles. But as the chin sank deeper and deeper—Charles had taken the precaution of removing his hat—the prophet bearded man began to stare at him, safe in the knowledge that his curiosity would not be surprised.

His look was peculiar: sizing, ruminative, more than a shade disapproving, as if he knew very well what sort of man this was (as Charles had believed to see very well what sort of man he was) and did not much like the knowledge of the species. It was true that, unobserved, he looked a little less frigid and authoritarian a person; but there remained about his features an unpleasant aura of self-confidence—or if not quite confidence in self, at least a confidence in his judgment of others, of how much he could get out of them, expect from them, tax them.

A stare of a minute or so's duration, of this kind, might have been explicable. Train journeys are boring; it is amusing to spy on strangers; and so on. But this stare, which became positively cannibalistic[3] in its intensity, lasted far longer than a minute. It lasted beyond Taunton, though it was briefly interrupted there when the noise on the platform made Charles wake for a few moments. But when he sank back into his slumbers, the eyes fastened on him again in the same leech-like manner[4].

You may one day come under a similar gaze. And you may—in the less reserved context of our own century—be aware of it. The intent watcher will not wait till you are asleep. It will no doubt suggest something unpleasant, some kind of devious sexual approach . . . a desire to know you in a way you do not want to be known by a stranger. In my experience there is only one profession that gives that particular look, with its bizarre blend of the inquisitive and the magistral; of the ironic and the soliciting.

Now could I use you?

Now what could I do with you?

It is precisely, it has always seemed to me, the look an omnipotent god—if there were such an absurd thing—should be shown to have. Not at all what we think of as a divine look; but one of a distinctly mean and dubious (as the theoreticians of the nouveau roman[5] have pointed out) moral quality. I see this with particular clarity on the face, only too familiar to me, of the bearded man who stares at Charles. And I will keep up the pretense no longer.

Now the question I am asking, as I stare at Charles, is not quite the same as the two above. But rather, what the devil am I going to do with you? I have already thought of ending Charles's career here and now; of leaving him for eternity on his way to London. But the conventions of Victorian fiction allow, allowed no place for the open, the inconclusive ending; and I preached earlier of the freedom characters must be given[6]. My problem is simple—what Charles wants is clear? It is indeed. But what the protagonist[7] wants is not so clear; and I am not at all sure where she is at the moment. Of course if these two were two fragments of real life, instead of two figments of my imagination, the issue of the dilemma is obvious: the one want combats the other want, and fails or succeeds, as the actuality may be. Fiction usually pretends to conform to the reality: the writer puts the conflicting wants in the ring[8] and then describes the fight—but in fact fixes the fight, letting that want he himself favors win. And we judge writers of fiction both by the skill they show in fixing the fights (in other words, in persuading us that they were not fixed) and by the kind of fighter they fix in favor of: the good one, the tragic one, the evil one, the funny one, and so on.

But the chief argument for fight-fixing is to show one's readers what one thinks of the world around one whether one is a pessimist, an optimist, what you will. I have pretended to slip back into 1867; but of course that year is in reality a century past. It is futile to show optimism or pessimism, or anything else about it, because we know what has happened since.

So I continue to stare at Charles and see no reason this time for fixing the fight upon which he is about to engage. That leaves me with two alternatives. I let the fight proceed and take no more than a recording part in it; or I take both sides in it. I stare at that vaguely effete but not completely futile face. And as we near London, I think I see a solution; that is, I see the dilemma is false. The only way I can take no part in the fight is to show two versions of it. That leaves me with only one problem: I cannot give both versions at once, yet whichever is the second will seem, so strong is the tyranny of the last chapter, the final, the "real" version.

I take my purse from the pocket of my frock coat. I extract a florin[9], I rest it on my right thumbnail, I flick it, spinning, two feet into the air and catch it in my left hand.

So be it. And I am suddenly aware that Charles has opened his eyes and is looking at me. There is something more than disapproval in his eyes now; he perceives I am either a gambler or mentally deranged. I return his disapproval, and my florin to my purse. He picks up his hat, brushes some invisible speck of dirt (a surrogate for myself) from its nap[10] and places it on his head.

We draw under one of the great cast-iron beams that support the roof of Paddington station. We arrive, he steps down to the platform, beckoning to a porter. In a few moments, having given his instructions, he turns. The bearded man has disappeared in the throng.

【注解】

1. Grogon: 希腊神话中三个蛇发女妖之一，人一见其貌便会变成石头。
2. Spurgeon: 即查尔斯·斯珀吉翁 (1834—1892)，伦敦基督教新教的讲道人。
3. cannibalistic: cannibal 一词指食人者。这里用它的形容词形式 cannibalistic 来形容人的眼神好像要把对方吞食掉一样。
4. leech-like manner: leech 是水蛭，一种水生吸血蠕虫，一旦附着在皮肤上，就很难被拔除。这里用来形容他的目光像水蛭叮人一样地紧紧附在查尔斯的身上。
5. nouveau roman: 新小说，指 20 世纪中期在法国兴起的实验小说。它们通常打破叙述常规，在叙述视角的革新、文本虚构性的凸现等方面进行了大胆的尝试。
6. I preached earlier of the freedom characters must be given：在小说的第十三章，叙述者，也就是小说的虚拟作者在阐发自己的创作理念时写道："倘若我希望他［查尔斯］是位真实的人物，我就得尊重他的自由，而废弃我为他规定的任何貌似神圣的计划。"
7. protagonist: 这个词在这里指的是小说的女主人公莎拉。
8. ring: 竞技场，拳击场。
9. florin: 一枚值两先令的英国硬币，1971 年起停止使用。
10. He picks up . . . from its nap: 此处意思是"查尔斯掸了掸灰尘，而实际上帽子上根本就没有灰尘，他这一动作是表示对我厌恶，想要把我和灰尘一样掸掉"。

【思考题】

1. Who is the bearded man in Chapter 55? Who is the "I" interfering into the narration at the second half of this chapter? What does the narrator mean when he says "I will keep up the pretense no longer"?
2. Why does the bearded man look at Charles with "the look an omnipotent god . . . should be shown to have"? What does it imply?
3. Charles is living in Victorian England. Do you think the bearded man who he meets on the train is Charles's contemporary? Where does the bearded man come from? Please comment on his presence and function in the novel.
4. Please make a comparison between the narrative voice in *David Copperfield*, which is a typical Victorian novel, and that in *The French Lieutenant's Woman*, which is pseudo-Victorian.
5. Which ending of *The French Lieutenant's Woman* do you prefer, and why?

【简评】

《法国中尉的女人》打破了常规的叙述手法。作者福尔斯为小说设置了数个结局。第一个结局中，主人公查尔斯和欧内斯蒂娜结了婚，生了一大群孩子，成为一个平庸的商人。这个结尾符合维多利亚时代的道德观，男主人公抵制住了“诱惑”，战胜了自己，但是他的生命却浪费在了毫无激情的婚姻和没有意义的生活中。难怪作者随即写道：“这个结尾不过是查尔斯一时的想象。”实际上，查尔斯所做的是情不自禁地追随着萨拉的脚步，赶到她下榻的旅馆。查尔斯决定和萨拉结婚，然而这时萨拉却离开了他。在小说的第五十五章中，小说的作者叙述者，也就是留着大胡子的男人出场了，他凝望着熟睡中的查尔斯，思考着该如何给故事结尾。一种可能是让查尔斯永远地留在去伦敦的车上，小说在这里戛然而止，让读者去揣测等待他的命运。然而这种开放性结尾显然不符合维多利亚时代小说的传统。叙述者又提出了另外两种可能。查尔斯没有找到萨拉，怀着失望的心情，去了美国。一年后，当他得知萨拉在伦敦后匆匆赶回。一个结局中，查尔斯发现萨拉为他生下了一个女儿，一家人幸福地团聚了；另一个结局中，萨拉表示她爱自由胜过一切，查尔斯伤心离去，却体会到了存在主义意义上的解脱和自由。

为了撰写《法国中尉的女人》，福尔斯对维多利亚时代进行了大量的研究，创造出一个高度仿真的维多利亚社会。但随着与查尔斯时代相隔百年的叙述者对文本的不断介入，福尔斯对维多利亚时代进行了解构，使小说具有了双重视角：读者不仅可以对维多利亚时代的道德观进行批判性审视，也可以通过审视维多利亚时代更好地理解现代社会的症结所在。

小说中叙述者的存在不仅突出了主题，而且使作品具有明显的后现代主义色彩。20世纪60年代，法国批评家罗兰·巴尔特提出了“作者之死”的著名论断，宣布作者对文本没有绝对的主宰权，文本的意义归于读者。而《法国中尉的女人》恰恰体现了这种革命性的观点。小说出现多重结尾，作为作者的叙述者要求读者自己作出选择，作者/叙述者在文本中与本应受到操纵的角色为情节的发展进行探讨、作出妥协，等等，这一创作技巧打破了作者对作品的垄断。而作者/叙述者和查尔斯在火车上的相遇，则突破了传统小说的时空界限，揭穿了文本所构筑的文学幻象，凸显了大多数叙事小说尽力想要掩饰的文本虚幻性。从这个意义上看，虽然《法国中尉的女人》具有传统小说的外表，其实质却是一部颠覆性的实验小说。

V. S. Naipaul

1932—2018

作者简介

V. S. 奈保尔于1932年出生于中美洲加勒比海南部的特立尼达岛。他的祖父母是印度婆罗门后裔，在19世纪80年代以契约劳工的身份从印度移民到特立尼达岛，在当地的甘蔗种植园工作。奈保尔的父亲是位事业并不如意的记者，因此奈保尔家里经济条件不算太好。七岁时，奈保尔一家搬到了特立尼达和多巴哥的首都西班牙港。奈保尔自幼接受英语教育，他在1950年获得奖学金，前往英国牛津大学读书。1952年在学校结识了帕翠西亚·安·黑尔 (Patricia Ann Hale, 1932—1996)，1955年与其结婚，之后加入了英国籍。

奈保尔在1957年和1958年接连出版了长篇小说《通灵的按摩师》(*The Mystic Masseur*) 和《全民选举》(*The Suffrage of Elvira*)，但真正让他在文学界脱颖而出的是1959年出版的短篇小说集《米格尔街》(*Miguel Street*)。《米格尔街》其实是奈保尔早在1955年就完成的作品，但出版商担心这位"外籍无名作家"的短篇小说集没什么市场，故而要求他先发表长篇小说，将它搁置了几年才出版。1961年，奈保尔出版了《毕司沃斯先生的房子》(*A House for Mr Biswas*)，以恢宏的眼界和讽喻笔法讲述了一位特立尼达岛的印度移民想要拥有一所房子的故事，生动展示了一个平凡人对梦想的追求及遭受的苦难与曲折。奈保尔随后又接连出版了小说《斯通与骑士伙伴》(*Mr Stone and the Knights Companion*, 1963)、《模仿者》(*The Mimic Men*, 1967) 和短篇故事集《岛上的旗帜》(*A Flag on the Island*, 1967)。1971年，奈保尔凭借《自由国度》(*In a Free State*) 赢得了布克奖，自此开始被越来越多的国外读者所了解。1975年《游击队员》(*Guerrillas*) 面世。1979年奈保尔出版了他的重要代表作《大河湾》(*A Bend in the River*, 又译《河湾》)。20世纪80年代至90年代，奈保尔的小说创作速度有所放缓，但也陆续出版了《抵达之谜》(*The Enigma of Arrival*, 1987) 和《世间之路》(*A Way in the World*, 1994)。奈保尔在2001年迎来高光时刻，作品《半生》(*Half a Life*) 使他荣获当年的诺贝尔文学奖。瑞典文学院对该作品给予了高度评价，在授奖词中称其"将深具洞察力的叙述和不受世俗侵蚀的探索融为一体，迫使我们去发现被压抑历史的真实存在"。2004年奈保尔出版了《半生》的续集《魔种》(*Magic Seeds*)，这也是他在长篇小说领域的封笔之作。

奈保尔在非虚构写作上同样取得了很高的成就。他在亚洲、非洲和美洲等地漂泊游历，撰写了多部游记和散文，如“印度三部曲”《幽暗国度》(*An Area of Darkness*, 1964)、《印度：受伤的文明》(*India: A Wounded Civilization*, 1977)、《印度：百万叛变的今天》(*India: A Million Mutinies Now*, 1977)，“美洲三部曲”《重访加勒比》(*The Middle Passage: The Caribbean Revisited*, 1962)、《失落的黄金国》(*The Loss of El Dorado*, 1969)、《南方的转折》(*A Turn in the South*, 1989)，以及描绘非洲风土人情的游记《非洲的假面剧》(*The Masque of Africa: Glimpses of African Belief*, 2010)，等等。2018 年，奈保尔在伦敦逝世。

奈保尔被誉为“文学世界的漂流者”，是英国后殖民文学和“流散文学”的杰出代表，他和石黑一雄、鲁西迪并称为“英国文坛移民三杰”。他的祖辈从印度移民到特立尼达和多巴哥，他本人又移民到英国，这种双重移民经历使他对种族、身份、独立、殖民、历史记忆和文明冲突等话题尤为关注。瑞典文学院在诺贝尔文学奖授奖词中对他这样评价：“奈保尔是康拉德的继承者，他从道德观的角度，也即从对人类造成何种影响的角度，记录了帝国的兴衰变迁。他作为叙事者的立足点在于他对其他已经忘却了的被征服国家的历史的记忆。”奈保尔不仅批判殖民主义，还以冷峻的态度对自己所在的地域文化进行审视与批判。奈保尔的写作生涯长达半个世纪，在写作过程中，他也见证了西方殖民体系在二战以后瓦解的历史进程。他的作品往往带有浓厚的纪实色彩，多以 20 世纪席卷全球的民族解放运动为视角，记录加勒比、印度、非洲等地的文化和历史变迁。

Half a Life

【题解】

《半生》出版于 2001 年，是奈保尔在世纪之交创作的一部半自传体小说。这部作品由三个部分组成，分别为“萨默赛特·毛姆来访”“第一章”和“第二次转变”。小说讲述了主人公威利·詹德兰在印度、英国和非洲等地生活的故事。威利的祖上是印度祭司，拥有最高种姓婆罗门的血统，父亲热爱文学，曾与英国作家毛姆相识，并在毛姆的游记作品中被提及。她的母亲则来自印度低等种姓家族。威利从小心思敏感，性格叛逆，对自己有低种姓血统而深感自卑。威利因父亲一位英国故交的提携获得了奖学金，被一所成人教育学院录取，于是他离开故乡来到伦敦。他在那里亲历了诺丁山种族骚乱，开始尝试写作，却未能实现作家梦。他结识了来自非洲葡属殖民地的女友安娜，跟随她去非洲生活了十八年，见证了葡萄牙殖民政府的倒台。后来又离开非洲，前往德国西柏林投奔妹妹萨洛姬妮。小说结尾处，威利对妻子安娜说起自己这半生："在伦敦求你的时候，我很害怕。我没地方可去。学期一结束，他们就会把我赶出去，而我不知道该怎么活下去。可现在，我生命中最好的时光已经过去，而我一事无成。"《半生》被称为奈保尔最伤感绝望的小说。诺贝尔文学家获得者 J. M. 库切说道："奈保尔是英语文学大师，《半生》的文字干净冷酷，犹如一把匕首，留给读者的不是笑料，而是悲凉"。

本文为小说第二部分"第一章"的开头。小说第一部分是威利父亲讲述自己的故事，讲到威利兄妹出生便结束。小说第二部分开始讲述威利兄妹在教会学校的学习和生活，那里的孩子大多出身于低种姓家庭，威利带着自卑又爱慕虚荣的心理，渴望去加拿大生活。他在写作文时按照美国漫画书的模式描写西方人的生活方式和说话语气，假装自己是加拿大人。他的作文得到加拿大籍老师的高度赞扬，被评为满分。威利想得到父亲的赞许，却又不敢直接拿给他看，只是偷偷把写有作文的练习册放到游廊的桌子上，因为父亲每天都会坐在那里喝咖啡。父亲对他之前写的两篇作文非常恼火，但是并没有告诉他自己的想法。威利又羞又怒，于是写了一篇新作文放在桌上，试图让父亲对其进行点评。

From Half a Life

Part 2

The First Chapter (excerpt)

A few days later the exercise book was on the verandah table[1]. Willie Chandran's father didn't hesitate. He flicked through the red-ticked pages to the last composition.

It was a story. It was the longest thing in the book and it looked as though it had been written at a great rate. The fast, small, pressing-down handwriting had crinkled[2] every page, and the teacher with the red pen had liked it all, sometimes drawing a red vertical line in the margin and giving one tick to a whole paragraph or page.

The story was set, like Willie's other stories or fables, in an undefined place, at an undated time. It began at a time of famine. Even the brahmins[3] were affected. A starving brahmin, all skin and bones, decides to leave his community and go elsewhere, into the hot rocky wilderness, to die alone, with dignity. Near the limit of his strength, he finds a low dark cavern in a cliff and decides to die there. He purifies himself as best he can and settles down to sleep for the last time. He rests his wasted head on a rock. Something about the rock irritates the brahmin's neck and head. He reaches back to touch the rock with his hand, once, twice, and then he knows that the rock isn't a rock. It is a hard grimy sack of some sort, full of ridges, and when the brahmin sits up he discovers that the rock is really a very old sack of treasure.

As soon as he makes the discovery a spirit calls out to him, "This treasure has been waiting for you for centuries. It is yours to keep, and will be yours forever, on condition that you do something for me. Do you accept?" The trembling brahmin says, "What must I do for you?" The spirit says, "Every year you must sacrifice a fresh young child to me. As long as you do that, the treasure will stay with you. If you fail, the treasure will vanish and return here. Over the centuries there have been many before you, and all have failed." The brahmin doesn't know what to say. The spirit says with irritation, "Dying man, do you accept?" The brahmin says, "Where will I find the children?" The spirit says, "It is not for me to give you help. If you are resolute enough you will find a way. Do you accept?" And the brahmin says, "I accept." The spirit says, "Sleep, rich man. When you awaken you will be in your old temple and the world will be at your feet. But never forget your pledge."

The brahmin awakens in his old home and finds himself well fed and sturdy. He also awakens to the knowledge that he is rich beyond the dreams of avarice. And almost immediately, before he can savour his joy, the thought of his pledge begins to torment him. The torment doesn't go away. It corrupts all his hours, all the minutes of all the hours.

One day he sees a group of tribal people passing in front of the temple compound. They are black and small, bony from starvation, and almost naked. Hunger has driven these people from their habitations and made them careless of old rules. They should not pass so close to the temple because the shadow of these people, their very sight, even the sound of their voices, is polluting. The brahmin has an illumination. He finds out where the tribal encampment is. He goes there at night with his face hidden by his shawl. He seeks out the headman and in the name of charity and religion he offers to buy one of the half-dead tribal children. He makes this deal with the tribal headman: the child is to be drugged and taken to a certain low cave in the rocky wilderness and left there. If this is fairly and honestly done, a week later the tribal man will find a piece of old treasure in the cave, enough to take all his followers out of their distress.

The sacrifice is done, the piece of old treasure laid down; and from year to year this ritual goes on, for the brahmin, and for the tribals.

One year the headman, now better fed and better dressed, with shiny oiled hair, comes to the brahmin's temple. The brahmin is rough. He says, "Who are you?" The headman says, "You know me. And I know you. I know what you are up to. I have known all along.

I recognised you that first night and understood everything. I want half your treasure." The brahmin says, "You know nothing. I know that for fifteen years you and your tribe have been carrying out child-sacrifice in a certain cave. It is part of your tribal ways. Now that you have all prospered and become townsmen you are ashamed and frightened. So you have come and confessed to me and asked for my understanding. I have given you that, because I understand your tribal ways, but I cannot say I am not horrified, and if I choose I can lead anyone to the cave with the bones of many children. Now get out. Your hair is oiled, but your very shadow pollutes this sacred place." The headman cringes and backs away. He says, "Forgive, forgive." The brahmin says, "And don't forget your pledge."

The time comes for the brahmin's annual sacrifice. He makes his way at night to the cave of bones. He turns over and polishes every kind of story in case the tribal chief has informed on him and people are waiting for him. No one is waiting. He is not surprised. In the dark cave there are two drugged children. The headman has, after all, behaved well. With a practised hand the brahmin sacrifices the two to the spirit of the cave. When he comes to burn the little corpses he sees by the light of his wood torch that they are his own children.

This was where the story ended. Willie's father had read without skipping. And when, mechanically, he turned back to the beginning he saw—what he had forgotten during the reading—that the story was called "A Life of Sacrifice."

He thought, "His mind is diseased. He hates me and he hates his mother, and now he's turned against himself. This is what the missionaries have done to him with Mom and Pop[4] and Dick Tracy[5] and the Justice Society of America comic magazine[6], and Christ on the Cross movies in Passion Week[7], and Bogart and Cagney and George Raft[8] the rest of the time. I cannot deal rationally with this kind of hatred. I will deal with it in the way of the Mahatma[9]. I will ignore it. I will keep a vow of silence so far as he is concerned."

Two or three weeks later the boy's mother came to him and said, "I wish you would break that vow of silence. It is making Willie very unhappy."

"The boy is lost. There is nothing I can do for him."

She said, "You have to help him. No one else can. Two days ago I found him sitting in the dark. When I put the light on I saw he was crying. I asked him why. He said, 'I just feel that everything in the world is so sad. And it is all that we have. I don't know what to do.' I didn't know what to say to him. It's something he gets from your side. I tried to comfort him. I told him that everything would be all right, and he would go to Canada.

He said he didn't want to go to Canada. He didn't want to be a missionary. He didn't even want to go back to the school."

"Something must have happened at the school."

"I asked him. He said he went to the principal's office for something. There was a magazine on the table. It was a missionary magazine. There was a colour picture on the cover. A priest with glasses and a wristwatch was standing with one foot on a statue of the Buddha. He had just chopped it down with an axe, and he was smiling and leaning on the axe like a lumberjack. I used to see magazines and pictures like that when I was at the school. It didn't worry me. But when Willie saw the picture he felt ashamed for himself. He felt the fathers had been fooling him all these years. He was ashamed that he ever wanted to be a missionary. All he really wanted was to go to Canada and get away from here. Until he saw that picture he didn't know what missionary work was."

"If he doesn't want to go to the mission school he doesn't have to go."

"Like father, like son."

"The mission school was your idea."

So Willie Chandran stopped going to the mission school. He began to idle at home.

His father saw him one day asleep face down, a closed copy of a school edition of *The Vicar of Wakefield*[10] beside him, his feet crossed, the red soles much lighter than the rest of him. There was such unhappiness and such energy there that he was overwhelmed with pity. He thought, "I used to think that you were me and I was worried at what I had done to you. But now I know that you are not me. What is in my head is not in yours. You are somebody else, somebody I don't know, and I worry for you because you are launched on a journey I know nothing of."

Some days later he sought out Willie and said, "I have no fortune, as you know. But if you want, I will write to some of the people I know in England and we'll see what they can do for you."

Willie was pleased but he didn't show it.

The famous writer after whom Willie was named was now very old. After some weeks a reply came from him from the south of France. The letter, on a small sheet of paper, was professionally typewritten, in narrow lines with a lot of clear space. *Dear Chandran, It was very nice getting your letter. I have nice memories of the country, and it is nice hearing from Indian friends. Yours very sincerely . . .* There was nothing in the letter about Willie. It was as though the old writer hadn't understood what was being asked of him. There would have been secretaries. They would have stood in the way. But Willie Chandran's father was disappointed and ashamed. He resolved not to tell Willie, but Willie had a good idea of what had happened: he had seen the letter with the French stamp arrive.

There was no reply from a famous wartime broadcaster who had come out to India to cover independence and partition and the assassination of the mahatma, and had been exceptionally friendly. Some people who replied were direct. They said they couldn't do anything. Some sent long friendly replies that, like the writer's, ignored the request for help.

Willie's father tried to be philosophical, but it wasn't easy. He said to his wife—though it was his rule to keep his depressions to himself—"I did so much for them when they came here. I gave them the run of the ashram. I introduced them to everybody." His wife said, "They did a lot for you too. They gave you your business. You can't deny it." He thought, "I will never talk to her about these matters again. I was wrong to break my rule. She is quite without shame. She is a backward through and through. Eating my salt and abusing me."

He wondered how he would break the bad news to Willie. Now that he had understood the boy's weakness, he didn't worry about the scorn. But—still a little to his surprise—he didn't want to add to the boy's suffering. He couldn't forget the picture of the ambitious, defeated boy sleeping face down with the dead old school text of *The Vicar of Wakefield* beside him, his feet crossed, feet as dark as his mother's.

But he was spared the humiliation of an all-round refusal. There came a letter in a blue envelope from London, from the House of Lords, from a famous man who had paid a brief visit to the ashram just after independence. His fame and his title had made him memorable to Willie Chandran's father. The big and fluent handwriting on the blue House of Lords paper spoke of power and display, and what was in the letter matched the handwriting. It had pleased the great man to display his power to Willie's father, to win gratitude and merit in that far-off corner, to wave a wand, to lift a little finger, as it were (all the other fingers being busy about greater matters), and set many little men in motion. The letter contained a little of the gold the little men had spun: a place and a scholarship had been found for Willie Chandran in a college of education for mature students in London.

And that was how, when he was twenty, Willie Chandran, the mission-school student who had not completed his education, with no idea of what he wanted to do, except to get away from what he knew, and yet with very little idea of what lay outside what he knew, only with the fantasies of the Hollywood films of the thirties and forties that he had seen at the mission school, went to London.

【注解】

1. the verandah table：威利的父亲每天都会坐在游廊上这张桌子旁喝咖啡。
2. crinkle：使……变皱，起皱纹。
3. brahmins：婆罗门，印度种姓制中的最高种姓，以僧侣、学者为主。
4. Mom and Pop：此处指教会学校教给威利的西式称呼。
5. Dick Tracy：指美国漫画家切斯特·古尔德创作的同名连载漫画中的人物，身份是一名警探。
6. Justice Society of America comic magazine："美国正义协会"，即美国DC漫画旗下的超级英雄团队。
7. Christ on the Cross Movies Passion Week："受难周"播放的"基督受难"主题的电影。
8. Bogart and Cagney and George Raft：指亨弗莱·鲍嘉、詹姆斯·卡格尼和乔治·拉夫特，均为美国电影明星。
9. The Mahatma: 圣雄甘地 (Mahatma Gandhi)。
10. *The Vicar of Wakefield*：《威克菲尔德的牧师》，英国作家哥尔德斯密斯于1766年出版的情感主义小说。

【思考题】

1. Why would Willie Chandran write the story of a brahmin?
2. What does the title of "A Life of Sacrifice" suggest to you?
3. In what ways have the western values changed and fashioned the mind of young Willie?
4. Do you think Mr. Chandran does a good job for his son Willie's education?

【简评】

《半生》是关于威利·詹德兰的故事，但小说第一部分都是威利父亲在讲述自己的经历，使用了第一人称叙述者形式。要写主人公威利的半生，却从他的父亲写起，这也意味着每个人都是自己家族血脉的一部分，和祖辈紧密相连，无法割裂与民族文化、民族传统的联系。选文描写的故事展现了小威利在求学时代对待身份和文化的态度问题。威利拥有父亲一脉的高贵婆罗门血统，为此自命不凡，同时他又因自己拥有母亲一脉的低种姓血统而深感自卑与愤恨，在学校看不起低种姓同学的所作所为。威利在家里和学校都受到西方殖民文化的影响，不自觉地向西方文化靠拢，想要按照他们的文化模式来写作与生活。而当他来到伦敦和非洲，又始终无法真正融入当地的文化和生活。在浑浑噩噩和兜兜转转之间，威利恍然发现自己的人生已经过去大半，却始终一事无成。奈保尔通过《半生》向人们展示了印度种姓制度所造成的巨大的社会裂隙，用批判的眼光审视西方殖民文化的强大渗透力，从哲理层面思考了人生的选择和生命的意义。

Julian Barnes
1946—

朱利安·巴恩斯是享誉世界的英国当代作家，1946 年出生于英国伦敦西郊阿克顿 (Acton) 地区的一个中产阶级家庭。哥哥乔纳森·巴恩斯 (Jonathan Barnes, 1942—) 为牛津大学哲学教授，父母均为法语老师。受父母影响，巴恩斯自童年起便常赴法国度假，对法国文化产生了浓厚的兴趣。巴恩斯中学时期就读于伦敦城市公学，大学考入牛津大学莫德林学院现代语言专业攻读法语，其间还半途转修过哲学。在大学期间，他以英语实习教师的身份在法国雷恩的一所天主教学校交流了一年。大学毕业后，巴恩斯用了三年时间参与《牛津英语大词典 (增补本)》(*The Oxford English Dictionary Supplement*) 的编撰工作，也参加过律师考试，尝试成为律师。1974 年，他开始涉足文坛，以自由记者的身份在《新批评》《新政治家》与《观察家报》等多家报社担任兼职编辑与评论员，用本名或笔名发表文学与文化类评论文章。其间他结识了不少英国当时的知名文人，包括小说家马丁·艾米斯、诗人詹姆斯·芬顿 (James Fenton, 1949—)、克雷格·雷恩 (Craig Rainc, 1944) 及评论家伊恩·汉密尔顿 (Ian Hamilton, 1938—)。在他的成长历程中，对法国文化的兴趣拓宽了他的写作视野，编撰字典的经历锤炼了他的文字触感，准律师生涯丰富了他对相关行业的描写，与知名文人的结交培养了他良好的文学品味。这些经历融汇一体，成就了他独特的个人创作风格。1979 年，巴恩斯正式开启小说创作生涯。

巴恩斯在三十余载的创作生涯中笔耕不辍，著作颇丰、成就斐然，至今仍活跃在英国文坛，与石黑一雄、麦克尤恩等并称“黄金一代的英国小说家”。1980 年，巴恩斯的第一部长篇小说《伦敦郊区》(*Metroland*) 问世，一举夺得毛姆文学奖。随后，他又凭借小说《福楼拜的鹦鹉》(*Flaubert's Parrot*, 1984) 初次入围英国布克奖，摘得杰弗里·费伯纪念奖，并斩获法国美第奇奖。小说《英格兰、英格兰》(*England, England*, 1998) 和《亚瑟与乔治》(*Arthur and George*, 2005) 也分别入围了布克奖，却遗憾地铩羽而归，不过，2011 年，凭借《终结的感觉》(*The Sense of an Ending*)，巴恩斯终于斩获布克奖，弥补了遗憾。同年，巴恩斯被授予大卫·科恩英国文学奖，此奖是对获奖作家终身文学成就的肯定。此外，巴恩斯也深受美国、法国等文学界的欢迎，在国际上同样享有声望。

巴恩斯的创作生涯大致可划分为三个阶段。他的早期作品集中表达了对历史的思考；中期作品基本以英国本土为空间背景，具有明显的“英国性”；近期作品聚焦记忆现象，探询个体的心理空间。就时间而言，巴恩斯创作三个阶段的主题均关乎过去；就空间而言，他作品的空间背景从世界各地回归英国本土，再收缩至个体的心理空间，由此形成了历史、英国性与记忆这三个不同阶段各自侧重的主题。无论主题如何变化，碎片化书写却是贯穿始终的不变特征。作为后现代时期作家，巴恩斯不得不面临西方传统思想遭到解构冲击之后的碎片化境地，他也不遗余力地在作品中通过种种碎片化写作手段表现后现代情境中历史、英国性及个体记忆的碎片化状态。在巴恩斯的笔下，碎片化书写既是叙事的形式特征，亦是叙事的内容特征。在这种碎片化书写中，巴恩斯阐述了他对后现代情境下西方社会人类生存境况的理解。在西方社会进入后现代时期之后，经过战争与解构思潮的冲击与洗礼，总体不复存在的破碎境况已基本成为共识。面对这一状况，欣然接受者有之，彷徨失措者有之。而巴恩斯的应对方式则带有复杂的悖论色彩。他一方面细致描绘了碎片化运动解构一切之后总体不复存在的破碎局面，另外一方面也借由笔下的人物积极寻求超越与突破之道。

由于作品形式的原创性和实验性，以及作品内容的丰富性和深刻性，在三十多年的创作生涯中，巴恩斯获得了各种各样的称号，比如“极具原创性的作家”“艺术大师”“挑战文学正统的元小说家”“天生的讽刺家”“思想小说家”“具有哲学头脑的小说家”，等等；而由于其写作风格易变、多样，巴恩斯也被称为“英国文坛的变色龙”。从整体上看，其作品体现出一种强烈的“异质性”特征。作为“黄金一代的英国小说家”之一，巴恩斯在大英帝国衰落和冷战的政治冲突等当代历史现实的阴影之下成长，同时也身处后现代文化和思潮中，这无疑对巴恩斯的写作产生了巨大的影响，使他的作品具有敏锐的历史意识和典型的后现代主义小说特征。巴恩斯常常对历史的本质进行思考，认为“一切都不确定，这就是历史的本质”。因此，巴恩斯常常被评论家称为“半个历史学家”，而他的小说则被认为是“对历史的注解，对已知的颠覆”。

A History of the World in $10\frac{1}{2}$ Chapters

【题解】

小说《十又二分之一章世界史》(*A History of the World in* $10\frac{1}{2}$ *Chapters*, 1989)以《圣经》中的挪亚方舟及方舟的变体为基本意象和情节主线，由十章构成，而第八和第九章之间的部分被称为“插曲”，不是独立的一章，故名“十又二分之一章”。所谓世界史，其实是十一篇幻想故事，有的带有历史色彩，有的则畅想未来世界。这些故事看起来彼此互不相干，各自独立，但细读起来又会让人觉得它们构成了一个整体。

巴恩斯选择挪亚方舟来作为一个具有极高概括性的意象，体现了西方作家在现当代文学创作中对救赎主题的普遍关注。挪亚方舟和方舟的变体在人类历史的不同时期一再出现，其意义不仅在于在洪水滔天的世界性灾难中救出的那些人与动物，还与人类的命运密切关联，它与死亡、灾难、救赎、爱情、精神追寻等人类的生存主题构成一幅幅高度概括化了的历史图景。在小说里，巴恩斯使用多种叙述人称，通过不同的视角和笔调来写世界历史，用怀疑主义的眼光看待世界历史。除了讨论历史的性质，巴恩斯也对“爱”进行了重新的思考。小说囊括了真实与虚构、现象与本质、物质与精神、灾难与拯救、爱情与死亡等哲学命题，也将宗教传说、故事新编、历史记载、个人叙述整合于一体，这种斑驳陆离的形态在带有后现代文学显著特征的同时，也构成了巴恩斯对人类生存境况的一种感知和体验。

下文为该书第一章“偷渡客”的前半部分。这部分是对《圣经》典故“挪亚方舟”的改编。作者把故事的叙述者设计成七只蛀木虫之一。蛀木虫不属于被保护的物种，所以不被允许搭乘挪亚方舟，但是它们还是设法偷偷上了船，并且目睹了狂妄自大的人类灭绝物种的行径。这段文字的许多地方与《圣经》的开篇《创世纪》相左。作者不无诙谐地质疑了宗教组织的权威性，内容颇具讽刺，见地犀利深刻，调侃了西方世界以宗教为依据，宣扬的所谓人类物种至上的思想，批判了人类中心主义，揭示了人类世界“十分残暴、同类相食、充满欺诈”的一面。上帝将动物分为“洁净的畜类”和“不洁净的畜类”，而在人类历史上也一直有一部分人被列为敌人、异族、他者，遭到排斥、压迫乃至杀戮。作者将蛀木虫作为故事的讲述者，以独特的视角对人类进行观察与思考。这一视角不仅新颖别致，也发人深省。

From A History of the World in $10\frac{1}{2}$ Chapters

Chapter 1

The Stowaway

THEY PUT THE BEHEMOTHS in the hold along with the rhinos, the hippos and the elephants. It was a sensible decision to use them as ballast; but you can imagine the stench. And there was no-one to muck out. The men were overburdened with the feeding rota, and their women, who beneath those leaping fire-tongues of scent no doubt reeked as badly as we did, were far too delicate. So if any mucking-out was to happen, we had to do it ourselves. Every few months they would winch back the thick hatch on the aft deck and let the cleaner-birds in. Well, first they had to let the smell out (and there weren't too many volunteers for winch-work); then six or eight of the less fastidious birds would flutter cautiously around the hatch for a minute or so before diving in. I can't remember what they were all called—indeed, one of those pairs no longer exists—but you know the sort I mean. You've seen hippos with their mouths open and bright little birds pecking away between their teeth like distraught dental hygienists? Picture that on a larger, messier scale. I am hardly squeamish, but even I used to shudder at the scene below decks: a row of squinting monsters being manicured in a sewer.

There was strict discipline on the Ark[1]: that's the first point to make. It wasn't like those nursery versions in painted wood which you might have played with as a child—all happy couples peering merrily over the rail from the comfort of their well-scrubbed stalls. Don't imagine some Mediterranean cruise on which we played languorous roulette and everyone dressed for dinner; on the Ark only the penguins wore tailcoats. Remember: this was a long and dangerous voyage—dangerous even though some of the rules had been fixed in advance. Remember too that we had the whole of the animal kingdom on board: would you have put the cheetahs within springing distance of the antelope? A certain level of security was inevitable, and we accepted double-peg locks, stall inspections, a nightly curfew. But regrettably there were also punishments and isolation cells. Someone at the very top became obsessed with information gathering; and certain of the travellers agreed to act as stool pigeons. I'm sorry to report that ratting to the authorities was at times widespread. It wasn't a nature reserve, that Ark of ours; at times it was more like a prison ship.

Now, I realize that accounts differ. Your species has its much repeated version, which still charms even sceptics; while the animals have a compendium of sentimental myths. But they're not going to rock the boat, are they? Not when they've been treated as heroes, not when it's become a matter of pride that each and every one of them can proudly trace its family tree straight back to the Ark. They were chosen, they endured, they survived: it's normal for them to gloss over the awkward episodes, to have convenient lapses of memory. But I am not constrained in that way. I was never chosen. In fact, like several other species, I was specifically not chosen. I was a stowaway; I too survived; I escaped (getting off was no easier than getting on); and I have flourished. I am a little set apart from the rest of animal society, which still has its nostalgic reunions: there is even a Sealegs Club for species which never once felt queasy. When I recall the Voyage, I feel no sense of obligation; gratitude puts no smear of Vaseline on the lens. My account you can trust.

You presumably grasped that the "Ark" was more than just a single ship? It was the name we gave to the whole flotilla (you could hardly expect to cram the entire animal kingdom into something a mere three hundred cubits long). It rained for forty days and forty nights? Well, naturally it didn't—that would have been no more than a routine English summer. No, it rained for about a year and a half, by my reckoning. And the waters were upon the earth for a hundred and fifty days? Bump that up to about four years. And so on. Your species has always been hopeless about dates. I put it down to your quaint obsession with multiples of seven.

In the beginning, the Ark consisted of eight vessels: Noah's[2] galleon, which towed the stores ship, then four slightly smaller boats, each captained by one of Noah's sons, and behind them, at a safe distance (the family being superstitious about illness), the hospital ship. The eighth vessel provided a brief mystery: a darting little sloop with filigree decorations in sandalwood all along the stern, it steered a course sycophantically close to that of Ham's[3] ark. If you got to leeward you would sometimes be teased with strange perfumes; occasionally, at night, when the tempest slackened, you could hear jaunty music and shrill laughter—surprising noises to us, because we had assumed that all the wives of all the sons of Noah were safely ensconced on their own ships. However, this scented, laughing boat was not robust: it went down in a sudden squall, and Ham was pensive for several weeks thereafter.

The stores ship was the next to be lost, on a starless night when the wind had dropped and the lookouts were drowsy. In the morning all that trailed behind Noah's flagship was a length of fat hawser which had been gnawed through by something with sharp incisors and an ability to cling to wet ropes. There were serious recriminations about that, I can tell you; indeed, this may have been the first occasion on which a species disappeared overboard. Not long afterwards the hospital ship was lost. There were murmurings that the two events were connected, that Ham's wife—who was a little short on serenity—had decided to revenge herself upon the animals. Apparently her lifetime output of embroidered blankets had gone down with the stores ship. But nothing was ever proved.

Still, the worst disaster by far was the loss of Varadi. You're familiar with Ham and Shem[4] and the other one, whose name began with a J; but you don't know about Varadi, do you? He was the youngest and strongest of Noah's sons; which didn't, of course, make him the most popular within the family. He also had a sense of humour—or at least he laughed a lot, which is usually proof enough for your species. Yes, Varadi was always cheerful. He could be seen strutting the quarterdeck with a parrot on each shoulder; he would slap the quadrupeds affectionately on the rump, which they'd acknowledge with an appreciative bellow; and it was said that his ark was run on much less tyrannical lines than the others. But there you are: one morning we awoke to find that Varadi's ship had vanished from the horizon, taking with it one fifth of the animal kingdom. You would, I think, have enjoyed the simurgh, with its silver head and peacock's tail; but the bird that nested in the Tree of Knowledge[5] was no more proof against the waves than the brindled vole. Varadi's elder brothers blamed poor navigation; they said Varadi had spent far too much time fraternizing with the beasts; they even hinted that God might have been punishing him for some obscure offence committed when he was a child of eighty-five. But whatever the truth behind Varadi's disappearance, it was a severe loss to your species. His genes would have helped you a great deal.

As far as we were concerned the whole business of the Voyage began when we were invited to report to a certain place by a certain time. That was the first we heard of the scheme. We didn't know anything of the political background. God's wrath with his own creation was news to us; we just got caught up in it willy-nilly. We weren't in any way to blame (you don't really believe that story about the serpent, do you?—it was just Adam's black propaganda), and yet the consequences for us were equally severe: every species wiped out except for a single breeding pair, and that couple consigned to the high seas under the charge of an old rogue with a drink problem who was already into his seventh century of life.

So the word went out; but characteristically they didn't tell us the truth. Did you imagine that in the vicinity of Noah's palace (oh, he wasn't poor, that Noah) there dwelt a convenient example of every species on earth? Come, come. No, they were obliged to advertise, and then select the best pair that presented itself. Since they didn't want to cause a universal panic, they announced a competition for twosomes—a sort of beauty contest cum brains trust cum Darby-and-Joan event—and told contestants to present themselves at Noah's gate by a certain month. You can imagine the problems. For a start, not everyone has a competitive nature, so perhaps only the grabbiest turned up. Animals who weren't smart enough to read between the lines felt they simply didn't need to win a luxury cruise for two, all expenses paid, thank you very much. Nor had Noah and his staff allowed for the fact that some species hibernate at a given time of year; let alone the more obvious fact that certain animals travel more slowly than others. There was a particularly relaxed sloth, for instance—an exquisite creature, I can vouch for it personally—which had scarcely got down to the foot of its tree before it was wiped out in the great wash of God's vengeance. What do you call that—natural selection? I'd call it professional incompetence.

The arrangements, frankly, were a shambles. Noah got behind with the building of the arks (it didn't help when the craftsmen realized there weren't enough berths for them to be taken along as well); with the result that insufficient attention was given to choosing the animals. The first normally presentable pair that came along was given the nod—this appeared to be the system; there was certainly no more than the scantiest examination of pedigree. And of course, while they said they'd take two of each species, when it came down to it . . . Some creatures were simply Not Wanted On Voyage. That was the case with us; that's why we had to stow away. And any number of beasts, with a perfectly good legal argument for being a separate species, had their claims dismissed. No, we've got two of you already, they were told. Well, what difference do a few extra rings round the tail make, or those bushy tufts down your backbone? We've got you. Sorry.

There were splendid animals that arrived without a mate and had to be left behind; there were families which refused to be separated from their offspring and chose to die together; there were medical inspections, often of a brutally intrusive nature; and all night long the air outside Noah's stockade was heavy with the wailings of the rejected. Can you imagine the atmosphere when the news finally got out as to why we'd been asked to submit to this charade of a competition? There was much jealousy and bad behaviour, as you can imagine. Some of the nobler species simply padded away into the forest, declining to survive on the insulting terms offered them by God and Noah, preferring extinction and the waves. Harsh and envious words were spoken about fish; the amphibians began to look distinctly smug; birds practised staying in the air as long as possible. Certain types of monkey were occasionally seen trying to construct crude rafts of their own. One week there was a mysterious outbreak of food poisoning in the Compound of the Chosen, and for some of the less robust species the selection process had to start all over again.

There were times when Noah and his sons got quite hysterical. That doesn't tally with your account of things? You've always been led to believe that Noah was sage, righteous and God-fearing, and I've already described him as a hysterical rogue with a drink problem? The two views aren't entirely incompatible. Put it this way: Noah was pretty bad, but you should have seen the others. It came as little surprise to us that God decided to wipe the slate clean; the only puzzle was that he chose to preserve anything at all of this species whose creation did not reflect particularly well on its creator.

At times Noah was nearly on the edge. The Ark was behind schedule, the craftsmen had to be whipped, hundreds of terrified animals were bivouacking near his palace, and nobody knew when the rains were coming. God wouldn't even give him a date for that. Every morning we looked at the clouds: would it be a westerly wind that brought the rain as usual, or would God send his special downpour from a rare direction? And as the weather slowly thickened, the possibilities of revolt grew. Some of the rejected wanted to commandeer the Ark and save themselves, others wanted to destroy it altogether. Animals of a speculative bent began to propound rival selection principles, based on beast size or utility rather than mere number; but Noah loftily refused to negotiate. He was a man who had his little theories, and he didn't want anyone else's.

As the flotilla neared completion it had to be guarded round the clock. There were many attempts to stow away. A craftsman was discovered one day trying to hollow out a priest's hole among the lower timbers of the stores ship. And there were some pathetic sights: a young elk strung from the rail of Shem's ark; birds dive-bombing the protective netting; and so on. Stowaways, when detected, were immediately put to death; but these public spectacles were never enough to deter the desperate. Our species, I am proud to report, got on board without either bribery or violence; but then we are not as detectable as a young elk. How did we manage it? We had a parent with foresight. While Noah and his sons were roughly frisking the animals as they came up the gangway, running coarse hands through suspiciously shaggy fleeces and carrying out some of the earliest and most unhygienic prostate examinations, we were already well past their gaze and safely in our bunks. One of the ship's carpenters carried us to safety, little knowing what he did.

For two days the wind blew from all directions simultaneously; and then it began to rain. Water sluiced down from a bilious sky to purge the wicked world. Big drops exploded on the deck like pigeons' eggs. The selected representatives of each species were moved from the Compound of the Chosen to their allotted ark: the scene resembled some obligatory mass wedding. Then they screwed down the hatches and we all started getting used to the dark, the confinement and the stench. Not that we cared much about this at first: we were too exhilarated by our survival. The rain fell and fell, occasionally shifting to hail and rattling on the timbers. Sometimes we could hear the crack of thunder from outside, and often the lamentations of abandoned beasts. After a while these cries grew less frequent: we knew that the waters had begun to rise.

Eventually came the day we had been longing for. At first we thought it might be some crazed assault by the last remaining pachyderms, trying to force their way into the Ark, or at least knock it over. But no: it was the boat shifting sideways as the water began to lift it from the cradle. That was the high point of the Voyage, if you ask me; that was when fraternity among the beasts and gratitude towards man flowed like the wine at Noah's table. Afterwards . . . but perhaps the animals had been naïve to trust Noah and his God in the first place.

Even before the waters rose there had been grounds for unease. I know your species tends to look down on our world, considering it brutal, cannibalistic and deceitful (though you might acknowledge the argument that this makes us closer to you rather than more distant). But among us there had always been, from the beginning, a sense of equality. Oh, to be sure, we ate one another, and so on; thc weaker species knew all too well what to expect if they crossed the path of something that was both bigger and hungry. But we merely recognized this as being the way of things. The fact that one animal was capable of killing another did not make the first animal superior to the second; merely more dangerous. Perhaps this is a concept difficult for you to grasp, but there was a mutual respect amongst us. Eating another animal was not grounds for despising it; and being eaten did not instill in the victim—or the victim's family—any exaggerated admiration for the dining species.

Noah—or Noah's God—changed all that. If you had a Fall, so did we. But we were pushed. It was when the selections were being made for the Compound of the Chosen that we first noticed it. All this stuff about two of everything was true (and you could see it made a certain basic sense); but it wasn't the end of the matter. In the Compound we began to notice that some species had been whittled down not to a couple but to seven (again, this obsession with sevens). At first we thought the extra five might be travelling reserves in case the original pair fell sick. But then it slowly began to emerge. Noah—or Noah's God—had decreed that there were two classes of beast: the clean and the unclean. Clean animals got into the Ark by sevens; the unclean by twos.

There was, as you can imagine, deep resentment at the divisiveness of God's animal policy. Indeed, at first even the clean animals themselves were embarrassed by the whole thing; they knew they'd done little to deserve such special patronage. Though being "clean", as they rapidly realized, was a mixed blessing. Being "clean" meant that they could be eaten. Seven animals were welcome on board, but five were destined for the galley. It was a curious form of honour that was being done them. But at least it meant they got the most comfortable quarters available until the day of their ritual slaughter.

【注解】

1. Ark：挪亚方舟，《圣经》中挪亚在上帝的指示下建造的一艘用于逃难的大船。
2. Noah：挪亚，《圣经》中的人物，被上帝告知建造方舟，在灭世大洪水中幸存。
3. Ham：含，《圣经》中的人物，挪亚的第三个儿子，闪和雅弗 (Japheth) 的弟弟。
4. Shem：闪，《圣经》中的人物，挪亚的长子。
5. Tree of Knowledge：智慧树，《圣经》中伊甸园里的一棵树，据称食用其果实可使人具备分辨善恶的能力。

【思考题】

1. Animals on the Ark are divided into two classes: the clean and the unclean. What is the significance of the "divisiveness of God's animal policy"?
2. In what way is the woodworm's story of Noah different from the version provided by men's archives?
3. In this fantastic tale of Julian Barnes, the attack on anthropocentrism is implied in between the lines, which is thought-provoking and serves as a warning to all mankind. It is also a hot debated topic nowadays in and beyond literature. What is your understanding of anthropocentrism? Can you find any examples in both Chinese and western literature or history to illustrate this point?

解读举例

1.《十又二分之一章世界史》深入探讨了历史叙事问题。在文本结构上，巴恩斯以一种碎片化的叙事方式拒绝了以往历史作品中常使用的宏大叙事。他将历史拆分成独立的十个完整章节和半个“插曲”，并将宗教、神话、艺术、信仰、爱等不同元素置于不同章节的主题中，从而构成了一部“世界史”。在叙述上，“虚构”是小说中建构历史的重要方式。

2.《十又二分之一章世界史》以弱势群体的视角来观察历史，颠覆了强势群体的权威。蛀木虫眼中的人类起源史必定异于传统的主流话语，但也未必不是一种真实存在的历史。弱势群体的发声更新了人们对历史真实性的认识，也意味着主流话语的控制权被打破。蛀木虫所代表的是主流话语之外的边缘声音。它们“讲述”的历史是对整个话语系统的颠覆，能带给读者更深的思考。

3.《十又二分之一章世界史》对以“主宰”“征服”“掠夺”为特征的人类中心主义进行了辛辣的讽刺与批判。通过对《圣经》中挪亚方舟的故事、中世纪动物审判法庭记录的戏仿，巴恩斯批判了人类为满足一己私利，掠夺、破坏自然的行为，呼吁人与自然和平相处、和谐共存，尊重自然界其他物种的生存权利并保持生态平衡，只有这样，人类自身的可持续发展才有可能实现。

4.《十又二分之一章世界史》表现了巴恩斯对法律的多层面关注。小说通过不断重复象征“契约”母题的方舟意象展现“法律”发生和运行的过程，并将人类历史中的若干矛盾冲突抽象概括为对立的法理价值。这些法理价值冲突体现了巴恩斯对于“自然法”概念的反思，“法律”和“自然”在巴恩斯笔下都是充满悖论的概念。这种悖论性也使小说中的法律和契约成为巴恩斯文学理念的“元叙事”表征。

Ian McEwan

1948–

伊恩·麦克尤恩是当代英国小说家、剧作家，出生于英国汉普郡的奥尔德肖特。父亲是苏格兰人，当过工人，入伍后长年驻扎在国外，因此麦克尤恩从小便有着丰

作者简介

富的异域生活经历。十二岁时，麦克尤恩回到英国，进入萨福克郡的伍尔弗斯通霍尔学校学习，1970年在苏塞克斯大学获得英国文学学士学位，之后在东英吉利大学获得文学硕士学位。

1975年，麦克尤恩出版短篇小说集《最初的爱情，最后的仪式》(*First Love, Last Rites*)，荣获毛姆奖，在英国文坛崭露头角。之后他又出版了短篇小说集《床笫之间》(*In Between the Sheets*, 1978)，以及两部长篇小说《水泥花园》(*The Cement Garden*, 1978) 和《只爱陌生人》(*The Comfort of Strangers*, 1981)。这些作品以日常生活中的情与爱为题材，挖掘人性深处的欲望与幻想，字里行间体现了弗洛伊德学说的影响，带有哥特小说的恐怖色彩。其作品惊心动魄，让人过目难忘。麦克尤恩因此得名"恐怖伊恩"(Ian Macabre)。

1987年，随着第三部长篇小说《时间中的孩子》(*The Child in Time*, 1987) 获惠特布莱德小说奖，麦克尤恩的创作进入了一个新阶段，作品的恐怖氛围渐趋舒缓，语言风格更为细腻传神、引人入胜。《无辜者》(*The Innocent*, 1990) 是一部冷战谍战小说。《黑犬》(*Black Dogs*, 1992) 聚焦纳粹倒台和冷战结束之后的欧洲。《爱无可忍》(*Enduring Love*, 1997) 讲述一个科普作家与一个被爱妄想症患者之间的离奇纠葛。《阿姆斯特丹》(*Amsterdam*, 1998) 讲述一位作曲家和一位报纸编辑各自逃避死亡却又走向死亡的故事，摘获当年的布克奖。《赎罪》(*Atonement*, 2001) 追踪一个家境优越的十三岁女孩的成长历程，探讨爱的阶级藩篱、宽恕、战争等话题，入围了布克奖短名单，荣获美国书评人协会奖。《星期六》(*Saturday*, 2005) 通过描述一位神经外科医生的遭遇，对威胁人类世界的暴力与非理性力量进行反思，获得了当年詹姆斯·泰特·布莱克纪念奖。中篇小说《在切瑟尔海滩上》(*On Chesil Beach*, 2007) 讲述一对相爱至深的新婚夫妇因轻易放弃彼此而错失一生的凄美故事，入围了布克奖短名单。麦克尤恩的作品无不与社会现实息息相关。长篇小说《追日》(*Solar*, 2010) 关注气候变化；《甜牙》(*Sweet Tooth*, 2012) 审视20世纪70年代的英国社会和文化；《儿童法案》(*The Children Act*, 2014) 与1989年英国议会通过的同名法案有关；《我这样的机器》探讨人工智能；《蟑螂》(*Cockroach*, 2019) 的灵感源自卡夫卡的《变形记》，主题与英国脱欧有关。此外，麦克尤恩也创作了《梦想家彼得》(*The Daydreamer*, 1994) 等儿童文学作品和一些剧本。

麦克尤恩以短篇小说成名，但成名后的创作以长篇小说为主。迄今出版的16部长篇小说大多畅销且颇受学界好评。麦克尤恩曾摘取布克奖等诸多文学大奖，也是诺贝尔文学奖的有力竞争者。他是英语文坛中在艺术和商业领域均取得成功的少数作家之一。这既得益于他对文学孜孜不倦的探求精神，又跟他深入社会现实的创作理念息息相关。麦克尤恩博览群书、涉猎广泛，每天坚持读报，了解时事热点。他的创作主题无所不包，不仅有爱情、婚姻、家庭、死亡等永恒的人生主题，而且有英国脱欧和9·11事件等政治性较强的话题，还涉及气候变化和人工智能等社会热点。麦克尤恩并不满足于以题材取胜，他更注重挖掘复杂的人性，作品能触及人的意识深处。他笔下的人物往往在身体、心理和性格方面具有某种缺陷。于他而言，只有通过这样的人物才能更好地挖掘人性。他乐于尝试各种叙述策略，游走于后现代小说和现实主义小说之间，不受拘束。他的作品既惊险刺激，又发人深省，带给读者丰富的情感体验，令人回味无穷。

Atonement

【题解】

《赎罪》是麦克尤恩的代表作之一，主干由第一、二、三部分和后记构成，依循犯错、忏悔与拯救的叙事主线，讲述了一个关于爱情、罪恶和战争的扣人心弦的故事。故事发生于三个时空，分别是1935年夏天的英国、第二次世界大战期间的英国和法国及1999年的英国。主人公布里奥妮·塔利斯是庄园主的小女儿，小说开始时年方十三，醉心于写作，沉溺于幻想。姐姐塞西莉亚和女佣的儿子罗比一起长大，互生情愫，却因阶级偏见陷入了爱与尊严不可兼得的尴尬境地。布里奥妮目睹了两人的恋爱进程，因涉世未深对罗比产生误会，在证据不足的情况下指认罗比是强奸表姐罗拉的罪犯，导致罗比锒铛入狱。姐姐随后便与家人断绝了关系。第二次世界大战爆发，罗比出狱到法国参战，姐姐当了战地医院护士。布里奥妮此时已意识到自己的错误，陷入了深深的自责和忏悔，于是追随姐姐进入战地医院，成为一名护士。她去看望姐姐，在姐姐那里遇到了休假的罗比。布里奥妮向两人承诺，她将启动法律程序，还罗比清白。小说至此完成主体部分，似乎是皆大欢喜的结局。然而在后记中，七十七岁的小说家布里奥妮在日记中透露，罗比在敦刻尔克大撤退中死于败血症，几个月后塞西莉亚死于伦敦大轰炸，两人并未团聚，更未见过布里奥妮。主体部分其实是布里奥妮撰写的小说。为了弥补自己的过错所造成的恶果，她虚构了大团圆的结局，以文字偿债的方式实现自己的赎罪。

《赎罪》可以说是布里奥妮的心灵成长史。小说主体部分采用第三人称叙述，着力描写布里奥妮由误会到省思再到忏悔的心路历程，作品描述细致入微、丝丝入扣。《赎罪》在第二次世界大战这样重大的历史事件中铺陈个人的成长史，实乃从微观层面介入历史叙事，为读者观照历史提供更多视角。小说的结尾出人意料，也因此成为众多评论的焦点。有评论者认为，作者在小说主体部分的创作中使用现实主义的表现手法，一个元小说式的结尾破坏了整体结构的美感；更多的评论者则视《赎罪》为后现代小说，因而元小说式的结尾可谓水到渠成；也有学者指出，英国后现代小说家的创作并未完全脱离现实主义传统，只是不同程度地使用元小说等后现代创作技巧。

以下内容节选自《赎罪》第一部分第一章，即小说的开场。这一部分从布里奥妮的视角介绍她为创作和上演剧本《阿拉贝拉的磨难》所做的一切，涉及表姐罗拉及其双胞胎弟弟的来访，以及布里奥妮与父母及哥哥姐姐的关系。

From Atonement

Part One，Chapter One

THE PLAY—for which Briony had designed the posters, programs and tickets, constructed the sales booth out of a folding screen tipped on its side, and lined the collection box in red crêpe paper—was written by her in a two-day tempest of composition, causing her to miss a breakfast and a lunch. When the preparations were complete, she had nothing to do but contemplate her finished draft and wait for the appearance of her cousins[1] from the distant north. There would be time for only one day of rehearsal before her brother[2] arrived. At some moments chilling, at others desperately sad, the play told a tale of the heart whose message, conveyed in a rhyming prologue, was that love which did not build a foundation on good sense was doomed. The reckless passion of the heroine, Arabella, for a wicked foreign count is punished by ill fortune when she contracts cholera during an impetuous dash toward a seaside town with her intended. Deserted by him and nearly everybody else, bed-bound in a garret, she discovers in herself a sense of humor. Fortune presents her a second chance in the form of an impoverished doctor—in fact, a prince in disguise who has elected to work among the needy. Healed by him, Arabella chooses judiciously this time, and is rewarded by reconciliation with her family and a wedding with the medical prince on "a windy sunlit day in spring."

Mrs. Tallis read the seven pages of *The Trials of Arabella*[3] in her bedroom, at her dressing table, with the author's arm around her shoulder the whole while. Briony studied her mother's face for every trace of shifting emotion, and Emily Tallis obliged with looks of alarm, snickers of glee and, at the end, grateful smiles and wise, affirming nods. She took her daughter in her arms, onto her lap—ah, that hot smooth little body she remembered from its infancy, and still not gone from her, not quite yet—and said that the play was "stupendous," and agreed instantly, murmuring into the tight whorl of the girl's ear, that this word could be quoted on the poster which was to be on an easel in the entrance hall by the ticket booth.

Briony was hardly to know it then, but this was the project's highest point of fulfillment. Nothing came near it for satisfaction, all else was dreams and frustration. There were moments in the summer dusk after her light was out, when she burrowed in the delicious gloom of her canopy bed, and made her heart thud with luminous, yearning fantasies, little playlets in themselves, every one of which featured Leon. In one, his big, good-natured face buckled in grief as Arabella sank in loneliness and despair. In another, there he was, cocktail in hand at some fashionable city watering hole, overheard boasting to a group of friends: Yes, my younger sister, Briony Tallis the writer, you must surely have heard of her. In a third, he punched the air in exultation as the final curtain fell, although there was no curtain, there was no possibility of a curtain. Her play was not for her cousins, it was for her brother, to celebrate his return, provoke his admiration and guide him away from his careless succession of girlfriends, toward the right form of wife, the one who would persuade him to return to the countryside, the one who would sweetly request Briony's services as a bridesmaid.

She was one of those children possessed by a desire to have the world just so. Whereas her big sister's room was a stew of unclosed books, unfolded clothes, unmade bed, unemptied ashtrays, Briony's was a shrine to her controlling demon: the model farm spread across a deep window ledge consisted of the usual animals, but all facing one way—toward their owner—as if about to break into song, and even the farmyard hens were neatly corralled. In fact, Briony's was the only tidy upstairs room in the house. Her straight-backed dolls in their many-roomed mansion appeared to be under strict instructions not to touch the walls; the various thumb-sized figures to be found standing about her dressing table—cowboys, deep-sea divers, humanoid mice—suggested by their even ranks and spacing a citizen's army awaiting orders.

A taste for the miniature was one aspect of an orderly spirit. Another was a passion for secrets: in a prized varnished cabinet, a secret drawer was opened by pushing against the grain of a cleverly turned dovetail joint, and here she kept a diary locked by a clasp, and a notebook written in a code of her own invention. In a toy safe opened by six secret numbers she stored letters and postcards. An old tin petty cash box was hidden under a removable floorboard beneath her bed. In the box were treasures that dated back four years, to her ninth birthday when she began collecting: a mutant double acorn, fool's gold, a rainmaking spell bought at a funfair, a squirrel's skull as light as a leaf.

But hidden drawers, lockable diaries and cryptographic systems could not conceal from Briony the simple truth: she had no secrets. Her wish for a harmonious, organized world denied her the reckless possibilities of wrongdoing. Mayhem and destruction were too chaotic for her tastes, and she did not have it in her to be cruel. Her effective status as an only child, as well as the relative isolation of the Tallis house, kept her, at least during the long summer holidays, from girlish intrigues with friends. Nothing in her life was sufficiently interesting or shameful to merit hiding; no one knew about the squirrel's skull beneath her bed, but no one wanted to know. None of this was particularly an affliction; or rather, it appeared so only in retrospect, once a solution had been found.

At the age of eleven she wrote her first story—a foolish affair, imitative of half a dozen folktales and lacking, she realized later, that vital knowingness about the ways of the world which compels a reader's respect. But this first clumsy attempt showed her that the imagination itself was a source of secrets: once she had begun a story, no one could be told. Pretending in words was too tentative, too vulnerable, too embarrassing to let anyone know. Even writing out the she saids, the and thens, made her wince, and she felt foolish, appearing to know about the emotions of an imaginary being. Self-exposure was inevitable the moment she described a character's weakness; the reader was bound to speculate that she was describing herself. What other authority could she have? Only when a story was finished, all fates resolved and the whole matter sealed off at both ends so it resembled, at least in this one respect, every other finished story in the world, could she feel immune, and ready to punch holes in the margins, bind the chapters with pieces of string, paint or draw the cover, and take the finished work to show to her mother, or her father, when he was home.

Her efforts received encouragement. In fact, they were welcomed as the Tallises began to understand that the baby of the family possessed a strange mind and a facility with words. The long afternoons she spent browsing through dictionary and thesaurus made for constructions that were inept, but hauntingly so: the coins a villain concealed in his pocket were "esoteric," a hoodlum caught stealing a car wept in "shameless auto-exculpation," the heroine on her thoroughbred stallion made a "cursory" journey through the night, the king's furrowed brow was the "hieroglyph" of his displeasure. Briony was encouraged to read her stories aloud in the library and it surprised her parents and older sister to hear their quiet girl perform so boldly, making big gestures with her free arm, arching her eyebrows as she did the voices, and looking up from the page for seconds at a time as she read in order to gaze into one face after the other, unapologetically demanding her family's total attention as she cast her narrative spell.

Even without their attention and praise and obvious pleasure, Briony could not have been held back from her writing. In any case, she was discovering, as had many writers before her, that not all recognition is helpful. Cecilia's enthusiasm, for example, seemed a little overstated, tainted with condescension perhaps, and intrusive too; her big sister wanted each bound story catalogued and placed on the library shelves, between Rabindranath Tagore[4] and Quintus Tertullian[5]. If this was supposed to be a joke, Briony ignored it. She was on course now, and had found satisfaction on other levels; writing stories not only involved secrecy, it also gave her all the pleasures of miniaturization. A world could be made in five pages, and one that was more pleasing than a model farm. The childhood of a spoiled prince could be framed within half a page, a moonlit dash through sleepy villages was one rhythmically emphatic sentence, falling in love could be achieved in a single word—a *glance*. The pages of a recently finished story seemed to vibrate in her hand with all the life they contained. Her passion for tidiness was also satisfied, for an unruly world could be made just so. A crisis in a heroine's life could be made to coincide with hailstones, gales and thunder, whereas nuptials were generally blessed with good light and soft breezes. A love of order also shaped the principles of justice, with death and marriage the main engines of housekeeping, the former being set aside exclusively for the morally dubious, the latter a reward withheld until the final page.

The play she had written for Leon's homecoming was her first excursion into drama, and she had found the transition quite effortless. It was a relief not to be writing out the *she saids*, or describing the weather or the onset of spring or her heroine's face—beauty, she had discovered, occupied a narrow band. Ugliness, on the other hand, had infinite variation. A universe reduced to what was said in it was tidiness indeed, almost to the point of nullity, and to compensate, every utterance was delivered at the extremity of some feeling or other, in the service of which the exclamation mark was indispensable. *The Trials of Arabella* may have been a melodrama, but its author had yet to hear the term. The piece was intended to inspire not laughter, but terror, relief and instruction, in that order, and the innocent intensity with which Briony set about the project—the posters, tickets, sales booth—made her particularly vulnerable to failure. She could easily have welcomed Leon with another of her stories, but it was the news that her cousins from the north were coming to stay that had prompted this leap into a new form.

That Lola, who was fifteen, and the nine-year-old twins, Jackson and Pierrot, were refugees from a bitter domestic civil war should have mattered more to Briony. She had heard her mother criticize the impulsive behavior of her younger sister Hermione, and lament the situation of the three children, and denounce her meek, evasive brother-in-law Cecil who had fled to the safety of All Souls College, Oxford[6]. Briony had heard her mother and sister analyze the latest twists and outrages, charges and countercharges, and she knew her cousins' visit was an open-ended one, and might even extend into term time. She had heard it said that the house could easily absorb three children, and that the Quinceys could stay as long as they liked, provided the parents, if they ever visited simultaneously, kept their quarrels away from the Tallis household. Two rooms near Briony's had been dusted down, new curtains had been hung and furniture carried in from other rooms. Normally, she would have been involved in these preparations, but they happened to coincide with her two-day writing bout and the beginnings of the front-of-house construction. She vaguely knew that divorce was an affliction, but she did not regard it as a proper subject, and gave it no thought. It was a mundane unraveling that could not be reversed, and therefore offered no opportunities to the storyteller: it belonged in the realm of disorder. Marriage was the thing, or rather, a wedding was, with its formal neatness of virtue rewarded, the thrill of its pageantry and banqueting, and dizzy promise of lifelong union. A good wedding was an unacknowledged representation of the as yet unthinkable—sexual bliss. In the aisles of country churches and grand city cathedrals, witnessed by a whole society of approving family and friends, her heroines and heroes reached their innocent climaxes and needed to go no further.

If divorce had presented itself as the dastardly antithesis of all this, it could easily have been cast onto the other pan of the scales, along with betrayal, illness, thieving, assault and mendacity. Instead it showed an unglamorous face of dull complexity and incessant wrangling. Like rearmament and the Abyssinia Question[7] and gardening, it was simply not a subject, and when, after a long Saturday morning wait, Briony heard at last the sound of wheels on the gravel below her bedroom window, and snatched up her pages and ran down the stairs, across the hallway and out into the blinding light of midday, it was not insensitivity so much as a highly focused artistic ambition that caused her to shout to the dazed young visitors huddled together by the trap with their luggage, "I've got your parts, all written out. First performance tomorrow! Rehearsals start in five minutes!"

Immediately, her mother and sister were there to interpose a blander timetable. The visitors—all three were ginger-haired and freckled—were shown their rooms, their cases were carried up by Hardman's son Danny, there was cordial in the kitchen, a tour of the house, a swim in the pool and lunch in the south garden, under the shade of the vines. All the while, Emily and Cecilia Tallis maintained a patter that surely robbed the guests of the ease it was supposed to confer. Briony knew that if she had traveled two hundred miles to a strange house, bright questions and jokey asides, and being told in a hundred different ways that she was free to choose, would have oppressed her. It was not generally realized that what children mostly wanted was to be left alone. However, the Quinceys worked hard at pretending to be amused or liberated, and this boded well for *The Trials of Arabella*: this trio clearly had the knack of being what they were not, even though they barely resembled the characters they were to play. Before lunch Briony slipped away to the empty rehearsal room—the nursery—and walked up and down on the painted floorboards, considering her casting options.

On the face of it, Arabella, whose hair was as dark as Briony's, was unlikely to be descended from freckled parents, or elope with a foreign freckled count, rent a garret room from a freckled innkeeper, lose her heart to a freckled prince and be married by a freckled vicar before a freckled congregation. But all this was to be so. Her cousins' coloring was too vivid—virtually fluorescent!—to be concealed. The best that could be said was that Arabella's *lack* of freckles was the sign—the hieroglyph, Briony might have written—of her distinction. Her purity of spirit would never be in doubt, though she moved through a blemished world. There was a further problem with the twins, who could not be told apart by a stranger. Was it right that the wicked count should so completely resemble the handsome prince, or that both should resemble Arabella's father and the vicar? What if Lola were cast as the prince? Jackson and Pierrot seemed typical eager little boys who would probably do as they were told. But would their sister play a man? She had green eyes and sharp bones in her face, and hollow cheeks, and there was something brittle in her reticence that suggested strong will and a temper easily lost. Merely floating the possibility of the role to Lola might provoke a crisis, and could Briony really hold hands with her before the altar, while Jackson intoned from the *Book of Common Prayer*[8]?

It was not until five o'clock that afternoon that she was able to assemble her cast in the nursery. She had arranged three stools in a row, while she herself jammed her rump into an ancient baby's high chair—a bohemian touch that gave her a tennis umpire's advantage of height. The twins had come with reluctance from the pool where they had been for three hours without a break. They were barefoot and wore singlets over trunks that dripped onto the floorboards. Water also ran down their necks from their matted hair, and both boys were shivering and jiggled their knees to keep warm. The long immersion had puckered and bleached their skin, so that in the relatively low light of the nursery their freckles appeared black. Their sister, who sat between them, with left leg balanced on right knee, was, by contrast, perfectly composed, having liberally applied perfume and changed into a green gingham frock to offset her coloring. Her sandals revealed an ankle bracelet and toenails painted vermilion. The sight of these nails gave Briony a constricting sensation around her sternum, and she knew at once that she could not ask Lola to play the prince.

Everyone was settled and the playwright was about to begin her little speech summarizing the plot and evoking the excitement of performing before an adult audience tomorrow evening in the library. But it was Pierrot who spoke first.

"I hate plays and all that sort of thing."

"I hate them too, and dressing up," Jackson said.

It had been explained at lunch that the twins were to be distinguished by the fact that Pierrot was missing a triangle of flesh from his left earlobe on account of a dog he had tormented when he was three.

Lola looked away. Briony said reasonably, "How can you hate plays?"

"It's just showing off." Pierrot shrugged as he delivered this self-evident truth.

Briony knew he had a point. This was precisely why she loved plays, or hers at least; everyone would adore her. Looking at the boys, under whose chairs water was pooling before spilling between the floorboard cracks, she knew they could never understand her ambition. Forgiveness softened her tone.

"Do you think Shakespeare was just showing off?"

Pierrot glanced across his sister's lap toward Jackson. This warlike name was faintly familiar, with its whiff of school and adult certainty, but the twins found their courage in each other.

"Everyone knows he was."

"Definitely."

When Lola spoke, she turned first to Pierrot and halfway through her sentence swung round to finish on Jackson. In Briony's family, Mrs. Tallis never had anything to impart that needed saying simultaneously to both daughters. Now Briony saw how it was done.

"You'll be in this play, or you'll get a clout, and then I'll speak to The Parents."

"If you clout us, *we'll* speak to The Parents."

"You'll be in this play or I'll speak to The Parents."

That the threat had been negotiated neatly downward did not appear to diminish its power. Pierrot sucked on his lower lip.

"Why do we have to?" Everything was conceded in the question, and Lola tried to ruffle his sticky hair.

"Remember what The Parents said? We're guests in this house and we make ourselves—what do we make ourselves? Come on. What do we make ourselves?"

"A-menable," the twins chorused in misery, barely stumbling over the unusual word.

Lola turned to Briony and smiled. "Please tell us about your play."

The Parents. Whatever institutionalized strength was locked in this plural was about to fly apart, or had already done so, but for now it could not be acknowledged, and bravery was demanded of even the youngest. Briony felt suddenly ashamed at what she had selfishly begun, for it had never occurred to her that her cousins would not want to play their parts in *The Trials of Arabella*. But they had trials, a catastrophe of their own, and now, as guests in her house, they believed themselves under an obligation. What was worse, Lola had made it clear that she too would be acting on sufferance. The vulnerable Quinceys were being coerced. And yet, Briony struggled to grasp the difficult thought, wasn't there manipulation here, wasn't Lola using the twins to express something on her behalf, something hostile or destructive? Briony felt the disadvantage of being two years younger than the other girl, of having a full two years' refinement weigh against her, and now her play seemed a miserable, embarrassing thing.

Avoiding Lola's gaze the whole while, she proceeded to outline the plot, even as its stupidity began to overwhelm her. She no longer had the heart to invent for her cousins the thrill of the first night.

As soon as she was finished Pierrot said, "I want to be the count. I want to be a bad person."

Jackson said simply, "I'm a prince. I'm always a prince."

She could have drawn them to her and kissed their little faces, but she said, "That's all right then."

Lola uncrossed her legs, smoothed her dress and stood, as though about to leave. She spoke through a sigh of sadness or resignation. "I suppose that because you're the one who wrote it, you'll be Arabella . . ."

"Oh no," Briony said. "No. Not at all."

She said no, but she meant yes. Of course she was taking the part of Arabella. What she was objecting to was Lola's "because." She was not playing Arabella because she wrote the play, she was taking the part because no other possibility had crossed her mind, because that was how Leon was to see her, because she was Arabella.

But she had said no, and now Lola was saying sweetly, "In that case, do you mind if I play her? I think I could do it very well. In fact, of the two of us . . ."

She let that hang, and Briony stared at her, unable to keep the horror from her expression, and unable to speak. It was slipping away from her, she knew, but there was nothing that she could think of to say that would bring it back. Into Briony's silence, Lola pressed her advantage.

"I had a long illness last year, so I could do that part of it well too."

Too? Briony could not keep up with the older girl. The misery of the inevitable was clouding her thoughts.

One of the twins said proudly, "And you were in the school play."

How could she tell them that Arabella was not a freckled person? Her skin was pale and her hair was black and her thoughts were Briony's thoughts. But how could she refuse a cousin so far from home whose family life was in ruins? Lola was reading her mind because she now played her final card, the unrefusable ace.

"Do say yes. It would be the only good thing that's happened to me in *months*."

Yes. Unable to push her tongue against the word, Briony could only nod, and felt as she did so a sulky thrill of self-annihilating compliance spreading across her skin and ballooning outward from it, darkening the room in throbs. She wanted to leave, she wanted to lie alone, facedown on her bed and savor the vile piquancy of the moment, and go back down the lines of branching consequences to the point before the destruction began. She needed to contemplate with eyes closed the full richness of what she had lost, what she had given away, and to anticipate the new regime. Not only Leon to consider, but what of the antique peach and cream satin dress that her mother was looking out for her, for Arabella's wedding? That would now be given to Lola. How could her mother reject the daughter who had loved her all these years? As she saw the dress make its perfect, clinging fit around her cousin and witnessed her mother's heartless smile, Briony knew her only reasonable choice then would be to run away, to live under hedges, eat berries and speak to no one, and be found by a bearded woodsman one winter's dawn, curled up at the base of a giant oak, beautiful and dead, and barefoot, or perhaps wearing the ballet pumps with the pink ribbon straps . . .

Self-pity needed her full attention, and only in solitude could she breathe life into the lacerating details, but at the instant of her assent—how the tilt of a skull could change a life!—Lola had picked up the bundle of Briony's manuscript from the floor, and the twins had slipped from their chairs to follow their sister into the space in the center of the nursery that Briony had cleared the day before. Did she dare leave now? Lola was pacing the floorboards, one hand to her brow as she skimmed through the first pages of the play, muttering the lines from the prologue. She announced that nothing was to be lost by beginning at the beginning, and now she was casting her brothers as Arabella's parents and describing the opening to them, seeming to know all there was to know about the scene. The advance of Lola's dominion was merciless and made self-pity irrelevant. Or would it be all the more annihilatingly delicious?—for Briony had not even been cast as Arabella's mother, and now was surely the time to sidle from the room and tumble into facedown darkness on the bed. But it was Lola's briskness, her obliviousness to anything beyond her own business, and Briony's certainty that her own feelings would not even register, still less provoke guilt, which gave her the strength to resist.

In a generally pleasant and well-protected life, she had never really confronted anyone before. Now she saw: it was like diving into the swimming pool in early June; you simply had to make yourself do it. As she squeezed out of the high chair and walked over to where her cousin stood her heart thudded inconveniently and her breath was short.

She took the play from Lola and said in a voice that was constricted and more high-pitched than usual, "If you're Arabella, then I'll be the director, thank you very much, and I'll read the prologue."

Lola put her speckled hand to her mouth. "Sor-reeee!" she hooted. "I was just trying to get things started."

Briony was unsure how to respond, so she turned to Pierrot and said, "You don't look much like Arabella's mother."

The countermanding of Lola's casting decision, and the laughter in the boys it provoked, made for a shift in the balance of power. Lola made an exaggerated shrug of her bony shoulders and went to stare out of the window. Perhaps she herself was struggling with the temptation to flounce from the room.

Though the twins began a wrestling match, and their sister suspected the onset of a headache, somehow the rehearsal began. The silence into which Briony read the prologue was tense.

This is the tale of spontaneous Arabella
Who ran off with an extrinsic fellow.
It grieved her parents to see their firstborn
Evanesce from her home to go to Eastbourne
Without permission . . .

His wife at his side, Arabella's father stood at the wrought-iron gates of his estate, first pleading with his daughter to reconsider her decision, then in desperation ordering her not to go. Facing him was the sad but stubborn heroine with the count beside her, and their horses, tethered to a nearby oak, were neighing and pawing the ground, impatient to be off. The father's tenderest feelings were supposed to make his voice quaver as he said,

My darling one, you are young and lovely,
But inexperienced, and though you think
The world is at your feet,
It can rise up and tread on you.

Briony positioned her cast; she herself clutched Jackson's arm, Lola and Pierrot stood several feet away, hand in hand. When the boys met each other's eye they had a giggling fit which the girls shushed at. There had been trouble enough already, but Briony began to understand the chasm that lay between an idea and its execution only when Jackson began to read from his sheet in a stricken monotone, as though each word was a name on a list of dead people, and was unable to pronounce "inexperienced" even though it was said for him many times, and left out the last two words of his lines—"It can rise up and tread." As for

Lola, she spoke her lines correctly but casually, and sometimes smiled inappropriately at some private thought, determined to demonstrate that her nearly adult mind was elsewhere.

And so they went on, the cousins from the north, for a full half an hour, steadily wrecking Briony's creation, and it was a mercy, therefore, when her big sister came to fetch the twins for their bath.

【注解】

1. her cousins：即下文提到的布里奥妮的表姐罗拉及其双胞胎弟弟杰克逊和皮埃罗，他们因父母离婚将寄居于布里奥妮家。
2. her brother：即下文提到的布里奥妮的哥哥利昂。
3. *The Trials of Arabella*：《阿拉贝拉的磨难》，即上文提到的剧本，作者是布里奥妮。
4. Rabindranath Tagore：即印度著名诗人、文学家、哲学家罗宾德拉纳特·泰戈尔。
5. Quintus Tertullian：即古罗马帝国时期北非杰出的基督教作家昆图斯·德尔图良。
6. All Souls College, Oxford：牛津万灵学院。
7. the Abyssinia Question：指意大利侵略埃塞俄比亚，是 1935 年的时事热点。"Abyssinia" 即埃塞俄比亚的旧称。
8. *Book of Common Prayer*：公祷书，圣公会的祈祷用书。

【思考题】

1. What does Chapter One reveal about Briony Tallis's character?
2. What is the function of *The Trials of Arabella* in this chapter?
3. Identify the narrator or narrative point of view of Chapter One.

解读举例

1. 《赎罪》是一部成长小说。小说开头，布里奥妮是十三岁的无知少女，结尾处已是七十七岁高龄的女作家。她的成长不仅体现在文学创作的成就上，更在于心灵和精神方面的自省——她逐渐认识到自己的错误给罗比和塞西莉亚造成的致命后果。她到战地医院当护士，用实际行动关爱他人，又创作《赎罪》作为忏悔录，借助文学想象完成了赎罪。

2. 《赎罪》是一部爱情小说，重点探究阶级与爱情之间的关系。塞西莉亚是庄园主的千金，罗比是女佣的儿子，阶级地位的差异是阻碍两人相爱的藩篱。除了塞西莉亚和罗比的母亲，所有人都相信布里奥妮对罗比的指控，印证了英国社会根深蒂固的阶级偏见。

3. 《赎罪》是一部战争小说。麦克尤恩的父亲参加过第二次世界大战。父亲讲述的从战经历与麦克尤恩自己的阅读调研，令《赎罪》中的战争描写格外逼真，异常震撼。通过虚构罗比、塞西莉亚和布里奥妮等人物的个人“小叙事”，麦克尤恩揭示了战争的残酷和罪恶，消解了所谓的敦刻尔克奇迹等官方历史“大叙事”。

4. 《赎罪》是一部介于现实主义小说和后现代小说之间的作品。该小说的主干部分秉承英国小说的现实主义传统，后记则通过布里奥妮的第一人称自反性叙述，揭示主干部分的虚构性：布里奥妮为了赎罪，虚构了罗比与塞西莉亚的团圆等情节。小说由此展示了“叙述既能创造真相又能操纵真相的威力”。

Kazuo Ishiguro

1954—

作者简介

石黑一雄是当今英语文坛的著名小说家，以国际化写作 (International Writing) 的理念享誉世界。1954 年，石黑一雄生于日本长崎。1960 年，石黑一雄随家人迁居伦敦以南的萨里郡，先后就读于当地的斯托顿小学、沃辛县文法学校。十三岁时，石黑一雄受摇滚乐手鲍勃·迪伦的影响，渴望投身音乐事业，学习吉他演奏与歌曲创作，广泛接触美国、苏格兰和爱尔兰的传统民谣，并与同龄好友组建音乐小圈子。中学毕业后，他出外游历一年，前往美国西海岸与加拿大哥伦比亚省，在此期间制作了一张独立唱片。返英后，石黑一雄基于北美的旅行体验，创作了两个短篇故事。

1974 年，石黑一雄进入肯特大学，研习英国文学和哲学，对普鲁斯特和卡夫卡产生了浓厚兴趣。1976 年 4 月，他暂缓学业，前往苏格兰伦弗鲁的贫民区担任社工，广泛接触当地工会组织与底层家庭，这一经历也唤起了他对社会弱势无权者的深刻同情，并开始创作第一部小说。半年后，石黑一雄复归肯特大学，深入研读夏洛蒂·勃朗特、简·奥斯汀、陀思妥耶夫斯基、托尔斯泰和柏拉图的作品。1978 年毕业后，石黑一雄搬到伦敦，辗转于当地酒吧和咖啡馆写歌与演唱，同时继续创作小说。此间，他在伦敦诺丁山地区的慈善组织工作，为无家可归者奔走呼吁，并与同为社工的妻子相遇相知。

1979 年，石黑一雄进入东英吉利亚大学，跟随文学评论家和小说家马尔科姆·布雷德伯里 (Malcolm Bradbury) 及导师安吉拉 · 卡特 (Angela Carter) 研习创意写作，开始在小型文学杂志上发表短篇小说。这些作品引起费伯出版社编辑罗伯特 · 麦克拉姆 (Robert McCrum) 的兴趣，将其收录于《费伯介绍 7：新作家的故事》(*Faber Introductions 7: Stories by New Writers*, 1981)。1980 年，石黑一雄获创意写作文学硕士学位，重归诺丁山慈善组织。1982 年，石黑一雄的第一部长篇小说《远山淡影》(*A Pale View of Hills*) 由费伯出版社出版。小说出版后备受好评，获温尼弗雷德 · 霍尔比纪念奖，也使年仅二十七岁的石黑一雄入围《格兰塔》(*Granta*)“最佳英国青年作家”名单，鼓舞其走上全职作家的道路。

1986 年，石黑一雄第二部小说《浮世画家》(*An Artist of the Floating World*) 出版，同样将背景设于日本长崎。主人公小野增二战前是受人尊崇的知名画家，为军国主义摇旗呐喊，战后却遭遇多方质疑。为逃避现实，他沉溺于往昔荣耀，否认将毕生奉献给错误的帝国事业，最终在梦醒后重新审视个人身份。石黑一雄将对战争、名誉与个人抉择的感悟融入耄耋画家的回忆，对军国主义进行反思，拷问了个人在历史洪流中的道德责任。小说成功入围当年英国布克文学奖短名单，获惠特布雷德年度最佳小说奖，使石黑一雄成为英国文坛一颗耀眼的新星。

由于石黑一雄的日裔身份，加之前两部小说均将背景设在日本，因此评论界初期普遍聚焦于石黑一雄作品的“日本性”。然而，石黑一雄虽坦诚作品中存在日本元素，但强调小说描绘的是“想象的日本”，是在脑海中回忆构建并由强烈情感维系的他国形象。为打破对其作品过度日本化的解读，石黑一雄在后期秉持国际化写作的理念，聚焦人类普世性的存在境况，创作了在不同文化背景下都能引起共鸣的世界文学。

在代表作《长日留痕》(*The Remains of the Day*, 1989) 中，石黑一雄偏离“日本性”的身份建构，将视线集中在两次世界大战之间的英国社会。主人公史蒂文斯以侍奉达林顿勋爵为荣，坚信自己这个小人物在服务贵族阶层时，也能为改变世界进程作出贡献，却在坚守理想管家的“尊严”中，牺牲掉爱情、亲情与独立判断，最终在与故交的谈话中反思自我，悔悟自己未曾察觉达林顿同情纳粹的绥靖行动。通过对史蒂文斯恪尽愚忠的描写，石黑一雄揭示了二战后英国社会普遍存在的对贵族传统及大英帝国殖民霸主地位的怀旧情结，展现了国际化写作的文学理念，将读者的关注焦点从日本文化特质引向人类共同的艺术价值。凭借此部作品，年仅三十五岁的石黑一雄一举斩获布克文学奖。

实现国际化写作后，石黑一雄佳作迭出，之后的每部作品都在新语境中探索人类的存在境况，包含基因技术伦理困境、中世纪奇幻世界及人工智能等多个主题。《无可慰藉》(*The Unconsoled*, 1995) 体现了人在异化社会中的生存困境和焦虑状态；《莫失莫忘》聚焦克隆话题，是一部具有反乌托邦色彩的科幻小说；《被掩埋的巨人》(*The Buried Giant*，2015) 伪托英国后亚瑟王时代的传说探讨民族与个人应以何种态度面对历史宿怨；《克拉拉与太阳》(*Klara and the Sun*，2021) 则反映了人工智能时代人类所面临的问题。

在石黑一雄的创作中，记忆伦理、创伤书写、历史反思与不可靠叙述始终处于其国际化写作的核心位置。他的作品善于从异质文化交织的边缘地带观察社会，在优雅克制的叙事中，融入普世人文关怀，使读者在舒缓的记忆回望中，剥离那些被自我欺骗所遮蔽的残酷真相，激发深刻不安的阅读体验。这一独特的叙事风格不仅使石黑一雄在当代英国文坛独树一帜，也让其蜚声世界文坛。2017 年，石黑一雄获得诺贝尔文学奖，获奖理由是“在具有强大情感力量的小说中，揭露我们与世界连结的错觉之下隐蔽的深渊”。

Never Let Me Go

【题解】

《莫失莫忘》是石黑一雄的第六部长篇小说，将故事背景设于 20 世纪 90 年代的英国，聚焦作为器官捐献者的克隆生命。全书分为三部分，讲述了克隆人学生凯西与好友汤米、鲁斯共同经历的短暂人生：他们在黑尔舍姆寄宿学校被抚养成人，然后短住在农场中接受器官捐献的前置培训，最后在康复中心被切除器官，直至生命终结。石黑一雄从克隆人凯西的视角切入，在隐忍伤感的记忆叙事中，带领读者亲历凯西认知世界的渐进过程，洞悉隐藏于祥和生活下的黑暗事实，拉近了读者与克隆人的情感距离，使读者体悟克隆人对希望的追寻及希望幻灭时的绝望，由此肯定了克隆生命的人性身份。下文节选自第二十二章，讲述了成年的凯西与汤米怀揣着延期捐献器官的希望向艾米丽小姐寻求帮助，却最终梦碎的情景。

From Never Let Me Go

Chapter Twenty-Two

“Marie-Claude is correct,” Miss Emily[1] said. “I’m the one to whom you should be speaking. Marie-Claude worked hard for our project. And the way it all ended has left her feeling somewhat disillusioned. As for myself, whatever the disappointments, I don't feel so badly about it. I think what we achieved merits some respect. Look at the two of you. You've turned out well. I'm sure you have much you could tell me to make me proud. What did you say your names were? No, no, wait. I think I shall remember. You're the boy with the bad temper. A bad temper, but a big heart. Tommy. Am I right? And you, of course, are Kathy H. You've done well as a carer. We've heard a lot about you. I remember, you see. I dare say I can remember you all."

"What good does it do you or them?" Madame[2] asked, then strode away from the wheelchair, past the two of us and into the darkness, for all I know to occupy the space Miss Emily had been in before.

"Miss Emily," I said, "it's very nice to see you again."

"How kind of you to say so. I recognised you, but you may well not have recognised me. In fact, Kathy H., once not so long ago, I passed you sitting on that bench out there, and you certainly didn't recognise me then. You glanced at George, the big Nigerian man pushing me. Oh yes, you had quite a good look at him, and he at you. I didn't say a word, and you didn't know it was me. But tonight, in context, as it were, we know each other . . . Now, I'll try and answer your questions the best I can. I've heard this rumour countless times. When we still had Hailsham[3], we'd get two or three couples each year, trying to get in to talk to us. One even wrote to us. I suppose it's not so hard to find a large estate like that if you mean to break the rules. So you see, it's been there, this rumour, from long before your time."

She stopped, so I said: "What we want to know now, Miss Emily, is if the rumour's true or not."

She went on gazing at us for a moment, then took a deep breath. "Within Hailsham itself, whenever this talk started up, I made sure to stamp it out good and proper. But as for what students said after they'd left us, what could I do? In the end, I came to believe—and Marie-Claude believes this too, don't you, darling?—I came to believe that this rumour, it's not just a single rumour. What I mean is, I think it's one that gets created from scratch over and over. You go to the source, stamp it out, you'll not stop it starting again elsewhere. I came to this conclusion and ceased to worry about it. Marie-Claude never did worry about it. Her view was: 'If they're so foolish, let them believe it.' Oh yes, don't show me that sour face of yours. That's been your view of it from the beginning. After many years of it,

I came not exactly to the same viewpoint. But I began to think, well, perhaps I shouldn't worry. It's not my doing, after all. And for the few couples who get disappointed, the rest will never put it to the test anyway. It's something for them to dream about, a little fantasy. What harm is there? But for the two of you, I can see this doesn't apply. You are serious. You've thought carefully. You've hoped carefully. For students like you, I do feel regret. It gives me no pleasure at all to disappoint you. But there it is."

I didn't want to look at Tommy. I felt surprisingly calm, and even though Miss Emily's words should have crushed us, there was an aspect to them that implied something further, something being held back, that suggested we hadn't yet got to the bottom of things. There was even the possibility she wasn't telling the truth. So I asked:

"Is it the case, then, that deferrals don't exist? There's nothing you can do?"

She shook her head slowly from side to side. "There's no truth in the rumour. I'm sorry. I truly am."

Suddenly Tommy asked: "Was it true once though? Before Hailsham closed?"

Miss Emily went on shaking her head. "It was never true. Even before the Morningdale scandal[4], even back when Hailsham was considered a shining beacon, an example of how we might move to a more humane and better way of doing things, even then, it wasn't true. It's best to be clear about this. A wishful rumour. That's all it ever was . . . Was there something else you wished to talk to me about? This is all strictly against regulations, of course, and Marie-Claude should never have asked you in. And naturally, I should have turned you out the second I knew you were here. But Marie-Claude doesn't care much for their regulations these days, and I must say, neither do I. So if you wish to stay a little longer, you're very welcome."

"If the rumour was never true," Tommy said, "then why did you take all our art stuff away? Didn't the Gallery exist either?"

"The Gallery? Well, that rumour did have some truth to it. There was a gallery. And after a fashion, there still is. These days it's here, in this house. I had to prune it down, which I regret. But there wasn't room for all of it in here. But why did we take your work away? That's what you're asking, isn't it?"

"Not just that," I said quietly. "Why did we do all of that work in the first place? Why train us, encourage us, make us produce all of that? If we're just going to give donations anyway, then die, why all those lessons? Why all those books and discussions?"

"Why Hailsham at all?" Madame had said this from the hallway. She came past us again and back into the darkened section of the room. "It's a good question for you to ask."

Miss Emily's gaze followed her, and for a moment, remained fixed behind us. I felt like turning to see what looks were being exchanged, but it was almost like we were back at Hailsham, and we had to keep facing the front with complete attention. Then Miss Emily said:

"Yes, why Hailsham at all? Let's answer the simplest one, and perhaps it will answer all the rest. Why did we take your artwork? Why did we do that? You said an interesting thing earlier, Tommy. When you were discussing this with Marie-Claude. You said it was because your art would reveal what you were like. What you were like inside. That's what you said, wasn't it? Well, you weren't far wrong about that. We took away your art because we thought it would reveal your souls. Or to put it more finely, we did it to prove you had souls at all."

She paused, and Tommy and I exchanged glances for the first time in ages. Then I asked:

"Why did you have to prove a thing like that, Miss Emily? Did someone think we didn't have souls?"

A thin smile appeared on her face. "It's touching, Kathy, to see you so taken aback. It demonstrates, in a way, that we did our job well. As you say, why would anyone doubt you had a soul? But I have to tell you, my dear, it wasn't something commonly held when we first set out all those years ago. And though we've come a long way since then, it's still not a notion universally held, even today. You Hailsham students, even after you've been out in the world like this, you still don't know the half of it. All around the country, at this very moment, there are students being reared in deplorable conditions, conditions you Hailsham students could hardly imagine. And now we're no more, things will only get worse."

She paused again, and for a moment she seemed to be inspecting us carefully through narrowed eyes. Finally she went on:

"Whatever else, we at least saw to it that all of you in our care, you grew up in wonderful surroundings. And we saw to it too, after you left us, you were kept away from the worst of those horrors. We were able to do that much for you at least. But this dream of yours, this dream of being able to defer. Such a thing would always have been beyond us to grant, even at the height of our influence. I'm sorry, I can see what I'm saying won't be welcome to you. But you mustn't be dejected. I hope you can appreciate how much we were able to secure for you. Look at you both now! You've had good lives, you're educated and cultured. I'm sorry we couldn't secure more for you than we did, but you must realise how much worse things once were. When Marie-Claude and I started out, there were no places like Hailsham in existence. We were the first, along with Glenmorgan House. Then a few years later came the Saunders Trust. Together, we became a small but very vocal movement, and we challenged the entire way the donations programme was being run. Most importantly, we demonstrated to the world that if students were reared in humane, cultivated environments, it was possible for them to grow to be as sensitive and intelligent as any ordinary human being. Before that, all clones—or students, as we preferred to call you—existed only to supply medical science. In the early days, after the war, that's largely all you were to most people. Shadowy objects in test tubes. Wouldn't you agree, Marie-Claude? She's being very quiet. Usually you can't get her to shut up on this subject. Your presence, my dears, appears to have tied her tongue. Very well. So to answer your question, Tommy. That was why we collected your art. We selected the best of it and put on special exhibitions. In the late seventies, at the height of our influence, we were organising large events all around the country. There'd be cabinet ministers, bishops, all sorts of famous people coming to attend. There were speeches, large funds pledged. 'There, look!' we could say. 'Look at this art! How dare you claim these children are anything less than fully human?' Oh yes, there was a lot of support for our movement back then, the tide was with us."

. . .

"But what I don't understand," I said, "is why people would want students treated so badly in the first place."

"From your perspective today, Kathy, your bemusement is perfectly reasonable. But you must try and see it historically. After the war, in the early fifties, when the great breakthroughs in science followed one after the other so rapidly, there wasn't time to take stock, to ask the sensible questions. Suddenly there were all these new possibilities laid before us, all these ways to cure so many previously incurable conditions. This was what the world noticed the most, wanted the most. And for a long time, people preferred to believe these organs appeared from nowhere, or at most that they grew in a kind of vacuum. Yes, there were arguments. But by the time people became concerned about . . . about students, by the time they came to consider just how you were reared, whether you should have been brought into existence at all, well by then it was too late. There was no way to reverse the process. How can you ask a world that has come to regard cancer as curable, how can you ask such a world to put away that cure, to go back to the dark days? There was no going back. However uncomfortable people were about your existence, their overwhelming concern was that their own children, their spouses, their parents, their friends, did not die from cancer, motor neurone disease, heart disease. So for a long time you were kept in the shadows, and people did their best not to think about you. And if they did, they tried to convince themselves you weren't really like us. That you were less than human, so it didn't matter. And that was how things stood until our little movement came along. But do you see what we were up against? We were virtually attempting to square the circle. Here was the world, requiring students to donate. While that remained the case, there would always be a barrier against seeing you as properly human. Well, we fought that battle for many years, and what we won for you, at least, were many improvements, though of course, you were only a select few. But then came the Morningdale scandal, then other things, and before we knew it, the climate had quite changed. No one wanted to be seen supporting us any more, and our little movement, Hailsham, Glenmorgan, the Saunders Trust, we were all of us swept away."

. . .

I don't know what made me say it. Maybe it was because I knew the visit would have to finish pretty soon; maybe I was getting curious to know how exactly Miss Emily and Madame felt about each other. Anyway, I said to her, lowering my voice and nodding towards the doorway:

"Madame never liked us. She's always been afraid of us. In the way people are afraid of spiders and things."

I waited to see if Miss Emily would get angry, no longer caring much if she did. Sure enough, she turned to me sharply, as if I'd thrown a ball of paper at her, and her eyes flashed in a way that reminded me of her Hailsham days. But her voice was even and soft when she replied:

"Marie-Claude has given everything for you. She has worked and worked and worked. Make no mistake about it, my child, Marie-Claude is on your side and will always be on your side. Is she afraid of you? We're all afraid of you. I myself had to fight back my dread of you all almost every day I was at Hailsham. There were times I'd look down at you all from my study window and I'd feel such revulsion . . . " She stopped, then something in her eyes flashed again. "But I was determined not to let such feelings stop me doing what was right. I fought those feelings and I won. Now, if you'd be so good as to help me out of here, George should be waiting with my crutches."

. . .

Madame watched the departing vehicles for a long time. Then she turned as though to go back into the house, and seeing us there on the pavement, stopped abruptly, almost shrinking back.

"We're going now," I said. "Thank you for talking to us. Please say goodbye to Miss Emily for us."

I could see her studying me in the fading light. Then she said:

"Kathy H. I remember you. Yes, I remember." She fell silent, but went on looking at me.

"I think I know what you're thinking about," I said, in the end. "I think I can guess."

"Very well." Her voice was dreamy and her gaze had slightly lost focus. "Very well. You are a mind-reader. Tell me."

"There was a time you saw me once, one afternoon, in the dormitories. There was no one else around, and I was playing this tape, this music. I was sort of dancing with my eyes closed and you saw me."

"That's very good. A mind-reader. You should be on the stage. I only recognised you just now. But yes, I remember that occasion. I still think about it from time to time."

"That's funny. So do I."

"I see."

We could have ended the conversation there. We could have said goodbye and left. But she stepped closer to us, looking into my face all the time.

"You were much younger then," she said. "But yes, it's you."

"You don't have to answer this if you don't want to," I said. "But it's always puzzled me. May I ask you?"

"You read my mind. But I cannot read yours."

"Well, you were . . . upset that day. You were watching me, and when I realised, and I opened my eyes, you were watching me and I think you were crying. In fact, I know you were. You were watching me and crying. Why was that?"

Madame's expression didn't change and she kept staring into my face. "I was weeping," she said eventually, very quietly, as though afraid the neighbours were listening, "because when I came in, I heard your music. I thought some foolish student had left the music on. But when I came into your dormitory, I saw you, by yourself, a little girl, dancing. As you say, eyes closed, far away, a look of yearning. You were dancing so very sympathetically. And the music, the song. There was something in the words. It was full of sadness."

"The song," I said, "it was called 'Never Let Me Go.'" Then I sang a couple of lines quietly under my breath for her. "Never let me go. Oh, baby, baby. Never let me go . . . "

She nodded as though in agreement. "Yes, it was that song. I've heard it once or twice since then. On the radio, on the television. And it's taken me back to that little girl, dancing by herself."

"You say you're not a mind-reader," I said. "But maybe you were that day. Maybe that's why you started to cry when you saw me. Because whatever the song was really about, in my head, when I was dancing, I had my own version. You see, I imagined it was about this woman who'd been told she couldn't have babies. But then she'd had one, and she was so pleased, and she was holding it ever so tightly to her breast, really afraid something might separate them, and she's going baby, baby, never let me go. That's not what the song's about at all, but that's what I had in my head that time. Maybe you read my mind, and that's why you found it so sad. I didn't think it was so sad at the time, but now, when I think back, it does feel a bit sad."

I'd spoken to Madame, but I could sense Tommy shifting next to me, and was aware of the texture of his clothes, of everything about him. Then Madame said:

"That's most interesting. But I was no more a mind-reader then than today. I was weeping for an altogether different reason. When I watched you dancing that day, I saw something else. I saw a new world coming rapidly. More scientific, efficient, yes. More cures for the old sicknesses. Very good. But a harsh, cruel world. And I saw a little girl, her eyes tightly closed, holding to her breast the old kind world, one that she knew in her heart could not remain, and she was holding it and pleading, never to let her go. That is what I saw. It wasn't really you, what you were doing, I know that. But I saw you and it broke my heart. And I've never forgotten."

Then she came forward until she was only a step or two from us. "Your stories this evening, they touched me too." She looked now to Tommy, then back at me. "Poor creatures. I wish I could help you. But now you're by yourselves."

She reached out her hand, all the while staring into my face, and placed it on my cheek. I could feel a trembling go all through her body, but she kept her hand where it was, and I could see again tears appearing in her eyes.

"You poor creatures," she repeated, almost in a whisper. Then she turned and went back into her house.

【注解】

1. Miss Emily：艾米丽小姐，小说中的人物，黑尔舍姆创立者之一，也是首席监护人。艾米丽年长于其他老师，言行举止坚定严厉，具有敏锐的洞察力。她的存在让克隆人学生产生安全感，因而受到敬重。
2. Madame：全名玛丽–克劳蒂 (Marie-Claude)，小说中的人物，黑尔舍姆学校的捐赠者与创建人。她偶尔前往黑尔舍姆挑选学生创作的艺术品，置于私人画廊里供人参观，坚信人类社会需要善待这些充当器官捐献者的克隆生命。
3. Hailsham：黑尔舍姆学校，小说中虚构的克隆人寄宿学校，向未满十六岁的克隆人学生提供人文通识教育，凯西 (Kathy H.) 曾在此就读。
4. the Morningdale scandal：莫宁代尔丑闻，石黑一雄在小说中虚构的人种提升事件。一位名为詹姆斯·莫宁代尔的苏格兰科学家试图通过基因改良技术，强化人类孩童的智力与运动机能，最终遭到社会的强烈抵制。莫宁代尔丑闻后，人们开始担心克隆人会取代自然人，致使主流社会希望将克隆生命遗忘在角落里，不再支持改善克隆人的生存环境。企业与政客发现民意转向后，陆续停止赞助黑尔舍姆等慈善机构，导致诸多同类机构因经费不足被迫关闭。在此，石黑一雄影射了21世纪之交的众多克隆技术事件。

【思考题】

1. What is the narrative point of view in this novel? Why does Kazuo Ishiguro use this point of view to illustrate this story?
2. What is the rumor among the donators (clones), especially among those students who grow up at Hailsham?
3. What is the function of the Gallery mentioned by Tommy and other Hailsham students?
4. As a child at Hailsham, Kathy one day is singing along to the song "Never Let Me Go" and dancing with it by swaying her pillow like a baby. Suddenly, Kathy realizes that Madame is watching her from the hallway. To her surprise, Madame is crying and leaves abruptly. How do Kathy H. and Madame interpret this scene respectively?
5. Why are so many clones reared in deplorable situation and treated so badly by people? With such rapid development of artificial intelligence, gene editing, and clone technology in the world, how should we treat all the "non-human" life in the possible future?

解读举例

1. 黑尔舍姆教育体制是强权社会的意识规训工具，监护人刻意隐瞒学生的身份与既定命运——强制的器官切除被描述为自主捐献，器官切除后的个体死亡被粉饰成使命终结。据此，黑尔舍姆学校摧毁了克隆人群体认知自我和外部世界的能力，"教化"学生漠然接受捐献器官的宿命。此外，黑尔舍姆虽如艾米丽小姐所说，希望冷漠的社会以更加人性与合理的方式来对待生命，但由于人性的自私，人类不会放弃扩展生存空间的可能性，即使这意味着牺牲其他物种的生存权利。这样看来，黑尔舍姆是一场注定失败的事业，人们不过是在"赞扬"(Hail)一个"空壳"(Sham)。

---

2. 黑尔舍姆虽然在学生洞察现实世界方面有所隐瞒，但其人道的理想追求是不容抹杀的。创始人艾米丽小姐和玛丽–克劳蒂带领监护人在黑尔舍姆营造了一个远离外部残酷世界的"伊甸园"，使这些克隆人孩子摆脱同类的悲惨命运，避免其在骇人现实中茫然无措，丧失人性尊严。通过接受学校的人文通识教育，这些克隆人群体拥有了艺术修养、创造意识和集体认同感，在潜移默化中拥有了反思主体和世界的能力。黑尔舍姆为克隆人洞察自我身份和打破人类社会的意识规训提供了必要的力量，更为他们日后应对人类社会的残酷压制提供了精神支撑。

---

3. 石黑一雄的《莫失莫忘》通过描写克隆人的悲惨境遇，揭示了施加于生命的隐性政治暴力。小说中的主权者通过孤立克隆人，实现将克隆人与人类社会相隔离的空间规划，使克隆人沦为失去身份认知的"赤裸生命"(bare life)，同时借助闭塞封闭的隔离状态，在黑尔舍姆、农场和康复中心等克隆人的生存场所悬置法律规定，剥夺其参与集体生活的权利。克隆人由此丧失公民身份，处于法律界限模糊的空间地带，降格为隐匿在公共视线之外、仅用于器官培养与捐献的"另类"他者。克隆人被迫接受或自愿臣服于强制性政治权力，最终被"合法"操控与剥夺。

附录

英语基本文学词汇表

Aesthetic Movement 唯美主义运动

19世纪后期出现在英国艺术和文学领域的一场组织松散的运动。它提倡"为艺术而艺术"，强调超然于生活的纯粹美，追求形式完美和艺术技巧，它的兴起是对社会功利哲学、市侩习气和庸俗作风的反抗。英国唯美主义的代表人物为奥斯卡·王尔德和阿尔加侬·查尔斯·斯温伯恩(Algernon Charles Swinburne)。

allegory 寓言

一种诗体或散文体的故事，其人物、行为或背景代表某些抽象的意义或伦理。因此每个寓言都有两层意义：字面意义和象征意义。约翰·班扬的《天路历程》就是一部著名的寓言。

alliteration 头韵

一组词中相同或相似辅音或辅音组的重复。有时该词仅指词首辅音的重复。如"The sun sank slowly."中即使用了头韵法——s音的重复。又如著名英国女作家简·奥斯汀的《傲慢与偏见》一书的书名(*Pride and Prejudice*)也是典型的头韵法。

allusion 典故

诗文中的暗指或引用，可以是人物、地点、事件或文学作品。如《麦克白》(*Macbeth*)第一幕中，罗斯(Ross)称赞麦克白在战斗中的勇敢与高超技艺，称他是"贝娄娜(Bellona)的新郎"，即是在引用典故，因为在罗马神话中，贝娄娜是战争女神。

analogy 类比

将两个事物相比以显示其间的相似之处。类比常用来解释(通过比较熟悉的事物来说明不熟悉的事物)或辩论。E. M. 福斯特在《论英国人的性格》("Notes on the English Character")一文中把英国人的性格与大海作了一番比较，所使用的手法即是类比。

antagonist 反面人物，敌手

故事中反对主人公的人物或力量，即主人公的对手。如伊阿古(Iago)是《奥赛罗》(*Othello*)中的主要反面人物，处心积虑地陷害主人公奥赛罗，是奥赛罗的敌人。

anti-hero/heroine 反英雄

戏剧或叙事作品的中心人物，但缺乏像传奇文学和史诗等传统文学中的主人公所具有的高贵品质。这类人物已经成为西方小说的一个重要特征。福楼拜的《包法利夫人》(*Emma*

Bovary) 中的包法利夫人和乔伊斯的《尤利西斯》中的布卢姆都因这种反英雄式的平凡和庸俗而成为反英雄的典型。反英雄也出现在现代戏剧中，例如阿瑟·米勒 (Arthur Miller) 的《推销员之死》(*Death of a Salesman*) 中的男主人公。

antithesis 对偶

对偶通常用一个对称的句子来表达，即用相同或相似的语法结构来表达相互比照的思想。如：亚历山大·蒲伯在其《批评论》中即用了一个很有名的对偶句 "To err is human, to forgive divine."。

aphorism 格言，警句

含有劝诫和教育意义的话语，通常较为精练，采取定义的形式。如弗朗西斯·培根的名言："Silence is the virtue of fools."。

apostrophe 呼语法

指在演说或文章中用第二人称称呼不在场的人物或拟人化事物。比如，拜伦在《恰尔德·哈罗德游记》中对海洋说 "Roll on, thee deep and dark blue Ocean—roll"，即是使用了呼语法。

aside 旁白

指戏剧中，剧中人物低声或直接对着观众所说的话，舞台上的其他人物被假设听不见。这种手法常被用来向观众披露人物的内心情感，因此旁白者被设定是在讲真话。

assonance 谐音

指相同或相似的元音的重复，尤指诗歌中元音押韵、辅音不押韵的情况。如约翰·济慈的《希腊古瓮颂》中的诗句 "Thou foster child of silence and slow time"。

atmosphere 基调，总体艺术效果

指文学作品所渲染的总体气氛或感觉。基调通常至少有一部分是通过描写背景来达成的。如在格林厄姆·格林的《过桥》(*Across the Bridge*) 中，通过描写故事的发生地——一个灰蒙蒙、脏兮兮的小镇，使小说具有一种没落、无聊的基调。

autobiography 自传

个人关于自己一生的记述。与日记、信件不同，自传是完整的。自传与回忆录也有所不同，回忆录通常会包括一些作者一生中发生的社会大事或其他重要人物的记述。

ballad 叙事诗歌，民谣

指以民间传说为主要题材，以口头吟唱世代相传的民歌式诗歌，通常含有生动的对话。一般采用四行诗节，其中第二和第四行押韵。中世纪晚期，民谣在欧洲许多地区出现，15 世纪时在苏格兰尤为盛行。自 18 世纪起，一些诗人开始模仿民谣体的形式与风格进行创作，柯勒律治的《老水手谣》就是典型的一例。

ballad stanza 民谣体诗节

一种四行诗节，第一行和第三行为不押韵的抑扬格四步音节，第二行和第四行为押韵的抑扬格三音步，一般以 abcb 表示。

biography 传记

指由他人撰写、关于一个人一生的详细记述。著名的传记有詹姆斯·鲍士威尔所著的《塞缪尔·约翰逊传》。

blank verse 无韵诗

指不押韵的抑扬格五音步诗。这种诗体非常灵活，接近日常讲话的节奏，适合写作长诗。很多著名的英国诗歌都是以这种诗体写成的，包括威廉·莎士比亚和约翰·弥尔顿的某些诗作。

caesura 停顿

诗行中根据意思而作的主要停顿，在英诗中常用 ‖ 号标记。如：Then be not coy, ‖ but use your time;/And while ye may, ‖ go marry . . . /To the Virgins, to Make Much of Time.

canto 诗章

长诗或其他叙述体诗歌的一个篇章，相当于长篇小说的“章”。

caricature 漫画手法

通过夸张或扭曲使一个人物显得滑稽可笑。身体的某个特征或某种怪癖，性格上的某种特点或某种行为，均可被当作漫画的对象加以夸张。狄更斯《艰难时世》中的托马斯·葛莱恩 (Thomas Gradgrind，此人只讲利益，把生活看作金钱买卖关系) 即是一个漫画式的人物。

characterization 人物塑造，性格描绘

指一个人物所展示的个性，亦指作者展示人物个性的方法。作者通常都是通过描绘人物的行为、思想、语言、外表、他人的看法等方式来展示人物的性格。

classicism 古典主义

指绘画、文学或音乐中的一种运动或倾向，该运动或倾向反映了古希腊和古罗马艺术所展现的原则。它强调传统性和广泛性，追求永恒的主题，注重理性、清晰、平衡和秩序，与强调情感和个人主题的浪漫主义相对。

climax 高潮

指文学作品中（尤其是戏剧中）最紧张、最富于意义或最具悬念的一刻。在这一刻，读者的反应最为强烈，同时故事也达到了转折点，接着必须引出结局。

comedy 喜剧

通常指结局圆满、主人公与周围环境达成友好妥协的文学作品。与主人公结局悲惨的悲剧 (tragedy) 相对。喜剧中的主人公可以是一个性格平常，能力泛泛的人物，而不一定要达到悲剧人物所必备的英雄式的高度。喜剧往往意在暴露人性的弱点，而智慧、幽默，以及一种喜庆的气氛则是它常备的要素。

conceit 奇喻

比喻的一种，所比较的两种事物截然不同，把它们放在一起会使读者感到诧异或有趣，从而达到其艺术效果。一个奇喻可以是一个简单的暗喻，但它通常可以为一首诗建立起一个框架。如约翰·多恩在其《别离辞：莫伤悲》(“A Valediction: Forbidding Mourning”) 中，把情人的灵魂与圆规相比，即用了奇喻。

conflict 矛盾冲突

小说、戏剧或叙事诗中两种相对的力量或两个相对的人物之间的斗争。冲突可以分为内部与外部冲突两种，并可以有多种形式，如：个人对个人、个人对社会、个人对自然、个人自身两种性格要素的抗争等。冲突是情节发展的重要元素，是悬念的基础。在故事情节中，通常是两种或多种冲突同时存在。如：《哈姆雷特》可以被看作是哈姆雷特自身性格的冲突，但无疑该剧也体现了他同命运和社会的冲突。

connotation 含义，隐含意义

指一个词或词组除了其直观的字面意思 (denotation) 外，所能引起的所有情感和联想。如 shroud，字面意义是裹尸布，但令人联想到死亡、黑暗、寒冷等，这些联想到的意义便是 connotation。至于一个词或词组所具有的多重含义中，哪一种或哪几种会在阅读中被激发出来，这取决于它所处的上下文，以及读者的个体经验。

consonance 辅音韵

指一组词中相邻位置上相同或相似辅音的重复，重复的辅音可以出现在词首、词中或词尾。如 "And all the air a solemn stillness holds" (Thomas Gray) 中的辅音［l］。现代诗歌中，辅音韵常出现在诗行的结尾，以替代全韵 (full rhyme)。

couplet 对句

指紧邻两行的尾韵相谐的诗句。如莎士比亚《麦克白》第二幕第一场结尾便是一个对句：Hear it not, Duncan; for it is a knell/That summons thee to heaven or to hell.

dactyl 扬抑抑格

指一个重读音节后跟两个弱读音节的音步。如哈代的《声音》("The Voice") 中的第一句 "Woman much missed, how you call to me, call to me."。

denotation 字面意义，本义

指一个词或词组的字面意思。

denouement 结局

指戏剧、小说及叙事诗中解决冲突、揭示秘密的部分，通常为戏剧的最后一幕，小说或故事的最后一章。

diction 措辞，用语

指文学作品中对词的选择。一个作者的措辞既可正式，也可非正式；既可抽象，也可具体；既可简单，也可华丽。具体因人因题而异。

dissonance (声音) 不和谐或刺耳

勃朗宁和哈代都常在诗歌中故意制造不和谐的声音，以达到某种特定效果。但如果是非故意造成的，则会成为一种缺陷。

dramatic monologue 戏剧独白，戏剧诗

一种诗体，在其中一个虚构的人物或历史人物——而不是诗人本人——向一个或多个人组成的沉默的"听众"讲话，借以揭示该人物的思想与性格。勃朗宁就以使用这种诗歌形式并将其发展完善而著名。

elegy 挽歌

表达诗人对死亡等严肃主题的思索的诗歌形式。这种思索可以是由某个人的死亡引发的，也可以是诗人对某种庄重或伤感情绪的总体观察与表达。著名的挽歌有约翰·多恩的《挽歌》(*Elegies*) 和托马斯·格雷 (Thomas Gray) 的《墓畔挽歌》("Elegy Written in a Country Churchyard") 等。

emblematic image 象征意义

用词语描写的形象，长期以来已被赋予道德或宗教含义。比如"鸽子"(dove)，因其在《圣经》中为躲避洪水的挪亚衔回代表洪水消退的橄榄枝而成为和平的象征。

epic 史诗

一种叙事体长诗，以一种宏大华丽的风格来颂扬某个传奇英雄的业绩，反映当时社会的价值观。著名的史诗有《荷马史诗》、维吉尔的《埃涅阿斯纪》。《贝奥武甫》(*Beowulf*) 是最早的古英语史诗。

epigram 机智的短诗，警句

指内含机智思想的短诗或散文体著作中出现的机智、简洁的警句。如本·约翰逊 (Ben Johnson) 曾写过"讽刺短诗"(Epigrams)，王尔德的作品中常出现警句。

epigraph 引言，格言

指出现在书、章节或诗歌开始部分的引语或格言警句，起到暗示作品主题的作用。

epilogue 收场白，尾声

指作品的结尾部分。在莎士比亚时代，戏剧的结尾部分常有一个人物直接向观众说话，请求给予掌声。说话的人物及他说的话都被称为收场白。在一些小说中，作者在收场白中简单介绍人物后来的命运，也称尾声。

epiphany 顿悟

该词本来在基督教神学中指上帝的显灵，后来引申为对事物真谛的突然领悟。詹姆斯·乔伊斯的许多作品都描写这种顿悟。

epitaph 墓志铭，纪念死者的短诗

墓志铭可以以死者的口吻写成，吸引路人的注意力，也可以描述死者生前的功德。塞缪尔·约翰逊和威廉·华兹华斯都曾将墓志铭当作一种文体形式来进行创作。

epithet 表述人或事物性质、特征的修饰语

可以是名词、形容词，也可以是短语；经常出现在历史人物的称号中，如 Catherine the Great、Ethelred the Unready 等。荷马史诗中出现过许多表述词。Homeric epithet 指的就是被反复用来描述同一个人或事物的形容词（通常是复合形容词），如 the wine-dark sea 和 rosy-fingered Dawn。

epode 古希腊抒情颂诗的第三节（即最后一节）

该词还被用来指一种长短诗行相间的古希腊抒情诗体。

exemplum 中世纪传教士布道时讲的劝喻性故事或寓言等

乔叟的《坎特伯雷故事集》中就曾通过人物之口讲述过这类寓言。

exposition 提示部分

指剧本、故事等的开头部分，常常通过先前发生的事件来介绍人物及他们所处的情境等重要的背景信息。

fable 寓言

以诗歌或散文形式写成的进行道德教诲的小故事，故事的人物多为拟人化的动物，但人和拟人化的物体也常出现在其中。寓言常在结尾部分以警句的形式点明寓意。著名的寓言有公元前 6 世纪的《伊索寓言》(*Aesop's Fables*)。

falling action 突降

小说、戏剧中情节的一部分。情节冲突发展至高潮后出现突降，接着引向冲突结束时的大结局。参见 **plot**。

farce 闹剧，滑稽戏

喜剧的一种，通常由俗套的人物形象 (stock characters)、滑稽的肢体动作和夸张荒谬的情节故事构成。

flashback(小说、戏剧或叙事诗的)倒叙

指在叙述过程中先讲述后来发生的事件，再讲述先前发生的事件。倒叙使叙述者能够补充说明人物和事件的背景信息。

foil 陪衬者

在戏剧中通过其品质和行动来与主人公形成鲜明对照的人物，如在夏洛蒂・勃朗特的《简・爱》中，简・爱幼年时好友，温顺、驯服的海伦・彭斯 (Helen Burns) 就是一个陪衬者，她同具有很强叛逆性的简・爱形成鲜明的对照。

foot 音步

指使诗歌保持节奏、不断重复的音节组合。最常见的英诗音步为抑扬格 (iamb)、扬抑格 (trochee)、扬抑抑格 (dactyl)、抑抑扬格 (anapest)。参见 **scansion**。

foreshadowing 预示，预兆

指小说或戏剧中为后来发生的事件作铺垫而预先营造的气氛或提供的信息，作家用此技巧来增加作品的趣味和设置悬念，如《哈姆雷特》第一幕的"闹鬼"情节为后来老国王鬼魂的出场作了铺垫，而《麦克白》开场时出现女巫的一幕则预示该剧后来发生的事情。

free verse 自由诗

一种背离了传统诗体的诗歌形式，无固定格律，诗行音步数目亦不相等，其节奏完全取决于诗人声音的抑扬顿挫。自由诗的形式最早在沃尔特・惠特曼 (Walt Whitman) 手中臻于完善，现已成为最为广泛使用的英诗诗体。

heroic couplet 英雄双韵体

一种抑扬格五音步对句，如蒲伯《夺发记》中的诗句：But when to mischief mortals bend their will, / How soon they find fit instrument of ill!

hyperbole 夸张法

指为了起到强调的效果而进行夸张的

一种修辞手法，不能按字面意思理解。如“I've been waiting here for ages.”一句就使用了夸张法。

iamb 抑扬格

即一个弱读音节后跟一个重读音节。主要采用抑扬格的诗歌被称作抑扬格诗 (iambic verse)，是现在常见的英诗形式之一。参见 **scansion**。

iambic pentameter 抑扬格五音步

即每行有五个音步，每个音步都是抑扬格。最常见的是十音节的抑扬格五音步，如丁尼生的诗句“Beyond the utmost bound of human thought.”。参见 **scansion**。

imagery 形象化描述

指通过表述具体、实在的物体、动作、场景或状态的词或词组，使读者在头脑中形成意象 (images) 或画面的一种描述手法。该词常同比喻（包括 metaphor 和 simile) 联系在一起，而使人联想到更为深层的含义。超出一般比喻意义的意象也就成了象征 (symbol)。

incremental repetition 渐增反复

指在诗歌（尤其是民歌）中，后一行诗（或诗节）重复前一行诗（或诗节）的一部分，以取得戏剧性效果的一种手法。渐增反复常出现在对话当中，如苏格兰民谣《兰多王》(“Lord Randal”)：

“What d'ye leave to your mother, Lord Randal, my son?
What d'ye leave to your mother, my handsome young man?”
“Four and twenty milk kye; mother, mak my bed soon.
For I'm sick at the heart, and I fain wad lie down.”
“What d'ye leave to your sister, Lord Randal, my son?
What d'ye leave to your sister, my handsome young man?”
“My gold and my silver; mother, mak my bed soon.
For I'm sick at the heart, and I fain wad lie down.”

in medias res（拉丁文）直奔本题

直接交代事件发展的进程（而非从头开始叙述）。

interlude 幕间幽默短剧

本来指在伦敦剧院出现以前，由一些职业演员在宴会和欢庆活动间歇时表演的短剧，后来演变成在幕间表演的幽默短剧，包括几类被认为是由道德剧 (the morality play) 向伊丽莎白时代的喜剧过渡的戏剧形式，如类似于道德剧、具有说教性质的道德短剧 (moral interludes)。一些幽默短剧接近滑稽戏。

internal rhyme 中间韵

指一行诗中间某些词押韵，或一行诗中某词与诗行末尾的词押韵。例如“We were the first that ever burst/Into that silent sea”中的“first”和“burst”。参见 **rhyme**。

inversion 倒装

指颠倒正常词语顺序的一种修辞手法，如 the body electric、sweetly blew the breeze 等。在诗歌中，颠倒词序可以使诗人保持诗行的押韵格式或音步，或者强调某些重点的词。

invocation（欲得到灵感而向缪斯等神的）祈求

是古希腊和拉丁诗歌（尤其是史诗创作）的一种传统，后来在文艺复兴时期和新古典主义时期，一些诗人也模仿这种做法。对神灵的祈求一般出现在诗的开头，但也可以在之后出现，比如在一个新章节的开始处。

irony 反讽

反讽可分三类：①言辞反讽 (verbal irony)，指作者或说话人说的与所要表达的意思完全相反；②戏剧性反讽 (dramatic irony)，指剧中人物或小说中人物未察觉而观众或读者却能领会的讽刺；③情景反讽 (irony of situation)，指作者显示出某种行为和情景的预期结局与实际结局的差异。

lyric 抒情诗

任何表达个人（可以是诗人本人，也可以是诗人在诗中创造出的人物）心情、感情或思绪的短诗都可被称作抒情诗，如挽歌、颂诗、十四行诗都属于抒情诗。抒情诗是英语诗歌中广泛使用的一种诗歌形式，它可以按任何韵律创作，主题也没有限制。常见的主题是抒发爱与悲伤等感情。

masque 假面剧

指 16 世纪末 17 世纪初盛行于欧洲贵族社会一种特殊的表演形式，综合了诗剧、音乐、舞蹈、歌唱、华丽的戏装和昂贵的舞台道具等因素。贵族们戴着面具入场，他们装扮成神话中的人物，表演简单的情节，最后摘去面具一起跳舞。莎士比亚在《暴风雨》(*The Tempest*) 中就穿插了一场假面舞会。

melodrama 传奇剧，音乐戏剧

一种戏剧形式，有着程式化的情节，夸张的情感。剧情往往是完美的主人公和凶恶的坏人之间的冲突，结局多是善有善报，恶有恶报。之所以也叫作音乐戏剧，是因为最初的情节剧中每个角色都有各自的主题音乐，一定的情节亦有相应的音乐相伴。

metaphor 隐喻

一种修辞格，对两个并不类似的事物进行比较。如“Life is a dream.”就是典型的隐喻。与明喻 (simile) 不同，隐喻不使用 like、as、resemble 这类的喻词。

metaphysical poetry 玄学派诗歌

特指盛行于 17 世纪的以多恩的诗作为代表的一个诗歌流派。它的特点是评议俏皮或充满机锋，结构精妙，格律多不规则，语言接近口语体，意象繁复细致，常常将看似迥异的各种概念熔于一炉。

meter 韵律

指诗歌中某种节奏模式的反复出现，

或是通过规则或较为规则地重复使用近似的声音模式而建立的节奏。长短律 (quantitative meter) 指由长短步组成的韵律，即长短音节规则地连续出现，构成音步 (feet)，这是最经典的韵律，常见于古希腊和拉丁诗歌中。重音律 (accentual meter) 指在一行诗或一组诗行中存在规则数量的重读音节 (非重读音节的数量不限)，在古英语和后来的英语诗歌中都可见到。音节律 (syllabic meter) 指在诗行中存在固定数量的音节，在法语和日语诗歌中常见。重读音节律 (accentual syllabic meter) 指诗行具有固定的总音节数 (包括重读和非重读音节)，其中重读音节的数量是固定的，常见于自乔叟以后的英诗中。

metonymy 换喻，转喻

一种修辞格，用和某一事物有密切关联的另一事物来代替或暗示这一事物，如用皇冠 (crown) 指代国王等。

miracle play 奇迹剧，圣迹剧

中世纪流行于英国的宗教剧，往往以圣人或圣母玛利亚的生平事迹或《圣经》中的历史片段为素材。

mock epic 诙谐史诗

一种喜剧性的文学形式，用庄严崇高的英雄式史诗形式来处理微不足道的主题事件，如英国文学中的著名诙谐史诗《夺发记》。

modernism 现代主义

20 世纪初期文学和其他艺术领域出现的先锋潮流的总称，包括象征主义、未来主义、表现主义、意象主义、达达主义、超现实主义等。现代主义文学旨在反抗 19 世纪的传统，例如小说中的现实主义和诗歌中的传统韵律等。现代主义作家试图摆脱资产阶级价值观，通过采用复杂难懂的艺术形式和风格使读者感到困惑，从而引发读者思考。代表作家有乔伊斯、伍尔夫，福克纳 (William Faulkner)、卡夫卡等人。

morality play 道德剧

由奇迹剧发展而来，15 世纪和 16 世纪在英国、法国和欧洲其他一些地区十分流行。道德剧其实是戏剧化了的寓言，在其中善和恶都被拟人化。

motif 主题，基调

指一部文学作品中反复出现的思想观念、人物类型、情节、场景等因素，通常它被用来深化和揭示作品的中心思想。

myth 神话

重点讲述神的故事，有时也涉及宗教仪式。神话体现了在科学不发达的时代人类对许多的事物的演绎和阐释。

narrative poem 叙事诗

指以叙述故事为主的诗歌，包括史诗、诗体骑士故事和某些民歌。

narrator 叙述者

指讲述故事的人。他可以是第一人称叙述者 (first-person narrator)，参与到作品之中，扮演主角或配角，也可以是第三人称叙述者 (third-person narrator)，置身于作品之外，常常是

一种全知型 (omniscient) 的叙述者，对所有的事情都很了解，不过有时他的视角也受到限制。也有个别作品采用的是第二人称叙述者(second-person narrator)。

naturalism 自然主义

指现实主义发展到极端时的一种文学流派。自然主义作家往往侧重描写生活的阴暗面，笔下的人物总是受到环境和传统的重重束缚，有时甚至到了悲观绝望的境地。著名的自然主义小说家有美国的西奥多・德莱塞 (Theodore Dreiser) 和弗兰克・诺利斯 (Frank Norris) 及英国的乔治・摩尔 (George Moore) 和乔治・吉辛 (George Gissing)。

neoclassism 新古典主义

盛行于 17 世纪和 18 世纪的一种文艺思潮，重新肯定古典主义的标准，推崇秩序、平衡与和谐。新古典主义思潮对文学产生了巨大影响。新古典主义者们认为艺术理想应当是秩序、逻辑、有节制的情感与精确，他们遵循一些固定的规则，如诗歌必须感情奔放，题材宏大，具有说教意义；散文必须精确，直观，流畅和灵活；而戏剧则必须采用英雄双韵体等。新古典主义的主要代表人物有约翰・德莱顿和蒲伯。

novel 小说

一种叙事性文学体裁。它以塑造人物形象为中心，通过展现故事情节，运用各种叙事方法，描绘具体环境来反映社会生活。叙事过程是小说区别于戏剧的重要特征。

octave（意大利十四行诗的）前八行

其余六行叫六行诗体 (sestet)。前八行通常按 abbaabba 押韵。

ode 颂歌

指篇幅较长，结构较复杂的抒情诗。它风格庄严，主题崇高，用以诵物志事，怀时抒情，或向某人致以敬意。珀西・雪莱的《西风颂》和约翰・济慈的《希腊古瓮颂》是颂歌中的精品。

onomatopoeia 象声，拟声

指词的发音某种程度上模仿它所指代的声音或暗示着它的含义。这种修辞手法在诗歌中被广泛使用。比如，在《老水手谣》中，柯勒律治利用拟声修辞再现了冰原的可怕响声：It cracked and growled, and roared and howled/Like noises in a swound!

paradox 矛盾修辞法

这种修辞法表面看似荒谬、自相矛盾，实则蕴涵的真理，如华兹华斯的著名诗句 “The Child is father of the Man” 就采用了典型的矛盾修辞法。

parallelism 排比

一种修辞手法，使用一连串结构类似的词、词组、从句等句子成分，甚至整个句子，来表示强调和层层深入。比如，莎士比亚在《理查二世》(*Richard II*) 中的诗句：I'll give my jewels for a set of beads，/ My gorgeous palace for a hermitage，/ My gay apparel for an almsman's gown，/ My figured goblets for a dish of wood . . .

parody 滑稽模仿

指对某部文艺作品或流派的诙谐模仿，因在模仿过程中加入夸张和嘲讽而取得幽默效果。模仿的范围包括作品的情节、人物、写作风格，甚至是主题。例如，塞万提斯的《堂·吉诃德》就是对中世纪骑士传奇文学 (chivalric romances) 的滑稽模仿。

pastoral 田园诗

指歌颂理想的田园牧歌生活的诗篇，一般描写牧羊人的爱情与悲伤。克里斯托弗·马洛的《多情牧童致爱人》("The Passionate Shepherd to His Love") 是其中的经典之作。

personification 拟人

一种把动物、抽象的思想或没有生命的事物人格化的修辞手法。例如菲利普·锡德尼爵士 (Sir Philip Sidney) 的诗句：Invention, Nature's child, fled stepdame Study's blows.

picaresque novel 流浪汉小说

这种小说产生于16世纪中叶，受市民文学的影响，多承袭现实主义传统，带有讽刺色彩，记录了社会底层流浪汉式人物的种种经历和奇遇。著名的流浪汉小说有英国丹尼尔·笛福的《摩尔·弗兰德斯》、亨利·菲尔丁的《弃儿汤姆·琼斯的历史》，以及美国马克·吐温 (Mark Twain) 的《哈克贝利·芬历险记》(*Adventures of Huckleberry Finn*) 等。

plot 情节

指小说、戏剧或叙事诗中的一系列行为或事件。情节可简可繁，可以结构松散，也可以紧凑，但每一个情节都必须由一系列相互关联的事件构成。情节包括阐明背景的展示部分 (exposition)、推进情节发展的冲突 (conflict)、情节发展至极致处的高潮 (climax)、高潮过后的突降 (falling actions)，以及冲突结束时的大结局 (denouement)。

point of view 视角

指叙述故事的角度。文学作品中最基本的两个视角是第一人称视角和第三人称视角。第一人称视角指作品中某一人物以"我"的角度对故事加以叙述，这种视角大多有局限性；第三人称视角的叙述者不再是故事里的人物，他可能是全知全能的 (omniscient)，也可能是受局限的 (limited)。

protagonist 主人公

小说、戏剧或叙事诗的所有情节都围绕主人公展开，读者也最容易被他（她）的命运打动。尽管该词在不少场合下和表示主角的 hero 一词意义相近，但 protagonist 的范围更广，词意更中立。主人公可以是好人，也可以是坏人；可以是英雄，也可以是普通人。

pun 双关

指通过使用具有两种不同意思的同一个词或两个读音相近的词来产生歧义的一种手法。双关语常能达意想不到的幽默效果。例如，在《麦克白》第三幕第二场中，"Come in tailor, here you may roast your goose." 中的

“goose”一词也指裁缝用的熨斗。

quatrain 四行诗节

英诗中最常用的诗节，它的韵脚常是abab, abba 或 abcd。

realism 现实主义

该词既可以指一种以细致、精确的描写为基础的写作手法，也可以指一种更为广泛的创作态度，这种态度摈弃了传奇文学的理想主义、避世主义和一些夸张的色彩，偏重对生活中现实问题的探讨，试图忠实客观地再现生活。作为一种文学流派，现实主义小说在 19 世纪最为盛行，如法国巴尔扎克的《人间喜剧》和英国乔治·爱略特的《米德尔马契》。在 19 世纪末和 20 世纪初，现实主义也成为戏剧中的主要流派，如萧伯纳就是出色的现实主义剧作家。

refrain 叠歌，副歌

某个词、词组，某行诗甚至几行诗在一首诗中有规律地反复出现。它多用在每个诗节的末尾。民谣和叙事诗多用叠歌营造一种歌唱式的韵律美，同时叠歌也可以用来烘托悬念或强调主题。

revenge tragedy 复仇剧

悲剧的一种，盛行于 16 世纪和 17 世纪的英国，以复仇为动机，充满暴力、恐怖以及各种激烈的感情。莎士比亚的《哈姆雷特》可以算是最有名的复仇剧。

rhyme 押韵

一首诗里间隔比较规律的几个词同韵，称为押韵。英诗中，押韵一般出现在句尾，形成尾韵 (end rhyme)；也可以在句中，形成中间韵 (internal rhyme)。如果词之间只有一个音节押韵，叫作阳韵 (masculine rhyme)，如 love / above；如果有两个音节押韵，叫作阴韵 (feminine rhyme)，如 whether / together；如果有三个音节押韵，叫作三重韵 (triple rhyme)，如 glamourous / amorous。

rhythm 韵律

指相同的强拍 (beat) 以相等 (或大致相等) 的间隔在诗行中反复出现而形成的一种声音模式。在多数英诗中，基本的韵律包括四个或五个强拍，由格律的形式体现出来，即诗行中出现一组有节奏的强拍和弱拍，控制着重读音节和非重读音节的间隔。韵律能赋予诗歌一种明显的音乐节奏感。

rising action 上升情节

小说、戏剧中情节的一部分，指发展部分的情节，包含各种冲突，最后导致高潮的出现。

romance 浪漫文学，传奇文学

指欧洲中世纪的浪漫传奇故事，讲述骑士奇异的冒险经历及他们同贵妇之间的浪漫爱情，比如讲述亚瑟王和他的圆桌骑士冒险经历的故事 (*King Arthur and His Knights of the Round Table*)，其中以《高文爵士和绿色骑士》(*Sir Gawain and the Green Knight*) 最为出色。

romanticism 浪漫主义

指 18 世纪末 19 世纪初发生在欧美文

学中的哲学和文学运动。该运动是对18世纪古典主义和理性主义的反叛，强调个人感情的自由抒发，并以真实、自然和独创性作为文学创作的新标准。英国浪漫主义运动以华兹华斯和柯勒律治于1798年共同发表《抒情歌谣集》为起点。

satire 讽刺文学

一种文学形式，通常用夸张的手法对个人、团体或整个社会的缺点或缺陷进行嘲讽。讽刺作家的目的是为社会设立一定的道德标准，他们利用读者的笑声来阐述他们的观点，并达到说教的目的。英国作家斯威夫特的《格列佛游记》就是讽刺文学作品的名篇之一。

Saga 萨迦；英雄传奇；家世小说

原指中世纪冰岛和挪威流传的故事、传说，通常和传奇领袖或英雄人物有关。后来该词在英语中用来指讲述两代或两代以上家世故事的长篇小说，例如劳伦斯的《虹》和高尔斯华绥的《福尔赛世家》三部曲。

scansion 韵律分析

对常规的韵律进行分析的方法。诗歌的韵律是以音步为单位来进行分析的，一个音步由一个重读音节和一个或两个非重读音节组成。一般来说，一行诗有多少个重读音节就有多少个音步。标准的诗歌音步主要有：抑扬格 (iamb)，即由一个非重读音节加上一个重读音节构成，如 report 一词；扬抑格 (trochee)，即一个重读音节加上一个非重读音节，如 pattern 一词；扬抑抑格 (dactyl)，即一个重读音节加上两个非重读音节，如 silently 一词；抑抑扬格 (anapest)，即两个非重读音节加上一个重读音节，如 undertake 一词。根据音步的数量和特点，诗歌韵律可分为五音步抑扬格 (iambic pentameter) 和四音步扬抑格 (trochaic tetrameter)。五音步抑扬格指该行共有五个抑扬格音步 (5 iambs)；四音步扬抑格 (trochaic tetrameter) 指该行共有四个扬抑格音步 (4 trochees)。常用的韵律分析标志符号有“ˊ”和“v”。“ˊ”表示重读音节；“v”表示非重读音节。

sentimentalism 感伤主义

英国18世纪60年代至18世纪80年代末出现的一种文学潮流。英国工业革命后，出现很多社会弊病，人们对资产阶级政权感到失望，但又无可奈何，便将许多不满与无奈诉诸艺术，由此产生一股新的文学潮流，由斯特恩的小说《感伤之旅》(*A Sentimental Journey*) 而得名。感伤主义文学在形式上注重心理感觉，因此成为19世纪浪漫主义的源头，也是20世纪现代主义文学的滥觞。

sestet 六行诗

通常指意大利十四行诗的最后六行，前八行称作八行诗体 (octave)。

setting 背景

即在故事、小说、戏剧及叙事诗中交代事件发生的时间和地点。背景可以是单纯交代必要的时间和地点，也可以是为了突出某个主题而特意用来创造必要的气氛。

simile 明喻

把一物比作另一物，运用了具体的比较词语，如 like、as、than、resemble 等。这两种事物必须在本质上不相像，否则就构不成明喻。“Susan is like her grandmother” 不是明喻，而 “Susan is like a golden flower.” 则是明喻。

soliloquy 独白

戏剧中的一个角色独自站在舞台上向观众直接表白他的内心感受。世界文学史上的著名独白当数莎士比亚的《哈姆雷特》中，哈姆雷特在第三幕第一场中所做的关于生还是死的独白。该词现在也用于诗歌和小说批评中。

song 歌谣

带有明显音乐节奏感的短小抒情诗。通常是为配乐而作，表达一种质朴而又强烈的情感。彭斯的《一朵红红的玫瑰》及《友谊天长地久》都是著名的歌谣。

sonnet 十四行诗

由十四行组成的一首抒情诗，通常是由押韵的五音步抑扬格诗行组成。通常一首十四行诗表达单一的主题或思想，其结构和押韵格式允许有不同的变化形式，但常见的有两种：彼特拉克或意大利十四行诗 (Petrarchan or Italian sonnet, 押韵格式为 abba abba cde cde) 和莎士比亚或伊丽莎白体十四行诗 (Shakespearean or Elizabethan sonnet，押韵格式为 abab cdcd efef gg)。十四行诗的另一种比较少见的形式是斯宾塞体十四行诗 (Spenserian sonnet)。其押韵格式为 abab bcbc cdcd ee。一组相互关联的十四行诗称为十四行组诗 (sonnet sequence)，如斯宾塞的《小爱神》(*Amoretti*)、锡德尼爵士的《阿斯特菲罗与斯黛拉》(*Astrophel and Stella*)，以及勃朗宁的《葡萄牙人的十四行组诗》(*Sonnets from the Portuguese*)。

Spenserian stanza 斯宾塞诗节

每节有九行，前八行用五音步抑扬格，末行为六音步抑扬格，该行也称为亚历山大式诗行 (Alexandrine)，押韵格式为 abab bcbc c。斯宾塞诗节是斯宾塞为史诗《仙后》而创造出来的。这种诗节后来也为彭斯、济慈、雪莱等浪漫主义诗人所采用。

sprung rhythm 跳跃韵

一种以讲话的正常节奏为基础的诗歌韵律。该词最先由英国诗人 G. M. 霍普金斯使用。在这种诗歌韵律中，一个重读音节可以自由地与一个或多个非重读音节搭配使用，因此每行音步很不规则，听起来像平常的自然讲话。

stereotype 陈规，老套；落入俗套

指文学作品中经常出现的、读者十分熟悉的一类人物或角色，又称常规角色 (stock characters)。常见的常规角色有喜怒无常的影视明星、健谈的出租车司机，以及留着小胡子的坏人等。

stream of consciousness 意识流

一种文学创作的方法或风格，以描写

人物的内心情感，表现意识的流动为主要内容，以内心独白、自由联想、现实与虚幻相互交织为主要方法。意识流文学兴起于20世纪初期，主要受到弗洛伊德精神分析心理学的影响，盛行于20世纪20年代和30年代。代表作家有乔伊斯、伍尔夫等。

strophe 诗节

(古希腊戏剧中)歌咏队从右向左回舞时唱的歌，尤指古希腊颂歌中的第一节。

style 写作风格

指一个作家作品的特点。一部作品的风格通常是由作家的遣词造句以及句与句之间的关系特征所决定。写作风格也是一个作家在写作过程中使用意象、修辞格，以及节奏的特殊方式。写作风格是一个作家及其作品从总体上区别于其他作家作品的重要标志。

suspense 悬念

指文学作品采用的一种策略，能让读者或观众急于想知道故事结局。恐怖、惊险和侦探类的小说、电影、戏剧等往往十分注重悬念的灵活运用。

symbol 象征

指用具体的事物表示某种特殊的意义。例如，玫瑰通常是爱情和美丽的象征；头盖骨往往象征着死亡；春天和冬天分别象征着青年和老年等。

symbolism 象征主义

19世纪后半期在法国最先流行的反现实主义文学思潮，后来对许多20世纪英国作家和诗人的创作产生了很大影响。在象征主义诗人看来，情感是不确定的，因此交流起来比较困难。他们往往避免直接说出所要表达的意义，而是通过强有力的象征手法来暗示某种意义或情感。

synecdoche 提喻

一种修辞格，以部分或局部代表整体，有时也以整体代表局部。如华兹华斯在名诗《序曲》中就用“手”和“脚”来代表“人民”。

terza rima 三行诗节隔句押韵法

意大利一种三行一节的诗体，其押韵格式为“aba bcb cdc . . .”，依次类推下去。英国浪漫主义诗人雪莱的《西风颂》就是以这种押韵格式写成的。

theme 主题

指一部文学作品中作者所要表达的总体思想和观点。文学作品的其他一切要素——情节、背景、人物塑造及语言的运用都要围绕主题的阐发而展开。

tone 基调，格调

指在一部作品中，作家对其作品的主题、人物或观众所持的基本态度。每部作品都有基调，可能是怀旧情绪的，可能是严肃正式的，可能是活泼俏皮的，可能是幽默讽刺的。一部作品的基调主要是通过遣词造句体现出来的。

tragedy 悲剧

通常指主人公结局悲惨的严肃戏剧(或小说)。与喜剧不同的是，悲剧中的主人公通常威严而又勇敢，其所作